GREAT LIVES

SIMON BOUGHTON

Doubleday
New York

GREAT LIVES

Editor: John Grisewood
Assistant editor: Nicola Barber
Illustrators: Russell Barnett pages 73, 80-1, 143, 198-9, 206-7, 247, 256-7; Owain Bell pages 172-3, 229; Norma Burgin pages 106-7, 154-5; Dave Etchell and John Ridyard pages 24-5.
Picture research: Jackie Cookson and Penny Warn.
Cover design: The Pinpoint Design Company.

Library of Congress Cataloging-in-Publication Data

Great lives.

Summary: Outlines the major achievements and events in the lives of 1000 men and women, from all over the world and from all walks of life, who have shaped history.
1. Biography—Juvenile literature, [1. Biography]
I. Boughton, Simon.
CT107.G74 1988 920′.02[920] 87-22147
ISBN 0-385-24283-2

Printed in Hong Kong
First edition in the United States of America, 1988

For permission to reproduce copyright material, acknowledgment and thanks are due to the following: Page 62: 12 lines from *The Miller's Tale* from THE CANTERBURY TALES by Geoffrey Chaucer, translated by Nevill Coghill (Penguin Classics, 1951, 1958, 1960), copyright © Nevill Coghill, 1951, 1958, 1960. Page 74: Copyright © 1956 by E.E. Cummings. Reprinted from his volume COMPLETE POEMS 1913-1962 by permission of Harcourt Brace Jovanovich, Inc.

Contents

Introduction

In this book you will find short biographies of over 1,000 men and women who have played an important part in history and have a story worth telling. They come from all over the world, and have many different claims to fame. There are kings and queens, emperors, presidents, politicians, and soldiers. There are also scientists, inventors, writers, artists, entertainers, and sportsmen and -women—and many others besides. Most are very well known, and the book will help you find out why. But there are also many names you may not have heard of. Browse through these pages and you are bound to discover something new and interesting, as well as things you may have forgotten.

The entries are arranged in three different ways. The main part of the book is set out like a dictionary: the people are listed alphabetically, all the way from Abelard to Zworykin. Each entry gives the full name, the year of his or her birth and death, and some details of the person's life. In several cases a name that is very familiar turns out not to have been its owner's real name. Mark Twain's real name, for instance, was Samuel Langhorne Clemens. In these cases the entry appears under the familiar name, but the real name is given as well, in brackets before the

date. In other cases, one or both of the dates are not known for certain. Then an abbreviation will tell you if the date is approximate (*c.*), or if what you see is the date of the person's birth (b.) or death (d.). At the end of the entries you will sometimes see other people's names in SMALL CAPITALS. This tells you that you can find out more on the same subject by looking up this second name.

In the pages before the main part of the book there is a chronological table of contents. All the people in the book are arranged here in historical order, from 2800 B.C. to the present. A page number tells you where to find them in the main text. Alongside, there is a list of important events, so that you can see what was happening around the world during their lives.

The third way in which the entries are arranged is according to subject, in the index at the end of the book. You can look up events in history, the names of countries, nicknames, the names of books, works of art, inventions, and many other things, as well as general categories such as "Poetry," "Physics," or "Architecture." If you look up an event, you will find a list of the personalities who took part in it; if you look up a book, you will find the name of the author—and so forth. There is also a glossary at the back of the book that lists some of the names, technical terms, and abbreviations used in the text.

Chronological Contents

This section lists the entries chronologically, and gives their page number in the book *(in italics)*.

1000 Fan Kuan, Chinese artist *98*
1014 Canute, English king *53*
1030 Lady Murasaki, Japanese writer *182*
1040 Macbeth, Scottish king *163*
1042 Edward the Confessor, English king *88*
1066 William the Conqueror, king of England *261*
Harold II, king of England *120*
1085 Roger I, king of Sicily *218*
1088 Pope Urban II *249*

1115 Abelard, French theologian *21*
Héloïse, French nun *21*
1141 Matilda, English queen *169*
1152 Eleanor of Aquitaine, English queen *92*
1154 Pope Adrian IV *21*
Henry II, English king *136*
1155 Frederick Barbarossa, Holy Roman Emperor *103*
1170 Saint Thomas à Becket *36*
1174 Saladin, sultan of Egypt *222*
1175 Genghis Khan, Mongol emperor *110*
1189 Richard I, English king *214*
1190 Chrétien de Troyes, French writer *29*
1198 Pope Innocent III *133*
1199 John, English king *136*

1200 Saint Dominic *85*
Maimonides, Jewish philosopher *164*
Marie de France, French poet *167*
1210 Saint Francis of Assisi *102*
1215 Snorri Sturluson, Icelandic poet *236*
1250 Saint Thomas Aquinas *28*
1257 Kubla Khan, Mongol emperor *150*
1264 Simon de Montfort, English lord *178*
1265 Niccola Pisano, Italian sculptor *203*
1267 Roger Bacon, English philosopher *33*
1271 Marco Polo, Italian explorer *206*
1285 Philip the Fair, French king *202*
1292 John Baliol, Scottish king *136*

1300 Duccio, Italian artist *87*
Cimabue, Italian artist *63*
1306 Giotto, Italian artist *112*
1307 Edward II, English king *89*
Dante, Italian poet *76*
1314 Robert Bruce, Scottish king *216*
1325 Ibn Batuta, Arab explorer *132*
1327 Edward III, English king *89*
Petrarch, Italian poet *201*
1350 Pedro the Cruel, Castilian king *197*
1352 Jean Froissart, French poet *104*
1358 Boccaccio, Italian poet *42*
1360 William Langland, English poet *151*
1369 Tamerlane, Tatar king *238*
1375 Saint Catherine of Siena *55*
1377 Richard II, English king *215*
1381 Wat Tyler, English rebel *248*
1382 John Wycliffe, English church reformer *265*
1386 Chaucer, English poet *61*
1388 Háfiz, Persian poet *118*
1399 Henry IV, English king *123*
1400 Andrei Roublev, Russian artist *220*
The "Gawain-Poet" *110*
1402 Owen Glendower, Welsh leader *192*
Ghiberti, Italian sculptor *111*
1412 Donatello, Italian sculptor *85*
1413 Henry V, English king *123*
1420 Filippo Brunelleschi, Italian architect *49*
Masaccio, Italian artist *169*
1429 Joan of Arc, French leader *140*
1432 Jan Van Eyck, Flemish artist *250*
1434 Cosimo de'Medici, Florentine leader *172*
1450 Luca Della Robbia, Italian artist *82*
Johannes Gutenberg, German printer *117*
1455 Paolo Uccello, Italian artist *249*
1460 Piero della Francesca, Italian artist *202*
1462 Ivan the Great, Russian ruler *133*
1470 Botticelli, Italian artist *45*
1471 Thomas Malory, English writer *165*
1475 William Caxton, English printer *58*
1478 Lorenzo de'Medici, Florentine leader *172*
1479 Ferdinand II, Spanish king *99*
1482 Leonardo Da Vinci, Italian artist and scientist *157*
1483 Richard III, English king *216*
1486 Bartolomeo Diaz, Portuguese explorer *83*
1492 Christopher Columbus *68*
Pope Alexander VI *23*

MAIN EVENTS

B.C.

2800 "Old Kingdom" in Egypt
814 Carthage founded by the Phoenicians
609 End of the Assyrian Empire
480 Persian invasion of Greece
334 Beginning of Alexander's military campaigns
264 First Punic War between Rome and Carthage
214 Construction of Great Wall of China
44 Assassination of Julius Caesar
31 Battle of Actium

A.D.

43 Roman invasion of Britain
101 Roman Empire reaches greatest extent
313 Edict of Milan allows Christianity in Roman Empire
452 Huns invade Italy
622 The "Hegira"—Muhammad flees from Mecca
800 Charlemagne crowned first Holy Roman Emperor
856 Viking invasions of Britain begin
1066 Norman invasion of England
1099 First Crusade
1210 Mongols invade China
1215 Magna Carta limits the power of English king
1325 Aztec capital Tenochtitlán
1348 Black Death ravages Europe
1368 Ming Dynasty begins in China
1429 Siege of Orléans
1438 Inca Empire in Peru
1455 Wars of the Roses
1492 Europeans discover America

1493 Torquemada, Spanish Inquisitor *243*
1494 Savonarola, Florentine leader *224*
1495 Baber, Mogul emperor *33*
1497 Amerigo Vespucci, Italian explorer *252*
Vasco Da Gama, Portuguese explorer *76*
John Cabot, Italian explorer *51*

1500 Giorgione, Italian artist *112*
Carpaccio, Italian artist *53*
1502 Montezuma, Aztec king *178*
1503 Pope Julius II *139*
Cesare and Lucrezia Borgia, Italian nobles *44*
1505 Michelangelo, Italian artist *174*
Giovanni Bellini, Italian artist *39*
Lucas Cranach, German artist *71*
1507 Ximenes, Spanish minister *265*
1509 Erasmus, Dutch scholar *95*
Raphael, Italian artist *211*
1513 Pope Leo X *156*
Niccolo Machiavelli, Italian writer *163*
1515 Ariosto, Italian poet *28*
Albrecht Dürer, German artist *87*
Thomas Wolsey, English minister *262*
Francis I, French king *101*
1517 Martin Luther, Protestant reformer *162*
1518 Zwingli, Protestant reformer *267*
1519 Magellan, Portuguese explorer *164*
Charles V, Holy Roman Emperor *61*
Cortés, Spanish conquistador *71*
1520 Sulaiman, sultan of Turkey *237*
1526 Hans Holbein, German artist *127*
1529 Thomas More, English minister *178*
1532 Francisco Pizarro, Spanish conquistador *203*
Titian, Italian artist *242*
1533 Thomas Cranmer, English minister *71*
Anne Boleyn, English queen *43*
1534 Henry VIII, English king *123*
1535 Jacques Cartier, French explorer *54*
1536 John Calvin, Protestant reformer *52*
1540 Saint Ignatius Loyola, Jesuits' founder *162*
1541 Saint Francis Xavier *265*
1542 Mary Queen of Scots *169*
1543 Copernicus, Polish astronomer *70*
1546 George Wishart, Protestant reformer *150*
1547 Edward VI, English king *89*
Ivan the Terrible, Russian ruler *133*
Nostradamus, French astrologer *189*
1550 Giorgio Vasari, Italian artist and writer *250*
Pieter Breughel, Flemish artist *47*
1555 Akbar, Mogul emperor *93*
1556 Philip II, Spanish king *201*
1558 Elizabeth I, English queen *93*
Cellini, Italian goldsmith *58*
1559 John Knox, Scottish Protestant reformer *150*
1562 Saint Theresa of Ávila *241*
1568 William the Silent, Dutch leader *261*
1570 Palestrina, Italian composer *193*
Palladio, Italian architect *193*
Tintoretto, Italian artist *242*
1571 Don John, Spanish prince *136*
1573 Veronese, Italian artist *251*
1575 Tasso, Italian poet *238*
1576 Tycho Brahe, Danish astronomer *46*
1580 Ronsard, French poet *219*
1584 Walter Raleigh, English sailor *211*
1587 Virginia Dare, American settler *77*
1588 Francis Drake, English sailor *86*
Christopher Marlowe, English dramatist *168*
1589 Henry of Navarre, French king *123*
1598 Boris Godunov, tsar of Russia *113*
1599 Edmund Spenser, English poet *232*

1600 William Shakespeare, English dramatist *228*
William Byrd, English composer 50
Nicholas Hilliard, English artist *124*
Fabricius, Italian scientist *98*
El Greco, Spanish artist *115*
1601 Kepler, German astronomer *146*
1603 Stewart family, Scottish royalty *234*
James I, British king *134*
1605 Cervantes, Spanish writer *98*
Guy Fawkes, English conspirator *98*
1606 Saint Rose of Lima *220*
1607 Monteverdi, Italian composer *178*
1610 Ben Jonson, English dramatist *138*
Henry Hudson, English explorer *130*
Frans Hals, Dutch artist *119*
1611 Gustavus Adolphus, Swedish king *117*
1613 Galileo, Italian scientist *105*
1616 Pocahontas, American Indian princess *204*
1617 René Descartes, French philosopher *83*
1618 Grotius, Dutch lawyer *116*
1620 Miles Standish, leader of *Mayflower* voyage *233*
1621 John Donne, English poet *86*
Peter Paul Rubens, Flemish artist *220*
1624 Richelieu, French minister *216*
1625 Domenico Cassini, French-Italian astronomer *54*
Charles I, British king *60*
Inigo Jones, English architect *138*
Saint Vincent de Paul *252*
1626 Orazio Gentileschi, Italian artist *111*
1628 William Harvey, English scientist *121*
1629 Bernini, Italian architect *40*
1631 Corneille, French dramatist *70*
1632 William Prynne, English writer *209*
Rabelais, French writer *210*
Anthony Van Dyck, Flemish artist *250*
1640 Georges de La Tour, French artist *152*
1642 Jules Mazarin, French minister *170*

Rembrandt, Dutch artist *214*
Abel Tasman, Dutch explorer *238*
1643 Torricelli, Italian scientist *243*
Vesalius, Belgian scientist *251*
Louis XIV, French king *160*
1645 Oliver Cromwell, English leader *72*
Robert Boyle, Irish scientist *45*
1651 Calderón de la Barca, Spanish writer *51*
Thomas Hobbes, English philosopher *126*
1654 Pascal, French scientist and philosopher *195*
1656 Christiaan Huygens, Dutch astronomer *131*
Velázquez, Spanish artist *250*
1658 Aurangzeb, Mogul emperor *32*
1659 Andrew Marvell, English poet *168*
1660 Charles Lebrun, French artist *153*
Jan Vermeer, Dutch artist *251*
Samuel Pepys, English writer *200*
1662 John Milton, English poet *176*
1664 Peter Stuyvesant, Dutch governor *236*
1665 Colbert, French minister *65*
Molière, French dramatist *177*
1669 Madame de Sévigné, French writer *227*
1670 André LeNôtre, French landscape gardener *156*
Spinoza, Dutch philosopher *232*
Aphra Behn, English dramatist *38*
1674 John Sobieski, Polish king *137*
1676 John Bunyan, English writer *50*
1677 Racine, French dramatist *210*
1678 Titus Oates, English conspiritor *190*
1680 Nell Gwynne, English courtesan *117*
1682 William Penn *197*
1687 Isaac Newton, English scientist *187*
1690 John Locke, English philosopher *160*
1696 Peter the Great, tsar of Russia *201*
1697 Charles XII, Swedish king *61*

1700 Antony van Leeuwenhoek Dutch scientist *156*
William Congreve, English dramatist *66*
1701 John Churchill Marlborough, English soldier *167*
1710 Christopher Wren, English architect *263*
Vivaldi, Italian composer *253*
George Berkeley, Irish philosopher *40*
1712 Alexander Pope, English poet *205*
1715 Scarlatti, Italian composer *224*
Fahrenheit, German scientist *98*
1717 Watteau, French artist *255*
1719 Daniel Defoe, English writer *79*
1721 Edmond Halley, English astronomer *119*
1722 Kang Xi, Chinese emperor *144*
1723 J. S. Bach, German composer *33*
1726 Jonathan Swift, English writer *237*
1728 Vitus Bering, Danish explorer *40*
Jean Baptiste Chardin, French artist *59*
1731 William Hogarth, English artist *127*
1733 Jethro Tull, English agriculturalist *248*
1735 David Hume, English philosopher *131*
1737 Stradivari, Italian violin maker *234*
1739 John Wesley, founder of Methodism *258*
1740 Maria Theresa, Habsburg empress *118*
Frederick II, king of Prussia *103*
1741 Lomonosov, Russian writer and scientist *160*
1742 Linnaeus, Swedish scientist *158*
George Frederick Handel, German composer *120*
Henry Fielding, English writer *100*
1744 Lamarck, French scientist *151*
1750 "Capability" Brown, English landscape gardener *48*
Canaletto, Italian artist *52*
1751 Denis Diderot, French writer *84*
1752 Benjamin Franklin, American writer, scientist *102*
1756 Robert Clive, British soldier *64*
1759 James Wolfe, British soldier *262*
Laurence Sterne, English writer *234*
Josiah Wedgwood, English pottery owner *255*
1760 La Salle, French explorer *152*
Voltaire, French writer *253*
1761 Haydn, German composer *122*
1762 Jean Jacques Rousseau, French writer *220*
Catherine the Great, tsarina of Russia *55*

MAIN EVENTS

1517 "95 Theses against the Sale of Indulgences": Beginning of Reformation
1522 First circum-navigation of the world
1533 Conquest of Peru
1545 Council of Trent begins reform of Catholic Church
1571 Battle of Lepanto: Venetians defeat Turks
1572 St. Bartholomew's Day Massacre
1581 Dutch Republic proclaimed independent of Spain
1588 Spanish Armada defeated by English navy
1598 Edict of Nantes: freedom for French Protestants
1607 Colony of Virginia founded
1616 First rounding of Cape Horn
1626 New Amsterdam founded by Dutch (later New York)
1642 Civil War in England
1644 Manchu Dynasty in China
1649 English King Charles I executed; Commonwealth begins (to 1660)
1701 War of Spanish Succession
1740 War of Austrian Succession: dispute over Austrian throne
1756 Seven Years' War between Britain and France for control of America
1757 British rule established in India
1759 Britain captures Quebec
1768 Europeans land in Australia

1763 John Wilkes, English politician *260*
1764 James Watt, Scottish engineer *255*
James Hargreaves, invents spinning jenny *120*
Robert Adam, English architect *21*
1765 Samuel Johnson, English writer *137*
Edmund Burke, English politician *50*
1766 Pitt the Elder, English politician *203*
1768 James Cook, English explorer *67*
Joshua Reynolds, English artist *214*
Thomas Gainsborough, English artist *105*
1770 Angelica Kauffmann, Swiss artist *144*
Marie Antoinette, French queen *166*
Beaumarchais, French writer *35*
1772 Scheele, Swedish scientist *224*
1774 Louis XVI, French king *161*
Goethe, German writer *113*
Joseph Priestley, English scientist *208*
1775 Daniel Boone, American pioneer *44*
Paul Revere, American revolutionary *214*
1776 Anthony Wayne, American soldier *255*
Adam Smith, Scottish economist *230*
George Stubbs, English artist *236*
1777 William Bligh, English sailor *42*
Marie Joseph La Fayette, French revolutionary *151*
1780 Benedict Arnold, U.S. soldier *29*
1781 Kant, German philosopher *144*
Frederick Herschel, German astronomer *124*
1782 Mrs. Siddons, English actress *230*
1783 Pitt the Younger, English politician *203*
John McAdam, Scottish engineer *163*
George Rogers Clarke, U.S. soldier *63*
1785 Jacques David, French artist *78*
1786 Robert Burns, Scottish poet *50*
1787 Lavoisier, French scientist *152*
1788 Necker, French minister *186*
1789 William Blake, English poet *41*
Jeremy Bentham, English philosopher *39*
George Washington, U.S. President *256*
1791 Mozart, Austrian composer *180*
James Boswell, English writer *137*
Luigi Galvani, Italian scientist *106*
Joseph Guillotin, introduced "guillotine" *117*
Toussaint l'Ouverture, Haitian leader *244*
1792 Ranjit Singh, Indian Sikh leader *211*
Thomas Paine, English radical *193*
Eli Whitney, invents cotton gin *259*
Mary Wollstonecraft, Irish writer *262*
1793 Robespierre, French revolutionary *217*
Jean Paul Marat, French revolutionary *166*
Charlotte Corday, French assassin *70*
1794 Danton, French revolutionary *77*
1796 Edward Jenner, English doctor *135*
1797 John Adams, U.S. President *21*
1798 William Wordsworth, English poet *263*
Samuel Taylor Coleridge, English poet *65*
Wolfe Tone, Irish leader *243*
1799 Talleyrand, French minister *238*
Robert Owen, Welsh reformer *192*
Friedrich von Humboldt, German scientist *131*
Napoleon Bonaparte, French emperor *184*

1800 Thomas Jefferson U.S. President *135*
Pierre Laplace, French scientist *152*
Schiller, German writer *224*
Beau Brummell, English dandy *35*
1802 Ingres, French artist *132*
Benjamin Constant, French writer *66*
Richard Trevithick, English engineer *244*
1803 Robert Fulton, U.S. inventor of the steamboat *104*
1804 Sacagawea, American Indian *222*
Washington Irving, U.S. writer *133*
Josephine, French empress *138*
William Cobbett, English writer *65*
1805 Marshal Ney, French soldier *188*
Horatio Nelson, English sailor *186*
Mehemet Ali, viceroy of Egypt *171*
1807 William Wilberforce, English politician *260*
1808 Joseph Gay-Lussac, French scientist *110*
Goya, Spanish artist *114*
John Dalton, English scientist *76*
1810 Phineas Barnum, American showman *34*
Joseph Mallord Turner, English artist *248*
Madame de Staël, French writer *232*
1811 Bernardo O'Higgins, Chilean revolutionary *191*
Avogadro, Italian scientist *32*
1812 Ludwig van Beethoven, German composer *37*
1813 Jane Austen, English writer *32*
Elizabeth Fry, English prison reformer *104*
1814 Percy Shelley, English poet *227*
Davy Crockett, U.S. frontiersman *72*
1815 Alessandro Volta, Italian scientist *253*
George III, English king *111*
Wellington, English soldier *258*
Humphry Davy, English scientist *79*
1816 James Monroe, U.S. President *177*
Hegel, German philosopher *122*
Byron, English poet *50*
1818 Walter Scott, Scottish writer *226*
1820 John Keats, English poet *145*
Oersted, Danish scientist *190*

1821 Simon Bolívar, South American revolutionary *43*
José de San Martín, South American revolutionary *223*
1822 Franz Schubert, Austrian composer *224*
1824 John Constable, English artist *66*
1825 John Quincy Adams, U.S. President *21*
Louis Braille, inventor of blind reading system *46*
George Cuvier, French scientist *75*
1826 James Fenimore Cooper, U.S. writer *70*
Telford, Scottish engineer *239*
J. P. Niepce, French photographer *188*
1827 Manzoni, Italian writer *165*
Ohm, German scientist *191*
1828 Noah Webster, American lexicographer *255*
Andrew Jackson, U.S. President *134*
Johnny "Appleseed," U.S. frontiersman *28*
1829 William Booth, British religious leader *44*
George Stephenson, English engineer *234*
Grimm brothers, German writers *116*
Mendelssohn, German composer *174*
1830 Hans Christian Andersen, Danish writer *27*
Daniel O'Connell, Irish leader *190*
Stendhal, French writer *233*
Paganini, Italian violinist *193*
1831 Heinrich Heine, German poet *122*
1832 Ralph Waldo Emerson, U.S. writer *94*
George Sand, French writer *223*
Marie Taglioni, Italian dancer *238*
1833 Michael Faraday, English scientist *98*
1835 Alexandre Dumas *père*, French writer *87*
Thomas Carlyle, English writer *53*
1836 Chopin, Polish composer *62*
Charles Dickens, English writer *83*
Gogol, Russian writer *113*
1837 Rowland Hill, invents postage stamp *124*
Georg Büchner, German dramatist *49*
Victoria, English queen *252*
1838 Grace Darling, English lifeboatwoman *77*
Johann Strauss the Elder, Austrian composer *235*
1839 Daguerre, French scientist *76*
1839 Longfellow, U.S. poet *160*
1840 Robert Schumann, German composer *225*
1841 Robert Peel, British politician *197*
George Everest, English mapmaker *95*
1842 Balzac, French writer *34*
John Frémont, U.S. explorer *103*
Verdi, Italian composer *251*
Kit Carson, U.S. frontiersman *53*
1843 Samuel Morse, invents telegraph *179*
Sören Kierkegaard, Danish philosopher *147*
1845 J. H. Newman, English churchman *187*
Edgar Allan Poe, U.S. writer *204*
1847 Jefferson Davis, American statesman *78*
Charlotte and Emily Brontë, English writers *47*
Brigham Young, Mormon leader *266*
1848 Pierre Joseph Proudhon, French revolutionary *208*
Dante Gabriel Rossetti, English artist *220*
Karl Marx, German philosopher *168*
Friedrich Engels, German writer *95*
Elizabeth Gaskell, English writer *110*
William Makepeace Thackeray, English writer *240*
J. S. Mill, English philosopher *175*
Lajos Kossuth, Hungarian leader *150*
1849 Gustave Courbet, French painter *71*
Giuseppe Mazzini, Italian leader *171*
Harriet Tubman, underground railroad leader *248*
1850 Nathaniel Hawthorne, U.S. writer *121*
Tennyson, English poet *239*
1851 Heinrich Steinway, piano maker *233*
Reuter, German newsman *214*
John Ruskin, English writer *221*
Joseph Paxton, English architect *196*
Herman Melville, U.S. writer *171*

MAIN EVENTS

1773 Boston Tea Party
1775 American Revolution begins
1776 American Declaration of Independence
1783 Treaty of Paris: British recognize American independence, war ends
1788 First convicts transported to Australia
1789 Storming of the Bastille; new Assembly formed
1793 Louis XVI and Marie Antoinette executed
Reign of Terror begins in France
1801 Act of Union formally unites England and Ireland
1804 First Empire in France: Napoleon crowned emperor
1805 Battle of Trafalgar: French navy defeated
1814 Napoleon exiled to Elba
1815 The Hundred Days: Napoleon escapes to lead French army; defeated at the Battle of Waterloo
1823 Monroe Doctrine: U.S. warns Europe not to interfere in U.S.A.
1833 Slavery abolished in all British colonies
1839 Opium War between Britain and China
1846 Potato famine in Ireland
1848 Revolutions throughout Europe
1850 Rebellion against Manchu Dynasty in China
1851 Great Exhibition held in London

1852 Napoleon III, French emperor *184*
Harriet Beecher Stowe, U.S. writer *37*

1853 Emily Dickinson, U.S. poet *84*
Wagner, German composer *254*

1854 Henry Thoreau, U.S. writer *241*
Alfred Wallace, English scientist *254*
Florence Nightingale, English nurse *188*

1855 Walt Whitman, U.S. poet *259*

1856 Elizabeth Barrett Browning, English poet *35*
Henry Bessemer, steel process *40*

1857 Charles Baudelaire, French poet *35*
Pasteur, French scientist *195*
Gustave Flaubert, French writer *100*
Liszt, Hungarian composer *159*

1858 Isambard Kingdom Brunel, English engineer *48*
Oliver Wendell Holmes, U.S. writer *127*
Saint Bernadette *40*

1859 George Eliot, English writer *93*
Charles Darwin, English scientist *80*

1860 Brahms, German composer *46*
Garibaldi, Italian leader *106*
De Lesseps, builds Suez Canal *157*
Abraham Lincoln, U.S. President *158*

1861 William I, Prussian king *261*
William Morris, English designer *179*
Victor Emmanuel I, Italian king *252*
Cavour, Italian minister *58*

1862 Ivan Turgenev, Russian writer *248*
Robert E. Lee, U.S. soldier *153*
Victor Hugo, French writer *131*

1863 Édouard Manet, French artist *165*
Jules Verne, French writer *251*
George Pullman, U.S. businessman *209*

1864 Maximilian, Austrian archduke *170*
William Tecumseh Sherman, U.S. soldier *227*
Jean Henri Dunant, founds Red Cross *87*
Salmon P. Chase, U.S. justice *61*
Cornelius Vanderbilt, U.S. businessman *249*
John Greenleaf Whittier, U.S. poet *260*
Sojourner Truth, U.S. abolitionist *245*

1865 Lewis Carroll, English writer *53*
Leo Tolstoy, Russian writer *242*

1866 Dostoevsky, Russian writer *86*
David Livingstone, Scottish explorer *159*

1868 Benjamin Disraeli, British politician *85*
William Gladstone, British politician *112*
Émile Zola, French writer *267*
Gregor Mendel, Austrian scientist *174*

1869 Robert Browning, English poet *48*
Susan Anthony, U.S. feminist *27*
Louisa May Alcott, U.S. writer *23*
Ulysses S. Grant, U.S. President *115*
Henry Morton Stanley, English explorer *232*

1870 Johann Strauss the Younger, Austrian composer *235*
Elizabeth Garrett Anderson, English doctor *110*
Camille Pissarro, French artist *203*

1871 Bismarck, German chancellor *40*

1872 Heinrich Schliemann, German archaeologist *224*

1873 Cetewayo, Zulu king *59*
Edgar Degas, French artist *82*

1874 Claude Monet, French artist *177*
Auguste Renoir, French artist *214*
Grieg, Norwegian composer *116*

1875 "Calamity" Jane, U.S. frontiers-woman *51*
Stéphane Mallarmé, French poet *164*
Ci Xi, Chinese empress *63*

1876 Pierre Larousse, French lexico-grapher *152*
Sitting Bull, American Indian warrior *230*
Crazy Horse, American Indian warrior *72*
General George Custer *75*
Alexander Graham Bell, inventor *38*
Robert Koch, German scientist *150*
Mark Twain, U.S. writer *246*

1877 Gerard Manley Hopkins, English poet *130*
Thomas Edison, U.S. inventor *90*
James Whistler, U.S. artist *259*
Tchaikovsky, Russian composer *238*
Mary Cassatt, U.S. artist *54*

1878 Ellen Terry, English actress *240*
John Davison Rockefeller *218*
Paul Cézanne, French artist *59*

1879 Henrik Ibsen, Norwegian dramatist *132*
F. W. Woolworth, U.S. merchant *263*
Mary Baker Eddy, founds Christian Science *88*

1880 Geronimo, American Indian warrior *111*
Mother Jones, U.S. union leader *138*
Alfred Krupp, German businessman *150*
Ned Kelly, Australian outlaw *145*
Winslow Homer, U.S. artist *127*
Joel Harris, U.S. writer *121*
Edward Lear, English artist & writer *153*
Guy de Maupassant, French writer *170*
Carl Fabergé, Russian jeweler *98*
Charles Stewart Parnell, Irish leader *195*

1881 Booker T. Washington, U.S. educationalist *254*
Henry James, U.S. writer *135*

1882 Henri Toulouse-Lautrec, French artist *243*

1883 Gottlieb Daimler, invents internal combustion engine *76*
Robert Louis Stevenson, Scottish writer *234*
Paul Gauguin, French artist *110*

1884 John Singer Sargent, U.S. artist *223*
George Eastman, invents roll film *88*

General Gordon, British soldier *114*
1885 Henri Rousseau, French artist *220*
Nietzsche, German philosopher *189*
1886 Thomas Hardy, English writer *120*
Auguste Bartholdi, French sculptor *35*
1887 James Clerk Maxwell, Scottish scientist *64*
1888 August Strindberg, Swedish dramatist *236*
Edward Gibbon, English writer *111*
William II, German emperor *261*
1889 Heinrich Hertz, German scientist *124*
Gustave Eiffel, French engineer *89*
1890 Vincent Van Gogh, Dutch artist *250*
1891 Marcel Dassault, French engineer *78*
1892 Beatrice & Sidney Webb, English writers *255*
1893 Puccini, Italian composer *209*
1894 Aubrey Beardsley, English artist *35*
George Bernard Shaw, Irish writer *227*
Claude Debussy, French composer *79*
Alfred Dreyfus, French soldier *87*
Nicholas II, Russian tsar *188*
1895 Stephen Crane, U.S. writer *71*
William Röntgen, German scientist *219*
Fridtjof Nansen, Norwegian explorer *183*
1896 Antoine Becquerel, French scientist *37*
Alfred Nobel, Swedish inventor *189*
1897 John Enders, American scientist *94*
Jean Sibelius, Finnish composer *227*
1898 George Curzon, British politician *75*
Auguste Rodin, French sculptor *218*
Anton Chekhov, Russian writer *62*
1899 Oscar Wilde, Irish writer *260*
Thorstein Veblen, U.S. economist *250*
Edward Elgar, English composer *92*

1900 Julia Howe, American suffragette *130*
William James, U.S. philosopher *135*
Hokusai, Japanese artist *127*
Gustav Mahler, Austrian composer *164*
Joseph Conrad, Polish writer *66*
Max Planck, German scientist *203*
Beatrix Potter, English writer *205*
Sarah Bernhardt, French actress *40*
Pierre Bonnard, French artist *44*
Anatole France, French writer *101*
Sigmund Freud, Austrian psychologist *103*
1901 Guglielmo Marconi, Italian scientist *166*
Theodore Roosevelt, U.S. President *220*
Andrew Carnegie, U.S. businessman *53*
Rudyard Kipling, English writer *147*
Edward VII, English king *89*
1902 Marie & Pierre Curie, Polish scientists *75*
1903 Horatio Kitchener, British soldier *150*
W. B. Yeats, Irish poet *266*
Orville & Wilbur Wright, U.S. aviators *264*
Emmeline & Christobel Pankhurst, English suffragettes *194*
Jack London, U.S. writer *160*
1904 Rasputin, Russian monk *211*
Pavlov, Russian scientist *196*
Brancusi, Romanian sculptor *46*
Helen Keller, U.S. writer *145*
1905 Gertrude Stein, U.S. writer *233*
Schweitzer, French missionary *225*
Henri Matisse, French artist *169*
Albert Einstein, German scientist
1907 Pablo Picasso, Spanish artist *202*
Lady Gregory, Irish dramatist *116*
Segovia, Spanish guitarist *226*
1908 Cartier-Bresson *54*
Escoffier, French chef *95*
Henry Ford, U.S. car manufacturer *101*
Robert Baden-Powell, founds Boy Scouts *33*
Asquith, British politician *30*
1909 Sergei Diaghilev, founds *Ballets Russes* *83*
H. G. Wells, English writer *258*
Louis Blériot, French aviator *42*
Robert Peary, U.S. explorer *196*
Pavlova, Russian dancer *196*

MAIN EVENTS

1854 The Crimean War: Britain, France, and Turkey against Russia
1857 Indian Mutiny
1860 Garibaldi invades Sicily
1861 Italy united (except for Rome and Venice)
1863 Abolition of slavery in U.S.A.
Battle of Gettysburg: Union defeats Confederacy
1865 Confederacy surrenders; end of American Civil War
Lincoln assassinated
1869 Suez Canal opened
1870 Franco-Prussian War
Italy annexes Rome: becomes new capital
1876 Battle of Little Big Horn: American Indians defeat U.S. Army
1884 Berlin Conference: European nations agree to divide Africa
1885 European nations begin "scramble for Africa"
1893 Women in New Zealand given right to vote
1894 Dreyfus Affair: scandal in France
1897 Greece and Turkey at war over Crete
1898 U.S.A. and Spain at war over Cuba
1899 Boer War: British and Boers fight for South Africa
1900 Boxer Rebellion: Chinese rebel against foreign powers
1903 First powered flight
1904 War between Russia and Japan
1909 North Pole reached
First flight across the English Channel

1910 Harvey Crippen, American murderer *72*
Isadora Duncan, U.S. dancer *86*
1911 H.D., U.S. poet *86*
Sun Yat-sen, Chinese revolutionary *237*
Richard Strauss, German composer *236*
Emiliano Zapata, Mexican revolutionary *266*
Joseph Pulitzer, U.S. journalist *209*
Ernest Rutherford, New Zealand scientist *221*
Maria Montessori, Italian educationalist *177*
Katherine Mansfield, New Zealand writer *165*
Roald Amundsen, Norwegian explorer *26*
Pancho Villa, Mexican leader *252*
1912 Frederick Hopkins, British scientist *130*
James Thorpe, American athlete *241*
Ferdinand von Zeppelin, airship designer *266*
Robert Falcon Scott, British explorer *225*
Woodrow Wilson, U.S. President *262*
Arnold Schoenberg, Austrian composer *224*
Nijinksy, Russian dancer *189*
Robert Service, Canadian poet *226*
1913 Stravinsky, Russian composer *236*
Cecil B. DeMille, U.S. film maker *82*
Marcel Proust, French writer *208*
Sylvia Pankhurst, English suffragette *194*
D. H. Lawrence, English writer *152*
Carl Gustav Jung, Swiss psychologist *139*
Emily Davison, English suffragette *79*
Robert Frost, U.S. poet *104*
1914 André Gide, French writer *111*
1915 James Frazer, Scottish anthropologist *103*
Jean Henri Fabre, French scientist *98*
Edith Cavell, English nurse *55*
Enrico Caruso, Italian singer *54*
1916 Douglas Haig, British soldier *118*
Michael Collins, Irish politician *65*
Maud Gonne, Irish politician *113*
1917 Lenin, Russian leader
Trotsky, Russian leader *154*
Alexander Kerensky, Russian leader *146*
Georges Clemenceau, French politician *64*
Jascha Heifetz, Russian violinist *122*
T. S. Eliot, English poet *93*
1918 Eduard Beneš, Czech statesman *39*
Ignace Paderewski, Polish politician & composer *193*
John Reed, U.S. writer *214*
T. E. Lawrence, British soldier *153*
Wilfred Owen, English poet *192*
Erich Maria Remarque, German writer *214*
1919 Jan Smuts, South African politician *230*
Eamon De Valera, Irish leader *83*
Walter Gropius, German architect *116*
Edwin Hubble, U.S. astronomer *130*
Nancy Astor, British politician *30*
1920 Gustav Holst, British composer *127*
Augustus & Gwen John, English artists *137*
Houdini, U.S. escape artist *130*
Armand Hammer, U.S. businessman & diplomat *119*
J. L. Lewis, U.S. union leader *157*
Sinclair Lewis, U.S. writer *158*
Colette, French writer *65*
1921 Luigi Pirandello, Italian dramatist *203*
Marianne Moore, U.S. poet *178*
Kandinsky, Russian artist *144*
Faisal I, king of Syria and Iraq *98*
1922 Niels Bohr, Danish scientist *43*
Le Corbusier, Swiss architect *70*
Coco Chanel, French fashion designer *59*
Willa Cather, U.S. writer *55*
James Joyce, Irish writer *138*
Benito Mussolini, Italian leader *182*
1923 Wallace Stevens, U.S. poet *234*
Rilke, German poet *216*
Pablo Neruda, Chilean poet *187*
Atatürk, Turkish leader *30*
Calvin Coolidge, U.S. President *67*
e. e. cummings, U.S. poet *74*
1924 Stalin, Soviet leader *232*
J. L. Baird, Scottish engineer *33*
Ezra Pound, U.S. poet *205*
Sean O'Casey, Irish dramatist *190*
Franz Kafka, Czech writer *144*
1925 Charlie Chaplin, English actor & film maker *59*
Virginia Woolf, English writer *263*
F. Scott Fitzgerald, U.S. writer *100*
Jacob Epstein, U.S. sculptor *95*
Sergei Eisenstein, Soviet film maker *92*
Theodore Dreiser, U.S. writer *87*
William R. Hearst, U.S. newspaper owner *122*
André Kertész, Hungarian photographer *146*
Louis Armstrong, U.S. jazz musician *29*
1926 Suzanne Lenglen, French tennis player *156*
A. A. Milne, English writer *175*
Stan Laurel & Oliver Hardy *152*
Hirohito, Japanese emperor *125*
1927 Vita Sackville-West, English writer *222*
Babe Ruth, U.S. baseball player *221*
Thornton Wilder, U.S. dramatist *260*
Greta Garbo, Swedish actress *106*
Martha Graham, U.S. dancer *115*
Charles Lindbergh, U.S. aviator *158*
Buster Keaton, U.S. actor *144*
1928 Walt Disney, U.S. film maker *85*
Alexander Fleming, Scottish scientist *101*

Johnny Weissmuller, U.S. swimmer *255*
Wolfgang Pauli, Austrian scientist *196*
Garcia Lorca, Spanish writer *160*
Margaret Mead, U.S. anthropologist *171*
Herbert Hoover, U.S. President *130*
1929 Salvador Dali, Spanish artist *76*
Teilhard de Chardin, French philosopher *239*
Jean Cocteau, French artist *65*
Richard Byrd, U.S. explorer *50*
1930 Mahatma Gandhi, Indian leader *108*
Haile Selassie, Ethiopian ruler *118*
Amy Johnson, English aviator *137*
Rudolf von Laban, Hungarian choreographer *151*
Edith Piaf, French singer *202*
1931 Karen Blixen, Danish writer *42*
William Walton, English composer *254*
Ninette de Valois, English dancer *249*
1932 William Faulkner, U.S. writer *98*
Franklin D. Roosevelt, U.S. President *219*
Salazar, Portuguese leader *222*
Howard Hughes, U.S. businessman *131*
Melanie Klein, Austrian psychologist *150*
Laura Ingalls Wilder, U.S. writer *132*
Amelia Earhart, U.S. aviator *88*
1933 Erwin Schrödinger, Austrian scientist *225*
Adolf Hitler, German leader *125*
1934 Prokofiev, Russian composer *208*
1935 George Gershwin, U.S. composer *111*
Robert Watson-Watt, Scottish scientist *254*
Lincoln Ellsworth, American explorer *94*
1936 Jesse Owens, U.S. athlete *192*
John Maynard Keynes, English economist *146*
Allen Lane, English publisher *151*
Margaret Mitchell, U.S. writer *176*
Paul Robeson, U.S. singer *217*
Jacques Cousteau, French diver *71*
Léon Blum, French politician *42*
Simone Weil, French philosopher *255*
Edward VIII, British king *89*
1937 W. H. Auden, English poet *31*
Zora Neale Hurston, U.S. writer *131*
Grandma Moses, U.S. artist *179*
1938 Gladys Aylward, English missionary *32*
Neville Chamberlain, British politician *59*
Benny Goodman, U.S. jazz musician *114*
Graham Greene, English writer *115*
Bertolt Brecht, German dramatist *46*
1939 Igor Sikorsky, helicopter engineer *230*
General Franco, Spanish leader *102*
Vladimir Zworykin, U.S. scientist *267*
Dorothy Parker, U.S. writer *194*
Flann O'Brien, Irish writer *190*
1940 Bing Crosby, American singer *73*
Alfred Hitchcock, English film maker *125*
Ernest Hemingway, U.S. writer *122*
Al Capone, U.S. mobster *53*
Winston Churchill, British politician *63*
Cole Porter, U.S. songwriter *205*
Vidkun Quisling, Norwegian leader *210*
Béla Bartók, Hungarian composer *35*
Orson Welles, U.S. film maker *258*
John Steinbeck, U.S. writer *233*
1941 Jorge Luis Borges, Argentinian writer *44*
Joe Di Maggio, U.S. baseball player *84*
Zhukov, Soviet soldier *267*
1942 Eero Saarinen, American architect *222*
Albert Camus, French writer *52*
Enrico Fermi, Italian scientist *100*
Quasimodo, Italian poet *210*
1943 Jean Paul Sartre, French philosopher *223*
James Thurber, U.S. writer & artist *241*
Robert Oppenheimer, U.S. scientist *191*
Wladyslaw Gomulka, Polish leader *113*
1944 Wilhelm Furtwängler, German musician *104*
Bernard Montgomery, British soldier *178*
Omar Bradley, U.S. soldier *45*
Aaron Copland, U.S. composer *70*
1945 Harry S. Truman, U.S. President *245*

MAIN EVENTS

1910 Revolution in Portugal: republic declared
1911 Chinese Revolution: Manchu Dynasty overthrown
1912 First Balkan War
Titanic sinks; 1,513 lives lost
1914 World War I
1916 Easter rising in Ireland
1917 February Revolution in Russia: tsar overthrown
October Revolution: provisional government of Russia overthrown by Bolsheviks
1918 Armistice between Germany and Allies: war ends
1922 March on Rome: Fascists take control in Italy
1927 Civil war in China
1929 U.S. stock market collapses
1933 Hitler appointed Chancellor of Germany
1934 Long March in China
1936 Spanish Civil War
1939 Germany invades Poland: beginning of World War II
1941 Pearl Harbor: Japan attacks U.S. fleet—U.S.A. declares war on Axis
1944 Normandy landings: Allies begin reconquest of France
1945 Hitler commits suicide; Germany surrenders
Atomic bombs dropped on Hiroshima and Nagasaki in Japan: World War II ends
United Nations founded

Tito, Yugoslav leader *242*
Werner Von Braun, German engineer *253*
Robert Goddard, U.S. engineer *113*
Anne Frank, German-Jewish writer *102*
Patton, U.S. soldier *195*
Douglas MacArthur, U.S. soldier *62*
George Marshall, U.S. diplomat *168*
Chiang Kai-shek, Chinese leader *62*
George Orwell, English writer *191*
Ho Chi Minh, Vietnamese leader *126*
1946 Herman Hesse, German writer *124*
Carson McCullers, U.S. writer *171*
Juan & Eva Perón, Argentinian politicians *200*
1947 Rebecca West, English writer *259*
Tennessee Williams U.S. writer *262*
Maria Callas, Greek singer *51*
Louis Mountbatten, British diplomat *179*
Nehru, Indian politician *186*
Jinnah, Pakistani politician *136*
Thor Heyerdahl, Norwegian explorer *124*
Humphrey Bogart, U.S. actor *43*
1948 David Ben-Gurion, Israeli politician *39*
George Balanchine, Russian choreographer *34*
Benjamin Britten, English composer *47*
Fred Hoyle, English astronomer *130*
1949 Zhou Enlai, Chinese leader *266*
Arthur Miller, U.S. dramatist *175*
Mao Ze-dong, Chinese leader *165*
Doris Lessing, Rhodesian novelist *157*
Ben Hogan, U.S. golfer *127*
1950 Eugène Ionesco, Romanian dramatist *133*
Edward Hopper, U.S. artist *130*
Soichiro Honda, Japanese motorcycle maker *130*
Flannery O'Connor, U.S. writer *190*
Henry Moore, English sculptor *178*
Pablo Casals, Spanish cellist *54*
Jackson Pollock, U.S. artist *204*
Ralph Johnson Bunche, U.S. diplomat *50*
Enzo Ferrari, Italian car designer *100*
Mother Theresa, missionary *240*
Duke Ellington, U.S. jazz musician *94*
1951 Kurosawa, Japanese film maker *150*
1952 Elizabeth II, British queen *94*
Samuel Beckett, Irish writer *36*
Dwight Eisenhower, U.S. President *92*
1953 Simone Signoret, French actress *230*
Francis Crick, English scientist *72*
Julius & Ethel Rosenberg, U.S. spies *220*
Dag Hammarskjöld, UN secretary-general *119*
Edmund Hillary, N.Z. mountaineer *124*
Tenzing Norgay, Nepalese mountaineer *239*
Nikita Khrushchev, Soviet leader *147*
Jonas Salk, develops polio vaccine *223*
1954 Simone De Beauvoir, French writer *79*
Dylan Thomas, Welsh writer *241*
Roger Bannister, English athlete *34*
James Baldwin, U.S. writer *34*
Linus Pauling, U.S. scientist *196*
William Golding, English writer *113*
1955 Prince Sihanouk, Cambodian leader *230*
1956 Imre Nagy, Hungarian minister *183*
Nasser, Egyptian president *183*
Elvis Presley, U.S. singer *208*
Frank Lloyd Wright, U.S. architect *264*
1957 Vivian Fuchs, British explorer *104*
Leonard Bernstein, U.S. composer *40*
Eugene O'Neill, U.S. dramatist *191*
Jack Kerouac, U.S. writer *146*
Andrei Gromyko, Soviet diplomat *116*
Fidel Castro, Cuban leader *54*
1958 Alec Guinness, English actor *117*
Pelé, Brazilian soccer player *197*
Kenneth Kaunda, Zambian president *144*
Charles De Gaulle, French president *82*
1959 Joan Sutherland, Australian singer *237*
Che Guevara, Argentianian revolutionary *116*
Billie Holiday, U.S. singer *127*
1960 Mary Quant, British fashion designer *210*
Federico Fellini, Italian film maker *99*
Ingmar Bergman, Swedish film maker *39*
Cecil Beaton, English photographer *35*
Sylvia Plath, U.S. poet *204*
Julius Nyerere, Tanzanian president *189*
Laurence Olivier, English actor *191*
J. F. Kennedy, U.S. President *148*
James Alfred Van Allen, U.S. scientist *249*
1961 François Truffaut, French film maker *245*
Nureyev, Russian dancer *189*
Margot Fonteyn, English dancer *101*
Yuri Gagarin, first man in space *105*
1962 Georges Pompidou, French president *205*
Marilyn Monroe, U.S. actress *177*
John Lennon & Paul McCartney, English pop musicians *156*
Rod Laver, Australian tennis player *152*
Mick Jagger, English pop musician *134*
U Thant, Burmese diplomat *240*
1963 Lyndon Johnson, American President *137*
Valentina Tereshkova, first woman in space *239*
Lee Harvey Oswald, U.S. assassin *192*
Jomo Kenyatta, Kenyan president *146*

Frederick Ashton, English dancer *30*
Nadine Gordimer, South African writer *114*
1964 Nelson Mandela, Black South African leader *165*
Bob Marley, Jamaican pop musician *168*
Leonid Brezhnev, Soviet leader *47*
Malcolm X, black American leader *164*
Philip Larkin, English poet *152*
1965 Ian Smith, Rhodesian leader *230*
Bob Dylan, U.S. singer *87*
Robert Lowell, U.S. poet *162*
1967 Moshe Dayan, Israeli soldier *79*
Christiaan Barnard, South African surgeon *34*
Gabriel Garcia Márquez, Colombian writer *168*
1968 Alexander Dubček, Czech leader *87*
John Updike, U.S. writer *249*
Pierre Trudeau, Canadian politician *245*
Bob Beamon, U.S. athlete *35*
Kawabata, Japanese writer *144*
Robert Kennedy, U.S. politician *145*
Yasser Arafat, Palestinian leader *28*
Martin Luther King, black American leader *149*
1969 Indira Gandhi, Indian leader *108*
Golda Meir, Israeli politician *171*
Willy Brandt, German politician *46*
Neil Armstrong, U.S. astronaut *24*
1970 David Hockney, English artist *126*
Henry Kissinger, U.S. politician *150*
Jack Nicklaus, U.S. golfer *188*
Marshall McLuhan, Canadian writer *171*
Yukio Mishima, Japanese writer *176*
Anwar el Sadat, Egyptian president *222*
Italo Calvino, Italian writer *52*
Milton Friedman, U.S. economist *104*
Germaine Greer, Australian writer *115*
Aleksander Solzhenitsyn, Russian writer *231*
1971 Dorothy Day, U.S. social reformer *79*
1972 Mark Spitz, U.S. swimmer *232*
Eddy Merckx, Belgian cyclist *174*
Ted Hughes, English poet *131*
1973 Stevie Wonder, U.S. pop musician *263*
Patrick White, Australian writer *259*
1974 Richard Nixon, U.S. President *189*
1975 John Malcolm Fraser, Australian politician *103*
Yehudi Menuhin, U.S. violinist *174*
Martina Navratilova, Czech tennis player *183*
Juan Carlos I, Spanish king *139*
1976 Jimmy Carter, U.S. President *53*
Saul Bellow, U.S. writer *39*
Bjorn Borg, Swedish tennis player *44*
J. Paul Getty, U.S. businessman *111*
1977 Deng Xiaoping, Chinese leader *82*
1978 Pope John Paul II *137*
Muhammad Ali, U.S. boxer *26*
1979 Margaret Thatcher, British politician *240*
Ayatollah Khomeini, Iranian leader *147*
1980 Ronald Reagan, U.S. President *211*
Lech Walesa, Polish labor leader *254*
1981 François Mitterand, French president *176*
1984 Rajiv Gandhi, Indian politician *106*
1986 Mikhail Gorbachev, Soviet leader, introduces *glasnost* (openness)
1987 Margaret Thatcher, British prime minister, elected for third term

MAIN EVENTS

1947 Indian independence: India (Hindu) and Pakistan (Muslim) set up
1948 Communist takeover in Czechoslovakia
State of Israel declared
Korea divided into North and South
Gandhi assassinated in India
1949 Communist government establishes control of China
Germany divided into East (Democratic Republic) and West (Federal Republic)
1956 Egypt nationalizes Suez Canal: British and French invade; UN calls cease-fire
1957 Treaty of Rome: European Community set up
1960 17 African colonies gain independence
1961 Berlin Wall built
Bay of Pigs invasion
1965 U.S. bombs North Vietnam
1966 Cultural revolution in China
1967 Six-Day War between Israel and Arabs
1969 First manned moon landing
1975 Vietnam War ends
1976 Soweto riots in South Africa
1979 Iranian Revolution: shah replaced by Muslim leadership
Russian invasion of Afghanistan
1980 Rhodesia becomes independent Zimbabwe
Uprising in Poland led by Solidarity union
1986 Chernobyl nuclear explosion

Abelard, Peter (1079–1142)
Peter Abelard was a great French theologian who is also remembered for his passionate love affair with **Héloïse** (*c.*1098–1164). He was born in Brittany, and became famous as a lecturer at the cathedral school of Notre Dame in Paris. The 17-year-old Héloïse was one of his pupils. Abelard romanced her and they fled to Brittany, where they were secretly married. Héloïse later renounced their marriage, because it prevented Abelard from continuing as a priest, and became a nun. Her uncle then had Abelard retired to an abbey to lead the life of a monk. As a monk, and later as a hermit, he was surrounded by people eager to hear his teaching, although he was twice condemned by the Church as a "heretic" (somebody whose beliefs disagree with the official teaching of the Church). After having lived a devout life for many years, he decided to go to Rome to defend his opinions; however, he died while on his way there, at an abbey near Châlons. Abelard was buried near his abbey in Brittany by Héloïse. Héloïse died in 1164, when she was buried beside him. Their story is preserved in the letters that he wrote to her.

Abraham (*c.*2000 B.C.)
Abraham was "the father of the Israelites." The Book of Genesis, the first book of the Bible, says that Abraham was born in the town of Ur (in Mesopotamia), one of the three sons of Terah. At God's command, Abraham went with his wife Sarah and the rest of his household to Canaan (Palestine) where he founded the Hebrew people.

In order to test Abraham's faith, God instructed him to sacrifice his only son Isaac. Abraham journeyed with Isaac to a distant mountainside where he built an altar and prepared to kill him. Satisfied that Abraham would obey him, God ordered him to replace his son with a ram.

Peter Abelard with Héloïse—romantic but tragic lovers. As a theologian Abelard taught that traditional beliefs should be questioned in the light of reason.

Adam, Robert (1728–92)
A Scottish architect who studied ancient Greek and Roman ruins and used what he saw in his designs for British houses and furniture. He believed that all the parts of a building, including the decorations and furniture, should be made in a similar style.
○ KAUFFMANN

Adams, John (1735–1826)
In 1797 John Adams became the second president of the United States. He was trained as a lawyer at Harvard College and became a strong supporter of American independence. Adams was present during the drafting of the Declaration of Independence, which he signed, and served as American ambassador in a number of European countries, including England. In 1789 he became the first vice-president of the United States under George Washington. His own presidency lasted from 1797 until 1801. ○ JEFFERSON, WASHINGTON

John Adams' son, **John Quincy Adams** (1767–1848), was president from 1825 until 1829. As a boy he traveled with his father on his trips abroad, and like his father he studied law and became a politician and a diplomat. He was chosen as president by the House of Representatives after the 1824 election had failed to produce a result. Later in life he was known as an opponent of slavery. He died at the end of a particularly energetic speech in the House of Representatives.

Adenauer, Konrad (1876–1967)
Chancellor of Germany from 1949 until his retirement in 1963. Adenauer was keen to strengthen relations between Germany and the rest of the world after the World War II, and led Germany's entry into NATO and the European Economic Community.

Adrian IV (*c.*1100–59)
Adrian IV was the only Englishman ever to become Pope. He was born with the name Nicholas Breakspear at Langley, near St. Albans, and became a monk, and later abbot, of a monastery near Avignon in France. He was a strict disciplinarian, which caused other monks to complain of him to Pope Eugenius III; Eugenius, however, was impressed by Breakspear, and made him cardinal of Albano. As Pope, Adrian granted Ireland to Henry II and crowned Frederick I emperor. ○ FREDERICK I

Aeschylus (*c.*525 B.C.–*c.*456 B.C.)
Aeschylus was the first great ancient Greek dramatist. He was an Athenian, and he fought as a soldier during the Persian wars. In ancient Greece, new plays were entered in drama contests. Aeschylus won his first contest in 485 B.C., and won 13 more before being defeated by the young Sophocles in 468 B.C. Aeschylus spent some years in Sicily before returning to Athens to win a final victory with his trilogy (group of three plays) called *The Orestia*. They tell of the return of the warrior Agamemnon from the siege of Troy, of his murder by his wife; then, in the second play, how he is avenged by his son and daughter; and finally how his son is pursued by spirits called "The Furies." Only seven of Aeschylus' plays, including the three of *The Orestia*, have survived. There is a legend that the playwright was killed when an eagle, mistaking his bald head for a rock, dropped a tortoise on it. ○ PERICLES, SOPHOCLES

Aesop (6th century B.C.)
According to tradition, Aesop was the writer of a famous collection of animal "fables"—short, simple stories about animals which contain a "moral" (or lesson) for their human readers. Very little is known for certain about Aesop's life, but it is said that he was a slave, born on the ancient Greek island of Samos, in the Aegean Sea. He was set free, and traveled around the islands and kingdoms of the eastern Mediterranean. Eventually he met King Croesus of Lydia, who employed him as a diplomat. He is said to have been ugly, clownish, but also very witty. Sometimes his wit got him into trouble. On a visit to the sacred oracle at Delphi, the priests got fed up with Aesop's ceaseless joking, and they threw him over a cliff.

It is not known when or where he began writing down his fables. In fact, it is unlikely that Aesop

Illustrations by Gustave Doré of two of Aesop's fables: The Hare and the Frogs *and* The Eagle and the Crow. *In his fables Aesop makes his animals talk and act like human beings with human virtues and weaknesses. The most famous of his fables are probably* The Hare and the Tortoise *and* The Goose That Laid the Golden Egg.

actually *wrote* any of them. Similar stories about animals exist in many other cultures; Aesop probably only collected them together. No books or manuscripts by Aesop are known to exist, and the only surviving ancient Greek version was not written until the second century A.D., some years after Aesop's lifetime. But whatever the truth about their author, "Aesop's Fables" quickly became known by that name, and were very popular with the ancient Greeks. They include "The Hare and the Tortoise," in which a fast-running hare and slow, plodding tortoise run a race. The hare is so sure that he will win that he stops for a rest part of the way through. Meanwhile, the tortoise just keeps going steadily. The hare falls asleep, the tortoise plods past and wins the race. The moral is that the slow but sure are bound to succeed. This and many similar tales have remained famous for centuries. They were translated into Latin during the Roman Empire, and were widely read in the Middle Ages. In the 17th century **Jean de la Fontaine** (1621–95) wrote a famous French version of the fables, and they are often read and retold today. ○ CROESUS

Agrippina (d. A.D. 33)
The wife of the Emperor Germanicus, who was almost certainly poisoned by his enemies. Agrippina was so popular with the Roman people that the Emperor Tiberius was suspicious of her and had her banished and two of her sons murdered. Her third son, Caligula, became emperor, and her daughter, **Colonia Agrippina** (d. A.D. 59), was the mother of the Emperor Nero. The younger Agrippina married and probably poisoned her uncle, the Emperor Claudius, and was so famous for her cruelty that Nero had her killed.
○ CALIGULA, NERO

Akbar (1542–1605)
Akbar, which means "The Great," was born with the name Jelal-ed-din-Mohammed, and succeeded his father as Mogul emperor of India at the age of only 13. He extended and reorganized his empire, built roads and created a new police force. He was born a Muslim, but he allowed and was interested in other religions, and late in his life he tried to reduce conflict between various religious groups by promoting a new religion which combined many existing beliefs.

Alaric (*c.*370–410)
A general in command of Gothic troops under the Roman Emperor Theodosius I. Alaric was elected King of the Visigoths, and when Theodosius died, he broke with Rome and invaded various parts of the empire, finally capturing Rome in 410. He then attempted to conquer all of Italy, but died before he finished the task.

Alban, Saint (d. *c.*209)
A Roman soldier said to have been the first Christian martyr in Britain. He was executed, probably by beheading, for sheltering a fleeing priest. A shrine, and later a cathedral, were built at the site.

Alcott, Louisa May (1832–88)
Louisa May Alcott was an American writer whose most famous book is the children's classic *Little Women*. She was born in Pennsylvania, but her family moved to the city of Boston, Massachusetts, while she was a young girl. Among the family's neighbors were the writers Henry Thoreau and Ralph Waldo Emerson, who helped Louisa's father give her an education. Her family were not wealthy, and she worked at sewing and teaching to help support them. She also wrote stories, plays, and fairy tales, some of which were published in magazines and books. In 1860 the Civil War began, and she became a nurse in an army hospital. Her letters home were published in a book called *Hospital Sketches* in 1863. After the war she traveled, edited a children's magazine, and wrote a successful novel called *Moods*. But it was the publication of *Little Women* in 1868 that made her famous. It tells the story of family life in Massachusetts, and was closely based on Louisa's own childhood. The book was a best-seller, and was soon being translated into other languages. Louisa May Alcott continued to write novels (including *An Old-Fashioned Girl* and *Little Men*, both of which were popular).

Alexander VI (1431–1503)
Alexander VI was the name taken by Rodrigo Borgia when he became Pope in 1492. He was notorious for keeping mistresses, and for using his office to enrich himself and his family and to improve the fortunes of his children. His main aim as Pope was to strengthen the military power of Rome. He probably died of fever, but there is a legend that he was killed by poisoned wine which he intended for some of his guests. ○ BORGIA

Alexander the Great (356 B.C.–323 B.C.)
Alexander was a king of the ancient Greek state of Macedonia, who conquered and ruled lands stretching all the way from Italy in the West to India in the East. He was the son of King Philip II and was educated by the philosopher Aristotle. At

(Continued on page 26)

Alexander the Great.

Man on the Moon

Armstrong, Neil (1930–)
The short history of manned space flight began on April 12, 1961, when a Soviet cosmonaut, Yuri Gagarin, made a single successful orbit of the earth in his tiny *Vostok 1* capsule. A few weeks later, President Kennedy officially launched the Apollo program, saying that within ten years America would put a man on the moon and return him safely to earth. Remarkably, his words came true: on July 21, 1969, Neil Armstrong stepped from the *Eagle* lunar landing craft onto the moon's surface and transmitted the words "That's one small step for man, one giant leap for mankind" back to earth.

The Apollo 11 flight that delivered Armstrong and his companions, Buzz Aldrin and Michael Collins, to the moon was the result of rapid advances in science and technology, as well as the expenditure of billions of dollars. In 1965 and 1966 ten manned "Gemini" missions proved that astronauts could live and work in space, and gave both them and the scientists on the ground the opportunity to experiment with equipment and practice different maneuvers. Meanwhile, engineers developed the giant Saturn V rockets, powerful enough to launch the lunar landing craft and send it on its way to the moon. The first craft to travel to the moon was Apollo 8, which circled it ten times at Christmas, 1968.

2. The command module separates and turns on its axis to dock with the lunar landing craft (lunar excursion module or LEM).

Neil Armstrong
1930 Born at Wapakoneta, Ohio
1962 Joins space program
1966 Commander, Gemini 8 mission
1969 Astronaut on board Apollo 11 mission; becomes first man on the moon

Edwin "Buzz" Aldrin
1930 Born at Montclair, New Jersey
1966 Astronaut on board Gemini 12 mission; sets new space-walk record
1969 Astronaut on board Apollo 11 mission; becomes second man on the moon

Michael Collins
1930 Born at Rome, Italy
1966 Astronaut on board Gemini 10 mission
1969 Astronaut on board Apollo 11 mission; remains in orbiting command module

1. Launch of the Apollo/Saturn rocket from Cape Canaveral. The launching pad stood over 360 feet in height.

3. The command module and the LEM linked together in flight. The third stage of the launcher has now been jettisoned.

4. The command module remains in orbit around the moon while the LEM descends to the surface.

5. The LEM on the surface of the moon.

6. Blast-off from the moon. The bottom section of the LEM acts as a launching pad and is left behind.

Apollo 11 was launched the following summer. On July 20, Armstrong and Aldrin crawled from the command module, in orbit around the moon, into the lunar landing vehicle. Collins remained behind, circling above as the two astronauts explored the lunar landscape. The landing was not easy: an error in the craft's computers meant that Armstrong had to juggle the controls to land safely. But once on the ground, he radioed a message back to the controllers waiting in Houston, Texas: "Houston—Tranquility Base here. The Eagle has landed."

The two men spent just a day on the moon's surface. Five more successful Apollo missions followed, together with one near disaster. In April 1970 an explosion on board Apollo 13 put the lives of three astronauts in grave danger. They circled the moon and returned to earth with barely enough oxygen to survive, but eventually made a safe splashdown, in the ocean. The last mission, Apollo 17, took place in 1972. The entire program had been a combination of remarkable scientific and technical skill, and the daring of a few men like Neil Armstrong.

○ GAGARIN, GLENN

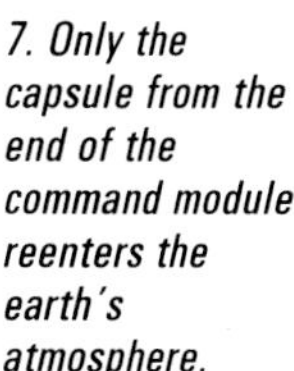

7. Only the capsule from the end of the command module reenters the earth's atmosphere.

8. Splashdown in the Pacific Ocean.

the age of 16 he was left in charge of Macedonia while Philip went to war with the Byzantines, and three years later he became king after Philip was assassinated during preparations for war with Persia. After crushing a rebellion in Greece, Alexander led his army into Persia. He won two great victories, at the river Granicus, and then in 333 B.C. at Issus, where he defeated King Darius and captured his family and treasure. From there, Alexander went on to conquer Syria and Palestine and to release Egypt from Persian rule. In 331 B.C. he founded the city of Alexandria on the river Nile, before returning northeast to defeat Darius a second time and capture the farthest corners of the Persian Empire. During his campaign he married a princess called Roxana, whom he had taken prisoner. But Alexander lost the support and friendship of his foster brother Clitus, whom he later killed in a drunken fight.

In 326 B.C. Alexander crossed the river Indus and entered India, where he defeated King Porus and captured the area known as the Punjab. His troops, now exhausted and few in number, refused to go farther, and Alexander returned to Babylon, where he ruled in great splendor from 325 B.C. until his death. Under Alexander, Greek culture spread throughout Asia and the Greeks increased their knowledge of geography and natural history. After his death, the empire was divided among his generals. ○ ARISTOTLE

Alfred the Great (849–*c.*900)
Alfred succeeded his brother Ethelred as king of Wessex (a kingdom in the southwest of England) in 871. At that time, much of the land was ruled by the Danes, who attempted to invade Wessex from the north and the east. In 878 Alfred was forced to retreat to marshland in the west of his kingdom. It was at this time that the story of his having allowed an old woman's cakes to burn arose. Later that year he defeated the Danish King Guthrum at a battle at Eddington, and took control of the Midlands and all of the country south of the Thames, allowing Guthrum to keep East Anglia. In 884 he began a new campaign against the Danes, and in 886 captured London and took control of Northumbria, making him the ruler of all England. As king, he reorganized the government and laws of the country and attempted to maintain peace. He was keen on education, and had many works translated from Latin into English. Toward the end of his reign, the country was again invaded by Danes. He died in between 899 and 901 and was buried at Winchester.

Ali, Muhammad (1942–)
Muhammad Ali, born Cassius Clay, is the only heavyweight boxer to have become world champion three times, the last in 1978. He was famous for teasing his opponents and entertaining his fans by predicting the round in which he would win a fight, and he pronounced his motto: "Dance like a butterfly—sting like a bee!"

Allende, Salvador (1908–73)
The first Marxist elected in a free election in the Western world, Allende served as president of Chile from 1970 until 1973, when an economic crisis resulted in a military coup led by General Pinochet, during which Allende was killed.

Alonso, Alicia (1920–)
A Cuban ballet dancer, famous for her interpretation of *Giselle.* She was the founder of the Cuban national ballet and school of dancing.

Amundsen, Roald (1872–1928)
Amundsen was a Norwegian explorer, famous for being the first man to reach the South Pole, in 1911. He also found the site of the magnetic North Pole, and commanded the first ship to navigate the Northwest Passage, the *Gjoa,* in 1903. As a boy, Amundsen's ambition was to be an explorer, and he gave up his schooling to join a Belgian Antarctic expedition. After the success of his Northwest Passage voyage, he was preparing an expedition to the North Pole when the news arrived that the American explorer Peary had already reached it. Amundsen decided to try to become the first to reach the South Pole instead, and in June 1910 he set out for Antarctica in a ship called the *Fram.*

Explorer Roald Amundsen—the first man to reach the South Pole, in 1911.

Scott, an Englishman, was also attempting to reach the South Pole, and its discovery became a race between the two expeditions. Using sledges drawn by dogs, Amundsen reached the Pole on December 16, 1911, a month before Scott. He left a

Norwegian flag and a message, and returned to his ship.

After the 1914–18 World War Amundsen made two attempts to fly over the North Pole. The second, made in 1926 in an airship with an Italian explorer called Umberto Nobile, was successful. In 1928 Amundsen was killed in a plane crash while searching for Nobile, who had been lost during a polar flight. He received many awards, and wrote a book called *The South Pole* about his Antarctic expedition. ○ PEARY, SCOTT

Andersen, Hans Christian (1805–75)
Hans Christian Andersen was a poet and storyteller who is most famous for his many children's stories and fairy tales. These include *The Ugly Duckling, Thumbellina, The Emperor's New Clothes, The Snow Queen,* and many more. He was born the son of a

Storyteller Hans Christian Andersen.

poor shoemaker in Odense, Denmark, and after his father's death worked in a factory. Andersen tried to improve his fortunes by traveling to Copenhagen. He attempted acting, singing, and writing plays, but failed at all these before a friend and minister called Collin found a place for him at a school, and then the university. Some of his poems had already been admired, and in 1830 he published a collected edition of his poetry. This was followed by a second, and then in 1833 by a traveling scholarship which enabled Andersen to visit Germany, Switzerland, and Italy. These visits inspired several stories. Over the next 20 years he wrote more than 160 stories and fairy tales, including all his most famous works. He also traveled widely, and became friends with the English novelist Charles Dickens. The storyteller fell in love with a famous Swedish singer called Jenny Lind, but failed to win her affection, and he never married. Hans Christian Andersen described his life in an autobiography called *My Life.*

Anderson, Elizabeth Garrett (1836–1917)
See Garrett Anderson, Elizabeth

Anne Boleyn (1504–36)
See Boleyn, Anne

Anthony, Susan Brownell (1820–1906)
Susan Anthony was one of the leaders of the campaign for women's rights in America during the second half of the 19th century. Early in life she petitioned for the abolition of slavery, and she believed that women, as well as slaves, should be granted the same legal rights as men. In 1854 Anthony collected 6,000 signatures on a petition which asked that women be given the vote, that they be allowed to keep any money they earned, and that they be able to keep their children if they were divorced. This petition, followed by several more, led to some reforms of the laws of New York State. After the Civil War, when slaves were freed and allowed to vote, women also expected to be granted a vote. This did not happen, and in 1869 Susan Anthony and **Elizabeth Cady Stanton** (1815–1902) formed the National Women Suffrage Association to campaign for votes for women. Although the Association was large and energetic in its campaigns, women did not gain the vote during Anthony's lifetime. She also lectured on temperance (abstaining from alcohol) and slavery. She retired in 1900.

Women's rights campaigner Susan Anthony.

Appleseed, Johnny (John Chapman, 1774–1845)
"Johnny Appleseed" was an American frontiersman. He was born in Massachusetts, but in about 1800 he moved west to Ohio, where he began planting apple trees. As settlers moved west, so Johnny Appleseed kept ahead of them, preparing the "wilderness" with fruit trees. In about 1828 he reached what is now Indiana, where he spent the rest of his life. He became famous not only for his tree planting, but for his gentleness with animals and his generosity. He is the hero of many American folk tales.

Aquinas, Saint Thomas (*c.*1225–74)
Thomas Aquinas was the most famous philosopher and theologian of the medieval church. He was born into a noble family near Aquino in Italy (which explains the name "Aquinas") and studied with Benedictine monks at the monastery of Monte Cassino, and at the University of Naples. In about 1244 he joined the Dominican order of monks. This angered his family, who kidnapped him and locked him up in the family castle. Thomas was undeterred; he escaped and traveled to Paris and Cologne, where he took his degree. He devoted the rest of his life to studying, teaching, and preaching, and always refused the church appointments that were offered to him. His two great works were the *Summa contra Gentiles*, which is about God and His creation, and the unfinished *Summa Theologica*. He believed in recording what he had learned for the benefit of others, and was a humble man; at the end of his life he said: "All I have written seems to me like so much straw compared with what I have seen and what has been revealed to me."

Arafat, Yasser (1929–)
Until 1983 the leader of the Palestine Liberation Organization (PLO), which seeks a homeland for the Palestinian people in an area free of Israeli occupation. Arafat was the first non-official government leader to address the United Nations.

Archimedes (*c.*287 B.C.–212 B.C.)
Archimedes, the greatest of ancient Greek mathematicians, was born in the city of Syracuse in Sicily. His many discoveries and inventions include the Archimedes screw, still used in many countries to lift water up from one level to another. He calculated the approximate value of the mathematical figure called *pi*, and is most famous for Archimedes' Principle. This explains that an object put into a fluid such as water will appear to *lose* an amount of weight equal to the weight of the amount (or "volume") of the fluid it displaces. He was killed when the Roman army invaded Syracuse in 212 B.C.

Ariosto, Lodovico (1474–1533)
Ariosto's *Orlando Furioso*, written between about 1505 and 1515, is one of the greatest poems in the Italian language. It tells how Orlando falls in love with a beautiful princess. When he discovers that she is married, he goes mad (*furioso* is the Italian for "mad")—but later returns to sanity and performs various heroic deeds. Ariosto also wrote comedies and satires, but *Orlando* is his greatest work.

Aristophanes (*c.*448 B.C.–*c.*388 B.C.)
Aristophanes was an ancient Greek playwright. Unlike the most famous of the other dramatists of his time, such as Sophocles or Euripedes, Aristophanes wrote comedies. Indeed, in some of his plays he makes fun of the great tragic playwrights. He also made politicians, statesmen, and philosophers the subjects of his jokes. Almost nothing is known about his life. He wrote over 50 plays, but only 11 have survived to this day. They include *Clouds* and *Wasps*, which are among his earliest plays, and *Birds* and *Frogs*, which were written later. In the *Lysistrata*, written in 411 B.C., a group of Athenian women refuse their husbands any favors until they stop fighting wars. Three of his sons, Araros, Nikostratos, and Philippos, also became comic playwrights. Aristophanes' plays have remained popular, and are frequently performed today.

Aristotle (384 B.C.–322 B.C.)
Aristotle was an ancient Greek philosopher whose ideas dominated European thought for many centuries. He was born in Stagira in northern Greece, where his father was a doctor working in the royal household of King Amyntas III, grandfather of Alexander the Great. At the age of 17, Aristotle traveled to Athens to study with the great philosopher Plato. He stayed at Plato's academy for 20 years, not leaving until the master's death in 347 B.C. In 342 B.C. he became tutor to the young Alexander. When Alexander set off to invade Asia, Aristotle returned to Athens, where he began a school called the Lyceum. He and his pupils came to be known as the "Peripatetics." The place where lectures were held was called "The Walk" (*Peripatos* in Greek), and Aristotle perhaps used to walk up and down *(peripateo)* while he spoke. After Alexander's death, Aristotle's enemies

attempted to have him arrested, and he fled to the island of Euboea, where he died. As well as philosophy, Aristotle studied biology and physics, proposed an ideal system of government, and set out rules for the writing of good drama.
○ALEXANDER, PLATO

Arkwright, Richard (1732–92)
Arkwright invented the spinning frame in 1768, the first machine able to make strong cotton thread. His designs were unscrupulously copied, and he was unpopular with the people because the machines took away jobs.

Armstrong, Louis (1900–71)
A black American jazz trumpeter and singer who learned to play the cornet when he was sent to an orphanage in New Orleans as a punishment for firing a revolver in the street. He began to make records in about 1925 and quickly became known as a virtuoso performer. By the time he had his last hit in 1964, "Satchmo," as he was known, was one of the most popular entertainers in the world.

A Victorian painting of the death of Arthur, the legendary king of the Britons. In the 12th-century chronicle of Geoffrey of Monmouth, Arthur is said to have died in 537 at the Battle of Camlan.

Armstrong, Neil (1930–)
See pages 24 & 25

Arnold, Benedict (1741–1801)
Benedict Arnold was an American soldier. He fought bravely in several important battles during the American Revolution, and was made commander of the city of Philadelphia. In 1780 he became head of the military academy at West Point, but he then decided to betray the Americans and become a British spy. When the plot was discovered he fled and joined the British army, and led attacks on the Americans.

Arthur
Arthur is the name of a legendary king of the Britons, said to have lived in about the 6th century A.D. He probably never existed, but many stories grew up about a hero who united the warring chieftains of the land and resisted invading Anglo-Saxon tribes after the departure of the Romans. The most famous of these were written or told during the Middle Ages, by poets such as Thomas Malory and the Frenchman **Chrétien de Troyes** (d. *c.*1190). In many versions, Arthur was a strong and holy king under whose rule the land was peaceful and the people content. He built a round

table for his council chamber so that none of his knights would seem more important than any other. Later, Arthur was betrayed by Guinevere, his queen, and Lancelot, his most famous knight, and the land fell into ruin. Another famous character in the legend is the magician Merlin, who protected Arthur when he was a boy and advised him when he became king. ○ GAWAIN-POET, MALORY

Ashton, Frederick William Mallandaine (1904–)
An English dancer and choreographer who became director of the Royal Ballet in 1963. Among his most famous ballets are *La Fille mal gardée* and *Cinderella,* in which he danced one of the ugly sisters. ○ VALOIS

Asoka (d. *c.*232 B.C.)
Asoka was an ancient Indian emperor who was responsible for spreading the Buddhist faith throughout India and much of Asia. He ruled from 264 until 232 B.C., and during the early part of his reign carried on a fierce and bloodthirsty campaign to bring the whole of India under his control. In about 257 B.C. he was suddenly converted to Buddhism, and in repentance for his past violence decided to bring Buddhist teaching to all his people. Lessons were painted on walls, and government officials told to ensure that people obeyed the faith. Asoka's ambassadors abroad became missionaries and by this means Buddhism eventually reached China and Japan. Many of the texts Asoka had painted can still be seen today. ○ BUDDHA

Asquith, Henry Herbert (1858–1928)
Asquith was a Liberal prime minister of Great Britain, serving from 1908 to 1916. He was a brilliant administrator, and his government included the reform of the Welsh Church, a bill for Irish home rule, and the introduction of National Insurance. ○ LLOYD GEORGE

Astor, Nancy Witcher Langhorne (1879–1964)
Nancy Astor was the first woman to sit as an MP (Member of Parliament) in the British House of Commons. She was born in Virginia, and went to England, where she met and married **William Waldorf Astor** (1879–1952), a politician. When he became Viscount Astor in 1919 and had to give up his seat in the House of Commons, she was elected to replace him. She was a Conservative, a supporter of the temperance movement, and of women's rights.

Ataturk, Mustafa Kemal (1881–1938)
Mustafa Kemal was the first president of modern Turkey. After World War I, in which he had been a successful commander, he opposed the dividing up of his country among the victorious nations and led a Turkish nationalist campaign. In 1920 Ataturk and his supporters separated from the powerless sultan and set up a new government. During the Turkish War of Independence, fought largely against the Greeks, Ataturk led his country to victory, and in 1923 he was elected president of the new Republic of Turkey. He attempted to modernize the country, introducing reforms such as the emancipation of women and the use of the Latin alphabet, and he encouraged people to adopt the Western habit of taking a surname. His own, "Ataturk," which he took in 1934, means "Father Turk."

Kemal Ataturk. He was elected the first president of the Turkish Republic in 1923.

Attila (*c.*406–53)
In 434 Attila became king of the scattered tribes known as the Huns who lived in Asia and central Europe. After murdering his brother, with whom he had at first ruled jointly, he led a vast army through southern Europe, and in 452 almost captured Rome itself. Negotiation with Pope Leo I, bribery, and the threat of plague and starvation which hung over Attila's army saved the city. This fierce warrior-chieftain died on or just after the day of his marriage to a princess named Ildeco. His death brought about the collapse of his empire, which at its height had stretched from Germany almost to China, and included a great many tribes.

Auden, Wystan Hugh (1907–73)
W. H. Auden was one of the most important English poets of the 20th century. During the 1930s, together with friends such as **Christopher Isherwood** (1904–86) and **Stephen Spender** (1909–), he became concerned about political problems like unemployment and the rise of fascism, and wrote about these things in his poems. In 1937 he went to Spain, where he drove an ambulance for the Republican army in the Spanish Civil War. The following year he traveled to China with Isherwood, where he wrote about the Japanese invasion. He emigrated to the United States, although he later became professor of poetry at Oxford University. Auden is most famous for the shorter poems he wrote during the 1930s. He also wrote scripts for operas by Stravinsky and his friend Benjamin Britten.
○ BRITTEN, STRAVINSKY

A drawing of the English poet W. H. Auden by the artist David Hockney. Auden became professor of poetry at Oxford University.

Augustine, Saint (354–430)
Saint Augustine is known as one of the great fathers of the Christian Church. He was the son of **Saint Monica**, but was not baptized and lived in Carthage with his mistress and their son for many years, before his search for a philosophy of life led him to Christianity. In 387 he was baptized and began a monastery in North Africa. Four years later he became a priest, and in 396 he was made Bishop of Hippo. As a bishop, he took great care of his people, looking after the poor and sick, preaching regularly, and acting as a judge in disputes. He wrote over a hundred books, the most famous of which is the *Confessions*, in which he describes his conversion to Christianity. He died during the siege of Hippo by the Vandals.

Augustus (63 B.C.–A.D. 14)
Augustus, who was born Gaius Julius Caesar Octavianus, became the first Roman emperor after Caesar's assassination and the downfall of the Roman Republic. At first he shared power with Mark Antony, Antony ruling the eastern half of the empire and Augustus the west. While Antony was enjoying himself in Cleopatra's court in Egypt, Augustus was attempting to secure his authority over the Romans. Augustus eventually fought and defeated Antony, making himself ruler of the entire empire. He was a cautious governor who concentrated on reforms in Rome and on keeping the peace abroad. He built new cities in various parts of the empire, and improved Rome: it was said that "Augustus found the city built of brick, and left it built in marble." Although his army suffered one major defeat at the hands of the Germans in 9 B.C., his reign remained fairly peaceful, and he was able to close the temple of Janus in Rome, at which offerings were made

Augustus, Rome's first emperor. He called himself "the first citizen of Rome."

during wartime. Poets and writers, including Virgil, Horace, and Ovid, flourished during Augustus' rule, known as "the Augustan Age." He died at Nola and was succeeded by his stepson, Tiberius.
○ BRUTUS, CLEOPATRA, HORACE, MARK ANTONY, VIRGIL

Aurangzeb (1618–1707)
A magnificent Mogul emperor whose name means "Ornament of the Throne." He came to power in 1658 by imprisoning his father and killing his brothers, Although Aurangzeb's rule was prosperous, he was himself hated and distrusted.

Austen, Jane (1775–1817)
Jane Austen is one of the greatest and most popular of English novelists. She was one of seven children born at a country rectory in Hampshire, where she and her family lived a quiet rural life. Entertainment was limited to reading, visiting, and sometimes putting on a play in a local barn. Jane Austen probably did her first writing for these family plays. Her first novels made fun of the "gothic horror" tales which were popular at the time by telling stories about ordinary heroines in ordinary situations, instead of about drama and danger, and she continued to write her novels about ordinary people like herself. Of her six books, four were published during her lifetime without her name being mentioned, and the other two after she died. Unlike most of her heroines, Jane Austen never married. After her father's death in 1805 she lived with her sister Cassandra in Southampton, and then in Chawton Cottage, near Alton in Hampshire, which is now a museum open to the public.

A portrait of Jane Austen by her sister Cassandra.

Jane Austen's Novels

Northanger Abbey 1797
Sense and Sensibility 1797
Pride and Prejudice 1813
Mansfield Park 1814
Emma 1815
Persuasion 1815

Chawton Cottage, Alton, Hampshire, where Jane Austen lived with her sister Cassandra.

Avicenna (980–1037)
Avicenna, also known as Ibn-sina, was a Persian philosopher, physician, astronomer, and poet. He was appointed royal physician and wrote more than a hundred books. His most famous work was his *Canon of Medicine*. It has been described as the greatest medical book ever written. It contains all the medical work of Aristotle and Galen, and describes treatment for pleurisy, lockjaw, and malaria. It also deals with experiments on animals and oral anesthetics. Avicenna also wrote many books on theology, philosopy, astronomy, and science.

Avogadro, Amadeo (1776–1856)
An Italian scientist who is famous for Avogadro's Law, which states that equal volumes of different gases will contain the same number of molecules when kept at the same temperature and pressure. Avogadro was born in Turin.

Aylward, Gladys (1903–70)
Gladys Aylward was an English missionary who worked in China. In 1938, during the war between China and Japan, she led almost a hundred refugee children on foot over the mountains away from the advancing Japanese.

B

Johann Sebastian Bach—one of the greatest composers of all time.

Baber (1483–1530)
Zahir ud-Din Mohammed, known as Baber, was the first great Mogul emperor of India. He described his conquests, which included Delhi and Agra, in his autobiography and in poetry.

Bach, Johann Sebastian (1685–1750)
A German composer born at Eisenach into a family which had already produced more than 50 musicians of various kinds. The young Bach was taught the violin by his father and then, after his father's death, the organ and clavier (an early version of the piano) by his elder brother. He was a devoted student: forbidden to go into his brother's music library, he got into the habit of secretly copying down music at night when there was no danger of discovery. In 1703 Bach became church organist at Arnstadt, and then later at Mulhausen, and got into trouble in both places because the music he composed was too complicated and too experimental. He next became court organist to the Duke of Weimar, but resigned from that post in 1717 when somebody he considered incompetent was promoted above him. While music master for Prince Leopold of Cöthen, a job he held until 1723, he composed the six famous Brandenburg Concertos for the Margrave of Brandenburg.

Bach married twice, first to a cousin called Maria Barbara in 1707 and then, after her death, to the singer Anna Magdalena Wilcken. He had a total of 20 children, 10 of whom survived, three to become famous musicians and composers. Among his works are instruction books and exercises he composed to teach them music. In 1723 Bach took charge of music at the Thomas-school at Leipzig, where he remained until his death. His house became a place of pilgrimage for other musicians and it was at this time that he wrote some of his great choral work, including the *St. Matthew Passion* and the *Mass in B Minor*. He died, almost totally blind, in 1750. ○ MENDELSSOHN-BARTHOLDY

Bacon, Francis (1561–1626)
An English philosopher who rejected the accepted philosophy of Aristotle and thought scientists should work out scientific explanations by observing nature.

Bacon, Roger (*c.*1214–92)
An English philosopher and scientist who studied in Paris and Oxford. He interpreted Aristotle's ideas, carried out research into optics, and invented the magnifying glass. He was suspected by many of being involved in magic; and he may have been imprisoned by the church authorities, who disapproved of his writings.

Baden-Powell, Robert Stephenson Smyth, Lord (1857–1941)
The founder of the Boy Scout movement in 1908, and in 1911, with the help of his sister **Agnes Baden-Powell** (1858–1945), of the Girl Guides. He was a soldier who served in India and Africa, and who wrote and illustrated about 30 books.

Baird, John Logie (1888–1946)
Baird was a Scottish engineer who pioneered the development of television in the 1920s. In 1924 he succeeded in transmitting television pictures, without the use of wires, across his room in London. He experimented with several other aspects of television including three-dimensional images and stereo sound, and in 1944 demonstrated a color picture.

Balanchine, George Melitonovich (1904–83)
A Russian-born American choreographer. The son of a Georgian folk musician, Balanchine studied at the Imperial Ballet School in Russia before joining Diaghilev's *Ballets Russes* while on a tour of Europe in 1924. In 1948 he cofounded the American Ballet School, later the New York City Ballet, for whom he choreographed 100 works. ○ DIAGHILEV

Balboa, Vasco Nuñez de (1475–1517)
A Spanish explorer and *conquistador* ("conqueror") who in 1513 was the first European to see the Pacific Ocean. Balboa lived in San Domingo in Spain, and in 1511 joined an expedition to the Central American province then called Darien (now Panama) as a stowaway. A mutiny enabled him to claim command of the party, and he proclaimed himself governor of the province. Europe's first view of the Pacific came at the end of an epic march across the country, led by Balboa. Meanwhile, his unofficial seizure of power had come to the attention of the Spanish king, and he was replaced as governor in 1514 by Pedrarias Davila. For a while he worked successfully with Davila, undertaking expeditions into the New World, and even married his daughter; but in 1517 Balboa was accused of conspiring against the governor, and beheaded.

The Spanish adventurer and explorer, Vasco Nuñez de Balboa. He was the first European to see the Pacific Ocean.

Balboa's discovery is celebrated in a famous poem by John Keats—but Keats made an equally famous mistake, saying that it had been another explorer, Cortés, who first saw the Pacific:

. . . like stout Cortez when with eagle eyes
He star'd at the Pacific—and all his men
Look'd at each other with a wild surmise—
Silent, upon a peak in Darien.

The lines are from a poem called "On First Looking Into Chapman's Homer," written in 1816. ○ KEATS

Baldwin, James (1924–)
An American writer whose novels, such as *Go Tell It on the Mountain*, and collections of essays, such as *Nobody Knows My Name*, deal with the position of blacks in America. He was very influential in the black civil rights movement during the 1950s and 1960s.

Balzac, Honoré de (1799–1850)
Balzac was a French novelist who had the idea of uniting all the novels and stories he wrote in one scheme, called *The Human Comedy*. This was intended to give a complete picture of French life; it includes scenes from the country, the city, the army, and many other aspects of society. Balzac was not immediately successful as a writer, and it took many years of hard work before he was able to live comfortably. He died just two months after his marriage to a rich Polish countess.

Bannister, Roger Gilbert (1929–)
An English athlete who was the first man to run the mile in under four minutes, on May 6, 1954. His time: 3 minutes, 59.4 seconds.

Barnard, Christiaan Neethling (1922–)
South African surgeon who in 1967 performed the first human heart transplant operation. His patient lived only 18 days after the operation, dying from infections contracted during surgery.

Barnum, Phineas T. (1810–91)
Phineas Barnum was an American showman who with James Bailey staged the world-famous circus known as "The Greatest Show on Earth." Barnum entered show business by exhibiting a black woman said to have been George Washington's nurse and to be more than 160 years old!

A Barnum and Bailey poster advertising their "Greatest Show on Earth."

Barrett Browning, Elizabeth Barrett Moulton (1806–61)
A 19th-century English poet and critic, whose work includes a novel written in verse called *Aurora Leigh* (1856) and a series of love poems addressed to the poet Robert Browning, whom she married in 1846. She was for many years a semi-invalid.
○ BROWNING

Bartók, Béla (1881–1945)
Hungarian pianist and composer who studied and later taught at the Budapest Academy. He spent a lot of time collecting folk songs, and these influenced his own compositions. He emigrated to New York in 1940, where he died in poverty.

Bartholdi, Auguste (1834–1904)
Bartholdi was a French sculptor. His most famous work is the giant Statue of Liberty, which stands on an island in New York Harbor. It was given as a gift to the United States by the French Republic, and was unveiled in 1886.

Baudelaire, Charles Pierre (1821–67)
Baudelaire was a 19th-century French poet. He went to school in Lyon and Paris, and as a young man he traveled to India and the French colony of Mauritius. On his return to France he read and admired the stories of the American writer Edgar Allan Poe and began the task of translating them into French. Baudelaire published his most famous work, a collection of poems called *The Flowers of Evil,* in 1857. The poems, which deal with scenes of great ugliness as well as great beauty, shocked many people, and Baudelaire and his publisher were prosecuted for "impropriety." He lived in poverty for most of his life, and died, addicted to drink and the drug opium, in Paris in 1867.

Beamon, Robert (1946–)
American athlete whose massive 29-ft. $2\frac{1}{2}$-inch long jump has stood as a world record since the 1968 Mexico Olympic Games.

Beardsley, Aubrey (1872–98)
An English illustrator who was associated with Oscar Wilde and an artistic movement known as the "English Aesthetic Movement" at the end of the 19th century. His style was unusual and extravagant, characterized by careful line drawing and lots of solid black coloring. Among his work are illustrations for Oscar Wilde's play *Salome* and Thomas Malory's King Arthur stories.
○ WILDE

Beaton, Cecil Walter Hardy (1904–80)
An English photographer, famous for his fashion pictures in magazines such as *Vogue,* his portraits of celebrities and of the British royal family. He also designed sets and costumes for films, and won Oscars for his work on *My Fair Lady.*

"Beau Brummell" (George Bryan Brummell, 1778–1840)
An English "dandy"—a man of wit and fashion—who lived in London at the end of the 18th century. A friend of the Prince Regent, he gambled away his fortune and died in France hiding from people to whom he owed money.

Beaumarchais, Pierre Augustin Caron de (1732–99)
Next to Molière, Beaumarchais is thought of as France's greatest comic playwright. He was the son of a Parisian watchmaker, who at the age of 21 invented a new watch mechanism which was stolen by a rival. The dispute over his invention led Beaumarchais to be noticed at the court of Louis XV, where he was given a job teaching the king's daughters the harp. He married twice, both times to wealthy widows, and increased his fortune by careful investment. When his banker and friend Duverney died in 1770, Beaumarchais gained a reputation as a champion of the people against the aristocracy in the dispute over his will. It was at this time that his best-known plays were written, including *The Barber of Seville* and *The Marriage of Figaro*—which were very successful, and were turned into operas by Rossini and Mozart. He lost his fortune in the French Revolution, became deaf, and died of apoplexy in Paris.

One of Aubrey Beardsley's illustrations for Oscar Wilde's drama Salome.

Becket, Saint Thomas à (1118–70)
Thomas à Becket was made Archbishop of Canterbury during the reign of King Henry II. He became bitterly involved in the constant struggle for power between the medieval Church and medieval kings, and as a result was murdered in Canterbury Cathedral. His assassination shocked Christians throughout Europe, and in 1173, only three years after his death, he was declared a saint by Pope Alexander III.

This stained glass window in Canterbury Cathedral shows Henry II and Thomas à Becket as friends.

Becket was born in London, where his father was a rich merchant. He had the best schooling available, studied in London and Paris, and was trained in the manners and habits of a knight at a country castle in England. In 1142 he joined the Archbishop of Canterbury's staff. He performed important missions to Rome, and in 1155 the young King Henry II made him lord chancellor, the most powerful minister in the land. He worked as a diplomat, fought in battles abroad, and governed with great skill. He was a lavish entertainer and one of the most brilliant figures at court, and he became close friends with the king. In 1162 he was made Archbishop of Canterbury. Instead of continuing his extravagant lifestyle, Becket gave up the job of lord chancellor, together with his privileges and luxuries at court. He devoted himself to the Church, and lived a simple, religious life. His job as archbishop soon brought him into conflict with the king: Henry attempted to limit the power of the Church and to keep priests under control, while Becket refused to recognize the king's authority in church affairs. Their disagreements reached a crisis at the Council of Clarendon, held at Northampton in 1164. Becket thought himself in danger, and tried to flee the country. Henry at first prevented his escape, and tried to fine him, but eventually Becket slipped away to France. The dispute continued. Becket appealed to the Pope for support, and in 1170 Henry was persuaded to allow his archbishop to return to England. Crowds gathered in Canterbury to greet Becket, who was popular because of his generosity and his resistance to the king and the nobles. Unfortunately, the peace did not last. Becket punished some bishops who had supported the king. When Henry heard about this, he is said to have muttered,"Will nobody rid me of this turbulent priest?" Four of his knights took this to be a royal command and went to Canterbury, where they murdered Becket in his own cathedral.

Beckett, Samuel (1906–)
Samuel Beckett is an Irish playwright, novelist, and critic who lives in France. In 1969 he was awarded the Nobel Prize for Literature. He was born in Dublin, from where he moved to London and then to Paris, where he became friends with the writer James Joyce. During World War II he was a member of the French resistance movement. After the war Beckett began to write more, and produced a number of novels and plays. These include *Malone Dies* (1956), a novel, and *Waiting for Godot*

This illustration shows Thomas à Becket being murdered on the altar of his own cathedral by four knights.

(1952), his best-known play. In it, two tramps do nothing but sit passing the time while they wait for a mysterious character named Godot, who never arrives. Like much of Beckett's writing, the play is about the slow passing of time, a lack of meaning in human life, and about death. Beckett usually writes in French and translates his work into English.

Becquerel, Antoine Henri (1852–1908)
One of a family of French scientists, Becquerel discovered in 1896 that uranium gave off radiation, which he called "Becquerel rays." His suggestions led the Curies to the discovery of radium, and he was jointly awarded the Nobel Prize for Physics with them in 1903. ○ CURIE

Bede (*c.*673–735)
Bede, or Baeda, is known as the "Venerable Bede" because of his huge contribution to early English history and learning. He was a monk at the Benedictine monastery at Jarrow, England, where he studied Latin, Greek, and Hebrew writing, as well as medicine, astronomy, and other subjects. His writing included hymns, lives of saints, a translation of Saint John's Gospel, and his famous *Ecclesiastical History of the English Nation*, which tells us most of what we know about early English history. King Alfred had it translated from Latin into Anglo-Saxon. Bede also helped to introduce the custom of dating events from the birth of Christ. ○ CAEDMON

Beecher Stowe, Harriet Elizabeth (1811–96)
An American novelist, most famous for writing *Uncle Tom's Cabin* in 1852, which helped increase support for the anti-slavery ("Abolitionist") movement. A second anti-slavery novel, *Dred*, was a best-seller in England. Her brother, **Henry Ward Beecher** (1813–87), was also a well-known opponent of slavery and a supporter of the "Votes for Women" campaign.

Beethoven, Ludwig van (1770–1827)
Ludwig van Beethoven is one of the most popular and influential composers in the history of Western music. At the age of 11 Beethoven was removed from school by his father, who attempted to turn his musical talents into a profit by advertising his playing as that of a "child genius" like Mozart. After some years as an organist in the orchestra of the Elector of Cologne he actually met, played for, and may have taken lessons from Mozart during a visit to Vienna. In 1792, during war with France, Beethoven went back to Vienna, where he remained for the rest of his life. His teachers included the composer Haydn, and he began to write his first successful music—although he stopped working with Haydn after the master had

Beethoven went to Vienna in 1787. He played for Mozart who was very impressed with him.

been critical of a piano piece. He was friendly with, and given money by, the most aristocratic members of Viennese society despite the fact that he was famous for his bad temper, untidiness, and loud manners.

Beethoven's first pieces were written in a style similar to that of earlier composers such as Mozart and Haydn. After about 1802, he began what came to be known as the "romantic" style: music which had less pattern and was more unpredictable and emotional than before. In 1803 he dedicated his Third "Eroica" Symphony to Napoleon, but angrily tore up the dedication when he found out that

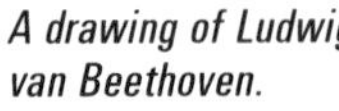

A drawing of Ludwig van Beethoven.

Napoleon had had himself crowned emperor. His only opera, *Fidelio*, was not a success when it was first performed in 1804 and had to be rewritten, but many of his most popular works date from this time. These include his violin concerto and the Sixth "Pastoral" Symphony. From 1812 Beethoven's deafness was becoming worse and he had very little money. His magnificent Ninth "Choral" Symphony and string quartets were written at the end of his life. He caught a bad chill while staying with his brother, who refused him a fire and charged him for lodging. After a journey back to Vienna in an open carriage he became ill and eventually died. His works remain among the most often performed pieces of music ever written.
○ HAYDN, MOZART

Beethoven's Life and Work

1770	December 12: Born at Bonn
1784	Joins the orchestra of the Elector of Cologne
1787	Visit to Vienna; meets and plays for Mozart
1792	Returns to Vienna; studies with Haydn and Salieri
1796	Beethoven first aware of his deafness
1797	Composes first piano concerto and piano sonatas
1800	First symphony
1804	Third "Eroica" symphony; first performance of opera *Fidelio*
1806	Composes violin concerto
1808	Composes sixth "Pastoral" symphony
1813	Meets the writer Goethe at Toplitz
1823	Ninth "Choral" symphony
1826	October: Stays at Gneixdorf with brother Johann; composes last string quartets
1827	March 26: Dies at Vienna

Behn, Aphra (1640–89)
The first English woman to earn a living by writing, author of 22 plays and 14 novels. She lived for a time in South America, worked as a spy in Holland, and began writing when she was put in prison for debt. Her play *The Forc'd Marriage* was the first written by a woman to be professionally performed in England.

Belisarius (505–65)
A Byzantine general during the rule of the Emperor Justinian. He carried out many successful campaigns against the Goths and Vandals in the West and the Persians in the East, and recaptured Rome in 536. Although brave and trustworthy, he was often accused by others of disloyalty and once imprisoned. The legend that he died blind and a beggar is untrue. ○ JUSTINIAN

Bell, Alexander Graham (1847–1922)
A Scottish-born American scientist who invented the telephone. He spent much of his life working with deaf-mute people and experimenting with sound. He produced and demonstrated the telephone in 1876, and the following year co-founded the Bell Telephone Company. Thomas Edison's microphone was built into the design in 1878, and Bell went on to improve Edison's phonograph device. He experimented with aviation, sonar devices, invented a new type of kite, and helped found the *National Geographic* magazine. ○ EDISON

Bellini, Giovanni (*c.*1430–1516)
The greatest of a family of painters who worked in Venice at the end of the 15th century. He was official painter to the Venetian government, for whom he made portraits and paintings of events in the city's history, and the finest of the *Madonnieri* — painters who produced pictures of the Madonna (Virgin Mary) for churches and chapels. Bellini's work is delicate and full of rich color. His pupils

The Madonna of the Meadow *by the Venetian painter Giovanni Bellini.*

included Titian and Giorgione, and he is thought of as the "father" of Venetian 16th-century painting. ○ GIORGIONE, TITIAN

Bellow, Saul (1915–)
An American novelist who has won the Nobel Prize for Literature (1976) and the Pulitzer Prize. His work includes *Henderson the Rain King* and *Herzog*. He is considered one of the leading 20th-century American writers.

Benedict, Saint (*c.*480–*c.*547)
Benedict is remembered as the patriarch (father) of Western monks because he was the first man to write down and put into effect rules for life in a monastery. Benedict was sent to Rome to study at the age of 14. He was disturbed by the corruption he saw there and soon left to live in religious solitude in the wild. His devotion made him famous: he gathered a large number of disciples, and from these he founded twelve small monasteries. In about 529 Benedict began the monastery of Monte Cassino near Naples—later to become the richest and most famous in Europe. His rule instructed monks not only to pray, but also to teach, learn, and carry out tasks such as growing their own food and copying manuscripts. The order he founded at Monte Cassino came to be known as the Benedictines. For many centuries Benedictine monasteries were among the only places of learning in Europe, because the monks took care to copy and preserve all kinds of writing and thought.

Beneš, Eduard (1884–1948)
Eduard Beneš was a Czech statesman, cofounder and second president of the Czechoslovakian Republic. Before World War I he was a leader of Thomas Masaryk's movement to achieve independence for Czechoslovakia from the Austro-Hungarian Empire. In 1918 the victorious Allies recognized Czechoslovakia's independence. During World War II, when Czechoslovakia was overrun, Beneš set up a Czech government in exile in London. After the war he was re-elected president in 1946. He resigned in 1948 when the Communists took control of the government.

Ben-Gurion, David (1886–1973)
The first prime minister of modern Israel. Head of the Israeli socialist party, Ben-Gurion was elected in 1948 and served almost continuously until 1963.

Bentham, Jeremy (1748–1832)
Bentham was an English philosopher who developed what is called "Utilitarian" philosophy. He believed that people always seek pleasure, and that for this reason good laws and actions are those which give the most pleasure to the largest number of people. Bentham was trained as a lawyer and campaigned for legal reforms such as the abolition of capital punishment, a national system for recording births and deaths, and universal suffrage (votes for all). When he died he asked that his skeleton, dressed in his clothes, be kept at University College in London, where it can still be seen. ○ MILL

Bergman, Ingmar (1918–)
Swedish film director who has won many honors and awards and been among the most influential figures in the history of cinema. His films include *Cries and Whispers* and *Fanny and Alexander.*

A stained glass window showing St. Benedict, the founder of the Benedictine order of monks.

Bering, Vitus Jonassen (1681–1741)
A Danish navigator and explorer who gave his name to the narrow strip of sea separating Russia and North America. In 1704 he joined the Russian navy. As a reward for his bravery during war with Sweden, Tsar Peter the Great asked Bering to lead an expedition to explore the seas around northeast Asia. He departed in 1728 and sailed north along the coast, passing through what is now called the Bering Strait, and reaching the most northeastern point in Asia. In 1741 he led a second voyage to explore the American side of the strait, but was shipwrecked and killed on the return journey.

Berkeley, George (1685–1753)
An Irish-born philosopher and bishop. He lived for a time in London, where he knew writers such as Swift and Pope, traveled in Europe, and went to America with the intention of founding a Christian college in the West Indies. His complicated ideas are explained in his *Principles of Human Knowledge*, published in 1710. He said that nothing exists unless it is perceived by some mind.

Bernadette, Saint (1844–79)
Bernadette was a visionary who claimed to have seen the Virgin Mary in a cave near Lourdes in southwest France. She was the small, sickly daughter of a poor miller called Francois Soubirous. In the spring of 1858, in a cave on the bank of the river Gave, she had several visions of a young and beautiful woman, who gave her messages and told her to pray. Later, the woman told Bernadette that she was the Virgin Mary. As a result of this apparition, Lourdes has become a place of pilgrimage for Christians looking for relief from pain or disease. Bernadette herself became the victim of both those who doubted her and those who were too eager to believe her. In 1866 she became a nun at Nevers, which helped her avoid publicity, and where she remained until her death at the age of 35. She was canonized (made a saint) in 1933, not for her vision itself but for her humility and trust in what she had seen.

Bernhardt, Sarah (1844–1923)
The most acclaimed actress of her time. She was born in Paris, where she performed in the Comédie Française and later in her own "Théàtre Sarah Bernhardt," in parts from Racine, Molière, Shakespeare, and others. Known as "The divine Sarah," she toured Europe and America and continued to act even after the amputation of a leg in 1915.

Bernini, Giovanni Lorenzo (1598–1680)
The most famous Italian Baroque sculptor and architect, born in Naples, from where he moved to work in Rome and Paris. His most famous creation is probably the magnificent colonnade which surrounds the square of St. Peter's in Rome.

Bernstein, Leonard (1918–)
Bernstein is an American conductor and composer whose work includes both symphonies and popular musicals such as *West Side Story*, which he wrote in 1957. He has toured all around the world and is a conductor laureate of the New York Philharmonic Orchestra.

Bessemer, Henry (1813–98)
An English scientist important in the Industrial Revolution for his invention in 1856 of the "Bessemer converter," which helped change molten iron into steel by passing air over it. He also helped to invent the first composing machine—a device which speeds up the process of printing a book or newspaper.

A photograph of Sarah Bernhardt—nicknamed by admirers "The Divine Sarah."

Billy the Kid (William H. Bonney, 1859–81)
"Billy the Kid" was a famous American bandit. He was born in New York, but as a young man moved out west to the new towns on the wild frontier. He became infamous for the holdups and robberies he and his followers carried out.

Bismarck, Prince Otto Edvard Leopold von (1815–98)
Bismarck was the first chancellor of the new German Empire in 1871, and the most important

An allegorical painting by William Blake of the scientist Isaac Newton.

Blackwell, Elizabeth (1821–1910)
Elizabeth Blackwell was the first American woman doctor. She was born in Bristol in England, but moved to the United States with her family at the age of 11. She began by teaching herself medicine, but it was many years before she could get into medical school. She finally graduated in 1849, and in 1851 she set up a practice in New York City.

German politician of the 19th century. Under Bismarck's influence, Germany was transformed from a collection of small separately governed states into a united and powerful nation. He entered politics as a member of the parliament of the state of Prussia, and became leader of the Prussian government in 1862. Bismarck saw that the best way to unite the Germans would be through war with other countries which would bring the separate states together against a common enemy. In 1863 he formed an alliance with Austria and fought and defeated Denmark in a war over control of the provinces of Schleswig and Holstein in the north. Bismarck then provoked the "Seven Weeks War" with Austria, which was won for Prussia at the Battle of Königgratz in 1866. The peace treaty created the North German Confederation, an alliance of German states under Bismarck's leadership. By fighting and defeating France in the Franco-Prussian War of 1870–71, Bismarck ensured that the German states would stay together and that the French would not interfere with his plans. At the end of the war, Bismarck was made chancellor of the new German Empire, with the Prussian William I as king. As chancellor, he introduced measures to increase Germany's strength and influence, and became known as the "Iron Chancellor." He was forced out of the leadership of the country in 1890 by the new king, William II, who wished to run things himself.

Blake, William (1757–1827)
William Blake was an English poet, artist, and illustrator. He was the son of a London stocking maker, and as a boy claimed that he could see angels. Blake became an apprentice engraver in 1771, and later went to the Royal Academy School and began doing illustrations for magazines. Among his early poems are the famous *Songs of Innocence* and *Songs of Experience* (published in 1789), which like most of his work were printed with his own illustrations. Blake believed that the human imagination should be completely free, and many of his later poems use strange and complicated characters and myths. His best

Bismarck, the first chancellor of the German Empire.

illustrations include those he did for the biblical Book of Job. He engraved his poems and illustrations on metal plates and hand-colored the prints made from them. Blake's genius was not recognized in his own time but despite this he remained happy and, with the help of friends, he managed to avoid poverty.

Blériot, Louis (1872–1936)
Blériot was a French engineer and aviator who made the first airplane flight across the English Channel. He was born at Cambrai, and devoted most of his personal fortune to the design and construction of monoplanes. His pioneering flight was made from Baraques on the French side to Dover in England on July 25, 1909, in a 24-horsepower plane, and took 37 minutes. The feat won him a £1,000 prize offered by an English newspaper, the *Daily Mail.*

Louis Blériot taking off near Calais in his monoplane on July 25, 1909. He was the first person to cross the Channel in a heavier-than-air aircraft. The flight took him 37 minutes and he won the £1,000 prize offered by the Daily Mail *newspaper.*

Bligh, William (1754–1817)
Captain William Bligh was an English sailor, famous as the victim of the "mutiny on the *Bounty.*" He was born in Plymouth and sailed around the world with Cook between 1772 and 1774. Three years later he was sent to Tahiti in the Pacific as captain of the *Bounty*, on an expedition to collect breadfruit trees. On the return voyage his crew mutinied, either because of Bligh's harsh discipline, or because they wanted to return to girlfriends in Tahiti. The mutineers, led by Fletcher Christian, put Bligh and eight others in an open boat with a small supply of provisions and cast them adrift before returning to Tahiti with the *Bounty*. Bligh managed without instruments or a chart to sail his boat the 4,000 miles to Timor, near Java, where he was rescued after seven weeks of incredible hardship. He returned to England, fought in the war against France, and was sent to Tahiti a second time. In 1805 he was made governor of New South Wales in Australia, where he suffered a second mutiny. He was unpopular because he was strict with the troops and because he tried to stop illegal trading in rum, and in 1806 he was arrested and put in prison by an army officer. The officer was later court-marshaled and dismissed, and Bligh was promoted to admiral. He died in London.
○ COOK

Blixen, Karen (1885–1962)
A Danish novelist. Karen Blixen lived in Kenya with her husband from 1914 until 1931, when she returned to Denmark. Her most famous book, *Out of Africa*, is based on her experience. She wrote under the name "Isak Dinesen."

Blum, Léon (1872–1950)
A French Socialist politician, prime minister twice between 1936 and 1938, and then for a short period after World War II. During the war he was imprisoned in Germany by the Nazis. Blum was responsible for the increase in the popularity of the Socialists in the 1930s, and the first Socialist prime minister of France since 1870.

Boadicea *See Boudicca.*

Boccaccio, Giovanni (1313–75)
Boccaccio is one of Italy's greatest poets. The illegitimate son of a merchant, he was born near Florence. He was sent to Naples to study law and commerce, but soon gave these things up so that he could devote his time to writing. For several years Boccaccio lived alternately in Naples and Florence, and in Naples fell in love with Maria d'Aquino, a daughter of the king. She is the subject of a novel in which she is given the name "Fiammetta" to hide her true identity. Boccaccio's other early stories include the *Teseide* and the *Filostrato,* both of which inspired poems by the English poet Chaucer. In about 1340 he moved permanently to Florence when his father faced bankruptcy. He became a diplomat, made friends with the poet Petrarch, and wrote his greatest work, the *Decameron,* which was completed in 1358. It tells how ten people are forced to leave Florence because of plague. During their ten-day

stay in a country villa they each tell a story—making 100 stories in all. Boccaccio took these stories from the popular fiction of his time, and retold them with great poetic skill. At the end of his life Boccaccio became very religious and concentrated on writing scholarly works. He was even tempted to destroy all his poetry, but Petrarch prevented him from doing this.
○ CHAUCER, DANTE, PETRARCH

Bogart, Humphrey (1899–1957)
An American actor, most famous for his performances as gangsters and tough guys with soft hearts. His best-known films include *The Maltese Falcon*, *Casablanca*, and *The African Queen*, for which he won an Oscar. He was married to the actress **Lauren Bacall** (1924–), with whom he starred in *The Big Sleep*.

Bohr, Niels Henrik David (1885–1962)
Bohr was a Danish scientist who made great advances in the understanding of the structure of the atom and helped develop the "quantum theory." He was professor of physics at Copenhagen University, and worked at Manchester and Cambridge in England. During World War II he made a dramatic escape from occupied Denmark and went to the United States, where he helped with research on the atomic bomb. He was awarded the Nobel Prize for Physics in 1922.

Boleyn, Anne (*c.*1504–36)
Anne was the second of the six wives of King Henry VIII of England. She was the daughter of Sir Thomas Boleyn and related to the powerful Duke of Norfolk. Between 1519 and 1521 she stayed at the French court, and on her return to England had a number of suitors, before the king attempted to win her hand. Henry was still married to Catherine of Aragon, and Anne at first refused him. But as the process of getting a divorce from Catherine grew more and more prolonged, they began an affair and were secretly married in January of 1533. In May Archbishop Cranmer proclaimed that Anne was legally Henry's wife, despite the objections of the Pope and the Roman Catholic Church, and she was crowned queen. It was soon after this that Henry apparently began to lose interest in Anne. Desperate for a son to inherit his throne, he was irritated by the birth of a daughter (Elizabeth, later Queen Elizabeth I) as their first child, and furious when their second, a boy, was stillborn. Henry had begun an affair with **Jane Seymour** (*c.*1509–37), later to become his third wife, and in May 1536 Anne was arrested and charged with committing adultery. It is almost certain that this was an invention, but she was found guilty and beheaded at the Tower of London on May 19. ○ CRANMER, ELIZABETH I, HENRY VIII, MORE

Simón Bolívar, the South American revolutionary leader. He was known as "The Liberator" because he led the expulsion of the Spanish from the continent.

Bolívar, Simón (1783–1830)
Bolívar was a South American soldier known as "The Liberator" because he led the expulsion of the Spanish from the continent and the creation of independent republics. The country of Bolivia is named in his honor. Between 1813 and 1821 he was in command of the army fighting for Venezuelan independence, which was finally achieved after the Battle of Carabobo. He was then chosen as president of the Republic of Colombia, which was then made up of Colombia, Venezuela, and New Grenada. In 1822 Ecuador joined, and two years later Bolívar drove the Spanish out of Peru and became dictator there. In later life he was distrusted for his dictatorial methods of government, and he resigned his presidency just before he died. ○ SAN MARTÍN

Bonaparte, Napoleon
See Napoleon I.

Bonnard, Pierre (1867–1947)
A French "Post-Impressionist" painter. At a time when many artists were becoming more interested in "abstract" painting (pictures made up only of color and pattern, not of scenes and objects), Bonnard continued to make pictures of landscapes, interior scenes, and people.

Boone, Daniel (1734–1820)
Boone was an American "frontiersman"—somebody who lived and often fought in the west of the United States when it was still wild and unsettled. He was born in Pennsylvania and moved to the frontier in North Carolina in 1750, where he worked as blacksmith in campaigns against the native Indians. In 1767 he began to explore and colonize what is now Kentucky. He lived in the forest, hunting, fishing, and fighting the Indians. He was captured on two occasions, and in 1775 built a fort at a place now called Boonesboro. For the next three years, the fort was under regular siege, and Boone persevered in its defense. Daniel Boone, dressed in his famous raccoon cap, is the subject of many paintings and illustrations, and is an important figure in the history and folklore of the American wild west.

Daniel Boone, the fearless hunter and frontiersman.

Booth, William (1829–1912)
William Booth was a British religious leader and founder of the Salvation Army, an evangelical mission organized on military lines. He was known as General Booth. Members of his family continue his work.

Borg, Bjorn Rune (1956–)
A Swedish tennis player. Borg's achievements included six French Open titles and five consecutive victories in the Wimbledon men's singles competition. He reached the final of the U.S. Open on four occasions. He retired in 1983.

Borges, Jorge Luis (1899–1986)
An Argentinian poet, critic, and storyteller, one of the most influential South American writers of the 20th century. He lived for three years in Madrid, where he was associated with avant-garde poetry. His first collection of poems appeared in 1923 and the first of his stories in 1941. Among his works are *Labyrinths* and *The Book of Imaginary Beings.*

Borgia, Cesare (1476–1507)
Borgia is the name of an ancient Spanish family who moved to Italy during the 15th century. Cesare Borgia was one of the third generation of the Italian branch of the family, the son of Rodrigo Borgia (who became Pope Alexander VI in 1492) and a Roman courtesan called Giovanni Catanei. It is likely that Cesare had his elder brother murdered in order to make sure of his own advancement in the Pope's government. As a soldier and a governor he was both brilliant and deceitful. He led the Roman army in successful campaigns against Romagna, Perugia, Urbino, Siena, and Piombino, making himself master of much of central Italy. He was planning a kingdom with himself as head when the death of his father and the election of his enemy Julius II to the papacy suddenly removed his support in Rome. His power gone, Cesare surrendered himself at Naples in return for a promise of his safety; he was, however, arrested and imprisoned in Spain. He later escaped and joined the army of the king of Navarre, in which he died at the siege of Viana in 1507.

Cesare's sister, **Lucrezia Borgia** (1480–1519), was equally important in the politics of her time. She was married three times: first to Giovanni Sforza, then, after her father, as Pope, had annulled this marriage, to a nephew of the king of Naples. When Cesare and Alexander saw the opportunity to marry her to Alfonso, Duke of Este, who would inherit the kingdom of Ferrara, they had her husband murdered, and she was married a third time. History has remembered her mainly for her vices. But in her own time she enjoyed the love and respect of her subjects, and under her influence Ferrara became a center of Renaissance culture and learning. ○ ALEXANDER VI, MACHIAVELLI

Detail of Botticelli's painting Lamentation over the Dead Christ.

Botticelli, Sandro (1444–1510)
Botticelli is one of the most famous painters of the Renaissance period in Italy. He painted a great many Madonnas and other religious subjects for churches and chapels in the city of Florence, as well as allegories and mythological scenes based on ancient Roman and Greek stories. He showed a talent for painting while still a boy, and was sent as a pupil to Filippo Lippi, who ran a large workshop in Florence. Some of Botticelli's early paintings are among his best and most famous, for example the *Birth of Venus* and the *Allegory of Spring*. They are delicate, colorful works filled with graceful figures. He was at first popular with Florentine patrons (buyers of paintings and other art), and did several pictures for the powerful Medici family. But in about 1500 his style was overtaken by the more rounded, three-dimensional figures of painters such as Leonardo da Vinci and Michelangelo. In addition to painting, he illustrated Dante's *Divine Comedy*.
○ LEONARDO, MEDICI, MICHELANGELO

Boudicca (c.A.D. 62)
Boudicca was the warrior-queen of an ancient British tribe called the Iceni who lived in East Anglia. When her husband Prasutagus died in about A.D. 60, the Romans occupied her land, killed many of her tribe, and ravished her and her daughters. In revenge, Boudicca assembled a huge army which destroyed the Roman settlement at Colchester, and then captured St. Albans and London. The Roman historian Tacitus says that as many as 70,000 Romans were killed by Boudicca's troops. Suetonius Paulinus, the governor, escaped because he was in Wales at the time of the attack; he now gathered his army to attack Boudicca. The Iceni were crushed and their queen, in order to avoid capture, killed herself by swallowing poison.

Boyle, Robert (1627–91)
An Irish scientist, often called the "father of modern chemistry" because he established chemistry as a subject separate from other scientific studies such as physics and medicine. He was born in Munster, Ireland, but spent most of his life in England. He first defined the term "element," as a substance which could not be broken up into other substances, and stated that all substances are made up of atoms. He is famous for "Boyle's Law," which describes the behavior of gases, and was a co-founder of the British Royal Society in 1645.

The Irish scientist Robert Boyle. He was famous for his work on the compression and expansion of gases.

Bradley, Omar Nelson (1893–1981)
An American general of World War II. Omar Bradley commanded in France, the Netherlands, Belgium, Austria, and Czechoslovakia the largest army ever assembled under the American flag. His concern for his men made him one of the most popular wartime generals.

Brahe, Tycho (1546–1601)
Brahe was a Danish astronomer. He first became interested in stars as a result of an eclipse which took place while he was a student. In 1576 he received a grant from King Frederick II to build an observatory on the island of Hveen, and over the next 20 years he made the first accurate records of the movements of stars and planets. He did not accept Copernicus' theory that *all* the planets, including the earth, revolve around the sun. In 1597 he left Denmark after a dispute with the government and built an observatory at Prague, where the young Johannes Kepler worked as his assistant. ○ COPERNICUS, KEPLER

Brahms, Johannes (1833–97)
Brahms was a 19th-century composer who resisted the "romantic" style of Beethoven and Wagner and based his music on the older "classical" style of composers such as Haydn. He was the son of a poor bass player in a Hamburg theater orchestra, and as a boy he played in dockside inns to earn a living. Success came in 1853, when Brahms accompanied a famous Hungarian violinist, Reményi, on a tour of Germany. He was able to begin composing, and later met the older composer Schumann, who encouraged him to write more and helped publish his piano sonatas. The two men became close friends, and after Schumann's death in 1856 Brahms remained devoted to his wife Clara—apparently in love with her, although they never married. Most of Brahms's great music was written late in his life: he was 44 when he finished the first of his four symphonies. His other work includes a violin concerto, piano concertos, songs and chamber music, and the choral work the *German Requiem*, finished in 1868. He spent the latter part of his life (from 1863) living in Vienna, composing, and giving occasional performances of his own work. Very little "bad" music by Brahms has survived, because he was a perfectionist who destroyed anything that he did not feel met his standards. ○ BEETHOVEN, HAYDN, SCHUMANN, WAGNER

Braille, Louis (1809–52)
The inventor of the system of raised "points," which allows blind people to write and read with their fingertips. Braille was born at Coupvray near Paris, and became blind in an accident at the age of three. He was sent to the school for the blind in Paris where he was first pupil, then a professor. He began work on his reading system at the age of 16, and continued to make improvements on it throughout his life.

Brancusi, Constantin (1876–1957)
Brancusi was a Romanian sculptor who had an important influence on 20th-century art. He thought of his sculptures as objects made into their simplest shape—for example, his "Egg," which he called *The Beginning of the World*. He left much of his work to the French nation, on the condition that his studio be kept as he had left it. It can now be seen reconstructed at the Musée de l'Art Moderne in Paris.

Brandt, Willy (1913–)
A West German statesman, Chancellor of Germany from 1969 until 1974. Brandt was a Socialist who fled from the Nazis in World War II. He entered politics in 1949 as a member of the German parliament, was elected mayor of West Berlin in 1957, and later became Chancellor. He attempted to bring about good relations between East and West and was awarded the Nobel Peace Prize in 1971. He was chairman of the Brandt Report on the world economy, published in 1980.

Right: Bertolt Brecht, the German dramatist (standing), with the composer Paul Dessau. Above: Willy Brandt.

Brecht, Eugen Bertolt Friedrich (1898–1956)
Brecht was a great German playwright, and is perhaps the most influential and important dramatist of the 20th century, both for his plays and for his ideas about how plays should be performed. He was born in Augsberg and studied at Berlin and Munich universities, where he produced his first work. He believed that plays should be able to "teach" their audiences something. In order for this to happen, they must realize that they are watching a play, and not imagine that what they see is "real life," so Brecht's plays do not pretend to be real: in *Mother Courage*

and Her Children, which he finished in 1938, the main character deliberately speaks the wrong lines to remind the audience that it is a play. *The Threepenny Opera,* which Brecht wrote with the composer **Kurt Weill** (1900–50), uses music to achieve the same effect.

Brecht remained a Socialist all his life. He left Hitler's Germany in 1933, and lived in Denmark and later the United States and Switzerland. In 1949 he returned to Germany to live and run a theater in East Berlin. Among the rest of his plays are *The Caucasian Chalk Circle* and *The Resistible Rise of Arturo Ui.*

Above: Children's Games *by Pieter Breughel. About 80 different games are shown including leapfrog, tag, and follow-my-leader.*

Breughel, Pieter (*c.*1520–69)
Breughel (or Brueghel) was a Flemish painter, probably born at the village of Breughel in the Netherlands. He is famous for his landscape pictures and for busy scenes from village life, such as his *Children's Games.* Breughel traveled widely in Europe, visiting France, Switzerland, and Italy, but he was influenced more by the scenery of these countries than by the paintings he saw, and his own pictures remained very individual and unusual in style. He is sometimes called "peasant Breughel" because so many of his paintings are crowded with peasant faces, but he was himself an educated city dweller. His two sons, Jan and Pieter, also became painters.

Brezhnev, Leonid Ilyich (1906–82)
Leader of the Soviet Union from 1964 until his death. Brezhnev united European Communist countries under Soviet leadership, and followed a policy of "détente" (reducing hostility) with the West, which led to the SALT agreements limiting numbers of nuclear weapons. ○ CARTER

Brian Boru (926–1015)
Brian Boru, which means "Brian of the Tribute," was an Irish warrior-king who lived to a great age and made himself master of the whole of his country. He became King of Munster in 976 after his brother had been murdered and immediately challenged the authority of the high king of Ireland, Malachy II. In a series of battles, Brian gained first the south, and eventually marched around the whole country, fighting and taking hostages. He was murdered after defeating the Danes at the Battle of Clontarf. His name has been preserved in the Irish surname of O'Brian.

Britten, Sir Edward Benjamin (1913–76)
An English composer and pianist. He wrote orchestral and choral music, but is best remembered for his operas, which include *Peter Grimes* and *A Midsummer Night's Dream,* based on Shakespeare's play. He worked on a number of projects with the poet W. H. Auden. ○ AUDEN

Brontë, Anne (1820–49), **Charlotte** (1816–55) and **Emily Jane** (1818–48)
Three sisters who between them wrote some of the finest English novels of the 19th century. Emily was author of the magnificent *Wuthering Heights;* Charlotte wrote *Jane Eyre.* They were the daughters of a clergyman, Patrick Brontë, and his wife Maria, and had two elder sisters (who both died during childhood) and a brother, Branwell Brontë. In 1820 the family moved to Haworth, a village on the edge of the beautiful and sometimes wild Yorkshire moors in England. Their mother died the following year. The Brontës were apparently happy children who spent their time exploring the countryside and making up stories for an imaginary world of their

The British composer Benjamin Britten. His works include the opera Billy Budd *(1951) and* War Requiem *(1962).*

The house in Haworth, Yorkshire, where the Brontë sisters and their brother Branwell grew up.

own which they called *Angria* or *Gondal.*

As young women, the three sisters were forced to look for work as teachers or governesses when Branwell began to get into debt. They were unhappy at being separated, and soon returned to Haworth with plans to start a school of their own. Charlotte took a job in a school in Brussels for two years in order to gain experience, but their scheme failed, and they next turned to writing as a way of earning money. A book of poems written by all three sisters sold only two copies, and Charlotte's first novel, *The Professor,* was rejected. Success came for Charlotte with *Jane Eyre,* which she finished in 1847. Meanwhile Anne had written two novels, *Agnes Grey* and *The Tenant of Wildfell Hall,* and Emily had finished her masterpiece, *Wuthering Heights.* This remained Emily's only novel, a passionate and wonderfully written love story set in the wild countryside around Haworth. She died from tuberculosis in 1848, and was followed a year later by her sister Anne; Branwell also died in 1848.

Charlotte wrote two more novels, *Shirley* in 1849, and *Villette* in 1852—which like *Jane Eyre* is based on parts of her own life. She married in 1854, but died during pregnancy only a year later, and thus Patrick Brontë outlived all of his children. All three sisters hid the fact that they were women by using false names: "Acton" (Anne), "Currer" (Charlotte), and "Ellis Bell" (Emily). Charlotte Brontë's biography was written by the novelist Elizabeth Gaskell. ○ GASKELL

Brown, Lancelot "Capability" (1716–83)
An 18th-century English landscape gardener who designed the gardens and parks of many country houses by exploiting the best features of their natural surroundings.

Browning, Robert (1812–89)
Browning was an English poet, born and educated in London. He traveled widely, and in 1846 secretly married the poetess Elizabeth Barrett. The couple lived in Italy until after her death in 1861, when Browning returned to England and wrote his greatest poem, *The Ring and the Book.* It is the story of a murder committed by an Italian nobleman told through the eyes of several different people. He was friendly with many of the writers of his time, including Charles Dickens and Thomas Carlyle.
○ BARRETT BROWNING

Brunel, Isambard Kingdom (1806–59)
Isambard Kingdom Brunel was one of the great engineers of the Industrial Revolution, a builder of ships, bridges, railways, and tunnels. His father, **Marc Isambard Brunel** (1769–1849), was also a successful engineer. He had worked in the United States, where he was chief engineer in New York City. He returned to London in 1799 and designed docks and other large projects. Young Isambard joined his father in his engineering practice, and helped him on one of his most ambitious schemes, a tunnel under the river Thames. This was never completed, but Isambard went on to become the greatest engineer of his day. In 1831 he began work on a suspension bridge over the river Severn at Bristol (which was not finished until after his death), and in 1833 he was made chief engineer for the Great Western Railway. His ship the *Great Western* was the first steamship to cross the Atlantic. In 1845 he designed the first large ship to use a screw propeller, and in 1858 he launched the *Great Eastern,* then the biggest ship ever built. Brunel personally supervised every step of its construction, which took over five years. He also worked on docks, barges, and guns.

The dome of Florence Cathedral was designed by Brunelleschi.

Brunelleschi, Filippo (1377–1446)
Brunelleschi was an Italian Renaissance engineer and architect, most famous for designing and building the dome of Florence cathedral. He began life as a sculptor and developed a theory of "perspective" for painters before becoming an architect. Work on the cathedral dome began in 1420 and was not completed until 1461, 15 years after Brunelleschi's death. Then the largest in the world, it was also the first to be built without the use of scaffolding to support it from the inside. Michelangelo used it as a model when he designed the dome of St. Peter's in Rome.

Brutus, Marcus Junius (85 B.C.–42 B.C.)
Brutus was a Roman soldier and senator who conspired with **Cassius** (d. 42 B.C) and others to assassinate Julius Caesar in 44 B.C. During the civil war in Rome both Brutus and Cassius took sides with Pompey, and after Pompey's defeat at the Battle of Pharsalia both were pardoned by the victorious Caesar. (○ JULIUS CAESAR, POMPEY) Brutus became the governor of part of Gaul and later praetor (magistrate) of the city of Rome. He is said to have been a thoughtful man, interested in philosophy and unwilling to become too involved in the dangerous politics of his time. Despite this, Cassius managed to persuade Brutus that Caesar was planning to make himself "king" of Rome and overthrow the republic. Brutus at last agreed to join the conspiracy against Caesar, and on March 15, 44 B.C. led the assassins who murdered him on the steps of the Senate. He was immediately forced to flee from Rome, pursued by Mark Antony and Augustus, and was defeated at the Battle of Philippi. To avoid capture he killed himself, while Cassius had one of his own troops kill him.
○ AUGUSTUS, MARK ANTONY

Büchner, Georg (1813–37)
A German playwright who died young and was forgotten until quite recently. His two outstanding plays, *Danton's Death* and *Woyzeck*, are powerful tragic dramas written in verse. *Woyzeck* was turned into an opera, *Wozzeck*, by the composer **Alban Berg** (1885–1935).

Buddha (*c.*460 B.C.–*c.*380 B.C.)
The name "Buddha" means "the enlightened one" and is the name given to Siddhartha Gautama, the founder of the Buddhist faith. He was the son of a prince of the Sakya tribe who ruled an area of northern India, and was brought up in great luxury. His father seems to have feared that the young man's thoughtful character might lead him to give up his princely lifestyle, and arranged for him to be married at an early age. It made no difference: Buddha left his wife and family and wandered the country seeking "truth." After six years, he is said to have become "enlightened" while sitting under a wild fig tree. He came to believe that all life is miserable, but that the faithful could reach a state in which suffering, and therefore "life," would cease. He called this "Nirvana." Buddha spent 40 years

A statue of Buddha in a temple in Bangkok.

spreading his teaching before he died at about the age of 80. The religion founded by Gautama—Buddhism—now has over 100 million followers, mainly in eastern countries.

Buffalo Bill (William Frederick Cody, 1846–1917)
Buffalo Bill became famous in the United States in the 1880s when he toured the country with his "Wild West Show"—a kind of circus in which scenes from life on the American frontier were re-enacted for the public. In fact, Buffalo Bill had little experience of the "Wild West." He was a scout for a short time in the Indian wars, and he got his nickname after killing thousands of buffalo to feed railroad workers (not very difficult because there were so many of the animals). He is best known as a showman.

Bunche, Ralph Johnson (1904–71)
A black American politician, winner of the Nobel Peace Prize in 1950 for his efforts to bring peace to the Middle East. He was a founding member of the United Nations administration, and its under-secretary from 1954 until 1967.

Bunyan, John (1628–88)
John Bunyan was an English Puritan preacher and the author of the *Pilgrim's Progress*. He was the son of a tinker, born near Bedford, and as a teenager served in Cromwell's Parliamentary army during the English Civil War. In about 1649 he was married, and it was soon after this that he began to have deep religious experiences. He joined a Puritan community in 1653 and began to preach. After the return of the monarchy to England in 1660 it was made illegal to preach without a license, and Bunyan was arrested and spent 10 years in Bedford prison. During this time he wrote his autobiography, called *Grace Abounding*. Bunyan was released, and then arrested again a year later. During his second stay in prison he wrote the first part of the famous *Pilgrim's Progress*. The second part was written about five years later. It is an "allegory," which means that characters in the story represent virtues or vices, for example faith, patience, or despair, and that their actions represent triumph, defeat, perseverance, or other qualities. Bunyan died in London after having been caught out in a rainstorm.

Burke, Edmund (1729–97)
An English politician and writer, remembered, among other things, for the great speeches he wrote for the House of Commons. He entered politics as a member of the Whig Party in 1765, and spoke out against the corruption of the ruling Tories. Later, after the publication of his book *Reflections on the French Revolution* in 1790, which opposed the revolution and supported the French king, he lost the support and friendship of many Whigs, and joined the Tories.

Burns, Robert (1759–96)
Burns is Scotland's greatest and most admired poet. He was born a farmer, and it was only when his family farm faced ruin that he considered publishing the poems he had been writing since he was a boy. The first book of his work, published in 1786, was a great success, and instead of emigrating as he had planned, he stayed in Scotland, married, and began another farm. Among his works are famous songs such as "Auld Lang Syne," as well as long poems such as *The Jolly Beggars* and *Tam o'Shanter*. Burns died in Dumfries, where he is buried.

Byrd, Richard Evelyn (1888–1957)
An American aviator and explorer who made the first flight over the South Pole in 1929. He also claimed to have made the first flight over the North Pole in 1925, although it is not certain that he actually did so. Byrd led two expeditions to Antarctica, and was able to map large unexplored areas from the air. On the second of these expeditions he spent five months alone in a weather station on Ross Island. His book *Alone* describes this experience.

Richard Byrd, the American aviator and explorer.

Byrd, William (1543–1623)
An English organist and composer. William Byrd is famous for madrigals, choral music, and pieces for instruments such as the harpsichord and virginals.

Byron, Lord George Gordon (1788–1824)
Byron was an English poet who was seen by his admirers as a "romantic hero": a man ruled by his moods and passions and in love with the idea of freedom, who wandered Europe having adventures. As a young man, Byron spent a lot of time trying to overcome lameness, and as a result became a strong swimmer. In 1809 he set out on a tour of Europe which inspired his first successful poem, *Childe Harold's Pilgrimage*. Back in London, he had several love affairs and an unhappy marriage, and in 1816 Byron returned to Europe. While living in Venice with an Italian countess he began his most famous poem, *Don Juan*, and in 1823 became interested in a movement whose aim was to free Greece from Turkish rule. He traveled to Greece to fight, but died of fever the following year.

Cabot, John (*c.*1450–*c.*1500)
John Cabot was an Italian navigator who discovered the mainland of North America. He was born in Genoa, moved to Venice and then to England, from where King Henry VII sent him on an expedition to the West. He sighted the coast of Nova Scotia on June 24, 1497. In 1498 he left on a second voyage, but never returned. Cabot's son, **Sebastian Cabot** (1474–1557), may have sailed with his father on the first voyage, and later became a mapmaker for King Henry VIII of England and Ferdinand V of Spain. He attempted to find the Northwest Passage and explored the coast of South America. A famous map which he made of his and his father's discoveries is preserved in Paris.

Caedmon (d. *c.*680)
Caedmon is said to have been the first English poet. The historian Bede wrote that he was an uneducated man who was told in a vision that he should become a poet so that he could spread God's word. Caedmon became a monk at Whitby Abbey in the north of England and learned to write. He spent the rest of his life writing poems on religious subjects, but the only work to have survived is a hymn which Bede repeats in his history. Other poems which were traditionally thought to be by Caedmon were probably written much later. ○ BEDE

Caesar, Gaius Julius (*c.*101 B.C.–44 B.C.)
See Julius Caesar

"Calamity" Jane (*c.*1852–1903)
The nickname given to Martha Jane Burke, an American "frontierswoman" (somebody who lived in the wild West before it was settled by Europeans). She became famous for her sharp-shooting, her skill on horseback, and for her habit of wearing men's clothes, which was at that time thought strange. She got the name "Calamity" because she threatened "calamity" to any man who tried to marry her.

Calderón de la Barca, Pedro (1600–81)
One of Spain's greatest poets and playwrights. Calderón was educated by Jesuit monks, became a soldier and then a sort of official dramatist for King Philip IV. He wrote over 100 plays for the court, Church, and public theaters. Among the most famous are *The Prodigious Magician* and *The Great Theater of the World*. In 1651 he became a priest and in 1653 moved to Toledo, but he continued to write throughout his life.

Caligula (A.D. 12–A.D. 41)
Caius Caesar Augustus Germanicus was the youngest son of the Roman Emperor Germanicus and his wife Agrippina. He got the nickname "Caligula," which means "little boots," from soldiers in his father's guard. Caligula became emperor of Rome after the death of Tiberius in A.D. 37. At first he seemed to be a careful and generous ruler, but a few months after he came to power an illness drove him mad. He managed to spend all of Tiberius' huge fortune in one year, banished or murdered almost all his relatives, and had many Roman citizens executed. There is a story that he made his favorite horse, called Incitatus, a consul of Rome. When he declared himself a god in A.D. 41 his subjects had finally had enough, and he was assassinated. ○ AGRIPPINA, CLAUDIUS I

Callas, Maria Meneghini (1923–77)
A Greek opera singer, born in New York. Maria Callas made her debut in 1947 and went on to sing at all the world's great opera houses. She retired in 1965.

"Calamity" Jane, the American frontierswoman.

John Calvin, one of the pioneers of the Reformation.

Calvin, John (1509–64)
Calvin was a French religious reformer. Together with Luther, he was one of the founders of the Protestant Church. He became a law student at Paris University, where he first encountered the teachings of Luther, and in 1533 he was suddenly converted to the new Protestant faith. France was officially a Roman Catholic country, and Calvin lived in constant danger of arrest. He fled to Switzerland, where he wrote a book called *The Institutes of the Christian Religion* in which he explained his ideas. Calvin believed that people were "predestined" for either heaven or hell—that is, that God had decided in advance who would be damned and who would be saved. This could not be changed, but good works were often a sign that somebody had been saved. In 1536 Calvin became governor of the city of Geneva, then the center of Protestantism. His rule was strict: public entertainment such as the theater was banned, people had to declare their faith, and there were even rules about how people could dress. He was at first unpopular and forced to leave the city, but in 1541 he returned to begin an even stricter government. Calvin is remembered as the first man to organize Protestant beliefs. He also founded what was to become Geneva University, and under his rule the city became prosperous. ○ LUTHER

Calvino, Italo (1923–85)
An Italian writer, born in Cuba. Among his many novels and stories are *Invisible Cities* and *If on a Winter's Night a Traveler . . .*

Camus, Albert (1913–60)
Camus was a French novelist and critic born in Algeria. During World War II he edited the journal of the French resistance movement, called *Combat*, and afterward wrote his most famous novels, *The Outsider* (1942) and *The Plague* (1947). He was also interested in the theater and wrote many plays. Camus died in a car accident in 1960. He was awarded the Nobel Prize for Literature in 1957.

Canaletto (Giovanni Antonio Canale, 1697–1768)
"Canaletto" was a painter famous for his views of Venice. His pictures are often dramatically lit by sunshine or shade, and are always very accurate in their detail. Most of them were bought by English visitors. He spent about ten years in London, but his pictures of the English capital were never as successful as those he did of Venice.

One of Canaletto's many famous views of Venice.

Canute (*c.*994–1035)
Canute or "Cnut" as he is sometimes called, was a Danish king of England, Denmark, and Norway. After his father, Sweyn of Denmark, died while conquering England in 1014, Canute was immediately proclaimed king by the troops. His English rival Ethelred at first chased him out of the country, but in 1015 Canute returned and led a violent campaign which gained him all of the north and west of England. Peace was finally made with Ethelred's successor, Edmund, but after Edmund's death in 1016 Canute made himself ruler of the whole country. After so much bloodshed, Canute suddenly became a wise and tolerant ruler who respected English customs and rights. The story is often told of how he tried to stop the tide coming in—but he did this not because he thought he would actually be able to stop it, but in order to demonstrate to his lords the limits of his power. Canute became King of Denmark on the death of his brother in 1018, and of Norway in 1030.

Capone, Al (1898–1947)
An American gangster whose gang is said to have made over $100 million from gambling, illegal alcohol, and other vices. He was responsible for many murders, but avoided arrest by bribing and threatening the police. He was finally jailed for not paying his taxes.

Carlyle, Thomas (1795–1881)
A Scottish historian and philosopher. His most famous work is the *History of the French Revolution,* written in the mid-1830s, which sees the Revolution as the work of dynamic, larger-than-life individual "heroes." He was among the most influential thinkers of his time. His essays were widely read and admired. The *History of the French Revolution* inspired Dickens' novel *A Tale of Two Cities.* ○ DICKENS

Carnegie, Andrew (1835–1919)
An American industrialist, born in Scotland, who built a vast empire of iron and steel industries. In 1901 he sold everything, making over $250 million, which he then invested in libraries, universities, and other philanthropic projects such as the Carnegie Endowment for International Peace.

Carpaccio, Vittore (*c.*1460–*c,*1523)
A Venetian painter, perhaps an assistant of Bellini. His crowded, colorful, and detailed pictures include a series illustrating the life of St. Ursula, and a charming life of St. George. ○ BELLINI

Carroll, Lewis
(Charles Lutwidge Dodgson, 1832–98)
"Lewis Carroll" was the pseudonym (false name) used by Charles Lutwidge Dodgson, most famous as the author of *Alice's Adventures in Wonderland* (1865) and *Through the Looking Glass* (1872). He was a lecturer in mathematics at Christ Church College, Oxford, and *Alice* contains many mathematical-type puzzles. Both books were written for Alice Liddell, the daughter of Carroll's friend Henry George Liddell, who was dean of the college. Carroll was a keen chess player, enjoyed word games and other puzzles, wrote books on mathematics and logic, and was a good photographer. As a writer of intelligent and "logical" nonsense, he was supreme. He introduced a whole vocabulary of ridiculous words into the English language.

One of Tenniel's illustrations to Carroll's Through the Looking Glass.

Carson, Kit (1809–68)
An American hunter, trapper, and frontiersman whose knowledge of Indian languages and habits led him to become a guide on Frémont's expeditions across the Rocky Mountains. He was later an Indian agent in New Mexico. ○ FRÉMONT

Carter, James Earl (1924–)
The 39th president of the United States from 1976 until 1980. As govenor of the state of Georgia Jimmy Carter did much to ease racial problems. While president, he negotiated the Camp David peace agreement between Egypt and Israel and helped détente by meeting Soviet leader Brezhnev. His popularity suffered when 50 Americans were held hostage during the Iranian revolution and he was unable to secure their release. ○ BREZHNEV, KHOMEINI, SADAT

Jacques Cartier's map of the St. Lawrence River in Canada.

Cartier, Jacques (1491–1557)
Cartier was a French explorer born at St. Malo who tried to find a northern sea route between the Atlantic and the Pacific oceans. On his first voyage in 1534 he explored Newfoundland and Labrador and claimed them for France. In 1535 Cartier led a second expedition and this time sailed up the St. Lawrence River—thinking it might take him to China—to the site of the city of Montreal. On a final voyage six years later, he failed to find anything new, but added information to his previous discoveries.

Cartier-Bresson, Henri (1908–)
Henri Cartier-Bresson—a French photographer of outstanding international events who has turned photographic reportage into an art form.

Caruso, Enrico (1873–1921)
An Italian opera singer, born in Naples. He sang throughout Europe and in New York, and owed his fame partly to his being one of the first singers to be recorded on a phonograph record.

Casals, Pablo (1876–1973)
A great Spanish cellist, who helped make the instrument and its music popular in the 20th century. He founded a famous music festival at Prades in France.

Cassatt, Mary (1845–1926)
Mary Cassatt was an American woman painter who became an influential member of the impressionist movement in France. She was born in Pittsburgh and decided to be a painter while still a girl, although her father, a banker, did little to encourage her. After touring Europe Mary Cassatt began to live and work in Paris, where in 1877 she met the painter Degas. He admired her work and invited her to enter her pictures in the Impressionist exhibitions. In addition to painting, Cassatt made prints and encouraged Americans to buy Impressionist pictures. Many of her own works are unsentimental pictures of mothers with their children or domestic scenes. By the time of her death, Mary Cassatt had become almost totally blind. ○ DEGAS

Cassini, Giovanni Domenico (1625–1714)
Cassini was a French-Italian astronomer who discovered four of Saturn's moons.

Castro, Fidel (1927–)
A Cuban revolutionary who overthrew the regime of President Battista and made himself leader of his country in 1958. As a young lawyer in the Cuban capital Havana, Castro defended cases on behalf of the poor. In 1953 he attempted to lead a revolution, was arrested, but later released under an amnesty. From 1956 Castro and a small group of followers fought a guerrilla war against the Cuban government, which was finally successful in December 1958. As a socialist leader, Castro attracted the hostility of the United States Government, who encouraged Cuban exiles to try and overthrow him at the "Bay of Pigs" invasion in 1961. Cuba became more friendly with the Soviet Union, and in 1962 President Khrushchev attempted to station Soviet nuclear missiles in Cuba. They were only removed when President Kennedy threatened war. Although unpopular with the United States and other Western governments, Castro has been influential in the politics of Africa and South America. Many Cuban troops and advisers are stationed in Angola and Ethiopia.
○ GUEVARA, KENNEDY, KHRUSHCHEV

Fidel Castro of Cuba—the head of the first socialist society in Latin America.

Cather, Willa Sibert (1873–1947)
An American novelist who was brought up on a ranch in the state of Nebraska. The people and landscape of the West are important features of her novels, which include *O Pioneers, My Antonia,* and *One of Ours,* for which she won a Pulitzer Prize in 1922.

Catherine II, "the Great" (1729–96)
Catherine the Great was Empress of Russia from 1762 until her death. She was an ambitious, calculating daughter of a Prince of Prussia, who saw that marriage (in 1745) to the future Tsar Peter III could make her powerful. Catherine hated her husband, who was a weak man, and they soon became enemies. Six months after Peter became Tsar in 1762 he was deposed and then murdered by two of Catherine's lovers, Count Grigory Orlov and Prince Grigory Potemkin. Catherine immediately declared herself empress, although her son was in fact next in line to the throne. She was an energetic and effective ruler. Wars with Turkey (in 1774 and 1792) and with Sweden (in 1790) increased the size of her empire, and when Poland was "partitioned" (divided up) Russia gained all of the area known as the Ukraine. Catherine abolished capital punishment for everything except political crimes, and planned to introduce a new education system and legal reforms. These last changes were never effective, and for many poor Russians life became worse under Catherine because there were more soldiers needed and therefore more taxes to pay. Her government was threatened by a revolt in 1773, led by a man who claimed he was Catherine's dead husband. Meanwhile, life in the royal court was extravagant and full of minor intrigues. Catherine herself recorded the events of her reign in her *Memoirs.*

Catherine the Great, Empress of Russia.

Catherine de'Medici (1519–89)
See Medici

Catherine of Siena, Saint (*c.*1347–80)
An Italian nun and "mystic" (somebody who has strange or deep religious experiences) who became involved in the religious politics of her time. She is said to have been beautiful, and her parents tried to make her get married. She refused, became a Dominican nun, and after a number of spiritual experiences began to gather disciples. During war between Florence and Rome in 1375 she tried to negotiate peace. She helped persuade Pope Gregory XI to return from France to Rome, and supported Pope Urban VI during the period known as the "Schism" when there were two men both claiming to be the true Pope.

Catullus, Gaius Valerius (*c.*84 B.C.–*c.*54 B.C.)
An ancient Roman poet, famous for his passionate love poems, and for poems making fun of politicians—including Julius Caesar. His work was lost for many centuries, and only rediscovered in Italy in the 1300s.

Cavell, Edith Louisa (1865–1915)
An English nurse and heroine of World War I. Edith Cavell became interested in nursing during a tour of Europe in 1883, and on her return to England she entered the London Hospital to begin training. In 1907 she became matron of a hospital in Brussels, and was left in charge there when World War I broke out and Belgium was invaded by the Germans. Soldiers of both sides were freely taken care of, but Cavell also used the hospital to hide escaping Allied soldiers. She was discovered. On August 5, 1915, she was arrested by the German army, brought to trial, and executed by firing squad two months later—despite the fact that her motives had been humanitarian and not political.

Chagall's Enchanted World

Marc Chagall and (opposite) one of his paintings, called Dance. *Chagall was particularly fascinated by circuses with their fantastic, topsy-turvy views of life. He was also deeply religious. In the early 1960s he designed stained glass windows for the synagogue at the medical center of the Hadassah-Hebrew university in Jerusalem.*

Chagall, Marc (1887–1985)
Marc Chagall was a Russian artist whose long life spanned the whole history of modern art. He was born at the end of the Impressionist period, and grew up during the era of the great Post-Impressionist painters such as Cézanne, Van Gogh, and Gauguin. In Paris in the 1920s and 1930s Chagall worked alongside Cubist painters such as Pablo Picasso, and he became an important influence over the Surrealist movement that followed.

Chagall was born in the Russian Jewish village of Vitebsk and studied painting at the Imperial School of Fine Art in St. Petersburg. He made his first visit to Paris in 1910, where he was able to see for himself the works of Picasso, Cézanne, and other western European artists. At the outbreak of war in 1914, he returned to Russia.

After the Russian Revolution of 1917, Chagall was made a "Commissar of Fine Arts" by the country's new Bolshevik leaders. He quarreled with his bosses and with other artists employed by the government, and soon left his job to work as a decorator and designer in Moscow's theaters. In 1923 he returned to France. At that time, Paris was the scene of intense experiment in painting, as well as literature, drama, and the other arts. Painters were developing new styles and new methods of interpreting on canvas the world they saw around them. Chagall was deeply influenced by these new artistic movements, particularly Cubism, with its strong, geometric designs and distorted composition and perspective. But he also brought the flavor of his Russian origins to his work.

Chagall was also fascinated with the subconscious part of the mind. His pictures often have a dreamlike appearance, and it was this interest in dreams that made him an influence over the Surrealist movement.

Another important aspect of Chagall's work is the art he created for public places. Later in his life he undertook huge decorative projects for buildings in Europe and the United States. In the 1960s he designed stained glass windows for the cathedrals of Metz and Rheims in France. He painted a ceiling for the Paris Opera House, and when the new Metropolitan Opera in New York City opened in 1966 it was decorated by Chagall's spectacular hangings.

○ BALANCHINE, CÉZANNE, PICASSO, STRAVINSKY

Chagall
Marc

Cavour, Camillo Benso di (1810–61)
When Cavour was a young man, Italy was divided into separately governed states and dominated by other countries such as Austria and Spain. It was Cavour who was most responsible for unifying Italy and freeing it from foreign rule. In 1852 he became prime minister of the kingdom of Piedmont and Sardinia in the north. His policies included free trade with other states, building roads and railways, and improving agriculture. These things helped strengthen links with other Italian states, and showed the rest of Europe that Italy could be independent and still survive. In order to remove Austrian power from Italy, Cavour needed the help of France, so he sent troops to aid the French in the Crimean War and promised France the states of Nice and Savoy in return for military help. In 1859, the Austrians were defeated by the French at the Battles of Magenta and Solferino, and Piedmont gained all of northern Italy except Venice. The following year, the central Italian states decided to join their powerful northern neighbor. Meanwhile, Garibaldi had liberated southern Italy, and he too joined Cavour. In 1861 Cavour became prime minister of all Italy (except Rome and Venice) and Victor Emmanuel king. Exhausted by his efforts, he died only a few months later. ○ GARIBALDI, MAZZINI, VICTOR EMMANUEL II

Caxton, William (*c.*1422–*c.*1491)
Caxton is remembered as the first English printer. He was born in Kent and became a merchant in various European cities, including Cologne, where he probably learned how to print. He moved to the Belgian city of Bruges, where in 1475 he produced the first book to be printed in English, called the *Recuyell of the Historyes of Troye*. In about 1476 Caxton set up the first English press at Westminster in London.

Cellini, Benvenuto (1500–71)
An Italian goldsmith who was a clever but apparently not very artistic craftsman. Few works by Cellini have survived, and he is remembered mainly for his *Autobiography*, in which he boasts of many adventures and gives a fascinating description of life in Renaissance Europe.

Celsius, Anders (1701–44)
Celsius was the Swedish astronomer and scientist who invented the centigrade thermometer for measuring temperature. He also investigated the Northern Lights and built a magnificent observatory at Uppsala University.

Cervantes Saavedra, Miguel de (1547–1616)
Cervantes was a Spanish writer, author of the great novel *Don Quixote*. His adventurous life began at Alcalá in Spain, where he was born into a family of seven children. In 1569 Cervantes was in Rome living in the household of a cardinal, and in 1571 he was a soldier at the famous naval battle at Lepanto, where he was shot three times and nearly lost his left hand. While returning to Spain in 1575, he and his brother were captured and imprisoned by Algerian pirates. He made several daring attempts to escape, but was only released when a ransom was paid for him in 1580. Back in Madrid, Cervantes wrote poems, plays, and stories, but he was unable to make any money, and in 1594 he became a tax collector. He was arrested and jailed when he failed to deliver all the taxes that were due to the government. After this, while living in great poverty in Seville, he began *Don Quixote*, which tells the story of an old knight of that name who wanders the countryside with his faithful squire, Sancho Panza. The first part, published in 1605, was a huge success, but it was only after the publication of a *false* second part, written by an anonymous author, that Cervantes got around to finishing his book. Meanwhile, in 1605, he had been in trouble again when the dead body of a man thought to be his daughter's lover was found in his

Don Quixote – the famous creation of the Spanish writer, Cervantes.

house. At the end of his life, Cervantes was happy and famous, although still poor. He died on the same day as Shakespeare, April 23, 1616.

Cetewayo (d. 1884)
King of the Zulu tribe of southern Africa from 1873. He fought and defeated the British in the Zulu War of 1879, but was later himself defeated. His own subjects deposed him in 1883.

Cézanne, Paul (1839–1906)
A French painter born in Provence, who studied in Paris and became friends with Impressionist painters such as Manet and Pissarro, and the novelist Émile Zola. Although he was associated with the Impressionists, Cézanne's ideas soon differed from theirs. Painters such as Pissarro were interested in the effect of light on their subjects. Cézanne, however, explored the shapes he saw in an object or scene, and how they could be represented by color alone. This was to influence painters such as Picasso and help begin the "Cubist" movement. He painted many landscapes, still lifes, and a few portraits. He remained almost unknown during his lifetime, but is now considered perhaps the greatest painter of the last 100 years.
○ MANET, PISSARRO

A landscape painting by Cézanne. His revolutionary use of color emphasized the volume of objects.

Chagall, Marc (1887–1985)
See pages 56 & 57

Chamberlain, Arthur Neville (1869–1940)
One of a family of British politicians, including his father **Joseph Chamberlain** (1836–1914), a 19th-century Liberal minister. Chamberlain became prime minister in 1937 and pursued a policy of "appeasing" (keeping the peace with) Adolf Hitler. At the Munich Conference of 1938, Chamberlain agreed not to oppose Hitler's invasion of Czechoslovakia in return for a promise of peace. He announced this agreement as a guarantee of "peace in our time"; however, war broke out in September 1939. ○ CHURCHILL, HITLER

Chanel, "Coco" (1883–1971)
Coco Chanel was the French fashion designer who developed the loose, low-waisted dresses that were popular in the 1920s, and that freed women from tight and uncomfortable corsets. She also created the famous "Chanel No. 5" perfume, introduced in 1922.

Chaplin, Sir Charles Spencer (1889–1977)
Charlie Chaplin was a British-born film director and actor, famous in many roles as a skinny tramp with a cane, a bowler hat, and a mustache. He was the son of a poor music hall performer in London. He traveled as an actor to the United States, where he made his first film for the Keystone Studio in 1914. Chaplin later became a director and writer, and founding member of the United Artists Corporation. Among his many fine films are *The Gold Rush*, (1925), *Modern Times* (1936), and *The Great Dictator* (1940), in which he played a sinister cartoon-like version of Hitler.

Charlie Chaplin in The Gold Rush. *Chaplin had a brilliant gift for mime.*

Chardin, Jean Baptiste Siméon (1699–1779)
A French painter, the son of the king's billiard-table maker, who was himself first a royal picture restorer and then a sign painter. He is famous for his still-life pictures and domestic scenes, with their delicate coloring and fine detail. Chardin lived in Paris all his life.

Charlemagne (742–814)
Charlemagne, who was also known as Charles the Great, was king of the Franks and the ruler of the largest European empire since the time of the Romans. He was born at Aachen in Germany, the son of King Pepin the Short and the grandson of Charles Martel. Charlemagne became sole king of the Franks after his brother's death in 771. Over the next 30 years ceaseless military campaigning made him ruler of Germany, Saxony, Bavaria, Lombardy in northern Italy, northeast Spain, and much of eastern Europe. In the year 800 he was called to Rome by Pope Leo III to help put down a rebellion there, and on Christmas Day the Pope crowned Charlemagne "Holy Roman Emperor" in St. Peter's, Rome. He used this title because it linked the idea of the great empire of the ancient Romans with the idea of Christianity. As emperor, Charlemagne continued to extend his territory. He also encouraged education, agriculture, manufacturing, and trade, and invited artists and scholars to his court. Although he could speak Latin and read Greek, Charlemagne never learned to write, but he did insist that new laws and regulations be written down and in that way preserved. Charlemagne's successors were weak men, and after his death the empire he had built fell apart. ○ CHARLES MARTEL, PEPIN III

Charles I (1600–49)
Charles I was king of Great Britain and Ireland from 1625. His inability to rule with the agreement of the country's Parliament led to the English Civil War and eventually to Charles's execution. Charles was the second son of King James I, and became heir to the throne after his elder brother's death in 1616. In 1625, shortly after he had become king, he married a French princess, **Henrietta Maria** (1609–69). She was a Catholic, and her arrival in England worried many people who wanted to make sure the country remained independent of the powerful Roman Catholic Church. Charles's main problem

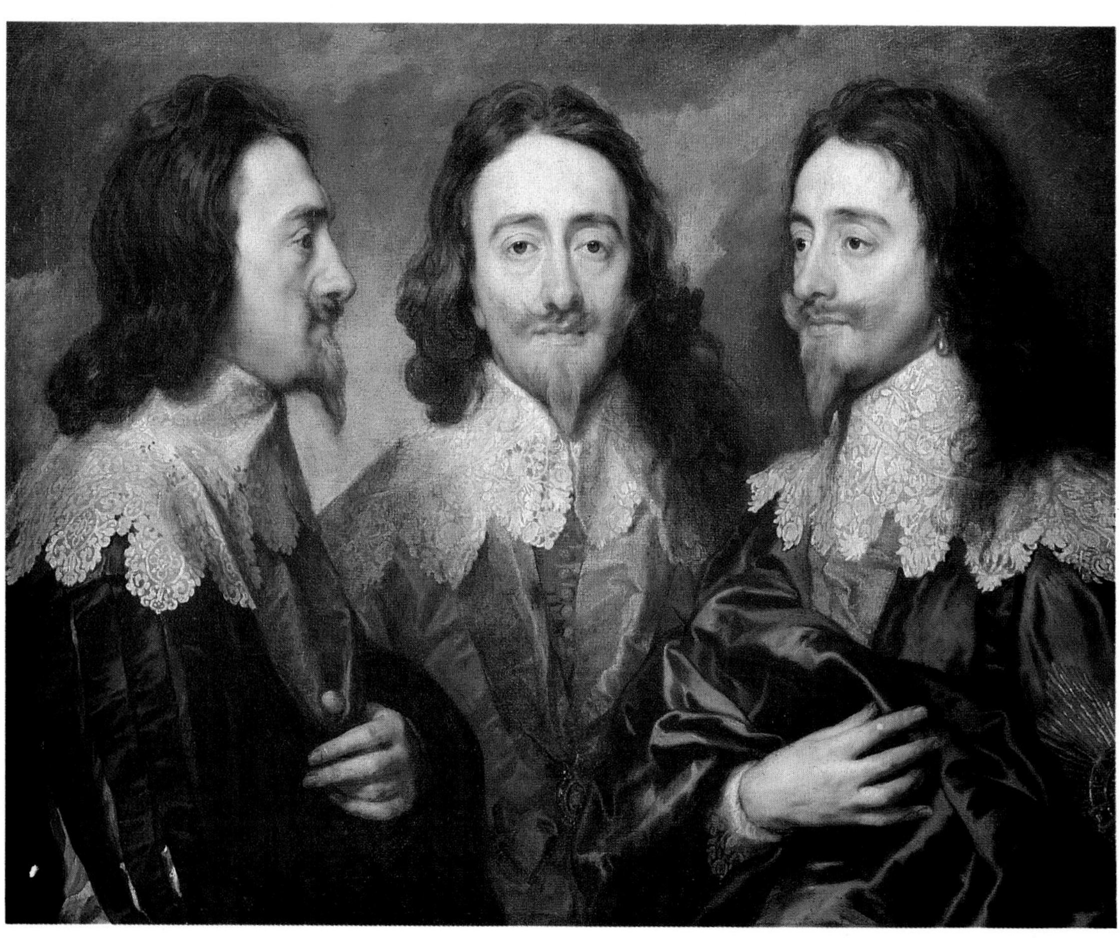

Charles I painted from three different angles by the Dutch portrait painter, Van Dyck.

was how to raise money for his household and army. On three occasions in the 1620s, Parliament refused to allow him to impose the high taxes he thought necessary, so in 1629 Charles decided that he could govern without their agreement, and Parliament was dismissed. One idea he had for raising money was a "ship tax," which was used to support the navy and was paid by towns which had a port. When Charles tried to extend this tax to inland towns with *no* port, he met great opposition. He was also unpopular when he tried to introduce a standard prayer book to all churches —especially in Protestant parts of Scotland. By 1640 his financial problems were so bad that he was forced to summon Parliament and try to persuade them to impose new, higher taxes. The first "Short Parliament" lasted only three weeks before Charles dismissed it, but it was soon recalled to form the "Long Parliament." In desperation, Charles agreed to a bill which said that Parliaments could only be dismissed by the king with their own agreement, in return for more taxes. Meanwhile, Queen Henrietta Maria was about to be arrested on suspicion of leading a Catholic plot against the country. She fled to Holland in February 1642, at the same time that Charles tried to have his five leading opponents in Parliament arrested. It was these events that led to civil war. (○ CROMWELL)

Charles was finally defeated at the Battle of Naseby in June 1645. He was held prisoner, and his refusal to recognize Parliament's authority, and his attempts to restart the war with foreign help, led to his being brought to trial for treason. Charles would not plead either guilty or not guilty, saying the court had no authority over him. On January 30, 1649, he was beheaded at Westminster.

○ CROMWELL, JAMES I

Charles V (1500–58)
Charles V was Holy Roman Emperor from 1519, and King Charles I of Spain. He inherited his claim to be Emperor from his father, the Emperor Maximilian, and became king of Spain through his mother Joanna, the daughter of Ferdinand and Isabella. As emperor, his rule was troubled by constant rivalry with King Francis I of France, who claimed some of the lands inherited by Charles. In addition, many of the states in Germany which belonged to the empire were influenced by the Protestant Reformation led by Luther and others. Charles, who was a devout Catholic, attempted unsuccessfully to oppose the new church. In 1555 he abdicated all his power and retired to a monastery. ○ FERDINAND II, FRANCIS I, LUTHER

Charles XII (1682–1718)
King of Sweden from 1697. As soon as he came to power, Charles found himself at war with the other northern powers—Russia, Poland, and Denmark. He defeated the Danes, then invaded Russia where at the Battle of Narva in 1700 he defeated 50,000 Russians with only 8,000 troops of his own. He conquered Poland, and his success continued until 1709 when the winter and the tsar's army combined to defeat him at the siege of Poltava. After failing to win Turkey's help against Russia, he returned to Sweden to begin a campaign against Norway, but was killed by a sniper at the siege of Frederiksten.

Charles XII of Sweden (above) was famous for his military campaigns.

The Holy Roman Emperor Charles V.

Charles Martel (*c.*688–741)
The ruler of the people known as the Franks from about 720. He conquered much of France, Germany, and the Netherlands. The name "Martel" means "The Hammer" and was given to Charles after his victory against a Muslim army at the Battle of Poitiers in 732. His grandson was the Emperor Charlemagne. ○ CHARLEMAGNE

Chase, Salmon Portland (1808–73)
A prominent American statesman who became Chief Justice of the United States Supreme Court. He served as secretary of the treasury under Abraham Lincoln and laid the basis of the country's national banking system. Chase was a founder of the Republican Party.

Chaucer, Geoffrey (*c.*1340–1400)
Chaucer is thought of as one of England's greatest poets. His works were among the first to be written and printed in the English language. He was the son of a wealthy London vintner (wine seller) and entered the royal household of Edward III as a

The plowman and the shipman—two of the pilgrims in Chaucer's Canterbury Tales.

page. During war with France in 1359 Chaucer was captured by the enemy, and the king himself paid £16 toward his ransom. In about 1366 he married one of the queen's ladies-in-waiting, and about this time wrote his first poem, *The Book of the Duchess,* which was dedicated to the wife of John of Gaunt. Chaucer became a diplomat, and during the 1370s traveled to France and Italy, where he may have met the Italian poets Boccaccio and Petrarch, whose stories and style influenced his own poems. He became a customs inspector and then a knight of the shire of Kent, and was able to spend more time writing. His *Troilus and Criseyde,* which tells the story of two lovers during the siege of Troy, was probably written in about 1380. In 1386 Chaucer lost all his public offices—perhaps because his friend and supporter at court, John of Gaunt, was abroad at the time. He became poor, and even had to ask the king for protection from arrest for debt. Despite this, it was at this time that he wrote his greatest poem, *The Canterbury Tales.* It is made up of stories told by a group of pilgrims as they travel to visit the shrine of St. Thomas à Becket at Canterbury. The pilgrims include a knight, a miller, a cook, a friar, a merchant, and many other characters, and their stories are told in many different styles. When he died, Chaucer was buried in the part of Westminster Abbey now known as "Poets' Corner." ○ BOCCACCIO, PETRARCH

THE MILLER (from *The Canterbury Tales*)

The *Miller* was a chap of sixteen stone,
A great stout fellow big in brawn and bone.
He did well out of them, for he could go
And win the ram at any wrestling show.
Broad, knotty, and short-shouldered, he would
boast
He could heave any door off hinge and post,
Or take a run and break it with his head.
His beard, like any sow or fox, was red
And broad as well, as though it were a spade;
And, at its very tip, his nose displayed
A wart on which there stood a tuft of hair
Red as the bristles in an old sow's ear.

GEOFFREY CHAUCER
(translated by Nevill Coghill)

Chekhov, Anton Pavlovitch (1860–1904)
Chekhov was a Russian short story writer and playwright whose writing has remained very popular throughout the world. He trained to be a doctor at Moscow University, supporting himself by writing stories for magazines. These were so successful that he decided to continue as a writer. His first plays were not well liked, and it was not until 1898, when *The Seagull* was successfully performed in Moscow, that he became famous as a dramatist. Among his other plays are *The Cherry Orchard* and *Uncle Vanya,* and his many hundreds of stories include "The Darling" and "The Duel."

Chiang Kai-shek (1887–1975)
A Chinese soldier and politician, who for many years disputed the leadership of the "true" China with Mao Ze-dong's Communist government. After the overthrow of the Manchu emperor in 1911, Chiang was sent by the new president, Sun Yat-sen, to subjugate the war lords of northern China. At the same time, he opposed the Communists in the new government, forcing them to leave the capital Canton and make the "Long March" into central China. After World War II, Chiang was for a short time president, but was defeated in a civil war by the Communists and forced to flee to Taiwan in 1950. He continued to insist that he alone represented the Chinese government until his death. ○ MAO, SUN YAT-SEN

Chopin, Frédéric (1810–49)
Chopin was a Polish pianist and composer whose music helped establish the popularity of the piano as a solo concert instrument. He was born near Warsaw, gave his first performance at the age of 8, and published his first composition at the age of 15. As a young man, Chopin visited Vienna and finally

settled in Paris, where he became a celebrated teacher and performer. In 1836 he met and fell in love with the woman novelist George Sand, with whom he lived until 1847. Chopin died at the age of 39 after suffering for many years from tuberculosis. At the end of his life he had been so ill that he had to be carried to his piano to give recitals. ○ LISZT, SAND

Chou En-lai (1898–1976)
See Zhou Enlai

Churchill, Sir Winston Leonard Spencer (1874–1965)
Churchill was a British politician, prime minister, and war leader. He was the son of a 19th-century Conservative minister, **Randolph Churchill** (1849–95). As a young man Churchill served in the army, then became a correspondent for the London newspaper the *Morning Post*. While covering the Boer War he was captured and escaped, making him a hero in Britain. He was elected to the House of Commons in 1900.

During the 1930s and Hitler's rise to power Churchill spoke out for a program of arming the country against the war he expected with Germany, and opposed Chamberlain's "appeasement" policy. When war broke out and Chamberlain resigned in 1940, he became prime minister. In a famous speech he said: "I have nothing to offer but blood, toil, tears, and sweat." Throughout the war, Churchill's determination to resist Hitler inspired many British and European people. He maintained good relationships with both Roosevelt and Stalin—although after the war Churchill was an opponent of Russian tyranny, and it was he who invented the phrase "Iron Curtain." In addition to being a politician, he was the author of many books on history, and in 1953 was awarded the Nobel Prize for Literature. He remained a member of the House of Commons until 1955. ○ CHAMBERLAIN, HITLER, ROOSEVELT, STALIN

> "Never in the field of human conflict was so much owed by so many to so few."
> Speech to House of Commons in 1940

Winston Churchill, British politician and war leader.

Cicero, Marcus Tullius (106 B.C.–43 B.C.)
Cicero was a Roman politician. He had several important posts in the government of the republic, but he was not always a successful politician. When **Catiline** (*c.*108 B.C.–62 B.C.) attempted to have Cicero and some other senators murdered and bring himself to power in 63 B.C., Cicero discovered the plot, denounced Catiline, and rounded up the other conspirators. But this success was spoiled when he illegally executed some of the gang, and he was exiled from Rome and had his property confiscated. It is for his great speeches that Cicero is best known. His contemporaries thought him the greatest of all Roman orators (speakers), and some of his speeches have survived and can be read today. He also wrote many letters and a number of books. He supported the plot to assassinate Julius Caesar in 44 B.C., although he did not take part in the murder. Later he became an opponent of Mark Antony, who had him killed to silence him. ○ JULIUS CAESAR, MARK ANTONY

Cimabue, Giovanni (*c.*1240–1302)
An Italian painter, possibly the teacher of Giotto, who owes his fame to the fact that he is mentioned in Dante's *Divine Comedy:* "Cimabue thought that he held the field in painting, but now Giotto is acclaimed and his fame hidden." ○ DANTE, GIOTTO

Ci Xi (1835–1908)
A formidable empress of China at the end of the 19th century. She was the mistress of the emperor Hien Fong who died in 1851, and took power when his son died in 1875. She introduced a number of reforms, and distrusted foreigners, restricting their movements in the country.

Clark, George Rogers (1752–1818)
An American military leader who conquered the Northwest from the British during the American Revolution. The area now covers the states of

Ohio, Indiana, Michigan, Illinois, and Wisconsin. By the Treaty of Paris, all this area was given to the United States.

Claudius I (10 B.C.–A.D. 54)
Claudius succeeded Caligula to become the fourth emperor of Rome. He escaped Caligula's notorious cruelty because he was a cripple and thought stupid, but in private Claudius is known to have written and studied history and ancient Greek writing. After Caligula's assassination in A.D. 41, Claudius hid himself in the imperial palace, where he was discovered by a party of soldiers. Instead of murdering him, as he apparently feared they would, they proclaimed him emperor. As ruler, he remained generous to the army, who rewarded him by securing the eastern frontier of the empire and beginning the conquest of Britain. Claudius also spent large amounts of money on new buildings, including the famous "Claudian Aqueduct." He is believed to have been poisoned by his second wife, Agrippina, so that she could ensure the succession of Nero, her son by an earlier marriage, to the throne. ○ AGRIPPINA, CALIGULA

Clemenceau, Georges Benjamin (1841–1929)
A French radical journalist and politician. During the 1880s and 1890s he was known as "The Tiger" for his fierce attacks on government ministers. He served in the French parliament for many years, and in 1917 was made prime minister and minister of war. Clemenceau was a strong, single-minded leader who lifted the morale of the French people during World War I.

Cleopatra (69 B.C.–30 B.C.)
Cleopatra was queen of ancient Egypt and the lover of both Julius Caesar and Mark Antony. It was her father's wish that she should share the Egyptian throne with her brother Ptolemy, but she was prevented from doing so by Ptolemy's guardians. When Julius Caesar arrived in Egypt during the civil war with Pompey, he is said to have been fascinated by Cleopatra's wit and beauty. He agreed to fight on her behalf, and in 48 B.C. Cleopatra was restored to her throne. Cleopatra bore Caesar a son, Caesarion (who was later killed by Augustus), and lived with him in Rome from 46 B.C. until 44 B.C. After Caesar's assassination, she met Mark Antony at Tarsus; he too was captivated by the queen, and traveled to Alexandria in Egypt with her. Although married to Octavia, Antony spent most of the next 12 years living in Egypt with Cleopatra. This made him unpopular in Rome, and led to the Battle of Actium, at which Antony was defeated by Augustus. Cleopatra attempted to negotiate with Augustus, but failed and, not wishing to be taken to Rome as a prisoner, killed herself. She is traditionally thought to have held an asp (a poisonous snake) against her breast, but she may simply have swallowed poison. ○ AUGUSTUS, JULIUS CAESAR, MARK ANTONY

Clerk Maxwell, James (1831–79)
A Scottish physicist. James Clerk Maxwell published his first scientific paper at the age of 15, and went on to become a professor at Aberdeen University, King's College, London, and the first Cavendish professor of physics at the University of Cambridge. He stated that the rings around the planet Saturn must be made up of tiny particles, and is most famous for his work on electricity and magnetism. ○ HERTZ

Scottish physicist James Clerk Maxwell.

Clive, Robert (1725–74)
Clive was a soldier and administrator responsible for establishing British power in India. He traveled to Madras with the "East India" trading company in 1743, was very unhappy, but after failing to commit suicide he trained a large army and fought several successful campaigns against French and Indian troops. In 1756 Clive was sent to punish the Nawab of Bengal and Calcutta for the "Black Hole of Calcutta" incident, in which 123 British people had suffocated when they were locked in a small room. Victory made him governor of Bengal and secured British power in India. When he returned to England for the last time in 1763 he was criticized for his methods of government, and he eventually killed himself.

Clovis (465–511)
A warlike king of the Franks, who conquered much of France, and in 493 married **Clotilda** (474–545). She was a Christian (later St. Clotilda) and wished to convert her husband. At a battle near Cologne in 496 Clovis seemed to face certain defeat, and

promised to worship Clotilda's God if he was granted victory. Clovis won the battle and he and his army were later baptized. He went on to conquer France as far south as Bordeaux, and made Paris the capital of his empire.

Cobbett, William (1763–1835)
An English politician and writer, famous for his interest in farming and the lives of the people who lived in the country. He was the son of a small farmer. His first job was to scare crows and his second was as a plowman, but in 1783 he left the countryside for London. Later, during a stay in the United States, he wrote articles under the name "Peter Porcupine" attacking the idea of democracy, and when he returned to England he began a paper called the *Weekly Political Register*. Cobbett at first supported the Tory government, but his paper quickly became more and more radical and championed the needs of the poor. The price of the *Political Register* was deliberately kept low so that the poor could afford it. Cobbett became a farmer and eventually a member of Parliament. His most famous book is *Rural Rides* in which he describes a journey around the countryside of England.

Cocteau, Jean (1889–1963)
A brilliant French artist, whose work included poetry, novels, plays, films, ballet, painting, and criticism. He was associated with Picasso, Stravinsky, Diaghilev, and others. His novels include *Les Enfants terribles* and his films *The Beauty and the Beast*.

Colbert, Jean Baptiste (1619–83)
A French politician who aimed to make France a strong nation by improving every aspect of government. Colbert was the chief minister of King Louis XIV. He reformed and improved the economy, built the navy, encouraged trade, and established new French colonies in Africa and America. He also founded the Academies of Art, Science, and Architecture. Colbert became unpopular because of the higher taxes he introduced to pay for these reforms. ○ LOUIS XIV

Coleridge, Samuel Taylor (1772–1834)
Coleridge was an English poet and philosopher who with William Wordsworth began what came to be known as the "romantic" movement in English poetry. The two men met in 1796, and in 1798 published *Lyrical Ballads*, a collection of poems which were intended to be free of the rigid rules and patterns of earlier poems. It contained Coleridge's "Ancient Mariner," the story of a seaman who is cursed when he shoots an albatross. His other work includes "Kubla Khan," which Coleridge said was part of a longer poem he heard in a dream while smoking the drug opium. ○ WORDSWORTH

Colette, Sidonie Gabrielle (1873–1954)
Colette was a French novelist. In 1893 she married the writer Henri Gauthier-Villars, who discovered her talent and kept her prisoner while she wrote her first four novels, which he then published under his own pen name of "Willy." Colette divorced her husband in 1906 and spent some years as an actress in the music hall before she returned to writing. Her first major success was the novel *Chéri*, published in 1920. She also continued to write stories about the character "Claudine," who had appeared in the novels stolen by her husband, including *Claudine in Paris* (1931). Colette's subject is almost always love, and many of her novels were thought scandalous when they were first published. She became very popular, and was given a state funeral when she died.

The French novelist Colette. Many of her novels were considered scandalous.

Collins, Michael (1890–1922)
Michael Collins was an Irish politician and soldier at the time when Ireland gained independence from the rest of Britain. During and after the rising of 1916 he was put in prison on several occasions

General Michael Collins in August 1922

because of his part in the independence movement. He became minister of finance in De Valera's government in 1919, and helped to negotiate the treaty with the British which recognized this government. When civil war broke out in 1922, Collins opposed De Valera's republican movement. He was killed in an ambush by soldiers belonging to the Irish Republican Army. ○ DE VALERA

Columbus, Christopher (1451–1506)
See pages 68 & 69

Confucius (K'ung Fu-tse, 551 B.C.–479 B.C.)
Confucius was a Chinese philosopher and teacher who is honored at shrines and in prayers throughout China. He is said to have been the son of a soldier and to have been very poor when he was young. Later he became an accountant in a grain store, and then a teacher, wandering the country discussing moral problems with people he met. Confucius' fame spread and he was followed by a growing party of disciples. In 501 B.C. he was put in charge of the city of Chung-tu. Under his guidance, the city became prosperous and its people famous for their manners and learning, but he was forced to leave by jealous neighboring lords. Confucius returned to his wandering life until he was invited to return to Chung-tu by a new duke in 482 B.C. His most famous saying is: "What you do not wish done to yourself, do not do to others," and all his teachings are based on ideas such as respect, loyalty, and obedience. After his death, a shrine was founded in his honor by a duke who wished to make amends for not having followed Confucius' ideals, and he has been honored in China ever since.

The Chinese philosopher Confucius. His philosophical and religious "system" spread from China to Japan and Korea.

Congreve, William (1670–1729)
An English playwright, famous for his comedies about love and manners. Congreve's best-known play is *The Way of the World*, first produced in 1700.

Conrad, Joseph (1857–1924)
Conrad was a Polish-born novelist who lived and wrote in England. He left Poland and became a seaman in 1874, eventually joining the British Merchant Navy and becoming a ship's master. His experiences at sea, especially around Singapore, Borneo, and Africa, provided the material for many of his novels. *Lord Jim* (published in 1900) tells the story of a seaman who, in a moment of weakness, leaves hundreds of pilgrims to drown on a sinking ship. Conrad's success as a writer is especially remarkable because English was only his fourth language. Among his other novels are *Nostromo* and *Heart of Darkness.*

Constable, John (1776–1837)
Together with Turner, Constable is thought of as the greatest English landscape painter. He was born and spent his childhood in the Suffolk countryside, which would become the subject of many of his paintings. In 1799 he entered the school of the Royal Academy in London, but it was in Paris (in 1824) that he had his first success, when his famous picture *The Hay Wain* won a gold medal in an exhibition. Meanwhile, Constable had inherited some money, and was able to give all his time to painting. His work includes a great many fine pictures of the village and canal at Flatford in Suffolk, where his father had been a miller. He had a great influence on the French painter, **Eugène Delacroix** (1798–1863). He was also important in the development of Impressionist painters.

Constant de Rebecque, Henri Benjamin (1761–1830)
Benjamin Constant was a French politician and writer. As a member of the French Tribunate he was critical of Napoleon, and in 1802 he was banished from France. He traveled Europe with Madame de Staël before returning to Paris in 1814. He is famous for his novel *Adolphe*, published in 1816. ○ NAPOLEON, STAËL

Constantine I, "the Great" (*c.*274–337)
Constantine was the first Christian emperor of Rome. He inherited control of the western half of the Roman Empire from his father, Constantius Chlorus, who died during an expedition to Britain in 306. There were many who refused to recognize Constantine as ruler, and civil war soon followed. In 312 Constantine defeated the general Maxentius, who had claimed to be emperor, at the Battle of Milvian Bridge. Before the battle he saw a vision of a cross, together with the words "In this sign shall you conquer." Constantine was converted to Christianity, and in 313 he announced the Edict of Milan which allowed Christians throughout his empire to practice their religion freely. After a series of wars with the eastern Emperor Licinius, Constantine gained control of the whole of the Roman Empire. He made Byzantium his capital, giving it the name "Constantinople" (the "city of Constantine"). Christianity became the state religion, although Constantine himself was not baptized until shortly before he died.

The Emperor Constantine, founder of the Byzantine Empire.

Cook, James (1728–79)
An English explorer who discovered Australia and Antarctica and greatly increased Europeans' knowledge of the Pacific. Cook was the son of a farm laborer in Yorkshire. He joined the British navy in 1755 and was quickly promoted because he was good at navigation. In 1768 he sailed the ship *Endeavour* to Tahiti, taking with him a party of astronomers who wanted to observe the planet Venus from the southern hemisphere. On the return voyage he sailed right around New Zealand and then landed at Botany Bay in southeast Australia. Cook led a second expedition between 1772 and 1775 on which he discovered Antarctica and explored New Zealand and the New Hebrides. He developed a method of controlling his crew's diet which stopped them from suffering from scurvy, and in all Cook's expeditions only one man died of illness. Cook himself was killed by Hawaiian natives on his third voyage in 1779.

Coolidge, John Calvin (1872–1933)
Calvin Coolidge was the 30th president of the United States, from 1923 until 1929. He believed that "the best government is the least government" and so used his authority as little as possible.

> James King, one of Cook's lieutenants, describes his death:
>
> *An accident happened which gave a fatal turn. The boats, having fired at some canoes, killed a chief. The [islanders] armed themselves and a general attack followed. Our unfortunate Commander was stabbed in the back, and fell with his face in the water. His body was immediately dragged ashore and surrounded by the enemy, who . . . showed a savage eargerness to share in his destruction. Thus fell our great and excellent Commander!*

Captain Cook explored the Pacific, where he discovered and mapped many tropical islands and also charted the coasts of Australia, New Zealand, and New Guinea.

The New World

The coat of arms the Spanish gave to Columbus to honor his discoveries.

CHRONOLOGY

1434 Cape Bojador rounded by the Portuguese
1487 Dias leaves Lisbon to sail around the Cape and enters the Indian Ocean (1488)
1492 Columbus discovers the Bahamas and explores the north coast of Cuba and Hispaniola (to 1493)
1493 Columbus explores the south coast of Cuba, thinking it is part of mainland China
1497 Da Gama sails to India (to 1499)
1498 Columbus discovers Trinidad and the coast of South America
1500 The Portuguese Pedro Cabral sees the coast of Brazil
1502 Columbus' last voyage (to 1504). He explores the coast of Central America
1519 First voyage around the world by Magellan's expedition (to 1522)

Columbus Christopher (1451–1506)
Columbus' voyage to America in 1492 was as daring as any ever made by man. He was sure that the earth was round, and that by sailing west instead of east he would eventually reach India and the wealthy trading ports of the Orient. But he did not know how far he would have to travel (and, in fact, his guess at the size of the earth was much too small), and he did not know what perils lay in wait in the Atlantic Ocean, a vast, unknown expanse of sea. Neither did he know that between him and his destination lay a huge unexplored landmass: the continent of America.

Columbus was an Italian, born in the coastal city of Genoa. He went to sea at the age of 14, and in 1470 he was shipwrecked in a battle near the Portuguese coast. He reached safety on a piece of wood, and decided to stay in Portugal, where he became a mapmaker. It was this work that led him to believe the world was round, and he began looking for somebody to finance a voyage westward to India. After many disappointments he was finally sent to Ferdinand and Isabella, the king and queen of Spain. After some delay they agreed to support him, and in 1492 a fleet of three small ships, the *Santa Maria*, the *Niña*, and the *Pinta*, and 120 men was gathered. Columbus set sail on August 3 and arrived at the Canary Islands at the beginning of September. From there he sailed due west, using a compass and guessing how far he had traveled each day. His crew was nervous, and Columbus had to keep their spirits up as they sailed across an empty ocean. On the thirty-third day out of the Canaries land was sighted ahead. It was a tiny, green island, surrounded by a reef, inhabited by a few naked (and surprised) people. For many years the site of Columbus' landfall in the New World was thought to be Watling Island (now known as San Salvador), but recent research has suggested that it was probably the tiny Samana Cay, some 56 miles to the south.

Columbus went on to sail to Cuba and then Haiti, which he named Hispaniola. He left a small settlement there and returned to Spain, where his discovery of the "West Indies" was greeted with great enthusiasm. In 1493 he set out on a second expedition, this time with 17 ships and over 1,000 men. He explored more of the islands of the West Indies, but it was not until his third voyage, begun in 1498, that he reached the mainland of America. Meanwhile, his fortunes in Spain had risen, fallen, and risen again. He was sent home from his third voyage in chains by the Spanish governor of Hispaniola, but Queen Isabella restored him to favor once he was back in Spain. His last voyage was made between 1502 and 1504, and took him south along the coasts of Panamá, Honduras, and Nicaragua in search of a passage west. Columbus didn't know that what lay before him was an impenetrable continent stretching across the globe, and when he failed to find a route through it he fell from favor once again. He died in poverty and disgrace in Spain, and was buried at a monastery near Seville.

Columbus set sail from Spain in three ships. The flagship was the Santa Maria. *It was 120 feet long and weighed 100 tons. The* Pinta *was a 50-ton caravel and was captained by Columbus' partner Martin Pinzon. The* Niña *was captained by Martin's brother, Francisco. The* Santa Maria *was destroyed on rocks near Haiti during a storm.*

Cooper, James Fenimore (1789–1851)
Cooper was an American writer, whose work includes over 30 novels. The family home was in a wild and beautiful part of New York State where Cooper's father was a wealthy politician and a Quaker. In 1803 Cooper went to Yale College, but was expelled and he eventually joined the navy. He began to write after abandoning the sea and marrying Susan De Lancey in 1811. His best novels are those about the sea or the American wilds, and include *The Last of the Mohicans* (1826) and *The Pathfinder* (1840). He was very popular in France, where he was a United States consul for a short time.

Copernicus, Nicolas (1473–1543)
Copernicus was a Polish scientist who is considered the founder of modern astronomy because he proved that the earth spins, and that it travels around the sun. At Cracow University he studied mathematics and optics, before becoming a student of law at Bologna in Italy. After visiting Rome (where he saw an eclipse of the moon in 1501) he traveled to Padua to study medicine. Copernicus eventually went to live with his powerful uncle, the Bishop of Ermeland, in a remote castle. He spent the next 30 years developing his theories about the movement of the planets, while at the same time working as a tax collector, judge, physician, military governor, and churchman. His book, called the *De revolutionibus*, which contains all his work on astronomy, was printed only hours before he died.
○ GALILEO

Copland, Aaron (1900–)
Copland is a leading 20th-century American composer. His music, which includes the famous ballet *Appalachian Spring*, has been influenced by jazz and by American folk music.

"Corbusier," Le (Charles Édouard Jeanneret, 1887–1965)
A Swiss architect, whose name means "the crow." He used strong modern building materials such as steel and concrete to design spacious, light-filled buildings, and was one of the most influential modern architects.

Corday, Charlotte (1768–93)
Charlotte Corday was a French noblewoman, born in the province of Normandy. When the French Revolution broke out in 1789 she was at first an enthusiastic supporter of the revolutionaries, but she was later horrified by the violence of "Jacobins" such as Robespierre and Marat. She decided to kill one of their leaders. On July 13, 1793, she gained an interview with Marat by pretending to have information about his enemies. When Marat (who was in his bath) said: "I will have them all guillotined in Paris," Corday plunged a dagger into his heart. Corday was then herself guillotined by the revolutionaries. ○ MARAT, ROBESPIERRE

A painting by David of the dead French revolutionary Marat. He was killed in his bath by Charlotte Corday.

Corneille, Pierre (1606–84)
Corneille was a great 17th-century French dramatist. After trying to become a lawyer at Rouen in Normandy he moved to Paris, where his first play was performed in 1631. For a while he wrote plays for the powerful Cardinal Richelieu, but in 1636 he quarreled with the cardinal over his most famous and successful work, *Le Cid*. Corneille continued to write until the end of his life, although he became less popular when his plays had to compete with those of the younger Racine. His brother **Thomas Corneille** (1625–1709) was also a successful playwright. ○ MOLIÈRE, RACINE, RICHELIEU

Cortés Hernán (1485–1547)
Cortés was the Spanish *conquistador* (conqueror) who defeated the Aztec empire in Mexico and claimed the land for Spain. The Aztecs were at that time a civilized, prosperous, and very numerous people. Cortés, with only 500 men and 10 cannons, landed in the area known as Yucatán in 1518, where he fought his first battles, founded a settlement, and burned his ships before beginning to march inland. The Aztec king Montezuma II was at first friendly—perhaps because he thought Cortés was the god Quetzalcoatl, who was said to be fair-skinned, bearded, and to ride a horse. In November 1519 Cortés reached the capital Tenochtitlán, a city of over 300,000 people built in the middle of a vast lake, which could only be reached by long causeways with drawbridges at their ends. Montezuma was easily taken prisoner, and forced to submit to Spain and give Cortés large sums in gold. However, when the Aztecs overcame their fear of the foreign invaders, Cortés and his men suddenly found themselves trappd. After much fighting, in which Montezuma was killed, the Spaniards were forced to flee from the city and about half of them were killed. Cortés recovered and returned to besiege Tenochtitlán. In August 1521 plague, starvation, and battle finally defeated the Aztecs. Cortés ruled as governor of "New Spain" until 1526, but eventually fell from power and died forgotten in southern Spain. ○ MONTEZUMA II

The French playwright, Pierre Corneille.

Courbet, Gustave (1819–77)
Gustave Courbet was a French painter who was largely self-taught. He was a realist painter who rejected all idealization in art. He believed that the noblest subjects for an artist were the worker and the peasant. Among his most famous pictures are *The Stonebreakers* (1849) and *The Burial of Ornans* (1850), a peasant funeral.

Cousteau, Jacques-Yves (1910–)
A French underwater explorer who helped invent the "Aqualung" breathing apparatus for divers in 1936. He has written many books about his voyages, and is famous for his color films about life beneath the seas.

Cranach, Lucas (1472–1553)
A German painter and woodblock printer. He painted a large number of religious subjects before becoming known as a portrait artist. Cranach may have been the first to paint portraits in "full length" (from head to toe), and his work includes several pictures of the Protestant leader Martin Luther. Luther and Cranach became friends, and Cranach made a number of woodblock prints for Protestant pamphlets. ○ LUTHER

Crane, Stephen (1871–1900)
Crane was an American novelist and poet. His most famous novel, *The Red Badge of Courage* (1895), is set in the Civil War, and its success led Crane to be appointed as a war correspondent during the Spanish-American War. From 1898 he lived in England, where he met the writers Henry James and Joseph Conrad.

Cranmer, Thomas (1489–1556)
Cranmer was Archbishop of Canterbury during the reign of King Henry VIII of England. While still a teacher at the Univeristy of Cambridge he pleased Henry by saying that he thought the king's reasons for divorcing his first wife, Catherine of Aragon, were good. Henry sent him to Europe to seek support for the divorce, and in 1533 made him archbishop. He declared Henry's marriage to Catherine invalid, and his marriage to Anne Boleyn (which had already taken place) to be legal. Cranmer never failed to support the king: he helped bring Anne Boleyn to trial, divorced Henry from Anne of Cleves, and favored the execution of Catherine Howard. After Henry's death, Cranmer's views became increasingly Protestant, and during the reign of the Catholic Queen Mary he was burned at the stake in Oxford. ○ BOLEYN, HENRY VIII

Crazy Horse (*c.*1840–77)
An Oglala Sioux Indian chief who took part in the defeat of General Custer and his troops at the Battle of the Little Bighorn in 1876. He was a quiet and careful warrior who was thought of by many Indians as their greatest chief. ○ CUSTER, SITTING BULL

Crick, Francis Harry Compton (1916–)
A British biologist who, together with J. D. Watson, explained the structure of DNA (deoxyribonucleic acid), the molecule that carries genetic information from one generation of living things to the next. This discovery, made in 1953, was one of the greatest advances in modern science. Crick and Watson were awarded the Nobel Prize for Medicine in 1962.

Crippen, Dr. Harvey (1862–1910)
Dr. Crippen was an American doctor and wife-poisoner who in 1900 settled in London. In 1910 he was questioned about the disappearance of his wife. He fled with his mistress Ethel Le Neve (who was disguised as a boy) on board the ocean liner *Montrose* bound for the United States. After his wife's remains were discovered in his house, Crippen was traced aboard the *Montrose* by wireless telegraphy (the first time it was used in criminal detection). He was later convicted of the murder and hanged.

Croce, Benedetto (1866–1952)
Benedetto Croce was an Italian philosopher and historian for whom the only reality is the mind or spirit, especially as seen in art.

Crockett, Davy (1786–1836)
Davy Crockett was an American pioneer who has become celebrated as a hero in many stories of the wild West. Most of these are exaggerated. Crockett was in fact a lawyer. In 1814 he fought against the Creek Indians, and was afterward elected to Congress. He died fighting at the Battle of the Alamo in Texas. Crockett was a skilled marksman with his long-barreled rifle "Betsy."

Croesus (d. 546 B.C.)
Croesus was the last king of the kingdom of Lydia in Asia Minor. He is remembered for his great wealth, his gold mines, and his conquests. After succeeding his father to the throne in 560 B.C., he first made the Greeks living in Asia Minor his subjects, then began to move eastward. He was defeated by Cyrus, king of Persia, and imprisoned. His death is a mystery. ○ CYRUS

Cromwell, Oliver (1599–1658)
Oliver Cromwell was the most important of the generals who led the parliamentary armies during the English Civil War. He signed the warrant for King Charles I's execution in 1649, and at the end of the war became Protector of England. His government was known as the "Commonwealth," and lasted until the return of the monarchy in 1660.

Cromwell's family were landowners in the flat fenlands around Cambridge and Ely in the east of England. He went to university at Cambridge, then studied law in London. In 1617, Cromwell's father died, and he returned to his family estate. One of the reasons for the outbreak of the Civil War was King Charles's refusal to cooperate with the nation's Parliament. Charles needed money to build a navy and to support his extravagant court, and so he tried to raise taxes. But Parliament hesitated to approve these new taxes, so in 1628 Charles dismissed them and decided to govern alone. By 1640 he had become desperate and was forced to recall Parliament. Cromwell sat in the Parliaments of both 1628 and 1640, and he spoke up as an opponent of the king. Another cause of the war was religion. Cromwell and many of those who joined the parliamentary side were "Puritans"—English Protestants who wanted to "purify" the English Church and abandon all elaborate ceremonies and rituals. Charles, although not a Catholic, often seemed to favor Catholic traditions, and his queen, Henrietta Maria, was a French Catholic who was accused of plotting with France to overthrow the English Parliament. War broke out in 1642. Cromwell returned to East Anglia, where he formed his army of "Ironsides": strictly disciplined and enthusiastic troops who became almost invincible. Cromwell was a skilled general, and he gradually rose to become the leader of the parliamentary army. Charles's "Royalist" army was finally defeated at the Battle of Naseby on June 14, 1645. The king fled to Scotland, but the Scots eventually handed him back to the English

Portrait of Oliver Cromwell.

parliamentarians, and he was imprisoned on the Isle of Wight. At first, Cromwell tried to reach agreement with the king, but the army wanted him brought to trial. After he was discovered plotting another war, he was tried and executed.

The country was now governed by Parliament or "Commonwealth," but over the next few years disputes between Parliament and the army, and between different factions within Parliament, led to power being placed in Cromwell's hands alone. First he was unable to agree with the "Rump" Parliament, which had survived from before the war, so he dismissed them. They were replaced by the strongly Puritan "Barebones" Parliament, but they, too, could not agree. In 1653 Cromwell was made Protector. Parliament was supposed to approve his decrees, but constant argument meant that Cromwell's word alone became law. He was a skilled governor. England had several successes abroad, and at home he was tolerant of all religions except Catholicism. Scotland became prosperous through its union with England, although in Ireland Cromwell put down a rebellion with great and unnecessary severity. He died in 1658 and was succeeded as Protector by his son, **Richard Cromwell** (1626–1712). But without Cromwell's strong personality, the Commonwealth collapsed. Richard was a weak ruler, and he was forced to resign by the army. In 1660 Charles II was returned to the throne, and the only period of republican government in England came to an end. ○ CHARLES I

Oliver Cromwell led the Puritan army to victory over King Charles I's forces in the Civil War. Charles was tried for treason in Westminster Hall. He was executed at Whitehall, and impressed everyone with his dignity.

Crosby, Bing (Harry Lillis, 1903–78)
Bing Crosby was an American singer and actor. He was a leading "crooner" of the 1930s and 1940s. In 1960 he received a platinum disk to commemorate the sale of his 200,000,000th record! He is famous for his films with Bob Hope and Dorothy Lamour, especially the "Road" series, among which are *The Road to Singapore,* and *The Road to Morocco.*

The American poet e.e. cummings. He was famous for his typography. He dropped capital letters except in unexpected places, chopped up words, and arranged the whole poems in patterns on the page.

jake hates
                    all the girls(the
shy ones,the bold
ones;the meek
proud sloppy sleek)
all except the cold
                                        ones

paul scorns all
                         the girls(the
bright ones, the dim
ones;the slim
plump tiny tall)
all except the
                              dull ones

gus loves all the
                              girls(the
warped ones,the lamed
ones;the mad
moronic maimed)
all except
                         the dead ones

mike likes all the girls
                                        (the
fat ones,the lean
ones;the mean
kind dirty clean)
all
       except the green ones

Cummings, Edward Estlin (1894–1962)
Cummings was a well-known 20th-century American poet. He liked to experiment with unusual uses of words and grammar, strange spellings, and other unconventional approaches to writing poetry. One of the most noticeable was his refusal to use capital letters or punctuation, and he even chose to sign his own name "e e cummings." He was born in Massachusetts and went to college at Harvard. He graduated during World War I. Although the United States had not officially entered the war, Cummings decided to volunteer, and in 1916 he went to France to serve as an ambulance driver. The following year he was imprisoned in a French concentration camp on a completely mistaken charge of spying. He spent six months there, and described his experiences in his first book, *The Enormous Room*. It was published in 1922, and became a great success. Cummings had also begun writing poetry. His first collection, *Tulips and Chimneys*, was published in 1923, and was quickly followed by two more. An important theme in his poetry is the celebration of individual, spontaneous human emotions, such as love and joy. While praising such qualities, Cummings also makes bitter fun of "dead," "soulless" people, who live not by the heart but only by ideas and the mind. He had a word for such a person: "unman." As well as poetry, Cummings also wrote plays. They include *Tom* (1935), which was based on the book *Uncle Tom's Cabin*. Other collections of his poetry include *No Thanks* (1935), *One Times One* (1944), and *95 Poems* (1958). He was a talented artist, and he exhibited and published his drawings and paintings. Like his poetry, they were unconventional in style, and caused some controversy when they appeared in public.

maggie and milly and molly and may

maggie and milly and molly and may
went down to the beach(to play one day)

and maggie discovered a shell that sang
so sweetly she couldn't remember her troubles,and

milly befriended a stranded star
whose rays five languid fingers were;

and molly was chased by a horrible thing
which raced sideways while blowing bubbles:and

may came home with a smooth round stone
as small as a world and as large as alone.

For whatever we lose(like a you or a me)
it's always ourselves we find in the sea

e. e. cummings

Curie, Marie (1867–1934)
A Polish-born scientist who discovered and isolated the element radium. She moved to Paris in 1891, where she worked as assistant to **Pierre Curie** (1859–1906), a professor at the Sorbonne university. They were married in 1895. After Becquerel had discovered radioactivity in 1896, the Curies worked together to discover the radioactive elements radium and polonium. In 1902 they managed to extract one gram of these substances from over eight tons of pitchblende. The Curies shared the 1903 Nobel Prize with Becquerel for their work. In 1906, Pierre Curie was killed in a road accident in Paris. Marie took over as professor of physics at the Sorbonne, and in 1910 she succeeded in completely isolating radium. She was awarded a second Nobel Prize in 1911.
○ BECQUEREL

Marie and Pierre Curie working in their lab.

Curzon, George Nathaniel (1859–1925)
George Curzon was a British politician. He entered Parliament as a Conservative in 1886. In 1898, at the age of 39, he was appointed viceroy of India. He held various offices under Lloyd George during World War I. In 1919 he was made foreign secretary. He was a traveler and scholar. Though he got a bad degree at Oxford, he exclaimed with characteristic extravagance: "I shall devote the rest of my life to showing the examiners that they have made a mistake." He spent vast sums of money on the restoration of Kedleston Hall in Derbyshire, a fine Robert Adam house, and on the magnificent Montacute House in Somerset. He married Mary Leiter, daughter of a U.S. millionaire.

Custer, George Armstrong (1839–76)
General Custer was an American cavalry officer who suffered a famous defeat at the hands of the Indians at the Battle of the Little Bighorn. He was born in Ohio, trained at the West Point military academy, and served in the American Civil War. In the spring of 1876 Custer's Seventh Cavalry unit was one of several sent to chase the Indians out of their homelands in the Montana Territory. The Indians, however, were prepared to fight. On June 25 Custer divided his troops and led 264 men in a reckless charge on a vast Indian camp next to the Little Bighorn River. The Indians, mostly Sioux and Cheyennes led by Sitting Bull and Crazy Horse, annihilated the cavalry, killing Custer and all his men. ○ CRAZY HORSE, SITTING BULL

A color photograph of General Custer. He passed into American legend after "Custer's Last Stand," the Battle of Little Bighorn.

Cuvier, Georges (1769–1832)
A French scientist who studied animal life and fossils. Unlike Darwin and his followers, Cuvier believed that different species were "fixed" in type; that is, that they did not "evolve" or change into other species. ○ DARWIN

Cyrus the Great (d. 529 B.C.)
Cyrus was the founder of the great Persian Empire that, by the time of his death, stretched all the way from the Mediterranean to India. He apparently came to power by conquering the various different peoples of Asia and then uniting them under his rule. He is mentioned in the Bible as "The Shepherd." ○ CROESUS

Da Gama, Vasco (*c.*1469–1525)
Da Gama was a Portuguese sailor who led the first fleet to sail around the Cape of Good Hope and reach India by sea. The expedition was made up of three ships and 168 men, and left Lisbon in July 1497. Four months later Da Gama rounded the cape and started to sail up the eastern coast of Africa, despite being troubled by hurricanes and then by a mutiny among his crew. He arrived at the African port of Melinda, where he found an Indian willing to guide him across the Indian Ocean. In May 1498 he landed at Calicut on the Indian mainland. At first the Indians were friendly, but they soon turned hostile, and Da Gama was forced to fight his way out of the harbor.

When Da Gama returned to Portugal the following year he received many honors, and a second expedition led by **Pedro Cabral** (*c.*1467–1520) was sent to found a settlement in India. Forty members of this expedition were killed by Indians and Da Gama was then sent with a fleet to avenge them. On his way east he founded the Portuguese colony of Mozambique, and on arrival in India bombarded Calicut and was able to return home with his ships loaded with spice and other precious commodities. Da Gama died in India after being made governor there in 1524. ○ DIAZ

Daguerre, Louis Jacques Mandé (1789–1851)
Daguerre was a French scientist who invented the first practical method of making photographs. He was first a tax official, and then worked as a scene painter for a Paris opera house. He began to experiment with photography, and in 1829 was joined by Niepce, who had already succeeded in making very poor photographs. In 1839 Daguerre announced what he called his "Daguerreotype" process, which produced good-quality pictures in just 20 or 30 minutes. One of the disadvantages was that no copies could be made. ○ NIEPCE

Daimler, Gottlieb (1834–1900)
A German engineer who patented the first gasoline-driven internal combustion engine in 1883. In 1895 he produced one of the first roadworthy cars and founded the Daimler automobile company. The first Mercedes was manufactured by him in 1900, and was named after his daughter.

Dali, Salvador Felipe Jacinto (1904–)
Dali is a flamboyant Spanish painter and member of the Surrealist movement. His pictures are supposed to represent the world of dreams and the subconscious mind, and are often painted with great attention to detail.

Dalton, John (1766–1844)
An English chemist. Dalton reintroduced the theory (first proposed in ancient Greece) that matter is made up of "atoms," experimented with gases, and investigated the force of steam. Dalton and his brother were both color blind, and he was the first man to describe this condition in detail.

Dante Alighieri (1265–1321)
Dante was an Italian poet. His great poem *The Divine Comedy* is one of the most admired works of literature in the world, and has been translated into almost every language. Dante was the son of a lawyer, born in the city of Florence, and at the age of only 9 he fell completely in love with the beautiful "Beatrice." In a series of poems called *La Vita Nuova* ("The New Life") he describes his enchantment with her, how they met occasionally when they were both aged about 18, and his sorrow when she died (in 1290). We do not know if "Beatrice" shared Dante's passion, and her true name is never revealed. The poet Boccaccio, who wrote a biography of Dante, says that she was Bice Portinari, who married a wealthy banker.

After her death, Dante himself married, and became involved in city politics. When his party fell from power in 1302, Dante was forced to leave Florence, and he never returned. He began work on *The Divine Comedy* in about 1307. In the poem Dante travels through *Hell, Purgatory,* and *Paradise,* where he recognizes many famous people of his own and other times and finally (in *Paradise*) sees Beatrice. It was the first important work of literature to be written in Italian. Boccaccio described Dante as the "singular splendor of the Italian race." He spent the last years of his life at Ravenna, where he died and is buried.
○ BOCCACCIO, CIMABUE

Danton, Georges Jacques (1759–94)
Danton was one of the most important figures of the French Revolution. In 1789, when revolution broke out, he founded the "Cordeliers' Club," which became a meeting place for radicals. Danton became famous for his thunderous speeches denouncing the aristocracy, and in 1792 he became minister of justice in the revolutionary government. With France and the revolution threatened by invasions from abroad, it was Danton's determination that inspired the people of Paris to resist. In January 1793 he was among those who voted to execute King Louis XVI. Later that year the moderate Girondist party were forced out of power, and Danton and the radicals took complete control of the government. Danton was a member of the notorious "Committee of Public Safety," which brought "enemies" of the revolution to trial, but he opposed too harsh a treatment of prisoners and urged moderate policies. This brought him into conflict with the more extreme character of Robespierre. In 1794 he left Paris to stay with his wife in the country. Meanwhile Robespierre and his friends made up charges of disloyalty against Danton. When he returned to the city he was arrested and brought to trial before a Revolutionary Tribunal, condemned, and guillotined. Danton was one of the few men of the French Revolution with true political intuition.

○ MARAT, ROBESPIERRE

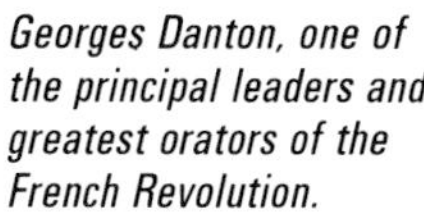

Georges Danton, one of the principal leaders and greatest orators of the French Revolution.

Dare, Virginia (1587)
Virginia Dare was the first European child to be born in America. She was the daughter of two members of the first settlement on Roanoke Island. Shortly after her birth in 1587, a group of settlers set sail for England to fetch supplies. When they returned two years later Virginia, her parents, and the rest of the community had all disappeared.

Darling, Grace (1815–42)
Grace Darling was the daughter of the lighthouse keeper on one of the Farne Islands off the coast of Northumberland in northeast England. On September 7, 1838, the steamship *Forfarshire* was wrecked on rocks nearby. Seeing survivors still clinging to the rocks, Grace and her father rowed out in heavy seas to rescue them. As a result she gained a great deal of publicity and admiration.

Darwin, Charles Robert (1809–82)
See pages 80 & 81

"All hope abandon, ye who enter here."
Divine Comedy: Hell

"In His will is our peace."
Divine Comedy: Paradise

The poet Dante towers over his native city of Florence in this painting in the city's cathedral. The imaginary landscape contains scenes from his greatest poem, The Divine Comedy.

Dassault, Marcel (1891–)
A French aircraft manufacturer, engineer, journalist, and publisher. His company, in which the state is now the major shareholder, produced Mirage jets.

David (*c.*1000 B.C.)
David (which in Hebrew means "Beloved") was the first king of all Israel. The Bible tells that he was the son of Jesse, and that he became a favorite of King Saul and a friend of Saul's son Jonathan. During a war with the people known as the Philistines David killed the giant Goliath with a stone thrown from a sling. He married Saul's daughter and became a military commander, but Saul then became jealous of the young man and he was forced to flee. For several years David led a band of soldiers and lived in a cave, but after Saul's and Jonathan's deaths he returned to the city of Hebron and ruled half of Saul's kingdom, while Saul's son Ishbosheth ruled the rest. When Ishbosheth died, David came to rule all the Israelites. He conquered the city of Jebus, where he built a new capital, calling it "Jerusalem," and went on to defeat the Philistines and many other tribes. David was a strong but sometimes corrupt leader. It is said that in order to have Bathsheba he ordered her husband to fight in the front of a battle, where he was killed. He is also said to have written many psalms and lyrics, although probably only some of those that have survived were actually written by him. He died in Jerusalem between 1018 B.C. and 993 B.C. and was succeeded by his son Solomon. ○ SOLOMON

David, Jacques Louis (1748–1825)
A French painter. David became popular in Paris in 1785 when his dramatic picture *The Oath of the Horatii* was exhibited. During the French Revolution David was a deputy in the government assembly and, as director of the arts, organized huge propaganda processions, and abolished the old French Academy. After Robespierre's death he was imprisoned for a time, but during Napoleon's government he again became an official painter. He made several portraits of Napoleon, including the huge scene showing his coronation in the cathedral of Notre Dame. After Napoleon's fall he fled to Switzerland and then to Brussels, where he died.

Davis, Jefferson (1808–89)
Jefferson Davis was president of the Confederacy, the Southern states whose breaking away from the United States caused the American Civil War (1861–65). When he entered the Senate in 1847, he defended the right of Southern states to own slaves against the Northern abolitionists. He came to believe that "Dixie" with its slaves and cotton plantations should be separate. When war broke out, Davis was soon elected president of the

Emily Davison throwing herself under the king's horse at the 1913 Derby.

Confederacy. When the South surrendered in 1865 Davis was jailed for two years. He spent his last years as a businessman in Mississippi.

Davison, Emily Wilding (1872–1913)
Emily Davison was an English suffragette (a campaigner for votes for women). She was a member of the Women's Social and Political Union, led by Emmeline Pankhurst. In 1913, in order to draw attention to her cause, she tried to grab the reins of a racehorse owned by the king as it ran toward the finish of the Derby race. She died a few days later from her injuries. ○ PANKHURST

Davy, Humphry (1778–1829)
An English chemist and researcher whose inventions included the miner's safety lamp (in 1815) and the diving bell. Davy was self-educated and lived a life of great energy and activity. In 1799 he discovered that nitrous oxide ("laughing gas") could be used as an anesthetic, and his most important chemical research involved isolating metal elements such as potassium, sodium, and calcium. ○ FARADAY, STEPHENSON

Day, Dorothy (1897–1980)
Dorothy Day was an American social reformer. She founded a newspaper called the *Catholic Worker* and spent most of her life caring for the poor and sick. She and her followers believed that helping the needy and resisting violence was true Christianity. She kept herself poor so that she would not have to pay taxes which would then be spent on weapons by the government.

Dayan, Moshe (1915–81)
Moshe Dayan was an Israeli soldier and politician. He was minister of defense in Golda Meir's government. He planned and commanded the Six-Day War in 1967. He was a key figure in the negotiations that led to the signing of the peace treaty between Israel and Egypt in 1979. ○ MEIR

De Beauvoir, Simone (1908–86)
De Beauvoir was a French feminist writer and novelist. She studied at the Sorbonne university in Paris, where she met the young Jean Paul Sartre. They remained together until Sartre's death, and developed a philosophy known as "existentialism" (○ SARTRE). De Beauvoir became a teacher, and published her first novel in 1943. She wrote several more novels, the most famous of which is *The Mandarins*, published in 1954, which won France's most important literary prize, the Prix Goncourt. In addition to novels, De Beauvoir wrote essays, travel books, and a long autobiography. Her most influential book is *The Second Sex*, published in 1949, in which she opposed marriage and motherhood because she saw them as ways in which women are oppressed by men.

Deborah (*c*.1100 B.C.)
An Old Testament prophetess, the only woman to become a judge of Israel (in about 1125 B.C.). She led an army which freed her people from oppression by the Canaanites. The *Song of Deborah* (in the Book of Judges) is one of the oldest parts of the Bible.

Debussy, Claude Achille (1862–1918)
A French composer, particularly famous for his piano pieces and chamber music. His experiments in composition led him to try to produce "pictures" made up of musical sound, and he began what is known as the "Impressionist" movement in music. Among his best-known work is *L'Après-midi d'un faune*, which was inspired by a poem by Mallarmé, the opera *Pelléas and Mélisande* (1902), and the three symphonic sketches, *La Mer* (1905). Even in his last works he continued to explore new and original harmonics.

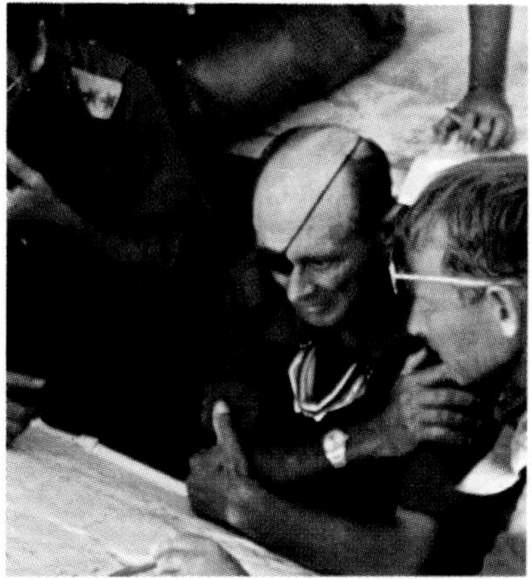

Moshe Dayan, the Israeli soldier and politician who commanded the Six-Day War in 1967.

Defoe, Daniel (1660–1731)
An English writer, whose most famous works are *Robinson Crusoe* and *Moll Flanders*. Defoe did not begin writing novels until he was 60 years old. For much of his life he ran a successful business and wrote political pamphlets in his spare time. In 1702 he made an attack on the Anglican Church, and as a result was locked in prison and made bankrupt by a heavy fine. When Defoe was released, he began a newspaper, and in 1719 published *Robinson Crusoe*.

(Continued on page 82)

The Origin of Species

Charles Darwin, the English naturalist who put forward the theory of evolution by means of natural selection. His ideas were very controversial because they challenged the accepted religious beliefs about how the world was created.

HMS Beagle, *the vessel in which Darwin set sail for South America and the Pacific islands, at anchor in the Galápagos Islands.*

Darwin, Charles Robert (1809–82)
In 1859 Charles Darwin published his great work *The Origin of Species*, in which he carefully set out his theory that the many different types of life on earth had not simply been "created" as they were, but had changed, adapted, and "evolved" over millions of years. The book was an immediate best-seller: the first edition sold out in a single day, and Darwin's name became well known throughout Europe. Just like Galileo three hundred years earlier, Darwin had challenged centuries of firmly held beliefs about the world—and people were anxious to find out about his ideas for themselves.

Darwin was born in the quiet English country town of Shrewsbury. He intended to become a doctor like his father, but disease and surgery disgusted him, and he soon abandoned medical school. Instead, he decided to enter the Church, and he went to Cambridge University to study theology. It was there that Darwin first became interested in nature and the science of biology. He took long walks in the Cambridge countryside with the university's professor of botany, collecting and studying different animals and plants. In 1832 the British navy asked the same botany professor if he could recommend a naturalist to sail around the world on HMS *Beagle* and study wildlife in the various places the ship would visit. He suggested Darwin, and so in 1831 the young man set sail for South America, the Pacific islands, and Australia.

It was on this voyage that Darwin collected the information on which he based his theory of evolution. In

the Galápagos Islands he noticed the huge variety of life forms. He also noticed that certain birds or tortoises were very slightly different on different islands. He wondered: were these *really* completely separate species?

The answer he gave to questions like this, after years of carefully studying his notes, was that different variations in species could develop from a single ancestor. For example, a particular tortoise might by chance be born with a characteristic which made it better able to survive. It could pass on this characteristic to its offspring—and so on, until, over many, many generations, a species of "better" tortoises with the new characteristic would develop, well adapted to survive in their environment. This simple idea, Darwin realized, could be extended to all species: characteristics that enable a plant or animal to survive in a particular way will be passed on from generation to generation.

He called this process "natural selection." The huge variety of different species even on a simple, grassy bank reflects the many different ways in which life could evolve and adapt to its surroundings. Darwin realized that although there were now many species, all surviving in their own way, millions and millions of years ago there must have been one simple ancestor for all life.

Many people were offended. God, they said, had created life, as described in the Bible. In particular, Darwin's theory suggested that man was not specially created by God, but, like all animals, had evolved—from the same ancestors as the ape. He discussed this idea in a later book, *The Descent of Man*, published in 1871.

Despite these objections, Darwin's theory gained acceptance, and remains one of the most revolutionary advances made by modern science.

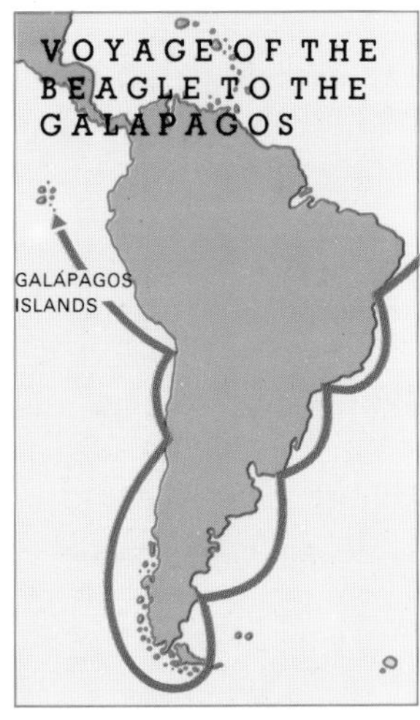

When we look at the plants and bushes enclothing an entangled bank, we are tempted to attribute their proportional numbers and kinds to what we call chance. But how false a view this is! . . . What a struggle between the several kinds of trees must have gone on during long centuries, each annually scattering its seeds by the thousand; what war between insect and insect—between insects, snails, and other animals with birds and beasts of prey—all striving to increase, and all feeding on each other or on the trees or their seeds or seedlings, or on the other plants which first clothed the ground . . . .

Charles Darwin, The Origin of Species, *Chapter III*

Its success led to *Moll Flanders* (1721) and several other stories and novels. Defoe also wrote of his travels around Britain and a great many essays and articles under his own and other names.

Degas, Edgar (1834–1917)
Degas was a French painter and sculptor. He was a pupil of Ingres, but was strongly influenced by Manet, and the first of the Impressionist painters. He was also interested in photography, and his paintings have an unposed appearance very similar to snapshots. In about 1873 Degas began to visit the ballet school and make the drawings and paintings of dancers for which he is best known. He experimented with materials such as crayon, chalk, and unusual mixtures of paint. Degas made friends with most of the great painters of his time and organized the Impressionist exhibitions held in Paris. He became more and more interested in sculpture as he got older, perhaps because his eyesight was getting worse and he could no longer see to paint. ○ INGRES, MANET

De Gaulle, Charles André Joseph Marie (1890–1970)
Charles De Gaulle dominated French politics in the years after World War II, and as President (1958–69) became a spokesman for French strength and

Charles De Gaulle, the French general and statesman who led the Free French movement after the fall of France in 1940 and later became president.

independence. When war broke out in 1940 De Gaulle escaped to Britain, where he organized the Free French movement and refused to recognize the Vichy government led by Pétain. In August 1944 De Gaulle returned to Paris with the army which liberated the city from German occupation and became head of the new government. He resigned two years later when the parties failed to agree on a new constitution, and founded his own political party, the RPF ("Rally of French People"). In 1958, during an economic crisis and the Algerian struggle for independence from French rule, De Gaulle was asked to become prime minister. The same year he was elected president under a new constitution which he had himself introduced. He granted independence to Algeria and the rest of France's colonies overseas, and helped the French economy recover. De Gaulle wanted France to remain as independent as possible, so he developed French nuclear weapons, withdrew French troops from NATO, and opposed British entry into the European Economic Community. He retired from the presidency in April, 1969, after failing to win support for changes to the French constitution.

De La Tour, Georges (1593–1652)
See La Tour, Georges de

Della Robbia, Luca (1400–82)
An Italian painter and sculptor who discovered a way of using the brightly colored glazes used by potters to decorate his sculptures. He began a workshop in Florence and made a large number of Madonnas and other decorations for churches and chapels using this method. His business was carried on by his nephew, **Andrea**.

DeMille, Cecil B. (1881–1959)
An American film director who, with **Samuel Goldwyn** (1882–1974), made the first American feature film, called *The Squaw Man*, in 1913. He went on to become famous for spectacular movies such as *The Ten Commandments* and *The Sign of the Cross*. DeMille also started the first passenger airline service in the United States in 1917.

De Montfort, Simon (1208–65)
See Montfort, Simon de

Deng Xiaoping (1904–)
Deng is a Chinese Communist politician. He took part in the Long March (1934–36) and held several government offices under Chairman Mao. During the "cultural revolution" he was denounced and lost his power. He was later reinstated and led China when Zhou Enlai became too ill to govern in

1973. Since 1977 he has been deputy prime minister and vice-president of the Chinese Communist party. ○ MAO, ZHOU ENLAI

Descartes, René (1596–1650)
Descartes was a French mathematician and philosopher and one of the most imporant thinkers in history. He was born at La Haye, near Tours, and educated by Jesuit monks. He was interested in mathematics but disliked study, and in 1617 became a soldier in order to find out more about what he called "the great book of the world." Descartes is famous for his saying: "I think, therefore I am." He believed that everything about life and the universe could be proved, like a mathematical problem. He found that the one thing which he could definitely prove was that he was thinking, and that therefore he must exist, and this led to his famous saying. His philosophy is called Cartesian philosophy. Descartes also made important discoveries in mathematics and geometry and experimented with optics. In 1649 he took a job as tutor to Queen Christine of Sweden, who was an admirer of his work. Unfortunately she liked to have her lessons at five o'clock in the morning, and within a few months Descartes had caught a chill and died.

De Valois, Ninette (1898–)
See Valois, Ninette de

De Valera, Eamon (1882–1975)
De Valera was an Irish nationalist politician who eventually became prime minister of the independent Irish nation. At the time of World War I, Ireland was still ruled by the British, but war in Europe reduced their ability to govern Ireland. In 1916 Irish nationalists, including De Valera, attempted to take over in the "Easter rebellion." This failed, but in 1919 the nationalists were able to set up a government of their own, with De Valera as leader. Some members of this government, such as Michael Collins, were in favor of a treaty with Britain, but De Valera opposed this, and civil war followed. In 1926 De Valera decided to give up his opposition and founded a new political party called Fianna Fail, which means "soldiers of destiny." He won the 1932 elections and became prime minister. During the 1930s almost all remaining ties with Britain were broken, until Ireland finally left the Commonwealth in 1948. De Valera remained prime minister for much of this time, and in 1959 became president of the Republic of Ireland. ○ COLLINS

Diaghilev, Sergei Pavlovich (1872–1929)
Diaghilev was the founder and guiding spirit of the famous *Ballets Russes*—a company of dancers and artists who introduced Russian ballet to the rest of Europe at the beginning of the 20th century. Among the dancers who performed for him were Nijinsky and Pavlova; he employed artists such as Matisse and Picasso to design stage sets, and composers such as Debussy, Stravinsky, and Ravel. ○ DUNCAN

Diaz, Bartolomeo (*c.*1450–1500)
A Portuguese explorer. In 1486 he set out with two ships to explore the west coat of Africa. Having already traveled farther south than anybody before him, he was caught in a violent storm and blown around the Cape of Good Hope—and so accidentally discovered the sea route to India. Discontent among his crew forced him to return, but his discovery enabled Da Gama to make his voyage to the east ten years later. ○ DA GAMA

Dickens, Charles (1812–70)
Charles Dickens' novels have been best-sellers ever since they were first published over 100 years ago. He was born at Portsmouth in England, where his father was a clerk in the navy yard. The family later moved to Chatham, but unluckily Dickens' father lost his job and was then put in prison for debt. Dickens, only 12 years old, left school and found a job labeling bottles in a factory in south London. After some years he became a clerk in a solicitor's

A photograph of novelist Charles Dickens. He wrote many of the outstanding social novels of the 19th century.

office and then, having taught himself shorthand, a reporter for a London paper. In the 1830s he wrote a series of successful articles about unusual people or places called *Sketches by Boz,* and this led him to write his first novel, *The Pickwick Papers.* Like almost all his work, it was published in weekly episodes in a magazine before it was printed as a book. *The Pickwick Papers* was very popular, and Dickens devoted the rest of his life to writing. He worked incredibly hard, not only writing novels for demanding publishers, but also at editing a newspaper and magazines; he wrote many stories (including *A Christmas Carol,* in which the character Scrooge appears), an account of his travels in the United States, and *A Child's History of England.* Dickens also gave public readings from his work to raise money for charity, and these were so exhausting that they contributed to his death. His last novel, *Edwin Drood,* was a murder mystery which he left unfinished—so the murderer is never revealed.

The Novels of Charles Dickens

The Pickwick Papers (1836)
Oliver Twist (1839)
Nicholas Nickleby (1839)
The Old Curiosity Shop (1841)
Barnaby Rudge (1841)
Martin Chuzzlewit (1843)
Dombey and Son (1848)
David Copperfield (1850)
Bleak House (1853)
Hard Times (1854)
Little Dorrit (1857)
A Tale of Two Cities (1859)
Great Expectations (1861)
Our Mutual Friend (1865)
Edwin Drood (1870)*

*Unfinished when Dickens died

Dickinson, Emily (1830–86)
Emily Dickinson was a great American poet. She was born and remained throughout her life at Amherst in Massachusetts, where her father was a lawyer. At the age of 23, she suddenly became a recluse, and would only speak to her family or her very close friends. Nobody is sure why she did this, although it has been said that she suffered an unhappy love affair. In her solitude Emily Dickinson wrote over 3,000 poems, most about love, nature, or God. They were unusual in style, and when they were published after her death she was immediately recognized as a great poet. Many American poets have been influenced by her work.

Diderot, Denis (1713–84)
Diderot was a novelist, critic, philosopher, and the creator of a great French encyclopedia. As a young man, he refused to become either a lawyer or a doctor as his father wished, so he was disinherited. He went to Paris, married a poor seamstress, and in 1751 began work on his *Encyclopedia.* The idea was to describe all the areas of human knowledge, and to show that they were related to each other. Many of the greatest writers of the time contributed articles, including Voltaire and Rousseau. Diderot was often in trouble with the government for his views, but eventually all 28 volumes were published. ○ ROUSSEAU, VOLTAIRE

Diesel, Rudolph (1858–1913)
A German engineer and the inventor of the type of internal combustion engine that bears his name (in 1892). His experiments with the engine nearly killed him when an early model exploded, and he eventually disappeared from a ferry in the English Channel.

DiMaggio, Joe (1914–)
Joe DiMaggio was a great American baseball player. He played for the New York Yankees from 1936 until 1951, and in 1941 set a record of 56 consecutive safe-hitting games. He was also a great outfielder.

Diogenes (412 B.C.–323 B.C.)
Diogenes was an ancient Greek philosopher. He was born at Sinope, a town on the Black Sea, and grew up in poverty. After many years of wandering, he arrived in Athens, where he led the life of a complete ascetic; that is, somebody who gives up all comforts and possessions in order to become completely free. He begged for food and slept on the ground. It is even said that he eventually made his home in a disused bathtub! The Athenians admired his teaching, and he became known as a "Cynic" philosopher, which meant one who lived "like a dog." He was so famous that Alexander the Great traveled to see him, and was so impressed that he left saying that if he had not been himself, he would have liked to have been Diogenes. ○ ALEXANDER THE GREAT

Dior, Christian (1905–57)
A French fashion designer. He became famous after World War II for what he called his "New Look" clothes. Dior also began a new trend in the fashion industry by introducing cheaper versions of his high-fashion clothes for the general public.

Disney, Walter Elias (1901–66)
Walt Disney was an American artist and motion picture producer. His best-known films are the cartoons for which he created characters such as Mickey Mouse, Donald Duck, and Pluto. Disney was born in the city of Chicago. In 1923 he made the world's first successful cartoon film, *Oswald the Rabbit*, but it was Mickey Mouse, who first appeared in 1928, that made cartoons really popular. The first Mickey Mouse movie was made in black and white; Disney's first color cartoon was *Snow White and the Seven Dwarfs* (1937). Several successful movies followed, many of which are still regularly shown, including *Bambi*, *Dumbo*, and *Pinocchio*. In the 1940s Disney began making color nature films (which won several Academy Awards, or "Oscars") and feature films for children such as *Treasure Island*, and *Mary Poppins*, in which cartoons and live actors are combined.

Mickey Mouse, the cartoon creation of Walt Disney.

Disraeli, Benjamin (1804–81)
Disraeli was a British writer and politician who served as prime minister in 1868 and then continuously from 1874 until 1880. As a young man he was well known in London society for his brilliant wit and fashionable clothes. Disraeli wrote a successful novel called *Vivian Grey* (published in 1826), and in 1837 he was elected to Parliament. When he was booed and laughed at by other MPs during his first speech, he finished by saying: "Though I sit down now, the time will come when you will hear me." His words came true. In the 1840s he attracted attention when he criticized Peel's government, and in 1852 he was made Chancellor of the Exchequer in Lord Derby's Tory government. He introduced the 1867 Reform Act, which gave more people the vote, and after Derby's death in 1868 became prime minister. Disraeli flattered Queen Victoria, proclaiming her Empress of India in 1867; he was keen to extend British colonies in Africa. In 1875 he bought half of the ownership of the new Suez Canal for Britain.
○ PEEL, VICTORIA

Dominic, Saint (*c.*1170–1221)
Dominic was the founder of an order of friars—the Dominicans—dedicated to converting people to Christianity by teaching, persuasion, and preaching. Dominic and his followers were "mendicants," which means they were not allowed to own property and led lives of complete poverty. They created a system of careful education in their monasteries, so that friars would be properly trained to preach to people outside.

Donatello (*c.*1386–1466)
Donatello was one of the greatest sculptors of the Renaissance period. He was the first to try to copy the style of the ancient sculptures which could be seen in Rome, and he introduced perspective into some of his carvings to make them seem more realistic. His figures influenced not only other sculptors, but also painters such as Masaccio and Bellini. ○ GHIBERTI, MASACCIO

A statue of St. George by Donatello.

Donne, John (1572–1631)
Donne was a great English poet of the 17th century. He wrote poems in many styles and on many subjects—religion, love, politics—and this reflects the many aspects of Donne's own life. He went to the universities at Oxford and Cambridge to study, and then returned to London, where he lived a wild life and was famous for his wit. In 1597 and 1598 he sailed in naval expeditions against the Spanish, then became secretary to a nobleman, Sir Thomas Egerton. In Donne's time poetry was usually written for wealthy men and women, rather than for publication in books. Donne became well known, but his career was spoiled when he fell in love with and secretly married Ann More. As a result, he lost his job and the favor of the wealthy, and was even thrown in prison. Donne and his wife had several children and lived in poverty for many years. In 1615 he became a priest in the Anglican Church. His talent as a writer brought him to the notice of the king, and in 1621 he became dean of St. Paul's Cathedral in London. The sermons he gave there are among the most remarkable ever written in English, but it is for his poetry that he is remembered.

Doolittle, Hilda ("H.D.") (1886–1961)
Hilda Doolittle was an American poet who wrote under the pen name of "H.D." She was born in Pennsylvania and in 1911 moved to London, where her friend Ezra Pound helped her publish some of her work. H.D. belonged to a group of poets known as "Imagists" because their poems often contain very short, clear descriptions of objects or scenes. ○ POUND

Sir Francis Drake, seaman and explorer.

Dostoevsky, Fyodor Mikhailovich (1821–81)
A great Russian novelist. Dostoevsky's life was plagued by misfortune. When he was only 18, his father was murdered by peasants on his country estate. Ten years later, after the success of his first novel (called *Poor Folk*, published in 1846), Dostoevsky was suddenly arrested and sentenced to death for being a revolutionary. He was reprieved only at the very last minute, and sent to prison in Siberia, where he became ill. He described his experiences there in a book called *The House of the Dead*. On his release, Dostoevsky found himself in debt and took to gambling. He twice had to leave Russia to escape from people to whom he owed money, but eventually, under the influence of his second wife, Anna Snitken, Dostoevsky's situation improved. He wrote his finest novels toward the end of his life. These include *Crime and Punishment* (published in 1866) and *The Brothers Karamazov* (1881).

Drake, Sir Francis (*c.*1540–96)
Francis Drake was an English seaman and explorer whose most famous exploit was the defeat of the Spanish Armada in 1588. As a young man he sailed the oceans attacking stray Spanish ships and taking whatever treasure he could find on board. Queen Elizabeth secretly approved of this, although in public she had to call it "piracy" because England and Spain were not officially at war at the time. In 1572, while raiding Spanish settlements in Panama, Drake saw the Pacific Ocean and decided he wanted to be the first Englishman to sail across it. He set sail from Plymouth with four ships five years later. By the time he had passed through the Strait of Magellan in South America (○ MAGELLAN) only his own ship remained. He renamed it the *Golden Hind* and continued north as far as California, before heading across the Pacific to Java, the Cape of Good Hope, and finally, in 1580, England again. Drake was knighted by Queen Elizabeth on board his ship in April 1581. By now Spain and England were almost at war. In 1587 Drake daringly entered Cadiz harbor and destroyed 33 Spanish ships. The following year the great Spanish Armada set sail to invade England. When it was sighted, Drake is said to have been bowling at Plymouth, and to have finished his game before going out to meet the Armada. The battle in the English Channel lasted about a week before the Spanish were defeated and forced to try to sail all the way around the north of Scotland to escape. Drake died of fever in the West Indies.
○ ELIZABETH I, FROBISHER

Dreiser, Theodore (1871–1945)
Dreiser was an American novelist. His childhood was spent in a poor, religious family in Indiana, and as a young man he worked as a reporter in the most depressed parts of Chicago and New York. His novels were highly realistic, and thought obscene by many people when they were first published. The best known is *An American Tragedy* (published in 1925), which describes how a boy's obsession with money and women lead him into becoming a murderer.

Dreyfus, Alfred (1859–1935)
The "Dreyfus Affair" was a scandal involving the government, army, and justice system in France at the end of the 19th century. Dreyfus was a Jewish army officer accused (in 1894) of spying for Germany. The evidence against him was false, but he was found guilty and sent to prison on Devil's Island. Many people, including the novelist Emile Zola, took up his cause. He was retried in 1899, but anti-Jewish officers in the army produced forged papers which led to his being found guilty again. The president of France immediately pardoned Dreyfus, but it was not until 1906 that the "guilty" verdict was withdrawn and Dreyfus restored to his rank in the army.

Dubček, Alexander (1921–)
Dubček became leader of Communist Czechoslovakia in 1968. He introduced a number of reforms, including greater freedom for the press, greater freedom of speech, and other political and economic reforms. He called this "Czechoslovakia's Road to Socialism"—but the Soviet government opposed the changes, and in August 1968 invaded Czechoslovakia. Dubček was forced to resign and his policies reversed.

Duccio di Buoninsegna (*c.*1260–*c.*1320)
A painter who perfected the flat, highly decorated Byzantine style of art in Italy. His greatest work is a series of 26 scenes from Christ's Passion in the cathedral at Siena.

Dumas, Alexandre (1802–70)
Dumas was a French playwright and novelist. Among the many hundreds of books that appeared under his name are *The Count of Monte Cristo* and *The Three Musketeers.* His first successes were plays on historical subjects, and in the mid-1830s he decided to try historical novels. Dumas almost never wrote a whole novel himself: he would invent the story and characters and write the important passages, but the rest of the work was given to assistants. Over 90 different writers worked for him at various times (not always happily), and he was able to produce over 1,500 novels in this way. His son, also called **Alexandre Dumas** (1824–95), was also a successful writer.

Dunant, Jean Henri (1828–1910)
The Swiss founder of the International Red Cross (in 1864) and the winner of the first Nobel Peace Prize (1901). The idea for an international organization to treat those wounded in war came to him after he had worked in a hospital at the Battle of Solferino in 1862.

Duncan, Isadora (1878–1927)
An American dancer who introduced an individual and very controversial style of dancing, performing barefoot, dressed in long robes based on ancient Greek costumes. She founded schools all over Europe. ○ DIAGHILEV

Dürer, Albrecht (1471–1528)
Dürer was painter, engraver, woodcut printer, and book illustrator—altogether one of Germany's greatest artists. He produced only a small number of paintings, but his realistic and highly detailed prints spread his influence all over Europe. He became court painter to the Holy Roman Emperor Maximillian I, produced the first book to have been created entirely by an artist, and made the world's biggest woodcut print—the *Triumphal Arch,* over 100 square feet in area.

A woodcut by the Renaissance German artist, Albrecht Dürer.

Dylan, Bob (Robert Allen Zimmerman, 1941–)
An American singer and songwriter, famous for his powerful "protest" songs and his harsh, gravelly voice. He became one of the idols of the 1960s with songs such as "Blowin' in the Wind," "Mr Tambourine Man," and "The Times They Are A-Changin'."

E

Earhart, Amelia (1898–1937)
An American aviator who in 1932 became the first woman to make a solo flight across the Atlantic. It took her $13\frac{1}{2}$ hours to make the trip from Newfoundland to Ireland in a single-engine Lockheed aircraft. She also became the first woman to fly across the United States alone, but disappeared during an attempt to fly around the world.

Eastman, George (1854–1932)
Eastman was an American inventor and philanthropist, who made photography a popular hobby at the beginning of the 20th century by inventing the "roll" film and selling cheap Kodak cameras. Together with Edison he experimented with movies, and he gave about $100 million to schools and universities. ○ EDISON

Eddy, Mary Baker Glover (1821–1910)
Mary Baker Eddy was the American woman who founded the Christian Science Church. She was born in the town of Bow in New Hampshire, and was a keen student of the Bible. In 1866 she received serious injuries in a fall. Her doctors gave her up as certain to die, but after reading the story of the Palsied Man in the Gospel of St. Matthew, Mary Baker Eddy claimed to have healed herself through prayer. She believed that a person's "spirit" (meaning the religious spirit, or God) could influence and heal the body. In 1879 she founded the First Church of Christ Scientist in Boston, which was devoted to this idea. Mary Baker Eddy remained the minister there until her death. In 1908 she began the newspaper *Christian Science Monitor*.

Edgar (943–75)
An early king of England, known as "Edgar the Peaceful." He ruled Northumbria and Mercia from 957, and in 959 inherited the throne of Wessex, making him king of most of England. He avoided fighting with the Danes and reformed church law.

Edison, Thomas Alva (1847–1931)
See pages 90 & 91

Edward the Confessor (*c.*1003–66)
Edward the Confessor was a king of England who is remembered as a peace-loving, religious ruler. He was canonized (declared a saint) by Pope Alexander III in 1161. Edward was the son of King Ethelred II and Emma, sister of the Duke of Normandy, and he spent most of his childhood in Normandy to avoid the fighting going on in England. When King Hardicanute, Edward's half brother, died in 1042, Edward's powerful uncle Earl Godwin ensured that it was Edward who inherited the throne. As king, he gained a reputation for being generous to the poor, performing miracles in which sick people were healed, and for living a life of religious devotion. But he was also a strong ruler. At that time peace in England was constantly threatened by foreign invaders such as the Danes, and by conflicts between powerful lords, but Edward's reign was one of calm. Edward married Earl Godwin's daughter Edith in 1045, but they remained childless and he was succeeded by Godwin's son Harold. ○ HAROLD II

An engraving of Edward the Confessor. His alleged promise to Duke William of Normandy caused the Norman invasion of England.

Edward II (1284–1327)
Edward became king of England in 1307 when his father (**Edward I,** 1239–1307) died while attempting to conquer Scotland. Instead of continuing the campaign as his father had wished, Edward returned to London where his friend and favorite Gascon Piers Gaveston had remained. Edward's liking for the proud and extravagant Gaveston angered the nobility, and when Edward left Gaveston in charge of the country while he visited France in 1312, Gaveston was captured and murdered. Edward's next misfortune came when he attempted to recapture the parts of Scotland his father had won. He was disastrously defeated at the Battle of Bannockburn by Robert the Bruce in 1314. This was followed by rebellions in Wales and Ireland, and by several years of famine. Eventually, Edward's wife, Isabella, organized a rebellion and forced Edward to abdicate and make his son (Edward III) king. Edward was then murdered in Berkeley Castle. ○ EDWARD III, ROBERT THE BRUCE

Edward III (1312–77)
King of England from 1327. After the chaos of his father, Edward II's reign, Edward III restored some prestige to the English throne. He first won an important battle against the Scottish army and was able to have Edward Baliol, who was friendly toward England, crowned king. Claiming that he should inherit the French throne, Edward and his son **Edward the Black Prince** (1330–1376) invaded France and began what became known as the "Hundred Years' War." They won great battles at Créçy (in 1346) and Poitiers (1356), and although Edward gained large areas of France, he never gained the French crown. His wars also made him unpopular in England because of the high taxes needed to pay for them. ○ EDWARD II, FROISSART

Edward VI (1537–53)
Edward VI, king of England, was the son of Henry VIII by his third wife, Jane Seymour. He came to the throne in 1547 with his uncle Edward Seymour as Protector. In Edward's reign Protestantism became more firmly established, and the Anglican prayer book was issued. He was sickly and died aged 16. He was succeeded by his half sister, Mary, a Roman Catholic.

Edward VII (1841–1910)
Edward VII was the son of Queen Victoria and became king of Britain on her death in 1901. Although he was likely to become king, Victoria did not include her son in any government affairs. As Prince of Wales he was a member of fashionable European society, a lover of wine and gambling, and he traveled all over the world. He became a popular king who promoted good relations with other European countries.

Edward VIII (1894–1972)
Edward VIII succeeded his father George V as king of Great Britain in January 1936, but reigned for less than a year. He had been very popular as Prince of Wales, but had also been involved with an American divorcee, **Mrs. Wallis Simpson** (1896–1986). This had been kept secret. When the king announced that he wished to marry Mrs. Simpson, the government and large numbers of the public objected because the king was head of the Church, and for that reason should not marry a divorced woman. The government also refused to pass a law by which Mrs. Simpson would not become queen if they did marry—so Edward was forced to choose between her and the throne. The "Abdication Crisis," as it was known, lasted until December 1936, when Edward resigned in favor of his brother, and married Mrs. Simpson.

The Duke and Duchess of Windsor (formerly King Edward VIII and Mrs. Wallis Simpson) signing Christmas cards.

Eiffel, Alexandre Gustave (1832–1923)
A French engineer who designed the 985-ft. Eiffel Tower in Paris. It was completed in 1889 and remained the world's highest structure until the development of skyscrapers in New York in the 1920s. Eiffel also helped design the structure of the Statue of Liberty in New York Harbor.

Einstein, Albert (1879–1955)
See pages 96 & 97

The Age of Electricity

Edison, Thomas Alva (1847–1931)
The 19th century is sometimes called the "Age of Steam": it was the age of the Industrial Revolution, of coal mining, railways, steel mills, and steamships, and the steam engine was for all these new industries the most important source of power. But at the beginning of the 20th century things began to change. The light bulb, the telephone, the radio, and other inventions made the new century the "Age of Electricity," and Thomas Edison was one of its most important pioneers. He was not a scientist, so much as a tireless inventor, constantly investigating the possibilities of electricity and developing new ideas and manufacturing new devices.

Edison was born in the town of Milan, Ohio, and grew up in the state of Michigan. At the age of 12, after only three months at school, he got a job as a newspaper boy on the railroad. His ingenuity soon showed itself, when he bought some old printing equipment and produced the first newspaper to be printed on a train (*see box*). Three years later he became a telegraph operator, and he soon saw several ways in which he might improve the telegraph system. The first was an automatic repeating device, which "repeated" a message when it arrived at a telegraph station, so that it could continue down the line without having to be retapped out by the telegraph operator. Other improvements followed, including a machine that printed out the telegraph messages. Meanwhile, Edison had moved to New York City, and received his first official patent, for an electric voting machine. Throughout

Thomas Edison's Inventions

During his life, Thomas Edison patented well over 1,000 inventions. Here are just a few:

Electrical vote recorder (1869)
Automatic repeating telegraph (1870)
Printing telegraph (1871)
Duplex telegraph (1872)
Phonograph (1877)
Light bulb (1879)
First hydroelectric power station (1882)
"Kinetograph" and "Kinetoscope," moving picture devices (1891)

The telephone, invented by Alexander Graham Bell, was improved by Edison.

Radio receiver, using an electronic tube.

Edison invented the electric light bulb in 1879 at the same time as the British scientist Joseph Swan.

When he was 30, Edison invented the phonograph. He called it a "talking machine."

The kinetoscope. The first film show took place at Edison's laboratory in 1891.

his life, Edison combined his technical skill with good commercial sense. On moving to New York he helped set up a small electrical engineering company, but in little more than a year he had sold his share—and used the money to establish a bigger firm, with more facilities for research and experimentation. In 1876 he built a brand-new factory and laboratory at Menlo Park in New Jersey.

Edison's inventions continued. He developed the carbon microphone, which greatly improved Alexander Graham Bell's telephone and made it practical for the first time. In 1877 he demonstrated his phonograph—the predecessor of the record player. At first he used a metal sheet to record the sound; later he tried a wax cylinder, and later still a flat disk, just like a modern record. In 1879 he perfected one of his most important ideas—the light bulb. His experiments with this also led the way for others to develop the radio tube. Other successful projects included a moving picture device, called a "kinetoscope," batteries, designs for electric railways and power stations, motors, dynamos, and much else. In all, Edison patented well over 1,000 ideas, all of them intended to be useful, and salable. Once he had an idea, Edison rarely gave up on it. He said that genius is "one percent inspiration and ninety-nine percent perspiration."

○ BELL, MORSE

The Grand Trunk Herald

At the age of only 12, Edison became a railroad newspaper boy. With the money he earned he bought some secondhand type from a printer, and from the railroad he gained exclusive rights to sell newspapers on the line. He then began printing the *Grand Trunk Herald*, the first newspaper actually to be printed on a train, which Edison sold to the passengers and at the stations along the route.

Thomas Edison at work in his laboratory on his phonograph. His first recording was of himself reciting "Mary had a little lamb."

Ike, as Eisenhower was affectionately known, with his wife, Mamie, casting their votes on election day, November 4, 1952.

Eisenhower, Dwight David (1890–1969)
Eisenhower was an American soldier who was Supreme Commander of the Allied invasion of Europe in 1944, and who became the 34th president of the United States in 1952. He was born in Texas and went to the West Point military academy to be trained as a soldier. Between 1935 and 1939 he served with the American army in the Philippine Islands, and was quickly promoted. In 1942 Eisenhower was chosen to command the Allied invasion of North Africa, which had been occupied by German and Italian troops. The campaign was a success, and he went on to lead the invasion of southern Italy. Because the Allied command included several strong personalities from different countries, there was always the danger of argument over strategy. Eisenhower was tactful and a good organizer, and under his command there was little dispute. In 1944 he was chosen as Supreme Commander of the Normandy landings and the invasion of Germany. At the end of World War II he returned to the United States, where he became chief of all the country's military forces. He became head of NATO in 1950, and in 1952 was elected as a Republican president. As president he concentrated on helping the economies of Europe and Japan recover after the war, although his government was spoiled by the persecution of Communists and other "un-American activities." He was re-elected for a second term in 1956. Eisenhower visited many countries to promote better understanding. He retired to his farm near Gettysburg, Pennsylvania, in 1961.

War leaders: Eisenhower, American general and Supreme Commander of Allied forces in Europe, with General Montgomery.

A U.S. postage stamp of Dwight D. Eisenhower, the 34th president of the United States.

Eisenstein, Sergi Mikhailovich (1898–1948)
A Russian film maker who has been one of the most influential figures in motion picture history. Instead of concentrating on an individual hero, his films are about crowds and groups of people. They include *Battleship Potemkin* (1925) and *Ivan the Terrible* (1944).

Eleanor of Aquitaine (*c.*1122–1204)
Eleanor was duchess of the lands of Aquitaine in southwest France, and queen of King **Henry II** (1519–59) of England. She had first been married in 1137 to the future king of France, Louis VII, but he had divorced her. She immediately married Henry (in 1152), and by doing so transferred all her lands in France to the English king. This was the first incident in the long series of disputes and battles between England and France that lasted for the next three centuries. Eleanor was a strong woman. After her husband's death in 1189 she kept the peace between her sons John and Richard (who became King Richard I). ○ RICHARD I

Elgar, Edward William (1857–1934)
Elgar was an English composer. He was born near the city of Worcester, where his father was a church organist. Elgar's only musical training was violin lessons, and he taught himself to compose. For several years he attracted no notice, but in 1899 his *Enigma Variations* were praised by the German composer Richard Strauss. He became famous very quickly, with other pieces such as *The Dream of Gerontius* adding to his reputation. He was the most successful English composer since Purcell

two hundred years earlier, and remains one of the most popular.

Eliot, George (Mary Ann Evans, 1819–80)
George Eliot was an English novelist of the 19th century. Her real name was Mary Ann Evans; she took the name "George Eliot" when she published her first stories in 1857. She was born in Warwickshire in the middle of England, and after the death of her mother in 1836 found herself in charge of looking after her whole family. She learned Latin, Greek, German, and Italian, read a great deal, and translated works of philosophy into English. After her father's death in 1849 she moved to London, and eventually became deputy editor of a magazine called the *Westminster Review*. Among the people she met was a journalist called George Henry Lewes. They lived together until Lewes's death, but because he was already married and unable to get a divorce, they never married. The success of her first stories encouraged George Eliot to write more, and in 1859 she published her first novel, *Adam Bede*. This was followed by others, including *The Mill on the Floss* and *Middlemarch*, all of which were highly praised. After Lewes's death in 1878 she stopped writing.

Eliot, Thomas Stearns (1888–1965)
T.S. Eliot was a poet, dramatist, and critic. With poets such as Ezra Pound he founded the "modern movement," in which poetry was supposed to be related to modern life and written in modern language. Eliot was born in St. Louis and studied philosophy at Harvard, Paris, and Oxford. In 1915 he settled in London and took a job in a bank. Meanwhile, he also wrote poetry and helped edit literary magazines, and in 1917 published his first work, called *Prufrock and Other Observations*. His next work was *The Waste Land*, a long poem in which Eliot describes what he saw as the decay of the modern world after World War I. It was published by Virginia and Leonard Woolf, who had just founded their Hogarth Press in London. Among his plays, which he wrote in verse, are *The Murder in the Cathedral* (1935) and *The Cocktail Party* (1950). In 1927, he became a British citizen. In the 1930s Eliot became a devout member of the Anglo-Catholic section of the Church of England. This faith influenced several of his plays, and his poem the *Four Quartets*, which many people consider his greatest work. He wrote a book of nonsense poems, *Old Possum's Book of Practical Cats*. In 1948 Eliot was awarded the Nobel Prize for Literature. ○ POUND, WOOLF

Elizabeth I (1533–1603)
Elizabeth was Queen of England from 1558 until her death. When she became queen people thought that a woman on the throne would mean weak government and instability, but Elizabeth proved herself strong, determined, and courageous. She said of herself that although she was a woman, she had "the heart and stomach of a king." Elizabeth was the daughter of Henry VIII amd Anne Boleyn. After her mother's execution in 1536 Henry disinherited her, and she studied and lived a quiet life for several years. But when Mary Tudor died it was Elizabeth who had the best claim to inherit the throne, and she became queen. Her first problem concerned religion. Mary had been a Catholic, and under her government Protestants in England had been persecuted. Elizabeth decided to separate the Church of England completely from the Roman Catholic Church, and to support Protestants, both in England and the rest of Europe. She made a law that church services must be read in English, and banned many Catholic rituals in England. Meanwhile, she allowed sailors such as Drake and Hawkins to attack ships from Spain and other Catholic countries.

Queen Elizabeth I was a skilled politician, calculating and devious. Above all, she loved England, and in return her people loved her. Her court celebrated her as "Gloriana," and the ordinary people as "Good Queen Bess."

Elizabeth was expected to marry and give birth to an heir to the throne, but although many men tried to win her hand, she always refused them. For

American-born poet T. S. Eliot, was, with W. B. Yeats, one of the twin poles of the modern movement in poetry.

this reason she became known as the "Virgin Queen." It also meant that Mary Queen of Scots was the proper heir to the throne. Mary was a Catholic, and many people hoped to see the old faith restored in England if she became queen. After the discovery of several plots to kill her, Elizabeth was persuaded to have Mary executed, in 1587. The following year, King Philip of Spain attempted to bring Catholicism back to England (and to stop Elizabeth supporting his Protestant enemies in the rest of Europe) by sending the Armada to invade the country. Drake and Hawkins, helped by the weather, defeated the Spanish in the English Channel and Elizabeth was able to pass the rest of her reign in safety. Elizabeth was a popular queen. During her government England became powerful and prosperous, and it was a period in which some of the country's greatest literature was written. She died at Richmond, and was succeeded by James VI of Scotland. ○ BOLEYN, DRAKE, ESSEX, FROBISHER, HENRY VIII, JAMES I, MARY, SHAKESPEARE

The Dutch scholar and philosopher Erasmus. He was sympathetic to many of the aims of the Reformation.

Elizabeth II (1926–)
Elizabeth II has been queen of the United Kingdom since 1952. During her reign the popularity of the English monarchy has increased both in Britain and abroad. Elizabeth II is also head of the Commonwealth, a friendly organization of countries which used to be part of the British Empire. She is married to Philip Mountbatten, the Duke of Edinburgh, and they have four children: Charles, Anne, Andrew, and Edward.

Ellington, "Duke" (Edward Kennedy) (1899–1974)
Duke Ellington was an American jazz pianist and composer. He was born in Washington, D.C., learned music while he was still at school, and as a

"Duke" Ellington and his band on their arrival in Britain in 1933 for a series of performances.

young man spent his days working as a sign painter and his nights playing in a nightclub. He became famous after moving to New York, where he formed a band. His music is unusual because it is fully composed, and does not allow the players to improvise as much as other jazz does.

Ellsworth, Lincoln (1880–1951)
American explorer, engineer, and scientist whose flights from Spitzbergen to Alaska in 1926 and across Antarctica in 1935 made him the first person to fly across both the Arctic and Antarctic.

Emerson, Ralph Waldo (1803–82)
Emerson was an American poet, writer, and lecturer. He went to Harvard University and became a minister in the Unitarian Church, but in 1832 gave up the Church after a dispute over a sermon he had preached. On a trip to England he met Thomas Carlyle, with whom he remained close friends, and on returning to the United States began publishing the essays on religious and philosophical subjects for which he is most famous. ○ CARLYLE

Enders, John Franklin (1897–)
John Enders, the American microbiologist,

discovered a method of cultivating viruses which led to the production of anti-polio vaccine.

Engels, Friedrich (1820–95)
Engels was a German socialist writer and close friend of Karl Marx. Together they wrote the *Communist Manifesto* in 1848. Engels was the son of a cotton manufacturer. When his father sent him to work in the English city of Manchester, he studied the lives of the poor people who lived there. He published his findings in a book called *The Condition of the Working Class in England* in 1844. ○ MARX

Epstein, Jacob (1880–1959)
An American sculptor who lived and worked in England. Many of his stone carvings were criticized or even laughed at when they were first unveiled, and he is best remembered for his bronze portrait statues.

Erasmus, Desiderius (1466–1536)
Erasmus was a Dutch writer, scholar, and theologian. He was one of the best-known and most influential men of his time, and his fame helped increase the value people gave learning in northern Europe at the end of the Middle Ages. The illegitimate son of a clerk, Erasmus was born in the town of Gouda. After his father's death he was sent to live in a monastery. He so disliked the experience that he made himself a fierce enemy of monks and monastic life in his later writings. Erasmus spent much of his life traveling, visiting Italy, France, Switzerland, and England. Among his works are *Praise of Folly*, in which he attacks corruption and superstition in society, and the *Colloquies*, a philosophical work. He was a brilliant scholar of ancient languages, and published an edition of the New Testament in Greek with his own Latin translation.

Eric the Red (*c.*950–*c.*1003)
A famous Norwegian adventurer. An Icelandic "saga" (story) tells how Eric was banished from Iceland for murder. He sailed west and discovered Greenland, spent three years exploring its coastline, and founded Norwegian settlements there. His son, Leif Eriksson, is said to have been the first European to visit North America. ○ LEIF ERIKSSON

Escoffier, Auguste (1846–1935)
A famous French chef. He worked first for a Russian duke, then as Napoleon III's chef during the Franco-Prussian War in 1871. He went on to the Grand Hotel in Monte Carlo, before being persuaded to move to London's Savoy Hotel. Among his inventions is the "Peach Melba," which he created in honor of the Australian opera singer, Nellie Melba.

Essex, Robert Devereux (1566–1601)
Essex was an English soldier and courtier during the reign of Elizabeth I. He quickly became one of Elizabeth's favorites, and was one of the heroes of the capture of Cadiz in 1596. But in 1598 he had a spectacular quarrel with Elizabeth: he called her laws "as crooked as her carcass" and turned his back on her. She reached out and boxed his ears—and went on to take away many of his offices and honors and sent him on a miserable mission to Ireland. After his return, Essex attempted to provoke a rebellion in London. He was tried for treason and beheaded. ○ ELIZABETH I

Euclid (*c.*330 B.C.–*c.*260 B.C.)
Euclid was an ancient Greek mathematician. Little is known about his life, and most of his works have been lost, but his *Elements of Geometry* has remained the basis of the teaching of geometry for over two thousand years. He is thought to have been a teacher in the city of Alexandria and to have founded a mathematical school there. Euclid also studied astronomy, optics, and music.

Euripides (*c.*480 B.C.–406 B.C.)
Together with Aeschylus and Sophocles, Euripides is one of the three great ancient Greek tragic playwrights. He began life as a painter, but gave this up to write plays. He is known to have written over 80 plays, and to have won drama competitions five times, but only 18 of his plays have survived. They include *Medea*, *Alcestis*, and *The Bacchae*. Euripides used the traditional features of Greek drama, such as the chorus, dancing, and singing, less than either Aeschylus or Sophocles, and preferred to concentrate on action and drama. He became more popular after his death than he had been during his lifetime. ○ AESCHYLUS, PERICLES, SOPHOCLES

Everest, George (1790–1866)
An English surveyor and mapmaker who measured the world's tallest mountain in 1841, and gave it the name by which it is known in the English-speaking world.

Eyck, Jan Van
see page 250

The Theory of Relativity

Ernest Rutherford, father of nuclear science.

Enrico Fermi.

An atomic test.

Einstein, Albert (1879–1955)
Einstein's theory of relativity is certainly one of the best known of all scientific theories. Although very few people can follow the complicated mathematics of the work itself, many have been fascinated by its strange and puzzling conclusions. Moreover, all our lives have been directly affected by it: it was Einstein who first understood the potential of the atom as a source of vast amounts of energy. Scientists have developed techniques to liberate this energy, in nuclear reactors used to generate electricity —and in the terrifying explosions of nuclear weapons.

In fact, Einstein published two theories of relativity: the "Special" Theory in 1905, and the "General" Theory in 1916. He was born in Ulm, in southern Germany, but his family moved several times, first to Munich, then to Milan in Italy. Eventually Einstein settled in Switzerland, where he studied at the university in Zurich and then took a job as a patent examiner in the capital, Berne. Meanwhile, he wrote several papers on theoretical physics. The publication of the Special Theory of Relativity in 1905 quickly made him famous. A special professorship was created for him at Zurich, and he went on to lecture and to hold important posts throughout Europe and the United States.

Special Relativity deals with basic mechanical and physical phenomena: mass and energy, time and space. The central principle is that all measurements *are relative to the motion of the measurer*. Imagine, for example, an aircraft flying at high speed above the earth's surface. The earth itself is also moving, so if we try to measure the velocity of the aircraft from the ground, the result will show not the motion of the aircraft alone, but its motion *in relation to* the motion of the earth. This is true of all measurements, because everything in the universe is in some way in motion.

The startling thing about the theory, however, was that Einstein was able to extend this principle to the concepts of *time* and *mass*. Time and mass had traditionally been thought to be absolute, unchangeable. Einstein showed that they, too, could only be measured in relation to their motion and that the measurements would vary according to the motion of the measurer. Imagine a clock on the fast-moving aircraft described above, and many other clocks arranged at regular intervals on the ground beneath its flight path. Einstein predicted that somebody on board the plane would find his clock slightly slower than those on the ground. The effect is extremely small, but scientists have proved Einstein correct. They took a hydrogen clock and flew it around the world on a high-speed aircraft. When the plane landed, they found that the clock on board was a tiny fraction slower than an identical clock left behind on the ground.

Einstein also predicted that an object moving at high velocity—almost the speed of light—would increase in mass. This, too, has been proved correct: when atoms are accelerated in a special machine called an "accelerator" to almost the speed of light, their mass does become greater. It is this relationship between energy (in this case the velocity of the atom) and mass that is expressed in the famous equation $E = mc^2$. "E" stands for energy, "m" for mass, and "c" for the speed of light. Because energy and mass are related in this way, they can theoretically be converted into each other. This is what happens in an atomic explosion: some of the mass of an atom is converted into energy. But despite the huge power of such an explosion, the energy released is only a tiny fraction (about one ten-thousandth if the atom is a uranium atom) of the total energy stored in the mass of the atom.

With Einstein's equation the nuclear age had truly begun. The theory of relativity also upset many well-established ideas about physics, showing that apparently absolute phenomena such as mass and time could not be relied upon to remain stable. It led in many directions—to new ideas about the vast and mysterious properties of the universe, and to new discoveries in the tiny world of the structure of the atom. Einstein, like Galileo and Newton, was one of the very few great thinkers who have fundamentally changed people's understanding of their world. ○ FERMI, GALILEO, NEWTON, RUTHERFORD

Above: A bust of Einstein by the sculptor Jacob Epstein.

A Curious Incident

In 1939 the fissionable properties of the uranium isotope 235 had been discovered. The Italian physicist, Enrico Fermi, and two Hungarian physicists then living in the United States, prevailed upon Einstein to write to President Roosevelt pointing out the danger of Nazi Germany getting ahead with the development of nuclear energy for military purposes. As a result of this letter the Manhattan Project for the development of the atomic bomb was set in motion. Thus to some extent Einstein's life devotion to world peace may have been ironically tragic.

Above: Albert Einstein, whose revolutionary theory of relativity was published in 1916.

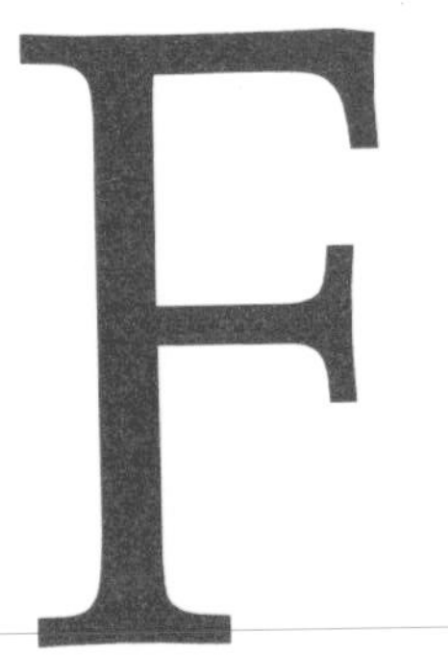

Fabergé, Peter Carl (1846–1920)
Fabergé was a Russian jeweler who became famous at the end of the 19th century for the costly, highly decorated ornaments he made for the royal families of Europe. He inherited a jewelry business from his father in 1870, but he soon gave up making ordinary things to concentrate on the fantastic and extravagant. Among his most famous creations are jeweled easter eggs he made for Tsar Alexander III.

Fabre, Jean Henri (1823–1915)
Fabre was a French entomologist—somebody who collects and studies insects. For many years he worked as a teacher in the south of France, before retiring to give all his time to insects. His detailed studies were published in 1925.

Fabricius, Hieronymus (1533–1619)
A 16th-century Italian scientist who studied medicine at the University of Padua and became one of the greatest physicians of his time. Among his many works are studies of the development of the human embryo during pregnancy, and of the circulation of the blood. William Harvey was one of his pupils, and used Fabricius' work to develop his own theory about circulation. ○ HARVEY

Fahrenheit, Gabriel Daniel (1668–1736)
Fahrenheit was a German scientist who came up with the idea of using mercury in thermometers. He invented the Fahrenheit temperature scale, according to which water freezes at 32 degrees and boils at 212 degrees.

Faisal I (1885–1933)
Faisal I was king of Syria and then (from 1921) of Iraq. He was one of the leaders of the Arab Revolt against Turkish rule during World War I, and was made king of Iraq when the country became a British territory after the war. Iraq became completely independent under his leadership in 1932. ○ LAWRENCE, T. E.

Fan Kuan (*c.*1000)
Fan Kuan was a great Chinese landscape painter, and a devout follower of the Taoist philosophy (○ LAO-TZU). His pictures have a "flat" style, without depth of perspective, that is quite different from Western landscape painting.

Faraday, Michael (1791–1867)
Faraday was an English scientist who is most famous for his research into electricity and magnetism. In 1813 he became one of Humphry Davy's assistants at the Royal Institution in London. Faraday had first been a bookbinder, and he had gained Davy's favor by presenting him with a bound copy of notes made at his lectures. By 1833, Faraday had become professor of chemistry at the Institution. He gave lectures on a great many subjects, including lighthouse lamps, mental illnesses, and underwater diving, and published papers on (among many other things) gases, light, and optics. His work on the relationship between electricity and magnetism enabled inventors to make the first electric motors and electrical generators. The "farad," which is a unit used to measure electrical capacity, is named after him. ○ DAVY

Faulkner, William Harrison (1897–1962)
Faulkner was one of the greatest American writers of the 20th century. He was born in the Southern state of Mississippi. During World War I he was a pilot in the Canadian Air Force, then returned to the United States where he did odd jobs and began writing poetry and stories. His first novel, *Soldier's Pay*, was published in 1926. He is best known for the series of books he wrote about the imaginary "Yoknapatawpha County" in Mississippi, which describe the conflicts between black and white and rich and poor people in the South. They include *The Sound and the Fury* (1929) and *Light in August* (1932). Faulkner was awarded the Nobel Prize for Literature in 1949.

Fawkes, Guy (1570–1606)
Guy Fawkes was the most famous member of the Gunpowder Plot gang who attempted to blow up the English king and Parliament in 1605. He was born in York, and although his parents were Protestants, the young Guy Fawkes became an enthusiastic member of the Roman Catholic Church. He joined the Spanish army and fought Protestants in the Netherlands in the 1590s, before returning to England in 1604. Queen Elizabeth I had been a supporter of Protestants all over

Guy Fawkes (Guido Fawkes in the illustration) and the other Catholic noblemen who planned to blow up James I and his government.

Europe, and had finally separated the English Church from the Roman Catholic Church. Her successor, James I, did not intend to change this, so Fawkes and a group of other Catholics planned to blow up James and his government during the opening of Parliament on November 5, 1605. They filled the building's cellars with barrels of gunpowder, but it is said that Fawkes warned a friend of his who was a member of Parliament to stay away on that day. The friend passed the information on to the army, and Guy Fawkes was arrested in the cellars as he was about to set light to the explosives. He was executed in January 1606. Guy Fawkes's Day has been commemorated in England with bonfires and fireworks ever since.
○ JAMES I

Fellini, Federico (1920–)
An Italian film maker, whose works have often caused great controversy. They include *La Dolce Vita* ("The Sweet Life," made in 1960) and *La Strada* ("The Road," 1957).

Ferdinand II (1452–1516)
Ferdinand II of Aragon, or "Ferdinand the Catholic," as he was sometimes known, became a powerful king of all Spain. He and his queen, **Isabella of Castille** (1451–1504), united the country under their government and supported the creation of Spanish colonies in America. Ferdinand became king of the province of Castille as a result of his marriage to Isabella. He inherited the throne of Aragon from his father, John II, in 1479, and conquered a third great kingdom, Naples, in 1504. This made him ruler of almost all Spain. He fought and defeated the Moors (a North African people) living in the south of the country and gained the territories of Roussillon and Navarre from France. To ensure greater unity among his people, he insisted that they all become Catholics, and set up

Ferdinand of Aragon and Isabella of Castille.

the notorious Spanish Inquisition to investigate and punish those who did not. Ferdinand and Isabella provided the money for Columbus' voyage of discovery to America, and as a result large numbers of Spanish settlements were founded in the New World. When Charles V became king of Spain in 1516 the country was united, and one of the most powerful in Europe. ○ CHARLES V, COLUMBUS

Fermi, Enrico (1901–54)
An Italian scientist, best known for his work on nuclear physics. In 1942 he constructed the world's first nuclear reactor. Fermi worked at universities in Pisa and Florence in Italy, where he made several important discoveries about the atom. In 1938 he was awarded the Nobel Prize, but did not return to Italy after the prize-giving ceremony because he was afraid the Fascist government there would persecute his Jewish wife. He moved to New York and then Chicago, where he built the first nuclear reactor in an abandoned squash court. During the war he took part in research which led to the development of the atomic bomb.

Ferrari, Enzo (1898–)
An Italian engineer and car designer, famous for the Ferrari racing and sports cars.

Fielding, Henry (1707–54)
Fielding was an English novelist and playwright. His most famous works are the novels *Joseph Andrews* and *Tom Jones*. He was the son of an English aristocrat, and went to school at Eton and then in Germany. On his return to England he began writing plays, and was so successful that he was able to open his own theater in 1736. Unfortunately, new laws were introduced to control London's theaters, and Fielding was forced to close. He turned to writing novels, and in 1742 published *Joseph Andrews*. It describes the adventures of a young man (the Joseph Andrews of the title) as he travels the countryside in search of his sweetheart, and was intended to make fun of other more conventional novels of the time. *Tom Jones* was published in 1749. Fielding also wrote for magazines, and was a magistrate in London.

Fitzgerald, Francis Scott Key (1896–1940)
F. Scott Fitzgerald was an American writer whose novels portrayed wealthy American society in the 1920s. His first book (called *This Side of Paradise*) was published in 1920, and its success made Fitzgerald a rich and fashionable member of society. He married Zelda Sayre and together they traveled to Europe, where Fitzgerald wrote his most famous novel, *The Great Gatsby* (1925). During the 1930s the couple got into some debt, Zelda became ill and Fitzgerald an alcoholic. These experiences formed the basis of his novel *Tender Is the Night*, written in 1934. Late in life, Fitzgerald tried to make money writing film scripts in Hollywood. He died leaving one novel, *The Last Tycoon*, unfinished.

Scott, Zelda, and Scottie Fitzgerald celebrate Christmas together.

Flaubert, Gustave (1821–80)
Flaubert was a French novelist. He was the son of a wealthy doctor, and was sent to Paris to study law. In 1844, however, he abandoned this and gave all his time to writing. His greatest work, *Madame Bovary*, published in 1857, is a realistic novel about a middle-class woman who tries to escape her dull married life by having an affair with another man. The novel caused a scandal, and the French government tried to ban it because they thought it was obscene. The court case that followed brought *Madame Bovary* much publicity and made sure of its success. Flaubert was an epileptic and spent much of his life in his country home near the city of Rouen. His other works include the *Sentimental Education*. ○ MAUPASSANT

Fleming, Alexander (1881–1955)
Fleming was a Scottish scientist who discovered penicillin, a drug that kills infections. Its manufacture and use has been one of the most

A drawing of the scientist, Alexander Fleming.

important developments in modern medicine. Fleming was a professor at the Royal College of Surgeons in London. He first noticed that the mold called *Penicillium notatum* was a powerful germ killer in 1928, but it was 11 years before he was able, together with two chemists named Howard Florey and Ernst Chain, to perfect a process by which the drug could be produced in large quantities. The three of them shared the Nobel Prize for Medicine in 1945.

Fonteyn, Margot (1919–)
Margot Fonteyn is an English ballerina. She first studied dance in Shanghai, where her parents were living, and on her return to England became a member of the Vic-Wells Ballet, run by Ninette de Valois. In 1934 she made her debut in *The Nutcracker*, and quickly went on to become the company's leading dancer. As well as classic roles such as *The Sleeping Beauty* and *Giselle*, Fonteyn performed in new ballets created especially for her by choreographers such as Frederick Ashton. In 1962, at the age of 43, she began her famous partnership with Russian dancer Nureyev. She is one of only three dancers ever to have been named "prima ballerina assoluta" by the Russian state ballet. ○ ASHTON, NUREYEV, VALOIS

Ford, Henry (1863–1947)
Henry Ford was an American engineer and founder of the Ford Motor Company. He took an interest in engineering from an early age, and in 1893 built his first gasoline-driven car while still employed by the Edison Company in Detroit. He began his own factory in 1899 and introduced his "Model A" car in 1903. His great success was the "Model T," first produced in 1908. It was relatively cheap, hard-wearing, and Ford was able to produce them in vast numbers on a production line. Over 15 million Model Ts were made before the car was withdrawn from sale in 1928.

A "Model T" braving a rough track.

Dropping the bodies onto the chassis in a "Model T" Ford assembly line.

France, Anatole (Anatole François Thibault, 1844–1924)
A French writer of novels and short stories, including *The Revolt of the Angels* and *My Friend's Book*. His style is simple and realistic. France was a supporter of the army captain Alfred Dreyfus during the "Dreyfus Affair," and often a fierce critic of his country's government and institutions.
○ DREYFUS

Francis I (1494–1547)
Francis I became king of France in 1515 by virtue of his marriage to the daughter of King Louis XII. In 1519 he failed to get himself elected Holy Roman Emperor, losing to Charles V of Spain, and so immediately declared war on Charles. Things began badly: Francis was defeated and eventually (in 1525) captured and held to ransom. After his release the conflict continued at intervals until 1544, when Francis was forced to accept a treaty by which he gained almost nothing he had not had in 1519 when the war began. ○ CHARLES V

Francis of Assisi, Saint (1182–1226)
Francis of Assisi was the Italian founder of the Franciscan order of friars. He is remembered as a man of great love for all God's creation, and some of the best-known stories about him are those in which he showed this in his care for animals. Saint Francis was the son of a merchant in the town of Assisi in central Italy. As a young man he lived a carefree life, until a serious illness made him turn to prayer and began his conversion. In 1205 he joined an army, but suddenly returned to Assisi to care for the poor and sick. The next year Francis heard a voice commanding him to rebuild the decaying Church of San Damiano in Assisi. To obtain money for the work he stole a bale of cloth from his father —with the result his father completely disinherited him. Francis then decided to give up all property and live a life devoted to God. He lived as a hermit and gathered 11 disciples, and in 1210 they were given permission by the Pope to begin an order of friars. The "Friars Minor," as they were known, grew in number very quickly, and monasteries were founded all over Europe and in North Africa. In 1223 Francis went to Egypt, where he persuaded the Sultan of Turkey to improve his treatment of Christians and to allow the Friars to guard the Church of the Holy Sepulchre in Jerusalem. He died in Italy in 1226 and was declared a saint two years later.

A detail of a fresco by Giotto showing St. Francis of Assisi feeding birds. St. Francis abandoned a life of ease and helped the poor, weak, and sickly. He founded the worldwide religious order of Franciscans.

Franco, Francisco Paulino (1892–1975)
General Franco was the leader of Spain from 1939 until his death. He was head of the only political party allowed in the country, the Falange (Fascist), and ruled as a dictator. In 1936 he had been governor of the Canary Islands and joined General José Sanjurjo in an attempt to overthrow the Republican government. This led to the Spanish Civil War, which Franco finally won in 1939, when he set up his government. During World War II he was friendly toward Germany, but remained neutral. Franco held power in Spain for 36 years, but he was criticized for his dictatorial methods. He declared that Spain would become a monarchy and named Prince Juan Carlos as his successor, but after his death many political reforms were introduced.
○ JUAN CARLOS

Frank, Anne (1929–45)
Anne Frank was a German Jewish girl who became a victim of the Nazis' policy of extermination. The diary she kept while hiding from the Nazis was published in 1947, under the title *The Diary of a Young Girl*. She was the daughter of a Frankfurt businessman. When the Nazis came to power in Germany the family moved to Amsterdam to escape persecution, but when the Netherlands was invaded in 1941 they once again found themselves in danger. They went into hiding in a sealed office in a warehouse in July 1942, and remained there for over two years, having food and news brought to them by friends. Anne kept her diary throughout this time, recording the family's feelings and fears. They were nearly discovered several times; then, in August 1944, they were found by the Nazis and sent to concentration camps. Anne, her sister, and her mother all died, but her father survived and preserved her diary.

Franklin, Benjamin (1706–90)
Benjamin Franklin is one of the great figures of American history. As a politician, he was one of those who helped write the Declaration of Independence; he was also a scientist and journalist. Franklin was the fifteenth of seventeen children, born in Boston, Massachusetts. His first trade was printing, and he made enough money to buy his own newspaper, the *Pennsylvania Gazette*, in 1728. Another of his publications, *Poor Richard's Almanac*, first issued in 1732, became enormously popular. At the same time, Franklin began a fire brigade, became a postmaster, and founded the Philadelphia Academy (later the university). He experimented with electricity, and in 1752 proved that lightning

Benjamin Franklin, the American statesman and scientist, experimenting with his lightning conductor in a storm.

and electricity were the same by flying a kite in a storm, and conducting lightning down the kite string to a bucket of water at his feet. This led him to invent the lightning conductor. He charted the paths taken across America by storms and the course of the warm sea current known as the Gulf Stream. Franklin visited England several times, and in 1764 went there as a diplomat to try to solve the disputes between Britain and the American colonies. He was a supporter of American independence, but also favored conciliation rather than war with Britain. After independence he was American ambassador to France, and on his return to Philadelphia in 1785 Franklin became president of the state of Pennsylvania. Before he finally retired from public affairs in 1788, he was one of those who helped to draw up the United States Constitution.

Fraser, John Malcolm (1930–)
An Australian politician. As leader of the Liberal Party he was asked to become prime minister after a crisis in the Australian government in 1975. He won three successive elections before being defeated by the Labour Party in 1983.

Frazer, James George (1854–1941)
A Scot who pioneered the study of anthropology (the customs, beliefs, and culture of societies) with his book *The Golden Bough*, in which he describes the beliefs and rituals of many peoples.

Frederick I "Barbarossa" (*c.*1123–90)
Frederick "Barbarossa" ("Redbeard") was one of the greatest medieval rulers of Europe. He became king of the German states in 1152 and was elected Holy Roman Emperor in 1155. As emperor, he found that his subjects in Italy refused to recognize his rule, and he also fell into dispute with the Pope. In 1162 he captured Milan and forced the northern Italian states to submit to him. He went on to capture Rome, and it seemed as though the Pope, too, would submit, but Frederick's army was suddenly struck by plague and he was forced to withdraw. Further battles with the Italians followed, and after a disastrous defeat at the Battle of Legnano in 1176 Frederick was forced to change his policy. Instead of fighting, he decided to persuade and conciliate his subjects. This worked. Frederick secured his rule over northern Italy and in 1177 agreed to recognize the Pope's rights if in return the Pope would recognize him as emperor. Frederick was drowned while crossing a river as he led the Third Crusade against the Muslims.
○ ADRIAN IV

Frederick II, the Great (1712–86)
Frederick II was king of Prussia from 1740. He and his father, Frederick William I, hated each other, and the young Frederick once tried to escape the harsh discipline of the Prussian court and travel to England. He failed, and was forced to conform. At the same time that he became king, Maria Theresa had become ruler of the Austrian Empire. Frederick took the opportunity to invade the territories of Silesia, which he won in 1742. But in 1756 the Seven Years' War broke out, and Frederick found himself faced by an alliance of Austria, France, and Russia. He led a brave and skillful campaign, but was outnumbered and eventually seemed to face defeat. He was saved by the death of the tsarina of Russia, which led to Russia's withdrawal from the alliance. By the Treaty of Hubertsburg he was able to retain the territory he had possessed when the war began, and he had forced other European nations to respect Prussian power. ○ HABSBURG

Frémont, John Charles (1813–90)
An American soldier and explorer who discovered the overland routes across America. He began exploring and surveying in 1838, first crossed the Rocky Mountains in 1842, and went on to explore the Great Salt Lake, the Columbia River, and the Rio Grande. He took part in the annexation of California for the United States, and was the first senator for the new state.

Freud, Sigmund (1856–1939)
Freud was an Austrian doctor who developed the theory of "psychoanalysis," a method of treating

Sigmund Freud, who developed psychoanalysis. He held that there was a deep, unexplored part of the human mind called the unconscious.

disturbed people by making them describe hidden or subconscious details of their lives. Freud was born and lived almost all his life in Vienna. He became interested in the things people said while they were under hypnosis, and from this got the idea of encouraging patients to relax and describe their dreams, fantasies, or details of their childhood. He found that this would sometimes reveal the problem that was disturbing the patient. Freud said that as a child grows it acquires an *ego*, a collection of memories and thoughts that help the child deal with the outside world. Among the many books he wrote about his work is the famous *Interpretation of Dreams*, published in 1900. ○ JUNG

Friedman, Milton (1912–)
An American economist, whose "monetarist" theories about the workings of a country's economy became fashionable in the 1970s. He believes that the best way of controlling the economy is by controlling the amount of money in circulation. ○ KEYNES

Frobisher, Martin (1535–94)
Frobisher was an English seaman and explorer during the reign of Queen Elizabeth I. He went on two expeditions to find a "Northwest Passage" between the Atlantic and the Pacific, and played an important part in the defeat of the Spanish Armada in 1588. ○ DRAKE, ELIZABETH I

Froissart, Jean (*c.*1333–*c.*1405)
A medieval French poet and historian. From the age of 19, Froissart traveled Europe collecting information for his famous *Chronicle*, which describes the royal households of Europe, and the wars they fought against each other. He also wrote poems, including a long work about King Arthur. ○ EDWARD III

Frost, Robert Lee (1874–1963)
Frost was an American poet who was sometimes called "the voice of New England" because his poems describe the landscape and people of the northeastern United States. He was in fact born in San Francisco in California, but went to college at Harvard in Massachusetts. He began publishing poems during a trip to England in 1913, and was immediately recognized as a great poet. Among his collections are *New Hampshire* and *From Snow to Snow*. He said of his poems that they should "begin in delight and end in wisdom."

Fry, Elizabeth (1780–1845)
Elizabeth Fry was an English prison reformer. She was the daughter of one wealthy Quaker businessman, and married to another. In 1810 she became a preacher in the Quaker community in London. During a visit to Newgate prison in 1813, she was outraged by the dirty and neglected conditions of the prisoners, especially the women, many of whom had children with them. She gave them clothing and read to them, and in 1817 formed an organization to campaign for reform of prisons throughout the country.

Fuchs, Sir Vivian (1908–)
Sir Vivian Fuchs, the British explorer and geologist, commanded a 12-man team of scientists and explorers who completed the first land crossing of the Antarctic continent as their contribution to the International Geophysical Year in 1957–58. The journey covered 2,158 miles and took 99 days.

Fulton, Robert (1765–1815)
An American engineer who was the first to design a successful steam-powered boat. He studied in London and Paris, where he produced many different inventions and ideas before demonstrating his steamboat on the river Seine in 1803. He returned to the United States, and in 1807 a steamboat he had designed (called *Clermont*) made the 150-mile journey up the Hudson River from New York to Albany. This marked the beginning of the end of sailing ships as the best way to travel by water.

Furtwängler, Wilhelm (1886–1954)
Wilhelm Furtwängler was a German conductor, pianist, and composer. He is particularly famous for his interpretation of German classics, notably Beethoven and Wagner. Despite his opposition to the Nazis, he was nevertheless criticized for remaining in Germany during World War II.

Gagarin, Yuri Alekseevich (1934–68)
Gagarin was a Soviet cosmonaut who in 1961 became the first man to travel in space. He was the son of a carpenter, born in a village near the city of Smolensk. After World War II he learned to fly and eventually joined the Soviet air force. The first manned space flight took place on April 12, 1961. Gagarin was launched into orbit aboard the spacecraft *Vostok 1* and completed a single circuit of the earth at a maximum height of 200 miles and a maximum speed of just over 17,000 miles per hour. The flight lasted one hour and 48 minutes before the craft landed by parachute. Gagarin made no other space flights, and was killed in an aircraft accident.

Gainsborough, Thomas (1727–88)
Gainsborough was an English landscape and portrait painter. He was born in the county of Suffolk, but moved to London to study. Many of his early pictures are landscapes containing small groups of people, and Gainsborough was much influenced by 17th-century Dutch landscape paintings. In 1760 he moved to Bath, which was then a fashionable resort town, where he became popular for his portraits of well-to-do members of society. In 1768 he was one of the founding members of the Royal Academy, and in 1774 he returned to London to live, where he painted several of the royal family. Among his most famous paintings are *The Watering Place* and *The Blue Boy.*

Galen (*c.* A.D. 130–A.D. 201)
Galen was an ancient Greek doctor and writer on medicine. He wrote a great deal, and gathered together all the medical knowledge of the ancient world. In A.D.157 he became the doctor attending the gladiators in ancient Rome, and later served Marcus Aurelius and several other emperors.

Galileo Galilei (1564–1642)
Galileo was a great Italian scientist of the Renaissance. He was born in Pisa, where he attended the university and studied medicine, mathematics, and physics. One of his first discoveries was that a pendulum will always take the same amount of time to complete its swing, no matter what the length of the swing, and he used this to build accurate clocks. Then, by dropping two different-sized rocks from the top of the "Leaning Tower" in Pisa, he showed that objects of *different* weights and sizes take the *same* amount of time to fall to the ground. In doing so, Galileo had disproved a law first put forward by Aristotle, and

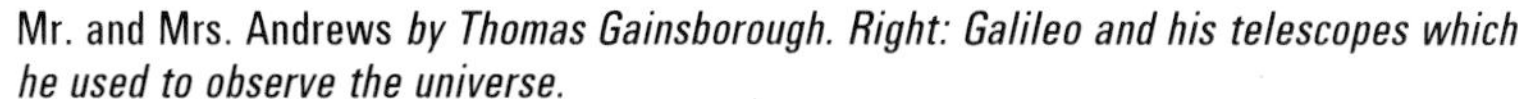

Mr. and Mrs. Andrews *by Thomas Gainsborough. Right: Galileo and his telescopes which he used to observe the universe.*

the other members of the university were so outraged that he lost his job. He moved to Padua (in 1591) where he invented the thermometer, and in 1609 made an improved version of the telescope (which had been invented in Holland a year earlier). Galileo was now able to observe the stars and planets, and he made several important discoveries. He found four moons circling the planet Jupiter, first saw the rings around Saturn, and concluded that the Milky Way was made up of many separate stars. He decided that the moon did not shine with its own light, but reflected that of the sun, and in about 1610 observed "spots" on the surface of the sun. When he noticed that these moved he concluded that the sun must rotate, and this, together with other discoveries, proved to him the truth of Copernicus' theory: that the earth spins, and rotates around the sun. When he published his ideas in 1613, he was immediately in trouble with the church authorities, and was ordered not to repeat them. For a while he was quiet, but in 1632 put forward his views a second time in his *Dialogue on the Two Chief Systems of the World*. He was tried (and possibly tortured) by the Inquisition, and eventually retracted all he had said. Galileo was now old and becoming blind, but he continued to work on other subjects until his death in the city of Florence. ○ COPERNICUS

Galvani, Luigi (1737–98)
An Italian scientist who became professor of anatomy at the University of Bologna. In 1791 he showed that a frog's legs would twitch when they were placed between two different types of metal. He believed that this was because there was electricity present in the animal, but Volta later showed that it was due to electricity passing from one metal to the other. ○ VOLTA

Gama, Vasco da (1469–1525)
See Da Gama, Vasco

Gandhi, Indira (1917–84)
An Indian politician. She was the daughter of Jawaharlal Nehru and took part in the movement for Indian independence, becoming a leading member of the Congress Party. When Prime Minister Shastri died in 1969, Mrs. Gandhi took over, and went on to win an election in 1971. In 1975 she declared a "state of emergency" which enabled her to rule almost as a dictator. This was unpopular, and she lost the next election in 1977. Mrs. Gandhi became prime minister again in 1980, but was assassinated by members of her own bodyguard in October 1984. Her son, **Rajiv Gandhi** (1944–), took over as prime minister and won a huge victory in elections later in the year. ○ NEHRU

Gandhi, Mohandâs Karamchand (1869–1948)
See pages 108 & 109

Garbo, Greta (Greta Louisa Gustafsson, 1905–)
A Swedish film actress who became a star of silent movies in films such as *Torrent* and *Flesh and the Devil*. She was equally successful in speaking roles (including *Mata Hari* and *Queen Christina*), but disliked publicity and insisted on living a very private life. After the failure of *Two-Faced Woman* in 1941 she retired and has become a complete recluse.

Garibaldi, Giuseppe (1807–82)
Garibaldi was an Italian guerrilla fighter who dedicated his life to one cause, the unification of the various states in Italy as one country, under Italian, not foreign, rule. As a young man he became a member of the Young Italy movement organized by Mazzini, and was sentenced to death after attempting to overthrow the government of the city of Genoa. Garibaldi escaped to South America, where he learned the tactics of guerrilla war and met and married the beautiful Anna Riviera de Silva. They returned to Italy in 1847,

and Garibaldi immediately joined the Italians fighting the Austrian army occupying Sardinia. In 1849 he took part in the revolution in Rome, and he and his men drove the French and Neapolitan troops out of the city. But the new government collapsed. Anna died and Garibaldi was forced to flee to New York, where he got a job as a candle maker. He returned once again in 1854, but this time instead of fighting he began a life as a farmer on the island of Caprera. When fighting between King Victor Emmanuel's Sardinians and the Austrian army broke out in 1859, Garibaldi went to the king's aid. For the first time Italian unity and independence seemed possible under Sardinian leadership. While the Sardinians conquered the north of the country, Garibaldi went south and invaded the island of Sicily, which was governed by Spanish rulers. In less than three months, Garibaldi and his "Red Shirts" had captured Sicily, and in August 1860 they crossed to the mainland and took control of Naples. When Victor Emmanuel and his army arrived from the north, Garibaldi gave up all his power, and so allowed him to become the first king of Italy. Garibaldi's remaining ambition was to bring Rome under Italian rule. An attempt to overthrow the government in 1867 failed, but in 1870 Rome became the nation's capital. ○ CAVOUR, MAZZINI, VICTOR EMMANUEL II

The Unification of Italy

1849 Victor Emmanuel II becomes king of Sardinia.

1852 Victor Emmanuel appoints Cavour chief minister. Adopts policy of uniting Italy under Italian rule.

1856 Sardinia gains French support against Austria.

1859 War between Sardinia and Austria. Austrians defeated at battles of Magenta and Solferino. Sardinia and Lombardy united under Sardinian government.

1860 Parma, Modena, Romagna, and Tuscany join Sardinia. Garibaldi captures Sicily and Naples and hands them to Victor Emmanuel.

1861 Victor Emmanuel crowned king of Italy.

1866 Venice joins Italy.

1870 French troops withdraw from Rome; Rome joins Italy and becomes the new nation's capital.

Garibaldi and his Red Shirt army entering the city of Naples on September 7, 1860. He is being welcomed and cheered by the King of Naples' troops.

Soul Force

Gandhi led the Indian struggle for independence from British rule.

When Mohandâs Gandhi returned to his native India from South Africa in 1915, the Indian poet Rabindranath Tagore greeted him with a new title: *Mahatma*. The word means, literally, "Great Soul," and is used by Hindus to describe the very greatest of their holy men. Gandhi first earned the title among the Indians living in South Africa; now, in India itself, his courage, faith, and example would inspire millions of his people to resist the British rule of their country. Gandhi was the Great Soul who led India to independence.

Gandhi, Mohandâs Karamchand (1869–1948) Mohandâs Gandhi was born in the town of Porbandar on the western coast of India. He began his career as a lawyer, first in London and Bombay, then, from 1893, in the South African province of Natal. His practice was successful and prosperous, and Gandhi himself was not, at first, the figure dressed in a simple white shawl that is familiar from so many photographs; instead, he appeared wearing fashionable European suits. But he took a deep interest in defending the rights of Indians against prejudice or abuse from white South Africans—often without receiving any payment. In 1906 a law was passed demanding that all Indians carry identification cards. Gandhi invented and led a unique campaign of resistance: Indians would not *fight* the new law—they simply would not obey it, peacefully refusing to do as they were required. These non-violent tactics led eventually to a compromise, making the carrying of identification cards voluntary.

He called the technique of passive resistance *Satyagraha*, a word from his native language combining "truth" and "love" with "firmness" and "force"—in short, "Soul Force." Soul Force was the key to Gandhi's attempts to liberate India. He believed that if the people showed resistance to their oppressors, but no violence, justice would inevitably prevail. The independence movement began, therefore, with Indians simply refusing to cooperate with the British: not buying British cloth and organizing boycotts of British businesses and institutions, combined with prayer and fasting as demonstrations of the Indians' wish to be free. The British, who feared a general revolt, often reacted badly: in April 1919 a British commander, General Dyer, ordered his men to fire on a peaceful demonstration in the city of Amritsar. Three hundred and seventy-nine Indians were killed.

Gandhi led the campaign by personal example. He had given up all worldly possessions, wore simple clothes, and ate only vegetables and fruit. He was imprisoned four times, but never offered any resistance, believing instead that the British condemned themselves by their own injustice. In 1930 he personally led a 200-mile march to the sea to gather salt. This was in defiance of the British monopoly on salt production, which tried to ensure that Indians had to buy salt from government-run agencies. But there was plenty of salt to be had for free on India's beaches. Gandhi went and scooped it up, and thousands of other Indians began doing the same.

This campaign of defiance eventually forced the British to take notice, and they at least appeared to be giving in. The first attempts at negotiation, however, at the "Round Table" conference in London in 1931, led nowhere. It was World War II in 1939 to 1945 that brought change. If the British were committed to freedom in Europe, said Gandhi, how could they ignore the Indians' desire for freedom in their own country? The force of this argument eventually prevailed. In 1947 India was made independent. Gandhi, however, was tortured by what was taking place in his country. The independence settlement established separate states (India and Pakistan) for Hindus and Muslims, and bitter violence erupted between the two groups. Gandhi fasted, and the possibility of his death stopped much of the fighting. But in 1948 he was assassinated at a prayer meeting by a Hindu who believed Gandhi's attitude to the Muslims to be too moderate.

○ JINNAH, NEHRU

Lord Mountbatten, the last viceroy of India, planned the British withdrawal in 1947.

Gandhi leading hundreds of his followers on a 200-mile march to the sea to gather salt in 1930. This was in defiance of the British monopoly on salt production.

Garrett Anderson, Elizabeth (1836–1917)
Elizabeth Garrett Anderson was the first woman doctor allowed to practice in England. She was born at Aldeburgh in Suffolk, and began studying medicine at the age of 24. At that time, male doctors strongly opposed the admission of women to their profession, but in 1865 Garrett Anderson finally passed her medical exams. In 1876 she became a doctor at the East London Hospital—which has since been renamed the "Elizabeth Garrett Anderson Hospital for Women" in her honor. She campaigned for allowing women to become doctors, and this led to the founding of the London School of Medicine for Women in 1874. She was also elected mayor of Aldeburgh—the first woman mayor in England.

Garrick, David (1717–79)
A celebrated English actor. He was a pupil and friend of Samuel Johnson, with whom he traveled to London in 1737. Garrick's first stage success was in Shakespeare's *Richard III,* and he went on to become the most popular and talented actor of his time, performing in all kinds of drama. He also wrote plays, and became manager of the Drury Lane Theater. ○ JOHNSON

Gaskell, Elizabeth Cleghorn (1810–65)
Mrs. Gaskell was an English novelist. She was born in London, and later moved to Manchester, where she studied the lives of working-class people and the industrial landscapes that appear in many of her novels. Her first novel, *Mary Barton,* was published anonymously in 1848. Among her other works are *Cranford* and *North and South,* and a famous biography of her fellow novelist Charlotte Brontë. ○ BRONTË

Gauguin, Eugène Henri Paul (1848–1903)
A French painter. In 1883 he left his wife and five children to devote his life to painting. He is most famous for the pictures he made during his visits to the south sea islands of Tahiti and Marquesas (where he died). They are strong, colorful pictures, and they helped introduce primitive people and their art to other European painters.

The French painter, Gauguin. He abandoned "civilization" to live and paint in Tahiti.

The **"Gawain-Poet"** (*c.*1400)
Nothing is known about the "Gawain-Poet" except that he lived somewhere in northeast England, and wrote one of the finest of all medieval English poems, *Sir Gawain and the Green Knight,* in about the year 1400. It tells the story of one of the knights of King Arthur's Round Table, Sir Gawain, and his encounter with a fearsome green man who tests his virtue. ○ ARTHUR

Gay-Lussac, Joseph Louis (1778–1850)
A French chemist who made many experiments into the chemical composition of different substances. He made balloon ascents (to a height of 21,000 feet) to examine the composition of the atmosphere, and together with Humboldt showed that water was made up of one part oxygen and two parts hydrogen. ○ HUMBOLDT

Genghis Khan (1162–1227)
Genghis Khan was a powerful Mongol emperor who conquered lands stretching all the way from the Black Sea and southeast Russia to China and the Pacific Ocean. He took command of his father's tribes at the age of only 13, and by conquest gradually extended his rule in Asia. In 1206 he gave himself his name, "Genghis Khan," which means "Very Mighty Ruler," and in 1212 brought much of China under his control. In about 1225 he returned home to Mongolia, but his generals continued his campaigns and enlarged the empire still farther. ○ KUBLA KHAN

Genghis Khan receiving dignitaries after his capture of Bukhara in 1220.

Gentileschi, Orazio (1563–1639)
Gentileschi was an Italian painter who worked in Paris, and then, from about 1626, in London as a court painter to King Charles I. He introduced some of the styles and effects of late-Renaissance Italian painting to northern Europe. His daughter, **Artemesia Gentileschi** (*c.*1597–1651), was one of the very few women painters of the time. She spent several years traveling Europe with her father before settling to live in the city of Naples. Her works include portraits and biblical subjects.

George, Saint
The patron saint of England, Portugal, and many churches and organizations (including the Boy Scouts). Little is known about his life. He was probably a soldier who died at Lydda in Palestine at the beginning of either the 3rd or 4th century. The most famous story about him tells how he saved a maiden from being eaten by a dragon at the town of Silene in Libya, but this is only a popular medieval legend. He was made patron saint of England by King Edward III.

George III (1738–1820)
George III was the third member of the German Hanover family to become king of Britain (his great-grandfather, George I, was the first), and the first to take an interest in the government of the country. Several very skilled politicians, including Lord North and the younger Pitt, served as his prime minister, and his reign saw such important developments as the French and American revolutions and the colonization of India. He became insane in 1815, and the country was governed by his eldest son, who became George IV after his death.

Geronimo (1829–1909)
"Geronimo" was the name given by the Mexicans to a famous American Indian chief (it is Spanish for "Jerome"). He led a band of Apache warriors in attacks on the U.S. army in the 1870s and 1880s, but he and his people were eventually defeated and forced to settle on reservations given to them by the U.S. Government.

Gershwin, George (1898–1937)
An American composer who combined traditional and more modern jazz elements in his compositions. His most famous works are the *Rhapsody in Blue* for piano and orchestra and the opera *Porgy and Bess*, which he wrote together with his brother **Ira Gershwin** (1896–1983).

Getty, Jean Paul (1892–1976)
An American oil company owner who became one of the world's richest men. At the time of his death his empire included over 100 companies. Much of his wealth has been used to finance the J. Paul Getty Museum in California, which contains a vast collection of art treasures.

Ghiberti, Lorenzo (1378–1455)
Ghiberti was an Italian sculptor and goldsmith. His most famous works are the relief sculptures he made for the doors of the Baptistery in the city of Florence. They depict scenes from the Old Testament, and are among the most beautiful of all the sculpture of the Renaissance. Michelangelo called them the "Gates of Paradise." Among Ghiberti's pupils were the sculptor Donatello and the painter Uccello. ○ DONATELLO, UCCELLO

A panel from the door of the Baptistery of Florence cathedral, the work of the goldsmith, Ghiberti.

Gibbon, Edward (1737–94)
Gibbon was an English historian whose great work *The Decline and Fall of the Roman Empire* (published in six volumes between 1776 and 1888) is still thought of as a masterpiece. The idea for the book came to him during a trip to Rome in 1764. Gibbon did not have an optimistic view of history; he said that it was a record of "the crimes, follies, and misfortunes of mankind."

Gide, André Paul Guillaume (1869–1951)
Gide was a French writer whose novels, poems, and other work have had a great influence on other 20th-century French authors. He was born in Paris and decided to become a writer at an early age, despite the opposition of his mother. His most famous works include the novel *The Vatican Cellars* (published in 1914), his autobiography and diaries, and his translations of Shakespeare. Although he was well known among French writers and other intellectuals, it was not until the 1920s that he was widely read by the public. Gide became involved in helping refugees during World War I and the

Spanish Civil War, and campaigned for better treatment of Africans in the French colonies. He was awarded the Nobel Prize for Literature in 1947.

Gilbert, Sir William Schwenck (1836–1911)
An English writer, famous for the many "Gilbert and Sullivan" operas he composed with Arthur Sullivan (1842–1900). These include *HMS Pinafore* (written in 1878) and *The Mikado* (1885). Sullivan composed the music for the operas, and Gilbert wrote the lyrics. Their partnership ended after a bitter quarrel between the two men in 1890.

Giorgione (Giorgio da Castelfranco, *c.*1478–1511)
Giorgione was an Italian painter who worked in Venice. Little is known of his life, and few of his pictures have survived, but it is certain he was a pupil of the famous Bellini and probably one of Titian's teachers. His greatest painting is *The Tempest*, with two unidentified figures in a stormy landscape. It is a small picture, and one of the very first to be painted for a collector, rather than for a church or public building. Giorgione died of plague, and many of his works were finished by other painters. ○ BELLINI, TITIAN

Giotto di Bondone (1267–1337)
Giotto was an Italian artist who is thought of as the founder of modern painting because he replaced the expressionless style of Byzantine art with pictures full of character and individuality. There is a story that at the age of only 10, Giotto was found in a field sketching a lamb by the famous artist Cimabue. Cimabue trained the boy, and he went on to become the greatest painter of his time. In about 1306 Giotto completed a series of pictures in the Arena Chapel in the city of Padua showing scenes from the life of Christ. They are delicate, colorful works, in which the expressions and gestures of the figures show their feelings. They can still be seen today, and are among the most beautiful paintings in all of Western art. Giotto painted another series illustrating the life of St. Francis in a chapel at the town of Assisi, as well as pictures of St. John the Baptist in the Church of Santa Croce in Florence, and several Madonnas. His fame spread; he was mentioned by Dante in the poem *The Divine Comedy*, and in 1334 he was put in charge of the building and decoration of Florence cathedral. He made several sculptures for the outside of the building, and designed the *campanile* (bell tower), known as "Giotto's Tower." ○ CIMABUE, DANTE, FRANCIS OF ASSISI

The Madonna in Majesty *by the Italian artist Giotto.*

Lamentations over the Dead Christ *by Giotto.*

Gladstone, William Ewart (1809–98)
A British Liberal politician who was prime minister four times: from 1868 until 1874, 1880 until 1885, in 1886 and then again from 1892 until 1894. He was born in Liverpool, and intended to become a clergyman, but in 1832 he entered Parliament as a member of the Tory Party. He was a minister during Peel's government, but abandoned the Tories to become a Liberal in the 1860s. As prime minister he introduced many important reforms, including an Education Act (1870), which established the first national school system in Britain; a Ballot Act (1872), which ensured that people could make their votes at election time secretly; and a Reform Act (1884), which gave many more men the vote. He also reformed the army and tried to tackle the Irish question—that of whether the British should continue to govern Ireland. ○ PEEL

Glenn, John Herschel (1921–)
An American astronaut and aviator, who in 1957 made a record-breaking flight across the United States at supersonic speed, and in 1962 became the first American to orbit the earth, in a Mercury space capsule. He is now a politician.

Goddard, Robert Hutchings (1882–1945)
An American engineer who realized that solid substances were too heavy to power rockets, and so designed the first liquid-fueled rocket. The American government was at first not interested in his ideas, but after his death Goddard's widow received over one million dollars for the use the government had made of his designs in the American space program.

Godunov, Boris Fyodorovich (1552–1605)
Boris Godunov was tsar of Russia from 1598 until his death. He became powerful during the reign of Ivan the Terrible, and ruled the country on behalf of Ivan's idiot son Fyodor from 1584 until 1598. As tsar, Boris was an efficient but tyrannical ruler. He was suspected of murdering Fyodor's younger brother in order to gain the throne, and was himself killed during a revolt. His life is the subject of a famous opera, *Boris Godunov*, by the composer Mussorgsky.

Goethe, Johann Wolfgang von (1749–1832)
Goethe was a playwright, poet, and novelist and perhaps the greatest writer in the history of German literature. He was an intelligent child, born in Frankfurt, and he quickly learned music and several languages. His father sent him to study law at the University of Leipzig in 1765, but Goethe had no liking for the subject and he soon became more interested in literature. His first success was a play, *Götz von Berlichingen*, written in 1771, which tells the story of a medieval knight. Goethe had been inspired to try to write drama which would have the same importance in German as Shakespeare's plays had in English, and he continued to write plays throughout his life.

Goethe, perhaps the greatest writer in the history of the German language.

In 1774 Goethe published a novel, *The Sorrows of Young Werther*, which was based on his own unhappy love affairs, and in 1775 he became chief adviser to Duke Charles Augustus of Weimar. He studied science, and discovered the similarity between the jawbones of humans and apes, and that the leaf was the structure on which all other parts of a plant are based. He was at first a supporter of the French Revolution, but later changed his mind and advised the duke to invade France and try to restore the king to the throne. His greatest work is *Faust*, which he wrote and re-wrote throughout his life. It tells the story of a magician, called Faust, who sells his soul to the Devil in return for knowledge and power. It was published in two parts, in 1796 and 1830. Among Goethe's other works are the novel *Wilhelm Meister* and the plays *Egmont* and *Iphegenie.*

Gogol, Nikolai Vasilyevich (1809–52)
Gogol was a Russian writer who lived and worked in the city of St. Petersburg. His most famous works are the play *The Government Inspector* (first performed in 1836), and a novel called *Dead Souls* (1837), which tells how some small landowners try to swindle the government by using the names of dead peasants when borrowing money. At the end of his life, Gogol became religious and destroyed many of his manuscripts.

Golding, William (1911–)
An English novelist, who won the Nobel Prize for Literature in 1983. His most famous novel is *Lord of the Flies* (1954), which describes what happens to a party of schoolchildren marooned alone on an island.

Gomulka, Wladyslaw (1905–82)
Gomulka was a Polish politician who led his country from 1943 until 1948 and from 1956 until 1970. During World War II he was a member of the Polish resistance, and after the defeat of Germany became prime minister. He wanted to develop a type of Polish socialism free of Russian domination, and opposed Stalin. For this he was imprisoned in 1948, but he returned to power after Stalin's death. Gomulka was forced to resign during riots about food shortages in 1970.
○ STALIN

Gonne, Maud (1865–1953)
Maud Gonne was an Irish nationalist politician. She was the daughter of an English army colonel, but campaigned for Irish independence from British

rule. She edited a newspaper called *Free Ireland* while living in Paris and married an Irish soldier, John MacBride. He was one of those executed after the 1916 rebellion in Dublin, and Maud Gonne then became a member of the Sinn Fein political party.

Goodman, Benny (1909–86)
Benny Goodman was a clarinetist and jazz band leader who became known as the "King of Swing." He and his musicians toured all over the world, starred in many films, and were among those to play in the very first jazz concert given at New York's Carnegie Hall in 1938.

Gorbachev, Mikhail Sergeyvich (1931–)
Gorbachev has been general secretary of the Soviet Communist Party and leader of the Soviet Union since the death of Konstantin Chernenko in March 1985. As leader he has tried to reform the Russian economy, and has traveled to several Western countries and met President Reagan of the United States. ○ REAGAN

Gordimer, Nadine (1923–)
A white South African novelist, whose many books deal with the way the "apartheid" system in South Africa affects people's lives. Among her works are *Occasion for Loving* and *July's People.*

Gordon, Charles George (1833–85)
General Gordon was a British soldier, surveyor, and engineer. In the 1860s he was in China, where he became well known for his exploits in suppressing a rebellion, after which he was known as Chinese Gordon. Then he then returned to London where he worked as an army engineer and gave much time to looking after the city's poor and sick. From 1874 he explored northern Africa, opening the upper Nile area to steamships and fighting the slave trade. Then in 1884 he was asked to evacuate Europeans from the Sudan, where they were in danger from an Arab rebellion. This he did, but remained to defend the city of Khartoum. The siege lasted five months; Gordon was finally defeated and killed only two days before the arrival of help.

Gorky, Maxim (1868–1936)
"Gorky" was the name used by the Russian writer Alexei Maximovich Peshkov. The word means "bitter" in Russian, and Gorky's novels describe the harsh realities of life for the Russian poor. He ran away from home and lived with the poor at the age of 12, and in 1905 became a revolutionary. He knew many of the leaders of the Bolshevik Party and supported them during the 1917 revolution. His works, which include *Sketches and Stories* and *My Childhood,* are famous in the Soviet Union.
○ LENIN

Goya y Lucientes, Francisco José de (1746–1828)
Goya was a Spanish painter who was born and lived in the city of Saragossa until a series of turbulent love affairs and violent quarrels forced him to leave. He studied in Madrid and Rome, and became famous after the publication of his engraved prints of Velasquez's paintings. He became head of the royal academy, and later chief painter to the Spanish royal family. It is surprising that he was not arrested, for his portraits, such as that of Ferdinand VII, make his subjects seem stupid, brutal, and arrogant. During the 1790s he suffered from a strange illness that made him deaf and produced hallucinations, and as he got older his pictures became more and more nightmarish. During the French occupation of Spain from 1808, Goya painted several pictures showing the horror and violence of war. As well as paintings, he produced a great many prints, and he influenced later 19th-century artists.

A portrait of Ferdinand VII by Goya.

Graham, Martha (1895–)
Martha Graham is an American choreographer who has become one of the most influential figures in modern dance. In 1927 she founded the Martha Graham School of Contemporary Dance, where she taught her pupils to use every aspect and part of their bodies and minds in their performances. She has produced over 170 pieces, many on American themes. The most famous is *Appalachian Spring*, which deals with native American myths and ways of life.

Grant, Ulysses Simpson (1822–85)
Grant was an American soldier who led the Union Army to victory in the American Civil War, and

General Ulysses S. Grant, victorious commander of the Union forces in the American Civil War, with some of his staff.

became the eighteenth president of the United States, from 1869 until 1877. He was born in Ohio, and became a cadet at the West Point military academy. He did not much like army life, and soon retired, only to be recommissioned as a colonel when the Civil War broke out in 1861. He led several successful campaigns, including the capture of the town of Vicksburg in 1863, where he took over 31,000 prisoners. In March 1864, Grant was put in charge of all the Union forces, and he masterminded the campaign that led to the Confederate surrender in 1865. His military exploits led to his being elected Republican president. During his government, a law guaranteeing a vote to all men, regardless of their race or color, was passed. But Grant was not a strong president: many of his officials were corrupt and inefficient, and the government was damaged by several scandals. At the end of his presidency, Grant became involved in banking but when the bank collapsed in 1884 it was discovered that he had been robbed by his partners. He took responsibility for the debts left by the failed bank, and tried to make money by writing his memoirs. He died of cancer of the throat, and had to dictate the last part of his book while in great pain. ○ LEE, LINCOLN

Greco, El (Domenikos Theotokopoulos, 1541–1614)
El Greco, whose name means, simply, "the Greek," was a painter who lived and worked for most of his life in Toledo in Spain. He was born in Crete, studied in Venice (perhaps with Titian), and visited Rome, where his arrogance offended many people. There is a story that he said that Michelangelo's *Last Judgment* should be demolished, and that he would paint a better version. His pictures are very unusual: they often contain strange, thin figures, and are brightly colored. The people who commissioned El Greco to paint for them were often disturbed by what they received, and sometimes refused to accept the pictures. His most famous work is *The Burial of Count Orgaz.*

Greene, Henry Graham (1904–)
Graham Greene is an English novelist. His first novel, *The Man Within,* was published in 1929, and since then he has written many novels, stories, and plays. His subjects are often the reasons for which people commit themselves to a particular cause or idea. Other Greene novels include *Brighton Rock* (1938) and *The Quiet American* (1955).

Greer, Germaine (1939–)
An Australian feminist writer who became a leading figure in the women's movement in 1970 with the publication of her book *The Female Eunuch.* She has remained a powerful spokeswoman for the movement, appearing on television and radio and publishing many books and articles.

Gregory I, Saint (*c.*540–604)
Gregory I, or "Gregory the Great" as he is sometimes known, was Pope from 590 until his death. He was responsible for many improvements in the organization of the Roman Catholic Church, spent large amounts of money on helping the poor, the sick, and the victims of war, and taught the need for the Church's ministers to care for their congregations as well as bring them the word of God. Gregory was for many years the chief magistrate of Rome. At the age of 35 he became a monk, and was sent as the Pope's representative to the city of Constantinople. He was a humble man, and tried to avoid being elected Pope, but he was eventually forced to accept the office. He wrote a number of books and treatises, and sent a mission to England to convert the people there to Christianity.

Gregory, Isabella Augusta (1852–1932)
Lady Gregory was an Irish playwright. She was a friend of the poet W. B. Yeats, and together they founded the Irish National Theatre Society and the Abbey Theatre in Dublin. She wrote several plays, including *The Rising of the Moon* (1907), as well as versions of Irish legends and translations of French drama, and supported other Irish playwrights. She believed that an Irish theater could help the political cause of Irish nationalism. ○ YEATS

Lady Gregory, Irish playwright and a founder of the Abbey Theatre, Dublin.

Grieg, Edvard Hagerup (1843–1907)
Grieg was a Norwegian composer. He studied music in Germany, where he was influenced by composers such as Schumann and Mendelssohn. In 1863 he settled in the Danish city of Copenhagen, because there were no opportunities for composers in Norway, and there he met other Scandinavian musicians and composers. Grieg developed a style inspired by northern landscapes and folk music. His works include the *Holberg Suite* and music for Ibsen's play *Peer Gynt*. From 1874 he lived in the Norwegian city of Bergen. ○ IBSEN

Grimm, Jacob Ludwig Carl (1785–1863) and **Wilhelm Carl** (1786–1859)
Jacob and Wilhelm Grimm, who are often called together the "Brothers Grimm," collected and published German fairy stories and folk tales and studied the development of the German language. Jacob was a librarian in the service of Jerome Bonaparte, the king of Westphalia, and then later secretary to the Elector of the kingdom of Hesse. In 1829 both Jacob and Wilhelm moved to the town of Göttingen, where Jacob became a librarian and professor at the university, and Wilhelm a junior librarian. When they protested at the king of Hanover's abolition of the state's constitution, they both lost their jobs, and so moved on to Berlin, where they became professors. They began their work of publishing folk tales in 1812, and continued to publish new volumes throughout their lives.

Gromyko, Andrei Andreyevich (1909–)
A Soviet politician. He became ambassador to the United States in 1943, during Stalin's leadership, and continued to serve as the Soviet Union's most important diplomat for over 40 years. He was made foreign minister in 1957, a position he retained until removed by Gorbachev in 1986. Gromyko is now "President" of the Soviet Union.

Gropius, Walter Adolf (1883–1969)
A German architect who pioneered the use of "functional" materials such as glass and concrete in his buildings. He was one of the founders of the Bauhaus School of design in Germany. ○ KANDINSKY

Grotius, Hugo (1583–1645)
Grotius was a Dutch lawyer who was one of the first men to write about international law—the laws governing relations between different countries. He was born in Delft, went to university at the age of 11, and became a diplomat in the service of King Henry IV of France at the age of 15. While practicing law in the city of The Hague he became involved in a religious dispute, and in 1618 he was arrested and sentenced to death for his views. He escaped when his wife smuggled him out of prison in a large trunk, and he fled to Paris. There he received support from King Louis XIII, published his ideas on the law, and campaigned for a reconciliation between different religious groups.

Guelph
Guelph was the name of a powerful political dynasty, or family, which originated in Germany. They became rulers of a number of German tribes, and were much involved in Italian politics, in the Middle Ages and Renaissance periods. The Guelphs supported the Pope's claim that the Church should be responsible for *all* government, and they and their supporters were often at war with the Ghibellines, who wanted to keep government separate from the Church.

Guevara, Che (1928–67)
Che Guevara was an Argentinian Communist and revolutionary, who together with Fidel Castro played an important part in the Cuban revolution in 1959. In 1956 he joined Castro's guerrilla army, and after the revolution became minister of industry in Cuba. He left Cuba in 1965, visited Africa and North Vietnam, and then became the leader of a guerrilla army trying to overthrow the Bolivian government. He was captured and killed by the Bolivian army. ○ CASTRO, PERÓN

Guillotin, Joseph Ignace (1738–1814)
A French doctor who became a member of the new French Assembly after the Revolution. In 1791 he recommended the use of the guillotine for executions, and the device was named after him. He did not, however, *invent* the guillotine: similar instruments had already been used in Scotland, Germany, and Italy.

Guinness, Sir Alec (1914–)
An English actor who has appeared in many plays and films, in many types of role. His films include *Great Expectations, The Ladykillers,* and *The Bridge on the River Kwai,* for which he won an Oscar.

Gustavus II (Gustavus Adolphus) (1594–1632)
Gustavus Adolphus was king of Sweden. He improved the Swedish government and reorganized the military, and campaigned to make Sweden the most important country in northern Europe. When Gustavus came to the throne in 1611, the country was at war with other northern states and the economy in disorder. He made a treaty with Denmark, fought and defeated the Russian army in 1617, and in 1629 ended a long war with Poland. As a result Sweden gained large areas of new territory. Meanwhile, Gustavus had introduced a new system of government in Sweden and reorganized and re-equipped his army. The soldiers had new uniforms, lighter, more efficient weapons, and were better disciplined than before. By the 1620s Sweden was already the most powerful country in the north, and in 1631 Gustavus joined the French side in the Thirty Years' War against the Holy Roman Empire, hoping to extend his power into Germany. He was immediately successful, and became the champion of Protestant Germans against the Catholic empire. After twice defeating the imperial army under General Tilly in 1632, Gustavus marched toward Austria. The imperial army at first retreated, but then at the Battle of Lützen turned to face the Swedes. During a desperate fight, Gustavus was suddenly separated from the rest of his army and killed. The Swedes revenged the death of their king by winning the battle.

Gustavus Adolphus, King of Sweden, who campaigned to make his country the most important power in northern Europe.

Gutenberg, Johannes Gensfleisch (1400–68)
Gutenberg is recognized as the first man to have printed books by using movable type. Little is known about his life. In the 1430s he was in Strasbourg, where he probably trained as a goldsmith, and may have experimented with printing. About 1450 he went into partnership with a man called Fust, who provided money to set up a printing press in the city of Mainz. The two men quarreled. Fust took possession of the press, and Gutenberg had to set up another press of his own. On this he was able to print his famous edition of the Bible, as well as copies of a Latin grammar book, the first printed books.

Above right: Gutenberg, the first person to have printed books by using movable type.

Gwynne, Nell (*c.*1650–87)
Nell Gwynne was an English courtesan who became the mistress of King **Charles II** (1630–85). She was born into a poor family in the town of Hereford, and later became an orange seller in London's Drury Lane district. From there she became an actress, and then Charles's mistress. She bore him two sons, and is said to have persuaded him to found the Chelsea Hospital for war veterans.

Habsburg

Habsburg (or Hapsburg) is the name of a family who dominated European politics for several centuries. Its members were elected Holy Roman Emperors continuously from 1440, when a German king, **Frederick III** (1415–93), received the crown, until 1806, when Napoleon abolished the empire. After that, Habsburgs remained rulers of the Austro-Hungarian Empire until **Charles I** of Austria (1887–1922) was deposed at the end of World War I (1914).

The family was founded by Albert, Count of Habsburg, in 1153, and took its name from the castle of Habsburg (meaning "Hawk's Castle") in Switzerland. During the Middle Ages the family gained control of much of Germany and then, under **Rudolf III** (1218–91), they extended their power into Austria and central Europe. When Charles V became king of Spain in 1516, the Habsburgs also gained the Spanish throne, which they held for the next 200 years. ○ CHARLES V, PHILIP II

One of the most famous members of the Habsburg family was **Maria Theresa** (1717–80).

The Empress Maria Theresa of Austria.

Her father, the Emperor **Charles VI** (1685–1740), attempted to make sure that she would inherit all the Habsburg lands from him through what was called the "Pragmatic Succession." He persuaded the other European countries to recognize her right to rule, but on his death in 1740 several countries went back on their agreement and claimed parts of the empire. Frederick the Great of Prussia invaded the state of Silesia in the north, and this began the War of Austrian Succession which lasted from 1741 until 1748. It was ended by the Treaty of Aix-la-Chapelle, in which Maria Theresa lost Silesia and some states in Italy, but kept the rest of her father's empire. She later attempted to regain Silesia in the Seven Years' War, but failed. In 1736 she married Francis of Lorraine, and when he was elected Holy Roman Emperor in 1745 Maria Theresa became empress. She was a wise and efficient ruler, who introduced reforms in the economy, education, and the legal system. Her daughter, Marie Antoinette, became queen of France by marrying Louis XVI, and she was succeeded by her son, Joseph III (1741–90). ○ FREDERICK II, MARIE ANTOINETTE

Hadrian (Publius Aelius Hadrianus, A.D. 76–A.D. 138)

Hadrian was Roman emperor from the year 117. He was born in Spain and educated in Rome, where he held important posts in the Roman government. After his father's death, the Emperor Trajan became his guardian. Hadrian accompanied Trajan during his campaigns, and after his death was proclaimed emperor by the army. He traveled throughout the Roman territories, where he introduced improvements in the army and government, and built fortifications such as Hadrian's Wall, which was intended to protect the Roman colony in England from attacks by the Scots. He was a just ruler, and a lover of the arts.

Háfiz (Shams ed-Din Muhammed, d. *c.*1388)

Háfiz was the name of a great Persian poet, known as *Chagarlab* (meaning "Sugar-lip") because of the sweetness of his verses. He was a Muslim, and a member of the sect (group) of mystic philosophers known as "Sufis." His poems are about ordinary, beautiful things, such as flowers, wine, or beautiful women, but as well as being love poems they also have a mysterious religious significance for people who understand Sufi ideas.

Haig, Douglas, 1st Earl (1861–1928)

A British soldier who became commander-in-chief of the Allied armies on the Western Front during World War I. He masterminded the battles at the Somme (1916) and Passchendaele (1917) as well as the offensive that finally won the war.

Haile Selassie (1891–1975)

Haile Selassie was emperor of Ethiopia from 1930 until 1974. Before becoming emperor, he was known as Prince Ras Tafari. In 1916 he led a successful revolution against the ruler Lij Yasu, and for the next 14 years acted as regent (governor) for the Princess Zauditu. When she died, Haile Selassie became emperor. After the Italian invasion of his country in 1936 he fled to Britain, where he remained until restored to his throne at the end of World War II. Haile Selassie attempted some economic and other reforms, such as abolishing the slave trade, and helped to found the Organization of African Unity. But Ethiopia remained poor and backward, and the emperor's extravagant lifestyle made him unpopular. He was overthrown in 1974 after years of famine and economic chaos, and replaced by a military government. Nonetheless, he is thought of by some Africans as a sacred figure.

Hale, Nathan (1755–76)
Nathan Hale was an American revolutionary soldier and hero. When the American Revolutionary War broke out, he was a schoolteacher in Connecticut. He joined the army fighting the British for independence, and was soon promoted for his bravery. In September 1776 he volunteered to travel behind the British lines to collect information. Disguised as a schoolmaster, he made the dangerous journey to the British garrison on Long Island. His mission accomplished, he was trying to return to safety when he was captured and brought before a British general. On the morning of September 22, 1776, he was hanged. His last words were: "I only regret that I have but one life to lose for my country."

Halley, Edmond (1656–1742)
Halley was an English astronomer whose most famous achievement was to predict the return of the comet that is named after him. After studying the movements of the planets and records of several comets, he said that the comet that had appeared in 1531, 1606, and 1682 would appear again in 1758. Halley did much else. He was the first to chart the stars that could be seen from the earth's southern hemisphere; he studied winds and weather patterns, surveyed the tides and coastline of the English Channel, invented the diving bell, and was the first to discover that a barometer could be used to measure altitude. In 1721 he became England's second Astronomer Royal.

Hals, Frans (*c.*1581–1666)
Hals was one of the greatest of all Dutch painters. He was born and lived in the city of Haarlem, and became a member of the guild of painters in 1610. His finest pictures are his portraits. Many of these show groups of people such as military officers, city officials, or families. Because each person in the picture contributed an equal share of the cost, Hals had to develop a technique of giving each one an expression of his own and an equal importance in the composition. Despite his success, Hals never became rich, and he lived a crowded, poor life. Two of his brothers were also painters.

Hammarskjöld, Dag Hjalmar Agne Carl (1905–61)
Secretary-general of the United Nations from 1953 until his death. Hammarskjöld was a professor at Stockholm University and a member of the Swedish government before becoming a delegate to the United Nations. He was involved in many attempts to bring peace to the Middle East through the United Nations. He died in an air crash while conducting negotiations in Africa, and was afterward awarded the Nobel Peace Prize.

Hammer, Armand (1898–)
An American businessman who has conducted successful trade with the Soviet Union since the 1920s, dealing in wheat, fur, coal, oil, caviar, and many other things. He has known every Soviet leader since Lenin, and has often helped arrange diplomatic links between the United States and the Soviet Union.

A 17th-century Dutch family painted by Frans Hals. Hals was one of the greatest of all Dutch portrait painters. One of his famous and less formal portraits is The Laughing Cavalier *(1624).*

Hammurabi (18th century B.C.)
Hammurabi was an ancient Babylonian king. He expanded the Babylonian Empire, and governed it with remarkable efficiency. An inscribed stone tablet (which can now be seen in the Louvre museum in Paris) records a system of laws which he established, and is thought to be one of the first legal documents in the history of mankind.

Handel, George Frederick (1685–1759)
Handel was a German-born composer who spent much of his life working in England. He composed

George Frederick Handel, composer of The Messiah.

and produced a great many operas, wrote instrumental music (including the famous *Water Music* and *Music for the Royal Fireworks*), and developed a new choral form called the "oratorio." Handel was born in Saxony and became a musician despite the opposition of his father, who was a barber-surgeon. He visited Italy, and then worked as a violinist and conductor in the city of Hamburg. In 1710 he became music master to the Elector of the kingdom of Hanover, but neglected his duties and was often absent on trips to London. This annoyed his employer, and it is said that the *Water Music* was composed as a peace offering. In 1719, the Elector became King George I of England, and Handel was able to move permanently to London. He founded the Royal Academy of Music, managed the King's Theatre, and later became involved with the Covent Garden opera house. Among his most famous works are the Concerti Grossi for orchestra, and the choral work *The Messiah*, composed in 1742. At the end of his life he became blind. When he died he was buried in Poets' Corner in Westminster Abbey.

Hannibal (247 B.C.–182 B.C.)
Hannibal was a Carthaginian soldier. Carthage was a kingdom in North Africa whose people were the sworn enemies of the Romans, and from the year 218 B.C. Hannibal led a series of daring campaigns against Rome in what is known as the Second Punic War. He traveled north through Spain to the river Rhone, and from there—with an army of several thousand men and a troop of elephants—across the Alps into Italy. He defeated the Roman army at battles at the river Trebbia, Lake Trasimene, and Cannae, but was not strong enough to capture Rome itself. Hannibal spent the next 14 years in southern Italy, defending himself against the Romans, but without relief from Carthage. Finally, in 203 B.C., he had to return to his native city to defend it from Roman invasion. He was defeated by Scipio at the Battle of Zana and eventually forced into exile, where he killed himself to avoid surrender. ○ SCIPIO

Hardy, Thomas (1840–1928)
An English poet and novelist. The countryside and people of southwestern England, where Hardy spent most of his life, usually form the subject of his work. Among his best-known novels are *The Mayor of Casterbridge* (published in 1886) and *Tess of the D'Urbervilles* (1891). *Tess*, which tells the story of a farm girl's life after her seduction by an aristocratic young man, was condemned as immoral, and Hardy became disillusioned with novel writing. His next book, *Jude the Obscure*, was also criticized, and he soon turned to writing poetry.

Hargreaves, James (1720–78)
Hargreaves was an illiterate carpenter and weaver from Lancashire in the north of England. In about 1764 he invented a machine called the "spinning jenny" which could spin several threads of cotton at once. This made him unpopular with other spinners, who thought they might lose their jobs, and his machine was broken by an angry mob.
○ ARKWRIGHT

Harold II (*c.*1022–66)
Harold II was the last Saxon king of England. Although he is remembered as the man who lost the Battle of Hastings in 1066, he was a brave, efficient, and energetic leader. He was the son of Earl Godwin of Wessex, and became Edward the Confessor's chief minister. During a visit to France in about 1063, Harold was forced to swear an oath of loyalty to Duke William of Normandy. In January 1066, Edward the Confessor died and Harold was proclaimed king. He immediately took back the oath he had made to William—and as a

The Bayeux Tapestry shows the Battle of Hastings in which King Harold of England was defeated by William of Normandy.

result William prepared to invade England. To add to Harold's troubles, his brother, Tostig, began a rebellion in the north, with the help of an army of Norsemen. Harold marched north and defeated Tostig at the Battle of Stamford Bridge, but meanwhile William had landed at Pevensey on the south coast. Harold's army returned south, and met the Normans near the town of Hastings on October 14. The Battle of Hastings lasted all day, and went well for Harold until the Normans pretended to retreat and tricked the Saxons into leaving a strong defensive position. Harold was shot in the eye by an arrow, and his army defeated. William "the Conqueror" thus became king of England. He was the last man to have successfully invaded the country. ○ EDWARD THE CONFESSOR, WILLIAM

Harris, Joel Chandler (1848–1908)
An American writer who achieved fame with his *Uncle Remus* (written in 1880), a collection of folk stories told in Negro dialect which featured characters such as Brer Rabbit and Brer Fox.

Harun al-Rashid (763–809)
Harun (or Haroun) al-Rashid was a famous caliph (ruler) of Baghdad. He is celebrated in the *Arabian Nights* as an ideal king, but the truth is that he could be cruel and extravagant. He left the government of his empire to a family called the Barmecides, and their skill and energy made Baghdad prosperous. Meanwhile, Harun became famous for his hospitality and learning, and artists and scholars flocked to his court. In 803, Harun was suddenly seized by jealousy or fear of the Barmecides, and he ordered that every member of the family be executed, even his close friends and favorites. Harun himself died while suppressing a rebellion in Khurasan.

Harvey, William (1578–1657)
An English doctor who discovered that blood circulates around the body, and is pumped by the heart. He studied at Cambridge in England, and then under the great Italian doctor Fabricius at the city of Padua. In 1628 he published *An Anatomical Exercise on the Motion of the Heart and the Blood in Animals*, in which he said that "the blood performs a kind of circular motion." He worked on this subject for much of the rest of his life, as well as being the doctor to two English kings, James I and Charles I. ○ FABRICIUS

Hawthorne, Nathaniel (1804–64)
Hawthorne was an American writer. He lived for some years in a remote, wooded part of the state of Maine and then in solitude in the town of Salem, Massachusetts. In 1839 he became a customs officer, and then joined an early socialist commune near Boston. In 1842 he was married and returned to his customs job in Salem. He wrote a great deal, but at first with little success. His most famous novel is *The Scarlet Letter*, completed in 1850, which is set in a community of Puritan settlers in New England. He also wrote a popular collection of children's stories, the *Tanglewood Tales* (1850). In 1853 Hawthorne became the United States consul in Liverpool, England, and from there visited Italy, which inspired his last complete novel, *The Marble Faun* (1860).

Nathaniel Hawthorne, one of America's greatest writers.

Haydn, Franz Joseph (1732–1809)
Haydn was an Austrian composer who had a great influence on European music, both in his own and later times. He wrote 104 symphonies, 50 concertos, and over 80 quartets, as well as choral works and other instrumental music; he was Mozart's teacher and friend, and for a short time Beethoven's teacher. Haydn was the son of a wheelwright, and as a boy he attended the choir school of St. Stephen's Cathedral in Vienna. His first jobs were playing in the city's street orchestras, but in 1761 he became music master for the wealthy Esterházy family, where he remained for 30 years. He first met Mozart in 1781, and in 1790 Haydn visited England, where his music was very popular. Among his greatest works are the choral pieces he wrote late in life, including *The Creation* (written in 1798) and a mass known as the "Nelson" Mass (1798). He died in Vienna.
○ BEETHOVEN, MOZART

Hearst, William Randolph (1863–1951)
An American newspaper owner who revolutionized journalism by introducing large amounts of illustration, huge "banner" headlines, and a sensational style of writing. He took over the San Francisco *Examiner*, which was owned by his father, in 1887, and by 1925 owned 25 papers in many cities.

Hegel, Georg Wilhelm Friedrich (1770–1831)
Hegel was a German philosopher whose ideas, together with those of Kant, dominated European thought in the 19th century. He was born in Stuttgart and first studied theology, although at the same time he wrote and edited articles on philosophy. Hegel became a professor at the university at Jena, but in 1806 Napolean closed the university and he had to work as a newspaper editor. From 1808 until 1816 he was the headmaster of a school, where he tried to teach his pupils some of his very complicated ideas! Finally, in 1818, Hegel became professor of philosophy at Berlin. One of his most important ideas was that of the "dialectic." Hegel said that the answer to a problem could be found by giving first one answer, then the opposite answer, and then combining *both* answers to discover the truth. This theory influenced many later thinkers, including Karl Marx and Jean Paul Sartre. Hegel remained at Berlin until his death. ○ KANT, MARX, SARTRE

Heifetz, Jascha (1901–)
Heifetz is a Russian-born violinist who now lives in the United States. He performed his first full concerto at the age of only 5, and was playing concerts in St. Petersburg at 10. After the Russian Revolution (1917) he traveled to the United States. He was famous for the accuracy and fine tone of his playing. William Walton's violin concerto was written for him. ○ WALTON

Heine, Heinrich (1797–1856)
Heine is considered one of the greatest German poets. He was born into a Jewish family in the city of Düsseldorf. He first tried to set up a bank, but when this failed went to university and studied law, literature, and philosophy. His first collection of poems, *Pictures of Travel*, was published in 1826, followed by the *Book of Songs* the next year. Both books were very successful, and Heine became well known. In 1825 he was baptized and became a Christian so that he could gain German citizenship, but in 1831 he traveled to Paris in support of the revolution taking place there, and he never returned to Germany. His poems are often about love or politics, and his own agonized feelings about these things. He tried, through his writing, to get the French and the Germans to recognize the things they had in common. In 1848 Heine began to suffer paralysis, and spent the rest of his life in great pain.

The American novelist Ernest Hemingway. A Farewell to Arms *(1929) and* For Whom the Bell Tolls *(1940) deal with the horrors of war. He was an ambulance driver in World War I.*

Hemingway, Ernest Miller (1899–1961)
Hemingway was an American novelist, born in the state of Illinois. He took part in World War I and the Spanish Civil War, and these experiences provided the inspiration for several of his books. Among the best known are *For Whom the Bell Tolls* (1940) and *The Old Man and the Sea* (1952), which won a Pulitzer Prize. Hemingway also wrote many fine short stories.

Henry IV (1367–1413)
Henry IV became king of England in 1399 by overthrowing **Richard II** (1367–1400). He was the son of the nobleman **John of Gaunt** (1340–1399) and a distinguished soldier. In 1397 King Richard was threatened by a rebellion led by the Duke of Gloucester. Henry supported the king, and as a reward he was made Duke of Hereford. But the following year Richard banished Henry and then confiscated his lands. Henry returned with an army, and in September 1399 forced Richard to renounce his crown. The former king starved to death in Pontefract Castle in Yorkshire. Meanwhile, Henry's reign was troubled by war and rebellion. Owen Glendower led an uprising in Wales, and there were invasion attempts from France. At the end of his life he became secretive.
○ HENRY V, OWEN GLENDOWER

Henry V (1387–1422)
Henry V succeeded his father, Henry IV, as king of England in 1413. His ambition was to recover the French kingdom which he believed to be rightly his. He invaded France in 1415 and at the Battle of Agincourt on October 25 defeated a greater French army. The French king, Charles VI, agreed that Henry should succeed him and marry his daughter Catherine of Valois (1401–37). He died two years later, leaving only the child **Henry VI** (1421–71) to succeed him. ○ EDWARD III, OWEN GLENDOWER

Henry VIII (1491–1547)
Henry VIII was king of England from 1509. As a young prince he was handsome, a skilled hunter, musician, and poet, and popular with the people, so when he became king there was plenty of rejoicing. Together with his minister Wolsey, Henry succeeded in making England a powerful European nation. First, he joined the "Holy League" of Spain and Pope Julius II against France, and defeated the French at the Battle of "the Spurs" in 1513. At the same time, the English defeated their enemies the Scots (who were allied with France) at the Battle of Flodden. Henry continued to support the Spanish, led by the Emperor Charles V, against the French until 1525, when he realized that Spain was becoming too powerful and changed sides so as to maintain a balance of power.

At about this time, Henry decided that he wanted to leave his first wife, Catherine of Aragon, and marry Anne Boleyn. The Pope refused to grant Henry a divorce. Wolsey was sent on a mission to Rome to try to persuade the Pope, but failed. The Archbishop of Canterbury, Thomas Cranmer,

King Henry VIII of England.

declared Henry's marriage to Catherine invalid in 1533 and, in defiance of the Pope, Henry married Anne. In 1534, the English Parliament agreed to break all links with the Pope, and declared Henry supreme head of the Church. This was the most important event of Henry's reign.

Henry had four more wives after Anne Boleyn was beheaded in 1536: **Jane Seymour** (1509–37), **Anne of Cleves** (1517–57), **Catherine Howard** (d. 1542), and **Catherine Parr** (1512–48).
○ BOLEYN, CHARLES V, CRANMER, ELIZABETH I, FRANCIS I, JULIUS II, MORE, WOLSEY

Henry of Navarre (1553–1610)
Henry, king of the kingdom of Navarre, became King Henry IV of France in 1589. He was a Protestant, and in 1572 he married **Marguerite de Valois** (1553–1615), the sister of the French King Charles IX. The wedding became the occasion of the Massacre of St. Bartholemew, in which 4,000 French Protestants (known as the "Huguenots") were killed by Catholics. Henry was forced to declare himself a Catholic, but in 1576 he escaped to the south, where he took command of an army and made himself the leader of the French Protestants. When King Henry III was murdered in 1589, Henry of Navarre found himself heir to the throne. Many Catholic noblemen opposed him, and he was forced to fight a four-year civil war before he could claim his crown. Even then, in order to enter Paris safely, he had to convert once again to Catholicism. He is believed to have said: "Paris is worth a mass." In 1598 he issued the Edict of Nantes, which guaranteed religious freedom to the Protestants in France.

Herod the Great (*c.*72 B.C.–4 B.C.)
"Herod" was the name of a powerful family that lived in Judea in the 1st Century B.C. Herod the Great was appointed to the post of procurator of Judea by Julius Caesar. In the year 40 B.C. he was given the title "Tetrarch" by Mark Antony, and then in 31 B.C. Augustus made him king. He was a cruel and suspicious ruler who murdered many rivals, and even members of his own family. The Bible tells how Herod, when he heard that a "king" named Jesus had been born at Bethlehem, ordered all the infants in the town to be slaughtered. This may or may not be true, but it is certainly possible because Herod committed so many other massacres. Herod had 10 wives and 14 children. One of his sons, **Herod Antipas** (d. *c.*A.D. 40), became Tetrarch of Galilee. It was to this Herod that Jesus was sent for trial by Pontius Pilate, although Herod refused to make any judgment. ○ PILATE

Herodotus (*c.*485 B.C.–425 B.C.)
Herodotus was an ancient Greek historian. He has been called the "father of history," because his work not only described events, but for the first time tried to explain why they had taken place. Herodotus was born in Halicarnassus. He traveled a great deal, collecting historical, geographical, and archaeological information, and then in 443 B.C. settled in the Athenian colony of Thurii. Here he wrote his great history of the wars between Greece and Persia, beginning with the reign of King Croesus of Lydia, and covering the two great wars between the two empires.

Herschel, Frederick William (1738–1822)
Frederick Herschel was a German-born astronomer who lived and worked in England, and who in 1781 discovered the planet Uranus. He was the son of a poor musician, and for many years made his own living playing the oboe. In 1776 he became an organist in the English city of Bath, where be began making telescopes. It was with his own 51-inch telescope that he first saw Uranus. At first he thought the object was a comet, but then realized it must be a planet. His discovery earned him a salary from the king, and Herschel was able to give all his time to astronomy. Together with his sister (**Caroline Lucretia Herschel**, 1750–1848) he made many catalogs and observed many new stars and nebulas. His son, **John Frederick William Herschel** (1792–1871), also became an astronomer. His most famous work was a catalog of the stars of the southern hemisphere, which he made while living at the Cape of Good Hope.

Hertz, Heinrich Rudolf (1857–94)
A German physicist. Hertz carried out experiments on the relationship between light and electricity, and proved that light is a form of electromagnetic radiation. His discovery of electromagnetic waves enabled Marconi to send the first wireless signals.
○ CLERK MAXWELL, MARCONI

Hesse, Hermann (1877–1962)
A German poet and novelist. Hesse was a bookseller in the Swiss city of Basel, and published his first novel in 1904. His works include *Steppenwolf* (1927) and *The Glass Bead Game* (1943). He was awarded the Nobel Prize for Literature in 1946.

Heyerdahl, Thor (1914–)
Heyerdahl is a Norwegian anthropologist and explorer. He has been particularly interested in ancient sea travelers, and has attempted to re-create and sail ancient ships. His most famous voyage was made in 1947 in a balsa wood raft called the *Kon Tiki* from Peru to Polynesia, in order to prove that Peruvian natives might have settled in the Polynesian Islands long ago. Heyerdahl has also sailed across the Atlantic in a reed boat and navigated ancient trade routes in the Far East.

Hill, Rowland (1795–1879)
Hill is thought of as the "inventor" of the modern postal system. In 1837 he suggested that letters could be sent throughout the British Isles for the cost of only one penny, and that the postage could be paid for in advance by buying a "stamp." Until then, the cost of sending a letter depended on the distance it was sent, but Hill's system made letter sending affordable for everybody.

Hillary, Sir Edmund (1919–)
Edmund Hillary is a New Zealand mountaineer and explorer who in 1953 became the first man to reach the summit of Mount Everest, the world's highest peak. He was born in Auckland, where he attended university and then joined the New Zealand air force. In 1952 he was a member of a British expedition which explored the area around Mount Everest, and then in 1953 he joined a team attempting to climb the mountain led by **John Hunt** (1910–). On May 29 he and a Sherpa, Tenzing Norgay, succeeded in reaching the top. In 1958 Hillary became the first man to reach the South Pole since Scott in 1911, and in 1977 he led an expedition which traveled from the mouth to the source on the Ganges River in India. ○ TENZING

The Conquest of Mount Everest

September 1952: Expedition planning begins.
March 1953: Expedition arrives at Katmandu in Nepal.
April 12, 1953: Climbers set up Base Camp at 17,900 feet. They begin establishing a series of camps higher up the mountain to serve as supply and resting points.
May 17, 1953: Camp 7 set up at 24,000 feet. Preparations for the summit attempt begin.
May 26, 1953: First attempt: Climbers reach "South Summit" of Everest before turning back.
May 28, 1953: Second attempt begins. Hillary and Tenzing camp at 27,900 feet.
May 29, 1953: Hillary and Tenzing reach summit.
May 31, 1953: Hillary and Tenzing return to base camp.
June 2, 1953: News of success reaches London.
June 7, 1953: Expedition leaves Mount Everest.

Sir Edmund Hillary and Tenzing Norgay.

Hilliard, Nicholas (1537–1619)
Hilliard could be said to have been the first great English painter. He was trained as a jeweler, and specialized in tiny, delicate "miniature" portraits of the English nobility. He worked for Queen Elizabeth I and King James I and was well known, although he does not seem to have become rich.

A painting by Nicholas Hilliard.

Hippocrates (*c.*460 B.C.–*c.*375 B.C.)
Hippocrates was an ancient Greek doctor. He is known as the "father of medicine" because he was the first person to make a science out of the study and treatment of illness. Hippocrates was born and worked on the island of Cos, where there was a medical school. He is named as the author of over 70 books and treatises, but many of these were probably written by his students. They contain descriptions of diseases, methods of treatment, and even of the surgical tools used by the ancient Greeks. His treatments included careful diet, a cautious use of drugs, and occasionally surgery. Hippocrates also wrote down a set of rules for doctors, and these survive today in the Hippocratic Oath taken by medical students in many countries when they qualify.

Hirohito (1901–   )
Emperor of Japan since 1926. Hirohito was the first Japanese prince to visit Europe (in 1921). His reign was marked by increasing militarism in Japan, and after World War II he gave up most of his powers and became a constitutional head of state.

Hitchcock, Sir Alfred (1899–1980)
Hitchcock was an English film maker famous for his thrillers. He became known as "the master of suspense." His first film was silent: *The Pleasure Garden*, made in 1925, but Hitchcock quickly began making the new "talkie" movies. The earliest of these included *The Lady Vanishes* (1938) and *The Thirty-Nine Steps* (1935). In 1940 he moved to Hollywood, California, where he had an immediate success with *Rebecca*. Hitchcock always appears somewhere in the films he directed—usually in the background or in a busy crowd scene. His other works include *Psycho* (1960) and *The Birds* (1963).

Hitler, Adolf (1889–1945)
Adolf Hitler was the leader of Germany from 1933 until 1945. His policies led directly to the outbreak of World War II. Hitler was born in the town of Braunau in Austria. At the beginning of World War I in 1914 he joined the German army, in which he became a corporal and was decorated with the Iron Cross.

In 1919, Hitler joined a tiny political party in Munich, which blamed the government for Germany's defeat in World War I and wanted to rebuild the country's military strength. He became the party's leader and renamed it the National

German leader (Führer) Adolf Hitler and British Prime Minister Neville Chamberlain met at Munich in 1938.

Socialist or "Nazi" Party. In 1923 Hitler spent nine months in prison after trying to overthrow the Bavarian government. He wrote a book called *Mein Kampf* ("My Struggle") in which he set out his political ideas. After his release, Hitler continued to strengthen the Nazi Party. He was given support by wealthy industrialists, who saw the Nazis as opponents of Communism. By 1932, over 200 members of the Nazi Party had been elected to the German parliament, and in January 1933 Hitler became the German Chancellor (prime minister). When a mysterious fire (probably started by the Nazis themselves) destroyed the parliament building in February 1933, Hitler claimed it had been the work of Communists, and declared himself complete dictator.

Hitler thought the Germans were "superior" to other peoples, and planned an empire which would completely dominate Europe. He built up the country's armed forces, made alliances with Italy and Japan, then occupied Austria and Czechoslovakia. Great Britain and France protested at the invasion of Czechoslovakia, and at the Munich Conference in 1938, Hitler agreed to keep the peace in future. But in 1939, German armies invaded Poland. Britain and France objected, and World War II began on September 3. Hitler quickly overran Poland, France, and the rest of Western Europe, but in the Battle of Britain in 1940 he was unable to defeat the British air force. In 1941 he invaded Russia, and was at first successful, but by the end of 1942 the vast strength of the Russians had begun to defeat the German army. American and British armies invaded France in 1944, and by April 1945 Hitler was trapped by the Russian army in his bombproof bunker in Berlin. There, on April 30, he shot himself. Hitler's plan for Europe had led to the extermination of over six million Jews, gypsies, Slavs, and others in concentration camps, and after the war many surviving Nazis were put on trial as "war criminals," ○ CHAMBERLAIN, CHURCHILL, STALIN

Hobbes, Thomas (1588–1679)
Hobbes was a great English philosopher. He met many of the best thinkers of his time, including Galileo, Descartes, and Bacon, and was tutor to the young Charles II of Britain. His most famous work is *Leviathan*, published in 1651.

The English philosopher Thomas Hobbes. He believed that social order should be based on human co-operation rather than ruling authority.

Ho Chi Minh (1890–1969)
Ho Chi Minh was a Vietnamese Communist leader, who served as president of Vietnam from 1945 until 1954, and then as president of North Vietnam from 1954 until his death. He left his home city of Annam in central Vietnam in 1911 and became a sailor, visiting the United States and Europe. For a time he worked for a photographer, and as an assistant to the famous French chef Escoffier. In 1920 he helped found the French Communist Party, and then visited Moscow, Hong Kong, and parts of China. He returned to Vietnam in 1935 to begin the Communist "Vietnam League for Independence," known as the "Viet Minh." During World War II Ho led guerrilla raids against the Japanese army, and after the Japanese defeat in 1945 he declared himself president of Vietnam. For eight years he was opposed by the French, and Vietnam was eventually divided into two parts, with Ho Chi Minh president of the north, and a French-supported leader in the south. In 1959 war began again between north and south, with the United States becoming involved on the side of the south. When Saigon was captured by the North Vietnamese in 1975, it was renamed Ho Chi Minh City in Ho's honor.

Hockney, David (1937–)
David Hockney is an English artist whose most famous works include portraits of Celia Birtwell

and Ossie Clark and *A Bigger Splash* (1970). In 1978 he designed a set for a production of Mozart's opera *The Magic Flute.*

Hogan, Ben (1912–)
An American golfer who won over 60 tournaments, including several U.S. Open titles. In 1949 he was seriously injured in a car accident and his doctors told him he would not be able to play again. However, his determination brought him back to win the U.S. Open only a year later.

Hogarth, William (1697–1764)
Hogarth was an English painter and engraver who is best known for his prints on moral subjects, which are rather like modern cartoons. These include *The Rake's Progress* and *A Harlot's Progress,* which illustrates the downfall of a country girl when she moves to London. Hogarth was strongly influenced by the literature of his time, and said: "My picture is my stage, and men and women my players."

Hokusai, Katsushika (1760–1849)
Hokusai was a Japanese artist. He became famous in Europe at the beginning of the 20th century for his delicately colored woodblock prints of Japanese city scenes, landscapes, and people. These include the beautiful *Views of Mount Fuji,* which show the famous Japanese mountain from many directions and in many moods. Hokusai amazed people with demonstrations of his artistic skill: it is said that he could paint the outline of a bird on a grain of corn. Hokusai greatly influenced European artists such as Toulouse-Lautrec and Gauguin.

View of Mount Fuji *by the Japanese artist Katsushika Hokusai.*

Holbein, Hans (1497–1543)
Hans Holbein "the Younger" was one of northern Europe's greatest painters. He was born in the German city of Augsburg, where his father, Hans Holbein "the Elder," was also a painter. In about 1515 he moved to Basel in Switzerland, where he produced portraits and prints, including illustrations for Luther's Bible. He met the scholar Erasmus, and in 1526 traveled to England, where he met—and later painted—Sir Thomas More. Among his works are many portraits of the English King Henry VIII. It was during his stay in London that he painted the famous *The Ambassadors,* a mysterious portrait of two English lords which includes a huge distorted skull in the foreground.
○ HENRY VIII, LUTHER, MORE

Holiday, Billie (1915–59)
An American jazz singer born in Baltimore. She was discovered singing in a club in the Harlem district of New York City and made her first records with Benny Goodman's band. She was never trained but became one of the most popular of all jazz artists. ○ GOODMAN

Holmes, Oliver Wendell (1809–94)
Holmes was an American writer and doctor. He studied law at Harvard University, but gave the subject up to become a doctor. He became a successful writer with the publication of a collection of essays, *The Autocrat of the Breakfast Table,* in 1858, and continued to write novels, poems, and articles. His son, also named **Oliver Wendell Holmes** (1841–1935), was an associate justice of the Supreme Court.

Holst, Gustav Theodore (1874–1934)
Gustav Holst was a British composer of Swedish descent. He was deeply influenced by English folk music. His most famous work is *The Planets.*

Homer
See pages 128 & 129

Homer, Winslow (1836–1910)
Winslow Homer was an American painter, best known for his watercolors of coastal and country scenes. He was born in Boston, where he made a living working as a magazine illustrator. During the American Civil War he worked as a reporter, sending drawings from the lines to *Harper's* magazine. His famous coastal scenes were painted in the 1880s during visits to the coast of the state of Maine.

Gods and Heroes

A bronze head of Apollo, the Greek god of poetry, the arts, and prophecy.

Menelaus, king of Sparta, with his wife Helen of Troy. Paris, a Trojan prince, persuaded Helen to elope with him to Troy. Menelaus and his brother Agamemnon gathered an army and attacked Troy. This started the Trojan War.

Homer

The ancient Greeks considered Homer the father of all literature. He was, according to tradition, the author of two great poems, the *Iliad* and the *Odyssey*, which became the source of countless stories, plays, and poems in later centuries. Moreover, Homer's poems dealt with the greatest event in Greek history: the Trojan War and the feats of the warrior-heroes who fought there.

There is no certainty as to when or where Homer lived, or even whether he existed at all. Many stories describe him as a blind poet, wandering from city to city, gathering audiences and speaking his poems out loud. Homer was not an author in the modern sense: he did not *write* his poems, but recited them from memory. It is very likely that the stories he told had been passed to him from earlier poets—and that he, in turn, passed them on to a younger generation. The *Iliad* and the *Odyssey* are very old, almost the oldest works in Western literature, but they were not written down until about the 6th century B.C., during the reign of the Athenian tyrant Peisistratus. "Homer" is the name that the Greeks and later peoples gave to the poet, but it is impossible to say how many times the stories had been retold and changed through the centuries.

The Trojan War began when Paris, a Trojan prince, seduced Helen, the wife of the Greek King Menelaus, and took her back to Troy. The Greeks assembled their finest warriors and set sail in pursuit. They camped for ten years outside the walls of Troy, waiting for the victory the gods had promised them. Finally they entered the city hidden in a huge wooden horse. As the Trojans slept, the Greek warriors emerged from their hiding place, and burned the city.

The *Iliad* tells the story of the Greek hero Achilles, who is angered when Agamemnon, the Greek commander, steals his mistress. Achilles refuses to fight, and persuades the gods to help the Trojans and show the Greeks how much they need him. But as the Greeks are forced to retreat toward their ships, Achilles' friend Patroklos is killed by Hector, a Trojan warrior. Achilles now puts on his armor and goes out to fight Hector. The two men face each other outside the walls of Troy: they are heroes of supernatural strength and agility—but nothing happens

Homer's Iliad *describes some of the events that occurred during the last year of the siege of Troy. The* Iliad *ends with Hector's burial. The fall of Troy is described in the* Aeneid, *an epic poem by the Roman poet Virgil. The Greeks built a huge wooden horse and placed it outside the walls of Troy. Odysseus and some other warriors hid inside the horse while the rest of the Greek army sailed away. The Trojans believed that the horse was sacred and would bring the protection of the gods. They pulled the horse into Troy. That night the Greeks crept out of the horse, opened the city gates, and let in the rest of the army who had returned. The Greeks took Helen and burned the city.*

> "Men in their generations are like the leaves of the trees. The wind blows and one year's leaves are scattered on the ground; but the trees burst into bud and put on fresh ones when the spring comes around." *Iliad*

without the will of the gods, and the gods have decided that Hector will be defeated. Hector flees, but is tricked by the goddess Athene into turning to face Achilles. That is the end of Hector, and Achilles drags his body through the dust of the battlefield before surrendering it to the Trojan King Priam.

The *Odyssey* returns to the story at the end of the war, when the Trojans have been defeated and the Greeks are preparing to leave. It tells of the wanderings of Odysseus, a Greek hero, as he tries to return home. He is beset by storms, strange temptations, and fearsome monsters as he travels around the Mediterranean. Finally, the gods allow him to return. ○ AESCHYLUS, EURIPIDES, PEISISTRATUS

Honda, Soichiro (1906–)
Honda is a Japanese engineer who began making motorcycles at the end of the World War II. He bought twelve engines and attached them to lightweight frames in a small shed. Today, the Honda company exports millions of efficient, reliable motorcycles all over the world.

Hoover, Herbert Clark (1874–1964)
The thirty-first president of the United States, from 1928 until 1932. He became well known as an organizer of famine relief in Europe at the time of World War I. As president, he was unpopular because he opposed government measures to improve the economy and help the unemployed during the Great Depression of the early 1930s. He was defeated by Roosevelt in 1932. ○ F. D. ROOSEVELT

Hopkins, Sir Frederick Gowland (1861–1947)
Frederick Hopkins was a British biochemist who in 1912 discovered the existence of vitamins.

Hopkins, Gerard Manley (1844–89)
Gerard Manley Hopkins was an English poet and a Jesuit priest. His bold technical innovation was a great influence on the development of modern English poetry. By his own wish his poetry was not published during his lifetime. His poems include *The Windhover* (1877) and *Pied Beauty*.

Hopper, Edward (1882–1967)
Hopper was an artist who painted bold, realistic pictures of American landscapes, buildings, and people. He lived for most of his life in New York. For many years he was unable to sell his paintings and made money illustrating advertisements and magazines. His pictures often convey a sense of loneliness, showing people alone in the city, restaurants, or hotels. But he also painted some fine rural scenes and seascapes, as well as pictures of the distinctive buildings to be found along the east coast of the United States.

Horace (Quintus Horace Flaccus, 65 B.C.–8 B.C.)
Horace was a Roman poet. He was the son of a slave who had been freed, and who had saved enough money to send the young Horace to school in Rome and then in Athens. During the civil war between Brutus and Mark Antony which took place after Caesar's death, Horace was an officer in Brutus' army. After Brutus' defeat he fled, but later returned to Rome, where he met the poet Virgil. Virgil introduced him to people in the Emperor Augustus' government, and he was given a villa and a salary so that he could write in peace. Among his works are the *Satires* and the *Odes*. Horace invented a new form of poem, the *Epistle*, in which the poem takes the form of a letter to somebody, and he invented many phrases that have survived as proverbs to this day. ○ AUGUSTUS, BRUTUS, VIRGIL

Houdini, Harry (1874–1926)
Houdini was a famous Hungarian-American escapologist—somebody who escapes from seemingly impossible combinations of locks, chains, and boxes. His ability made him famous throughout the world at the beginning of the 20th century.

Howe, Julia Ward (1819–1910)
Julia Howe was an American author, lecturer, and suffragette. She wrote *Battle Hymn of the Republic.* She was an active campaigner for women's rights, world peace, and other reforms.

Hoyle, Sir Fred (1915–)
An English astronomer and mathematician. He became famous in 1948 for the "steady-state" theory of the universe, in which he stated that the *density* of matter in the universe would remain constant, because new matter is created as the universe grows bigger. He has become a successful writer.

Hubble, Edwin Powell (1889–1953)
Hubble was an American astronomer whose research led to new discoveries about galaxies, and about the nature of the universe. From 1919 he worked at the giant Mount Wilson telescope in California. He discovered other galaxies similar to the earth's own galaxy, and showed that they are all traveling away from each other at great speeds, so the universe is in fact expanding.

Hudson, Henry (d. 1611)
Hudson was an English explorer who made several voyages into the Arctic oceans trying to find a northerly route to India. In April 1610 he left England in the *Discoverie*, sailed to Greenland, and from there up the Hudson Strait and into the great bay that is named after him—Hudson Bay. He decided to spend the winter in the bay, but eventually he and his crew began to run out of food. The crew mutinied and cast Hudson adrift in

a small open boat. Hudson was never seen again, but his crew returned safely to England.

Hughes, Howard (1905–76)
Howard Hughes was a mysterious and eccentric American millionaire who became involved in the oil business, film making, and aviation. His great wealth came from his father's oil-drilling equipment company. In 1926 Hughes suddenly decided to make films, including *Hell's Angels* and *Scarface*. Six years later he left the film industry and became involved in aviation, founding the Hughes Aircraft Company. He designed and flew his own planes, and three times broke the world speed record. During the 1940s he made some more films, then returned to designing aircraft and built the giant *Spruce Goose*, a seaplane intended to carry troops, but which only flew once, for less than a mile, piloted by Hughes himself. He was the principal owner of the airline TWA, although he eventually sold his shares for over $500 million. At the end of his life Hughes became a complete recluse, surrounded by mystery and rumor.

Hughes, Ted (1930–)
Hughes is an English poet. His work includes *The Hawk in the Rain* and *Crow*, as well as a number of children's books. He was married to the American poet, Sylvia Plath. In 1984 he became England's poet laureate. ○ PLATH

Hugo, Victor Marie (1802–85)
Victor Hugo was a French novelist, poet, and playwright. He was the son of a general in Napoleon's army, and spent much of his boyhood traveling around Europe. He won prizes for his poems while he was still a teenager, and published his first novel at the age of 17. His first successes were plays, including *Hernani*, which was first performed in 1830 and enjoyed a long run on the Paris stage. At about the same time he was writing his famous novel *Notre Dame de Paris*, about the love of the hunchbacked bell ringer Quasimodo for the beautiful Esmeralda. Hugo's greatest novel is *Les Misérables* (published in 1862). He wrote a vast quantity, as well as being involved in French politics.

Humboldt, Friedrich Heinrich Alexander von (1769–1859)
Humboldt was a German scientist and explorer. In 1799 he sailed on an expedition to Central and South America, visiting Mexico, Cuba, and the Amazon forest. He collected samples of wildlife, recorded the weather, investigated geography and geology, made maps, and studied the stars. On his return to Paris, Humboldt began the work of organizing and publishing his research, while at the same time conducting experiments with Gay-Lussac on the composition of the atmosphere. In 1829 he made a journey to Asia to investigate the geography of that region. ○ GAY-LUSSAC

Hume, David (1711–76)
Hume was a Scottish historian and philosopher. Between the ages of 20 and 25 he wrote his greatest work, the *Treatise of Human Nature*, which has remained one of the most important works in all of British philosophy. Hume was an "empiricist," which is to say that he believed that all ideas are based on people's experiences. He lived in Edinburgh, France, and England, and for a time worked as a diplomat.

Hurston, Zora Neale (*c.*1900–60)
Zora Neale Hurston was a black American writer. She wrote novels, stories, and articles, as well as collecting the folk stories told by black people in the American South. Her most famous book is *Their Eyes Were Watching God*, first published in 1937.

Huygens, Christiaan (1629–95)
A Dutch astronomer who developed the techniques of making lenses and invented an eyepiece for the telescope. This enabled him to investigate, among other things, the rings around the planet Saturn. He also improved the design of pendulum clocks.

The first working pendulum clock was invented in Holland in 1657 by Christiaan Huygens.

I

Ibn Batuta (1304–68)
Ibn Batuta was a great Arab traveler and explorer, who visited many of the same parts of the world as Marco Polo had just 50 years earlier. He was born in Tangier, and in about 1325 began exploring North Africa and the Middle East. From Persia and Mesopotamia he went on to cross the Black Sea and ventured into India. After having many adventures, he finally reached China, before returning home to Morocco in 1349. He wrote a description of his journey called *Travels in Asia and Africa.*

Ibsen, Henrik Johan (1828–1906)
Ibsen was a great Norwegian playwright. His plays deal realistically with ordinary men and women and the problems they face living in modern society. Ibsen was born in the town of Skien. As a young man he worked as an apothecary's apprentice, a journalist, and then as a theater manager. During this time he wrote several historical plays, before leaving Norway in 1864 to live in Italy and Germany. He returned two years later, and continued to write plays and work in the theater. Ibsen's famous works were written late in his life. They were often controversial, and offended many people who saw them because they dealt frankly with social issues such as divorce and disease. *The Doll's House,* first performed in 1879, tells the story of a woman who feels humiliated by her married life, and so leaves her husband and children. Many of the play's audience found this unacceptable and immoral. Ibsen's other works include *Ghosts* (1881), *The Wild Duck* (1884), and *Hedda Gabler* (1890). Ibsen suffered a stroke in 1900 and was unable to write any more. His work influenced many other European writers, and he is one of the most important of all modern playwrights.

The Norwegian playwright, Henrik Ibsen. His plays dealt with contemporary society and situations.

Imhotep (*c.*2800 B.C.)
Imhotep was an ancient Egyptian doctor and wise man. He was an adviser to the Egyptian King Zoser, and was probably the designer of the famous "step" pyramid at Saqqara, near Cairo. The ancient Greeks linked him with their own god of medicine, Aesculapius, because of his fame as a doctor.

Ingalls Wilder, Laura (1867–1957)
Laura Ingalls Wilder was the author of a famous series of children's books that describe life on the American frontier at the end of the 19th century. She was born in the state of Wisconsin, where her family lived a rugged pioneer life, living from the land and the woods and moving from place to place. Her books include *The Little House in the Big Woods* (1932) and *The Little House on the Prairie* (1935). In *Farmer Boy,* published in 1933, she describes her husband Almanzo Wilder's childhood, and in *These Happy Golden Years* (1934) she describes their courtship and marriage.

Ingres, Jean Auguste Dominique (1780–1867)
Ingres was a 19th-century French painter. He was born at the town of Montaubon, where his father was a sculptor. His father recognized the young

Oedipus and the Sphinx *by the French artist Ingres.*

Ingres's skill at drawing and sent him first to art school, then to Paris to study with the great Jacques David. Ingres's first success was a painting called *Ambassadors of Agamemnon,* which won a prize in an exhibition in Rome in 1802. He continued to live in Italy for several years, painting portraits and the nude figures for which he is most famous, before returning to Paris in 1841. He considered the ability to draw a painter's most important skill, saying "a thing well drawn is well enough painted." ○ DAVID

Innocent III (1161–1216)
Innocent III was one of the most important popes of the Middle Ages. He was elected in 1198, and his leadership made the Roman Catholic Church powerful throughout Europe. Innocent thought the Church should take part in the everyday government of countries. He brought England and Ireland under his influence after excommunicating King John, and was able to have the king of his choice elected Holy Roman Emperor in Germany. He was in favor of the spread of monasteries, and during his reign the Fourth Crusade captured Constantinople from the Muslims. ○ JOHN

Ionesco, Eugène (1912–)
Ionesco was a Romanian-born playwright who lived and worked in France. He is famous as one of the pioneers of the "theater of the absurd"—plays which do not immediately seem to make sense. His most famous work is *The Bald Soprano,* (1950).

Irving, Washington (1783–1859)
Washington Irving was an American writer and diplomat. He was born in New York, but in 1804 he was sent to Europe because of poor health. He visited several countries, including Italy, France, and Britain, where he made friends with the writer Walter Scott. He is remembered for essays and articles, collected in books such as *The Sketch Book* and *Tales of a Traveller,* but his best-known works are *Rip Van Winkle,* and *The Legend of Sleepy Hollow.*

Isaiah (*c.*700 B.C.)
Isaiah was an important Hebrew prophet. He began making prophecies in the Temple in Jerusalem in about the year 747 B.C., and remained there until about 700 B.C. Little is known of his life, although there is a story that he was sawn to death during a period of religious persecution. His prophecies are recorded in the Book of Isaiah in the Old Testament. Among them, he foresees the coming of the Messiah.

Ivan III, "the Great" (1440–1505)
Ivan III became Grand Duke of Moscow (then known as Muscovy) in 1462. He led successful military campaigns in which he chased the Tartar tribes out of Russia, and then conquered several small northern kingdoms. In 1472 he married a Byzantine princess named Sophia, and declared himself ruler of all Russia. Under his government, many artists visited Moscow and were employed decorating the city's churches and palaces.

Ivan IV, "the Terrible" (1530–84)
Ivan the Terrible was the grandson of Ivan III, and the first Russian ruler to use the title "tsar." He was an energetic, efficient, and cruel monarch. Ivan came to power in 1547, at the age of only 17. He led the conquest of the provinces of Astrakhan and Siberia, which considerably enlarged his empire, and during the early part of his reign he introduced reforms which improved the systems of law and government in the country. In 1553 he made a treaty with Queen Elizabeth I of England, which regulated trade between the two nations after English merchants had found their way to the far northern port of Archangel. He even offered to marry the English queen. In the 1560s Ivan became increasingly suspicious of those around him. He introduced a secret police force and began a reign of terror in which thousands of people were slaughtered. In 1580 he killed his own son. It is said that this brought him to his senses, and that he afterward died of sorrow.

Ivan III, known as "the Great," laid the foundation of the Russian Empire whose first self-styled emperor was his grandson, Ivan IV, a vicious and cruel autocrat.

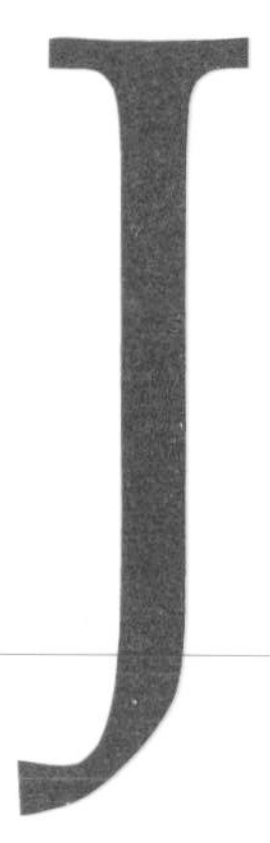

Jackson, Andrew (1767–1845)
Jackson was the seventh president of the United States. He was born in the state of South Carolina and became involved in politics in Tennessee. He was a successful soldier in the War of 1812 against the British and in battles against the native Indians. In 1824 Jackson, who was nicknamed "Old Hickory," was nominated for the presidency but lost to John Quincy Adams. He was elected in 1828, and served two terms. ○ ADAMS

Jackson, Thomas Jonathan, "Stonewall" (1824–63)
"Stonewall" Jackson was a Confederate general during the American Civil War who received his nickname for the strength of his defense at the Battle of Bull Run. He captured 13,000 Union troops at Harpers Ferry in 1862, and then saved General Robert E. Lee from defeat at the Battle of Sharpsburg. He died from a wound the following year. ○ LEE

Jagger, Mick (1943–)
Mick Jagger is the singer in the rock group the Rolling Stones. Together with **Keith Richards** (1943–) he has written most of the group's songs, including "Satisfaction" and "Jumpin' Jack Flash." The group first performed in 1962.

James I (1566–1625)
James was the only child of Mary Queen of Scots. When she was forced to abdicate from the Scottish throne in 1567 he became King James VI of Scotland. Then, after the death of Queen Elizabeth I, he became King James I of England and Scotland. Because James was only an infant when he inherited the Scottish crown, the country was ruled instead by powerful lords. When James took control in 1581, different groups of lords began competing for his favor. It was several years before the king was able to impose his authority.

Because Elizabeth I of England died without leaving an heir, James found himself next in line to the English throne. With his coronation in 1603, England and Scotland were properly united under one ruler for the first time. The kingdom was still divided by the religious disputes of Elizabeth's reign, and James tried to compromise between Protestant and Catholic factions. He listened to Protestant complaints about the Church of England, and sponsored the writing of a new "Authorized Version" of the Bible. But he abandoned Queen Elizabeth's anti-Catholic foreign policies, and even tried to arrange marriage between his son Charles and a Spanish princess. James believed in the "divine right of kings," meaning that he thought kings were responsible only to God and not to the Parliament or people. This did not always make him popular. He was a learned man, but he did not always govern wisely, and somebody once said that he was "the wisest fool in Christendom."
○ CHARLES I, ELIZABETH I, FAWKES, MARY

James VI of Scotland became in 1603 James I of England. From then on the crowns have been united.

James, Henry (1843–1916)
Henry James was an American novelist. He was born in New York but educated in Europe, and in 1869 he left the United States and lived for much of the rest of his life in England. Many of his novels are about the differences between American and European people and their manners. These include *The Europeans,* a charming story about a European princess and her brother who visit their cousins in New England, and *The Ambassadors,* which is about Americans in Paris. His other works include *Portrait of a Lady, The Golden Bowl,* and *The Turn of the Screw.* James's brother, **William James** (1842–1910), was a philosopher.

Jefferson, Thomas (1743–1826)
Jefferson was the third president of the United States. He was born in Shadwell, Virginia, and as a young man studied history, mathematics, and science, as well as learning several ancient and modern languages. He eventually became a lawyer, and in 1769 entered politics as a member of the Virginia state assembly. Jefferson soon joined the revolutionary party, which wanted to achieve independence for America. In 1775 and 1776 two Continental Congresses were held with this aim. At the second, it was Jefferson who made the first draft of the famous Declaration of Independence, which was signed by the delegates to the Congress on July 4. He returned to Virginia, where he helped establish the state's constitution and legal system. He was state governor from 1779 until 1781, then later a member of the United States Congress and an American diplomat in France.

In 1796 Jefferson became vice president after losing the election to John Adams. He was elected president in 1800, and then again in 1804. As president, he abolished the slave trade in the United States (1808), and in 1803 brought about the Louisiana Purchase by which the U.S. gained the French territories in the south of the country. In 1809 he retired from politics, although he continued to act as an adviser to the government. He spent the time making plans for the University of Virginia, which was opened in Charlottesville in 1825, and writing his autobiography. It was Jefferson who said: "The pen is mightier than the sword." ○ ADAMS, FRANKLIN, WASHINGTON

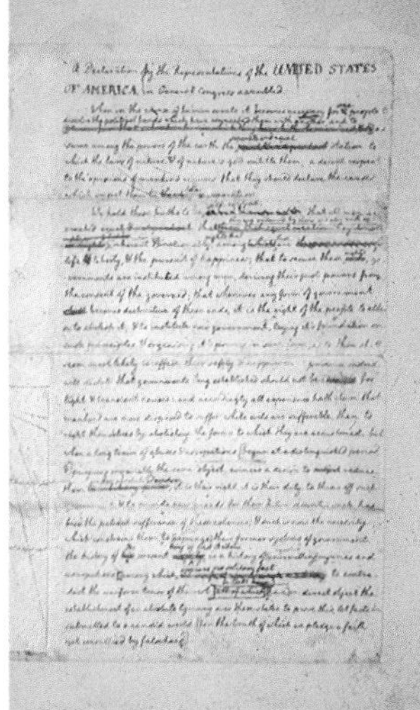

A Declaration by the Representatives of the UNITED STATES OF AMERICA, in General Congress assembled.

Thomas Jefferson, the third President of the U.S.A. It was Jefferson who made the rough draft of the Declaration of Independence (above).

Jenner, Edward (1749–1823)
Jenner was an English doctor who discovered the effectiveness of vaccination in preventing disease. After studying in London he returned to his country home in the county of Gloucestershire. He decided to investigate the local "superstition" that milkmaids who had suffered from the disease cowpox were immune to smallpox. He found that it was true: cowpox is a mild form of smallpox found in cows, and those who had had the disease were protected against the dangerous human version. The next step was to *inject* a small boy with cowpox and see if he would be protected. The experiment worked, and vaccinations of this sort quickly reduced the numbers of deaths from smallpox.

A mosaic of Jesus Christ. Byzantine artists specialized in this method of picture making.

Jesus of Nazareth (*c.*4 B.C.–A.D. 30)
Jesus was the founder of the Christian religion. The story of his life is told in the four gospels of the New Testament, written by Saints Matthew, Mark, Luke, and John. Jesus is also mentioned briefly by the Roman historians Suetonius and Tacitus. According to the gospels, he was born in the town of Bethlehem. His mother was Mary and his foster father was Joseph, a carpenter. Jesus was descended from the family of King David, and after his birth Herod, hearing of the new "king," ordered that all the infants in Bethlehem be killed. Jesus' parents escaped with him to Egypt, and then returned to their home in the town of Nazareth in Galilee. Little is told of his childhood, other than at the age

of 12 he astounded the scribes in the Temple in Jerusalem with his knowledge of the Scriptures.

Jesus was baptized at the age of about 30 by his cousin, John the Baptist. He gathered a party of twelve disciples and spent the next three years preaching in Galilee. He taught love, humility, and charity, and was reported to have healed the sick and performed other miracles. One of the best known was the feeding of 5,000 people who had gathered to hear him preach with only a few loaves and fishes. He attacked the Jewish leaders. Eventually he was forced to leave Galilee for a while, but on his return to Jerusalem just before the feast of the Passover he was greeted by huge crowds. The Jewish leaders decided to act against him. After the "Last Supper" he was betrayed to the authorities by one of his disciples, Judas Iscariot. He was tried and sentenced to death by Pontius Pilate, but it is said that three days after his crucifixion he rose from the dead. Over the next 40 days he appeared at various times to his disciples before ascending to heaven. ○ HEROD, JOHN THE BAPTIST, PILATE

> Consider the lilies of the field how they grow;
> they toil not neither do they spin:
> And yet I say unto you, That even Solomon in
> his glory was not arrayed like one of these.
> *Matthew 6:25*
>
> Father, forgive them; for they know not what
> they do. *Luke 23:34*

Jinnah, Mohammed Ali (1876–1948)
Jinnah was an Indian politician who became the first governor-general of Pakistan in 1947. Jinnah was a lawyer who became a member of the Indian National Congress and a supporter of Indian independence, although for many years he opposed Gandhi's campaign of "civil disobedience." He was a Muslim, and he came to believe that Muslim interests were being ignored in India. He wanted to establish a separate Muslim state after Indian independence. In 1947 he achieved this, and Pakistan was formed as a home for Indian Muslims. The movement of so many people to Pakistan caused huge refugee problems, and there was also bitter fighting between Muslims and Hindus.
○ GANDHI

Joan of Arc, Saint (*c.*1412–1431)
See pages 140 & 141

John (1167–1216)
John became king of England in 1199. He was the youngest son of King **Henry II** (1133–89) and succeeded his brother, Richard I, to the throne. He once tried to steal the crown while his brother was abroad, but the attempt failed. When John was crowned it was in preference to his nephew Arthur, who had a better claim to the throne. This caused a long and unsuccessful series of wars with the French King **Philip II** (1165–1223), who supported Arthur. In England itself, John found himself in conflict with the Pope when he refused to accept the Pope's choice of a new archbishop. John was eventually forced to submit. He was next humiliated by the English barons, who forced him to sign the Magna Carta ("Great Charter") in 1215. This document guaranteed the barons certain privileges, but was seen as a symbol of the liberties of the people over those of the king. When John died, he was still fighting the country's barons.
○ INNOCENT III, RICHARD I

John of Austria (1547–78)
"Don John," as he was known, was the illegitimate son of the Emperor Charles V. He was made a prince after his father's death by his half brother, Philip II, and sent on a number of military expeditions against the Muslims. His most famous victory was the sea battle of Lepanto in 1571, when a fleet made up mostly of Venetian ships defeated the Turks. He captured the city of Tunis in 1573, and decided he might make himself ruler of a new kingdom in North Africa. Philip II prevented this by sending him on more diplomatic missions. He died suddenly at Namur, but the story that Philip had him poisoned is probably untrue.
○ CHARLES V, PHILIP II

John the Baptist, Saint (*c.*27 B.C.)
John the Baptist was the son of a priest, Zacharias, and his wife Elizabeth, and a cousin of Mary, the mother of Jesus. In about 27 B.C. he began preaching near the river Jordan, and foretold the coming of Jesus. It was John who baptized Jesus. He was executed by King Herod at the request of a dancer, Salome. John's story is told in St. Luke's Gospel. ○ HEROD, JESUS

John Baliol (1249–1315)
John Baliol was king of Scotland from 1292 until 1296. He was chosen as king by Edward I, who dominated Scotland at the time, and forced to swear an oath of loyalty to England. When he realized that he would have no real power as king, John abandoned his oath and went to war with Edward. He was quickly and easily defeated, imprisoned, and forced to give up his crown. He

was kept in the Tower of London for three years before being released and allowed to go to France, where he died.

John Paul II (1920–)
John Paul II was the name taken by Cardinal Karol Wojtyla when he was elected Pope in 1978. He is the first non-Italian to have become Pope since the 16th century. John Paul was born near Krakow in Poland, where he worked for the resistance movement during World War II. At the same time, he studied theology, and became a priest in 1946. Since becoming Pope, John Paul II has traveled to many parts of the world, including the United States, Africa, South America, Korea, Ireland, and his home in Poland.

John Sobieski (1624–96)
John Sobieski was king of Poland from 1674. He was a soldier, born in the region of Galicia. He rose to the rank of commander in the Polish army, and in 1673 defeated the Turks at the Battle of Khotin. His success made him famous, and the next year he was chosen as king. John became well known throughout Europe ten years later when he led his army to the rescue of the city of Vienna, which was being besieged by the Turks. Despite the fame the victory brought him, Poland suffered as a result. John spent many years in an unsuccessful war with Turkey, and at the same time was troubled by threats to his authority at home from rival lords. He is sometimes known as "Jan III" or "John III."

John, Augustus Edwin (1878–1961)
Augustus John was an English painter, famous for his portraits. He was influenced by the Impressionist movement, and spent much time traveling Europe. His sister, **Gwen John** (1876–1939), was also a painter. Her pictures are often of people, but are more delicate in style than her brother's. She lived in France, where she was a close friend of the sculptor Rodin. ○ RODIN

Johnson, Amy (1903–41)
Amy Johnson was an English woman aviator who set new records for long-distance flights. In 1930 she made a solo flight from London, England, to Port Darwin in Australia in a De Havilland Moth aircraft. The trip took 191 days, including many stops for repairs, but when she arrived in Australia Amy Johnson was greeted with great excitement. In 1931 she flew to Japan and Siberia, and in 1936 she broke the record for the fastest flight between London and Cape Town. During World War II she flew transport planes. She is thought to have died when she parachuted into the estuary of the river Thames, but her body was never recovered.

Johnson, Lyndon Baines (1908–73)
Lyndon Baines Johnson was the 36th president of the United States. Vice president in John F. Kennedy's administration, he became president on November 22, 1963, when Kennedy was assassinated. He carried on the policy begun by Kennedy with a sweeping civil rights bill and the "War on Poverty" program. He became unpopular over his commitment of U.S. troops and equipment to Vietnam.

Johnson, Samuel (1709–84)
"Doctor Johnson" was an English poet, critic, and writer who dominated literary life in London in the mid-18th century. His favorite occupation was simply to talk with his friends, and many of his sayings and opinions were recorded by **James Boswell** (1740–95) in his *Life of Samuel Johnson*. Johnson is remembered for remarks such as: "When a man is tired of London, he is tired of life" and "A man will turn over half a library to make one book." He wrote and edited articles for magazines and spent eight years compiling his *Dictionary*, one of the first and most famous in English. In 1765 Johnson published an edition of Shakespeare's works. He traveled to Scotland with Boswell, and both men published descriptions of their experiences. His most famous poem is *The Vanity of Human Wishes*, published in 1749. ○ GARRICK

Amy Johnson, the first woman to fly solo from England to Australia.

Jones, Inigo (1573–1652)
Inigo Jones was an English architect. He was born in London, and visited Italy, where he studied buildings designed by the great Palladio. He was the first to introduce Italian styles of building to England. Among his works are the Whitehall Banqueting Hall in London, the "Queen's House" in Greenwich, and part of St. Paul's Cathedral. Together with Ben Jonson, Jones also designed elaborate pageants and plays for both King James I and King Charles I, and was the first person to use movable pieces of scenery in the theater.
○ JONSON, PALLADIO

Jones, John Paul (1747–92)
John Paul Jones was an American sailor who led a number of daring attacks on British ports and ships during the American Revolutionary War. He was born in Scotland and spent several years at sea before settling in Virginia. In 1778 he was captain of a ship that attacked parts of the British coast. Later, he led a force of French ships in support of the Americans and even managed to capture two British battleships in a battle off the east coast of England. Eventually he left America and joined the Russian navy. He died in Paris.

Jones, Mary Harris, "Mother" (1830–1930)
"Mother" Jones was an American union organizer at the end of the 19th century. She was horrified by the conditions in which miners, railroad workers, children, and other people were forced to work, and she devoted her life to organizing strikes against owners to gain better conditions. She continued campaigning until she was well over 80.

Jonson, Ben (1572–1637)
Ben Jonson was an English playwright and poet who was working at about the same time as Shakespeare. Before he began writing plays he was a soldier, a bricklayer, and an actor. In 1598 his play *Every Man in His Humour* was performed with great success in London, but Jonson was put in prison when he killed an actor in a duel. His greatest plays include *Volpone*, written in 1606, which makes fun of greed and lust, and *The Alchemist* (1610). As well as pieces for the public theater, Jonson also wrote "masques" for the royal family. These were complicated mythological plays in which the king and queen sometimes performed. They required elaborate costumes and scenery, and Jonson worked with the architect Inigo Jones on several productions. As he became older, Jonson was less successful in the theater. ○ JONES, SHAKESPEARE

Josephine (Marie Josèphe Rose Tascher de la Pagerie, 1763–1814)
Josephine was the wife of Napoleon and empress of France from 1804 until 1809. She was born on the

Josephine in 1798, two years before her marriage to Napoleon.

island of Martinique, where her father was a plantation owner. In 1779 Josephine married the Vicomte de Beauharnais, but he was executed during the French Revolution. After the fall of Robespierre and the end of the "Terror," she became a well-known member of Paris society, where she met Napoleon. They were married in 1796. However, the couple had no children, and Napoleon wished to leave an heir to his empire. In 1809 he divorced Josephine and married an Austrian duchess. She kept the title "Empress," remained loyal to Napoleon, and eventually tried to join him on the island of Elba after his downfall.
○ NAPOLEON, ROBESPIERRE

Joyce, James Augustine Aloysius (1882–1941)
James Joyce was an Irish author, whose experiments with unusual ways of writing novels and stories made him one of the most important writers of the 20th century. He was born in the city of Dublin. In 1903 he went to Paris, where he first studied medicine and then began training to be a concert singer. Joyce lived in a number of different European cities, and only returned to his home in Dublin occasionally. All his stories are about Irish people. The first were published in a collection called *Dubliners* in 1914. His first novel was the *Portrait of the Artist as a Young Man*, which

described his own early life. Joyce wanted to give a realistic description of every detail of life. His great work *Ulysses*, which was published in 1922, is a long novel which describes a single day in the lives of its characters in great depth. Some people found the book's realism offensive, and it was banned in Britain and America for many years. In his last book, *Finnegans Wake*, Joyce experimented with making writing like music. His work was greatly admired by other writers such as T.S. Eliot, Virginia Woolf, and Samuel Beckett.

Juan Carlos I (1938–)
Juan Carlos is the king of Spain. He was named as successor by General Franco in 1969, and took over the leadership of the country on Franco's death in 1975. After almost 40 years of dictatorship, Juan Carlos has played a major part in bringing about a return to democracy in Spain. His government has survived two attempted military coups d'état (takeovers). ○ FRANCO

Judith
Judith was an ancient Jewish heroine. The Book of Judith in some versions of the Bible tells us that her town was threatened by Nebuchadnezzar's armies. Judith gained admission to the tent of the general Holofernes, seduced him and then killed him, and so saved the town.

Julius II (1443–1513)
Julius II was the name taken by Giuliano della Rovere when he became Pope in 1503. He set out to impose his authority throughout Italy and to unite the kingdoms and territories that owed him allegiance. In the war of the League of Cambrai, he forced the state of Venice to surrender territory to him. He then formed the Holy League with Spain and England and forced the French army to withdraw from Italy. He also brought the cities of Bologna and Perugia under his control. As well as increasing the power of Rome, Julius was also a patron of the arts. Michelangelo and Raphael were among the artists he employed. ○ HENRY VIII, MICHELANGELO

Julius Caesar (*c.*101 B.C.–44 B.C.)
See pages 142 & 143

Jung, Carl Gustav (1875–1961)
Jung was a Swiss psychologist. He studied at universities in Zurich and Basel, and for several years worked and exchanged ideas with the Austrian psychologist Sigmund Freud. The two men quarreled when Jung published his book *The Psychology of the Unconscious* in 1913. Jung categorized people as belonging to different psychological types, such as "extrovert" or "introvert." ○ FREUD

Justinian I (*c.*482–565)
Justinian was a Byzantine emperor who is remembered for his military success and for organizing and reforming the whole system of Roman law. He was the son of a peasant, but his uncle was a soldier who eventually became the Emperor **Justin I** (450–527). When Justin died in 527, Justinian became sole emperor. With the help of talented generals such as Belisarius he conquered North Africa, Italy, Spain, and some of Persia. Within a few years the Byzantine territories were almost as great as the old Roman Empire. In 532 there was an attempted rebellion in Justinian's capital, Constantinople. He and his generals suppressed it with great ferocity. Justinian published the first version of his new legal system, the *Codex Justinianus*, in 529, but the work of revising and improving it continued for many years. He reformed the system of government, and built the great cathedral of Santa Sophia. Justinian's wife, Theodora, was an important figure throughout his reign. ○ BELISARIUS, THEODORA

The Emperor Justinian with his lords-in-waiting. This mosaic comes from the apse of the Church of San Vitale in Ravenna, Italy.

The Maid of Orléans

Joan of Arc (1412–31)

Joan of Arc's Life

1412 Born January 6 at Domrémy

1421 English army occupies area around Joan's home (they leave in 1424).

1425 Joan receives message from heaven to rescue France from the English.

1429 March: Persuades Charles to allow her to join French army.
April 29: Joan leads French army in defeating the English at the siege of Orléans.
July 17: Charles crowned Charles VII of France at Rouen.

1431 Joan attempts to relieve region of Compiègne. Captured and sold to the English.
February 21: Joan's trial for witchcraft and heresy begins.
May 30: Joan burned at the stake in Rouen.

Inspired by Joan, the French stormed the English forts.

The Hundred Years' War between England and France began when the English King Edward III claimed the French throne for himself in 1337. For the next 113 years, through the reigns of five French and five English kings, the two countries fought over the issue. Joan of Arc entered the war at a turning point. At a moment when the French lacked strong leadership and seemed threatened on all sides, she inspired a great victory at the siege of Orléans and turned the tide of the war in favor of France.

Joan was born in the tiny village of Domrémy in the region of northern France called Champagne. Although she had no schooling of any kind, she was an intelligent child. When she was nine years old the English army occupied the area around her home, remaining for almost three years. When she was 13 she began hearing "voices" telling her to go to France's rescue. Convinced that she had received a command from God, Joan managed to get an audience with the Dauphin (Prince) Charles, the heir to the French throne. He was at first suspicious of her, and so disguised himself and hid among a crowd of his attendants listening to her speak. Joan, although she had never seen him before, is said to have recognized him immediately. This convinced Charles that she really had received a command from heaven. She was given a magnificent suit of armor and was sent to join the army. On April 29, 1429, she arrived at the city of Orléans, which was besieged by the English army. Within ten days Joan, the "Maid of Orléans," had chased the English out of the city and forced them to retreat. Inspired by her leadership and determination, Charles and the French army marched through English territory to the city of Rheims, where Charles was crowned king in July.

Joan now tried to persuade Charles to press home his advantage and defeat the English once and for all, but she found that the new king was satisfied with what had been achieved and unwilling to fight any more. So Joan herself led an army to the south. It was then that she was captured and sold to the English. After nine months in prison, she was brought to trial by a religious court for heresy and sorcery. The charges were absurd, but Joan was found guilty and sentenced to death. On May 30 she was burned at the stake in the marketplace of the city of Rouen. Charles had done nothing to help her, although later he tried to persuade the Pope to overturn the guilty verdict. This was finally done in 1456; in 1920 she was declared a saint. ○ EDWARD III, HENRY V

The Ides of March

Julius Caesar, Gaius (*c.*101 B.C. – 44 B.C.)
Julius Caesar was the greatest military and political leader of ancient Rome. During his lifetime the frontiers of the empire were pushed forward and secured; Rome was transformed from a republic into a government with a single ruler, and Caesar was its first dictator. He wrote some of the finest works of history in Latin, describing the campaigns he fought in Gaul and the civil wars; he was an architect, a mathematician, and one of the ancient world's finest orators. There is no doubt that Caesar was ambitious and that he enjoyed the great power placed in his hands. It is said that he wished to be crowned king. This was the reason that the conspirators led by Cassius and Brutus gave for his murder: that Caesar had become too powerful and a danger to the survival of the republic. But his assassination, on the "Ides of March" (March 15) in 44 B.C. merely hastened the fall of the republic and the rise of the Roman emperors.

A statue of Julius Caesar as a general.

On the Ides of March, Julius Caesar was stabbed by a party of senators led by Cassius and Brutus (right).

Caesar was born into an old noble family, and grew up with all the many advantages his powerful relatives could bring him. For a time, Caesar's life was threatened by his family's political enemies, and he spent three years living abroad. But in 78 B.C. he returned to Rome and became the leader of the democratic party in the Senate. In 65 B.C. he was "aedile," the organizer of games and festivals in the city. The games he arranged were magnificent, and he became popular. Caesar was soon one of the two most powerful men in Rome. The other was Pompey, and at first they cooperated. Caesar was given command of a huge army sent to conquer lands to the north and west of Italy. His brilliance as a military leader brought Rome new territories in Gaul (France), and he twice invaded Britain. But his success also threatened to make him more powerful than Pompey. The two men quarreled, and in 49 B.C.

Pompey persuaded the Senate to order Caesar to disband his army. Caesar refused. Instead, he crossed the river Rubicon, the frontier between Italy and Gaul, and in doing so declared war on Pompey and the republic. Pompey's armies were scattered in territories to the east, and Caesar soon took control of Rome, while Pompey retreated to Epirus (modern Albania). Pompey was defeated at the great Battle of Pharsalus in 48 B.C. and fled to Egypt, where he was murdered.

Caesar's authority was now unchallenged. After defeating Pompey's remaining supporters, he returned to Rome to be greeted with great enthusiasm. His statue was placed in the city's temples, his portrait appeared on coins, and he was even declared to be divine. More important, he was made dictator of Rome for life, and given the title "Father of His Country." He proved himself a skillful and generous leader, and he introduced several reforms. In 44 B.C. he was offered the title "king." He refused, but some were already suspicious of Caesar's ambition. Prophets and astrologers warned him to take care, but Caesar took no notice. On the "Ides of March" he went to the Senate as usual, where he was stabbed by a party of senators led by Cassius and Brutus. ○ AUGUSTUS, BRUTUS, CLEOPATRA, MARK ANTONY, POMPEY

The Fall of the Roman Republic

49 B.C. Civil War between Caesar and Pompey.

48 B.C. Pompey defeated at Battle of Pharsalus.

47 B.C. Pompey murdered in Egypt.

46 B.C. Caesar returns to Rome. Seeks title "king" and adopts Octavius (later Augustus) as heir.

44 B.C. Caesar assassinated by Republican senators. Mark Antony, Octavius, and Lepidus form "triumvirate" to govern Rome.

42 B.C. Caesar's murderers defeated at Battle of Philippi.

38 B.C. Mark Antony returns to Egypt to live with Cleopatra.

31 B.C. Octavius fights and defeats Mark Antony at the Battle of Actium.

30 B.C. Octavius becomes emperor and takes name "Augustus."

Kafka, Franz (1883–1924)
Franz Kafka was a German writer who lived and worked in the Czech city of Prague. His stories and novels were influenced by his tormented relationship with his father, and by his years working in the government Workers' Accident Insurance office—which made him scornful of bureaucrats and officials. Kafka published many short stories during his lifetime, but his three great novels remained unfinished and unpublished when he died. They include *The Castle* and *The Trial.* He asked that the manuscripts be destroyed after his death, but they were rescued by his friend Max Brod and eventually printed. Many other 20th-century writers have been influenced by Kafka. His writings describe humans tortured by impersonal powers. Desperation is the prevailing mood.

Kandinsky, Wassily (1866–1944)
A Russian artist who developed his own style of "abstract" painting—pictures which use pattern and color and do not represent recognizable objects. For some years after the Russian Revolution he worked with the new government, but in 1921 he moved to Germany, where he joined the Bauhaus school, and then to France. His ideas appear in his book *On the Spiritual in Art.*
○ GROPIUS

Kang Xi (1662–1722)
Kang Xi was a Chinese emperor belonging to the Chi'ing Manchu dynasty. He was one of the first Chinese emperors to allow Westerners into China, and during his reign many missionaries and others arrived in the country.

Kanishka (d. *c.*152)
Kanishka was a Tatar king of western India who came to his throne in about 144. He is famous for ordering the construction of Buddhist monuments throughout his kingdom and for organizing a council of wise men to discuss Buddhist beliefs.

Kant, Immanuel (1724–1804)
Kant was a very influential German philosopher. He was born in the town of Könisberg, and remained there all his life, eventually becoming professor at the university. As well as philosophy, he was interested in mathematics and science, and he developed a theory about the creation of the solar system. In 1781 Kant published his great philosophical work, the *Critique of Pure Reason.* He said that people gain knowledge only by experience of the world around them, and he wrote a great deal about how people categorize their experiences. Kant was also interested in politics, and supported the American and French revolutions. ○ HEGEL

Kauffmann, Angelica (1741–1807)
Kauffmann was a Swiss woman painter who lived in the 18th century. She became well known for her portraits and mythological pictures, and in the 1770s she lived in England. She painted decorations for several houses designed by Robert Adam. ○ ADAM

Kaunda, David Kenneth (1924–)
Kaunda is the first president of modern Zambia. He founded the Zambia African National Congress in 1958 to fight for independence for his country, and was for a short time put in prison for his activities. In the first election held in Zambia he was voted prime minister, and when the country became independent later that year, Kaunda became president.

Kawabata Yasunari (1899–1972)
Kawabata was a Japanese novelist who won the Nobel Prize for Literature in 1968. He experimented with both European and Japanese styles of writing, but eventually adopted a traditional Japanese method. His works include *Thousand Cranes* (1949) and *The Sound of the Mountain* (1971). Kawabata often wrote about man's confrontation with death, and in 1972 he committed suicide.

Keaton, "Buster" (1895–1966)
Buster Keaton (whose proper name was Joseph Francis Keaton) was the star of many silent films in the 1920s. He was born in Kansas and made his first film in 1917. He is remembered for the "deadpan" expression he wore on his face, no matter what difficulties or dangers confronted him. Keaton both acted in and directed films such as *The General* (1926) and *Steamboat Bill Junior* (1927).

When talking films were introduced he was quickly forgotten, but became popular again in the 1960s, when many of his pictures were re-shown.

Keats, John (1795–1821)
John Keats is among the best known of all English poets. He was born in London, where his father was a stable keeper. After his father's death, the 16-year-old Keats was apprenticed to an apothecary (a type of old-fashioned chemist). He eventually began working in London's hospitals, but the horrors of surgery in the days before the widespread use of anesthetics eventually persuaded him to leave.

Keats had remained devoted to poetry since his schooldays, and while working as an apothecary he met several young poets, including Shelley. He published his first collection of poems in 1817. In 1818 he published *Endymion*, a very long work which was praised by some readers, but attacked by many others. His greatest works were written over the next two years and published as *Lamia and Other Poems* in 1820. They include the "Ode on a Grecian Urn" and the famous "Ode to a Nightingale." But Keats was becoming dangerously ill with consumption. In September 1820 he traveled to Italy where he hoped the climate would help him recover, but in February of the following year he died. He was buried in an anonymous grave in Rome. Keats is also remembered for the moving letters he wrote to his family, friends, and to Fanny Brawne, with whom he had a long love affair. ○ SHELLEY

Keller, Helen Adams (1880–1968)
Helen Keller was a deaf and blind author and teacher whose determination to overcome her handicaps made her an American heroine. She was born in Alabama, and became deaf and blind at the age of only 19 months as the result of an attack of scarlet fever. She was educated by a woman named Anne Sullivan, and learned to speak and to read Braille. In 1904 she graduated from Radcliffe College in Massachusetts with a B.A., and as an adult wrote several books and toured the world giving lectures.

Helen Keller with Anne Sullivan who taught her "to speak."

Kelly, Ned (1855–80)
Ned Kelly was a famous Australian outlaw. He was the son of a convict who had been transported to Australia from Ireland, and grew up to become a bushranger in New South Wales. Ned and his brother Dan started stealing horses, and after a shoot-out in 1878 in which Ned killed three policemen, they fled to the outback. After 18 months Ned Kelly was finally caught and hanged in Melbourne. His last words are said to have been: "Such is life!"

Kemal Ataturk (1881–1938)
See Ataturk, Mustafa Kemal

Kennedy, John Fitzgerald (1917–63)
See page 148

Kennedy, Robert Francis (1925–68)
Robert Kennedy was the younger brother of President John F. Kennedy. He was a lawyer and became well known for bringing corrupt union leaders to trial. He managed his brother's successful election campaign and afterward became attorney general of the United States. In 1968 he entered the race for the presidency as a Democrat, but on June 5, he was shot by a Jordanian, Sirhan Sirhan. He died the next day.

The shooting of Senator Robert Kennedy on June 5, 1968. He died the next day.

Kenneth Macalpine (*c.*850)
Kenneth Macalpine was a king of Scotland about whom little is known. His father was named Alpin and ruled a tribe in the north of the country. Kenneth succeeded him in about 834, and led his army to victory against a Danish invasion. He then conquered the tribe known as the Picts. By about 850 he was ruler of a kingdom covering most of modern Scotland, as far south as the river Clyde and the Forth.

Kenyatta, Jomo (*c.*1889–1978)
Jomo Kenyatta was the first president of Kenya after the country became independent from Britain in 1963. He went to university in London, and during World War II he worked on an English farm. He also studied in Russia, but in 1946 returned to Kenya where he led the Kenya African National Union, a political party dedicated to gaining independence for the country. In the early 1950s he took part in the Mau Mau rebellion against the British, but was caught and sent to prison. After his release Kenyatta became an MP, and in 1963 he was elected prime minister. When the country became independent, he became its first president.

Jomo Kenyatta, the father figure of independent Kenya, at the Independence Day celebrations in 1963.

Kepler, Johann (1571–1630)
Kepler was a German scientist who is thought of as one of the founders of modern astronomy. He was born in the German state of Württemberg and went to the University of Tübingen, with the intention of becoming a Protestant minister. But Kepler found himself fascinated by science, and instead of entering the Church he was made professor of mathematics at Graz in 1594. At about the same time he began exchanging ideas with the famous astronomer Tycho Brahe, and in 1600 he traveled to Prague to become Brahe's assistant. After Brahe's death in 1601, Kepler took over his position as royal astronomer to the Emperor Rudolf II. Unfortunately, he was not paid very well or very often, and in 1612 he left Prague to become a mathematics teacher in the Austrian city of Linz. Kepler believed Copernicus' theory that the earth orbits the sun, and he was able to devise laws which explained the motion of the earth and other planets. These are known as "Kepler's Laws," and they helped Newton develop his theory of gravity. Kepler was also the first to suggest that tides were caused by the gravitational pull of the moon.
○ BRAHE, COPERNICUS, NEWTON

Kerensky, Alexander (1881–1970)
Alexander Kerensky was the first person to lead the new Russian government after the 1917 revolution. He was a lawyer, and had become an outspoken critic of the tsar's government. He was leader of the Social Revolutionary Party, and when the tsar was finally overthrown in March 1917 he was made minister of war. In July he became prime minister. Kerensky decided to continue Russia's involvement in World War I against Germany. This made him unpopular because the country's army and economy had been severely weakened by the fighting. In September 1917 he successfully defeated a military revolt, but in November Kerensky was overthrown by the Bolsheviks led by Lenin. He left Russia and lived for the rest of his life in France and the United States.
○ LENIN

Kerouac, Jack (1922–69)
Jack Kerouac was an American novelist who became one of the most famous of the "Beat Generation"—the discontented young people of 1950s America. His most famous novel is *On the Road*, published in 1957.

Kertész, André (1894–)
André Kertész is a Hungarian-born photographer who has pioneered both "news" and "art" photography in the 20th century. His early pictures were of the people and streets of Budapest and Paris. After World War II he moved to New York, where he has worked for popular magazines and as a fashion photographer.

Keynes, John Maynard, 1st Baron (1883–1946)
Keynes was a British economist whose theories have had a great influence on governments throughout the world. He was born in Cambridge,

where he went to university, and during World War I he worked in the British Treasury (the ministry responsible for the economy). He was an adviser at the Versailles peace conference in 1918. The Treaty of Versailles ordered Germany to pay huge sums in damages to the victorious nations. Keynes opposed this because he said that it would make the German economy weak, and the Germans would become hostile to the rest of Europe. The rise of Hitler in the 1930s proved him right. Meanwhile, the Great Depression which began in 1929 was causing high unemployment in Britain and the United States. In the *General Theory of Employment, Interest and Money*, published in 1936, Keynes suggested that governments spend money on "public works"—building roads, bridges, and other things. This would provide people with jobs and wages. In addition, as people spent their wages there would be more demand for other products, and the economy would gradually improve. This theory provided the basis for the economic policies of many different governments after World War II.

Khomeini, Ayatollah Ruhollah (1900–)
Khomeini is the leader of Iran. The word "Ayatollah" means "religious leader," and he has governed Iran on traditional Islamic principles. Khomeini lived in Paris for many years, but

Ayatollah Khomeini, the leader of Iran.

returned to Iran to lead his people after the fall of Shah Mohammed Reza Pahlevi in 1979. ○ CARTER

Khrushchev, Nikita Sergeyevich (1894–1971)
Khrushchev was leader of the Soviet Union from 1953 until 1964. He was the son of a shepherd and worked as a farmer, a locksmith, and a plumber. It is said that he could neither read nor write until he was 25. During World War II he led guerrilla attacks on the German army, and afterward he planned the rebuilding of devastated territory. His power in the Communist Party gradually increased, and after the death of Stalin in 1953 he became First Secretary of the Party. In 1956 he denounced Stalin's leadership and removed many of the former leader's associates from their jobs. Khrushchev attempted to increase Soviet influence abroad, by diplomacy and by force. In 1961 he shipped nuclear missiles to Cuba, only miles from the mainland of the United States. President Kennedy threatened war if the missiles were not removed, and Khrushchev eventually agreed to withdraw. He was deposed by other top Communists in 1964

Rudyard Kipling, the English poet and storyteller.

and forced to retire. He was replaced by Leonid Brezhnev. ○ BREZHNEV, CASTRO, KENNEDY, STALIN

Kierkegaard, Sören Aaby (1813–55)
A Danish philosopher, born in the city of Copenhagen, where he attended university. Kierkegaard had trained in theology, but did not become a priest, and in his later writings he attacked the Christian idea of faith.

Kipling, Rudyard (1865–1936)
Kipling was an English writer who is remembered for his poems, and for his stories and novels about India during the period of British rule there. He was born in the city of Bombay, where his father was a teacher, but went to school in England. Kipling returned to India in 1880, where he wrote articles for magazines and newspapers. He became well known as a writer of short stories, including *Plain Tales from the Hills*, published in 1888. In 1889 he went back to London, and in 1901 published his most successful novel, *Kim*, which tells the story of an orphan's adventures growing up in India. Kipling wrote many fine children's stories, including *The Jungle Book* and the famous *Just So Stories*.

America's Youngest President

President John F. Kennedy in his office in the White House. He was elected 35th president of the United States in 1960.

Kennedy, John Fitzgerald (1917–63)
In November 1960 John Kennedy defeated Richard Nixon in the election for the United States presidency and became both the youngest and the first Roman Catholic ever to hold the office. His victory was the result of a long campaign, and came at the end of years of service as a congressman and senator. The election was very close—the closest since 1916—but Kennedy went on to become a popular president.

At his inauguration Kennedy said: "Ask not what your country can do for you—ask what you can do for your country." His short presidency was distinguished by its energetic attempts to solve many of America's social problems. He introduced liberal reforms intended to improve education, medical care, and housing in the country's cities. As the black civil rights movement grew in strength, he supported policies aimed at removing discrimination against blacks and ensuring that they were able to exercise the same rights as white people. Kennedy attempted to increase American aid to poor countries. It was during his presidency that the Peace Corps was set up to encourage volunteers to use their teaching or technical skills in projects abroad. He also encouraged funding for the Apollo space program which put an American on the moon in 1969.

In April 1961 Kennedy and the United States were humiliated by the failure of the "Bay of Pigs" invasion—an attempt to overthrow the government of Cuba by force by American-trained Cuban exiles. But his prestige recovered in October 1962 when the United States discovered that Soviet nuclear missiles were being installed in Cuba. He threatened war unless they were removed, and, after several tense days in which the world seemed on the brink of a nuclear conflict, the Soviet Union agreed to remove the missiles.

Kennedy's presidency came to a violent end on November 22, 1963, when he was assassinated in Dallas, Texas, by Lee Harvey Oswald. His youth, energy, and confidence had made a deep impression on Americans, and seemed to many to represent the spirit of the country in the early 1960s. ○ ARMSTRONG, CASTRO, ROBERT KENNEDY, KING, KHRUSHCHEV, NIXON, OSWALD

At 12.30 p.m. on Thursday, November 22, 1963, Jo F. Kennedy was shot by an assassin as he drove through the streets of Dallas, Texas. Doctors worke desperately to save the President but he died at 1

Civil Rights in the U.S.A.

King, Martin Luther (1929–68)
The American Civil War freed black Americans from the degradation of slavery. A hundred years later, at the beginning of the 1960s, many black people in the United States were still the victims of racial discrimination and lived in conditions much poorer than those of the white population. The civil rights movement grew up to try to put an end to racial discrimination, to make sure that blacks both had and exercised the same rights as whites.

Dr. Martin Luther King, the American civil rights leader. His non-violent program reached a high point on August 28, 1963 when more than 200,000 people marched through Washington D.C. from the Washington Monument to the Lincoln Memorial. King told the crowd: "I have a dream that one day this nation will rise up and live out the true meaning of its creed: 'We hold these truths to be self-evident; that all men are created equal.'"

Martin Luther King was one of the movement's most important leaders. He was a young Baptist minister in Montgomery, Alabama, in 1955 when a black woman, Rosa Parks, was arrested for refusing to give up her bus seat to a white man. King and the other blacks in Montgomery organized a boycott of the bus companies, and eventually the state was forced to make segregated buses illegal. In 1957 King became the president of the Southern Christian Leadership Conference, which organized civil rights protests throughout the South. At first he favored non-violent tactics, although later the movement adopted a policy of confrontation with whites and the authorities. One of their most important campaigns was to encourage blacks to register their votes, and so take an active part in politics. In 1963 King led thousands of blacks in the March on Washington, where

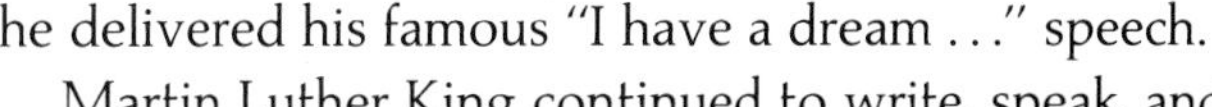

he delivered his famous "I have a dream ..." speech.

Martin Luther King continued to write, speak, and act on behalf of his people. In 1968 he was taking part in a campaign to improve working conditions for the black employees of the government of Tennessee when, on April 4, he was assassinated at his motel by James Earl Ray.

Martin Luther King is buried near Ebenezer Baptist Church in Atlanta. These words from a spiritual song are carved on his tombstone: "Free at last, free at last, thank God Almighty, I'm free at last."

King's short career greatly advanced the cause of civil rights in the United States. His campaigning helped the passage of the Civil Rights Act of 1964 and the Voting Rights Act of 1965. "Injustice anywhere," he wrote while in prison in Birmingham, Alabama, "is a threat to justice everywhere." ○ KENNEDY, MALCOLM X

rlanded Martin Luther King on a non-violent civil hts march in Selma, Alabama, in 1965.

Kissinger, Henry Alfred (1923–)
An American politician, who served as Secretary of State under Presidents Nixon and Ford. He helped negotiate cease-fires between North Vietnam and the U.S. forces in the south, and between Israel and Egypt. ○ NIXON

Kitchener, Horatio Herbert (1850–1916)
Lord Kitchener was British commander-in-chief during the Boer War in South Africa. He later held the same post in India (1903–09). He organized the British army in World War I (1914–18). He died when his ship was sunk by a German submarine.

Klein, Melanie (1882–1960)
Melanie Klein was an Austrian psychologist who was particularly interested in children's behavior. Until 1925 she worked in Berlin, and then moved to London where she spent the rest of her life. She studied young children at play, and was able to develop theories about their anxieties and desires. Melanie Klein published her findings in *The Psychoanalysis of Children* in 1932.

Knox, John (*c.*1513–72)
John Knox was a Scottish religious reformer who worked for the foundation of a separate, Protestant Church of Scotland. He was born in East Lothian and was for many years a priest in the Roman Catholic Church. But in about 1544 he met **George Wishart** (1513–46), a Protestant reformer who was eventually burned at the stake for his beliefs. Knox joined the Protestants, but in 1547 he was taken prisoner by French troops who supported the Catholic rulers of Scotland. He was released at the request of the English King Edward VI, and traveled to Geneva, where he worked with the Swiss reformer Calvin for the next three years. In 1559 Knox returned to Scotland. He preached in the towns of Perth and St. Andrews, and converted his congregations to the Protestant cause. Eventually, it seemed that civil war would break out between Protestants and Catholics in Scotland, but the English army entered Edinburgh and ensured victory for Knox and his supporters. As a result, the Church of Scotland was established. Knox wrote several books, and remained a tireless supporter of the Protestant cause throughout his life. ○ CALVIN

Koch, Robert (1843–1910)
Koch was a German scientist whose work led to great improvements in vaccination and the treatment of disease. He identified the bacteria that causes tuberculosis, as well as those causing cholera and anthrax. He also did important work on malaria and bubonic plague.

Kossuth, Lajos (1802–94)
Kossuth was a Hungarian revolutionary. He campaigned against Austrian rule of Hungary, and in 1848 helped pass laws that abolished the privileges of the nobility. The following year Hungary declared itself independent of Austria, and Kossuth became governor. But the combined strength of the Russian and Austrian armies soon defeated the revolution, and Kossuth fled to Turkey.

Kreisler, Fritz (1875–1962)
Austrian-born virtuoso violinist who became an American citizen in 1943. His tours of the United States established his fame as a master of his instrument and also as a composer.

Krupp, Alfred (1812–87)
The founder of a vast iron, steel, and arms-manufacturing empire in Germany. Members of the family retained control through both world wars (which contributed to their fortune), but the company was finally taken into state ownership in 1968.

Kubla Khan (1214–94)
Kubla Khan was the grandson of the great Genghis Khan, and became Mongol emperor in 1259. His territory extended right across Asia, but it was in China that he was most at home. He made Cambaluc (the site of modern Peking) his capital, adopted Chinese manners, and proclaimed himself the first emperor of the Yüan dynasty. His armies conquered northern China, Tibet, and entered Burma. Meanwhile, Kubla Khan ruled in great splendor. He encouraged art and science and welcomed foreigners at his court. Marco Polo, the Venetian explorer, spent 17 years there. ○ GENGHIS KHAN, POLO

Kung Fu Tse
See Confucius

Kurosawa, Akira (1910–)
A Japanese film director who has become one of the most admired figures in modern motion pictures. Among his films are *Rashomon* (1951), *The Seven Samurai* (1954), which inspired the famous Western *The Magnificent Seven*, and *Ran*, a film based on Shakespeare's *King Lear*.

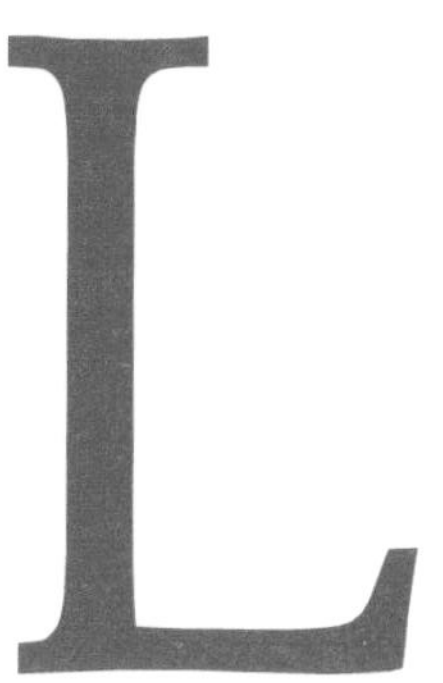

Laban, Rudolf von (1879–1958)
A Hungarian-born choreographer and dance teacher who played an important part in the development of modern dance. He invented a system of recording the steps in a ballet called "Labanotation."

La Fayette, Marie Joseph Paul Yves Roch Gilbert Motier (1757–1834)
La Fayette was a French political reformer who played an important part in both the American War of Independence and the French Revolution. He was a member of an aristocratic family, born in the castle of Chavagnac in the district of the Auvergne. He became a soldier, and in 1777 sailed to America to aid the independence movement. He met George Washington and took command of a division of soldiers. Next he returned to France to persuade the French government to support the American rebels by declaring war on Britain, then went back to America and fought at the Battle of Yorktown in 1781. La Fayette had by now gained a reputation as a liberal and a reformer, and at the beginning of the French Revolution in 1789 he was elected to the new National Assembly. He set up the National Guard, an army of citizens created to protect the revolution, and suggested a new constitution based on the American Declaration of Independence. However, La Fayette was not a violent revolutionary, and when the policies of the French revolutionaries became more extreme he left the country. During the 1820s he was a member of the Chamber of Deputies in France, and in 1830 he supported the revolution that replaced King Charles X with Louis Philippe. ○ WASHINGTON

Lamarck, Jean Baptiste Pierre Antoine de Monet (1744–1829)
Lamarck was a French biologist who developed a system of classifying species and put forward some of the first ideas about evolution. He was a soldier in the French army, and afterward worked in a bank. In 1744 he became keeper of the royal gardens in Paris and began giving his famous lectures on plants. It was Lamarck who introduced the term "biology" to describe the study of living things.

Lane, Sir Allen Willams (1902–70)
An English publisher and the founder of Penguin Books. Lane's idea was to make a large number of books available at low cost by printing them in cheap paperback editions. The first Penguins, issued in 1936, cost only a few cents.

Langland, William (*c.*1332–*c.*1400)
Langland was an English poet remembered for his one great work, the *Vision of Piers the Plowman,* which first appeared about 1360. It is a long religious work, written in difficult language, but it gives fascinating glimpses of life in medieval England. ○ ROBIN HOOD

La Fayette, the French political reformer. He helped the American colonists during the War of Independence.

Lao-Tzu (*c.*600 B.C.)
Lao-Tzu, which means "Old Philosopher," was the founder of the ancient Chinese philosophy known as Taoism (*Tao* means "the way"). He was probably born in the city of Honan, where he was the keeper of the royal library. Confucius may have met Lao-Tzu there. His book, the *Tao te Ching,* describes the philosophy of Taoism: accept things as they are, and go about life quietly, without striving. Together with Buddhism and the philosophy of Confucius, Taoism is the most important set of beliefs in China, although it is incorrect to think of it as a religion. ○ CONFUCIUS

Laplace, Pierre Simon (1749–1827)
A French mathematician and astronomer who made a number of important discoveries about the movements of the planets and put forward a theory of the origin of the solar system. He was the son of a poor farmer. He was made a member of the French Academy of Sciences, and was also a member of Napoleon's government.

Larkin, Philip (1922–86)
Larkin was an English novelist and poet. His collections of poetry include *The Whitsun Weddings* (1964) and *High Windows* (1974). He worked for many years as a librarian at Hull University.

Larousse, Pierre (1817–75)
Pierre Larousse was a French lexicographer who compiled the 15-volume *Universal Dictionary of the 19th Century* (1876).

La Salle, René Robert Cavelier (1643–87)
La Salle was a French explorer who made a famous voyage down the Mississippi River in the 1670s. He was born in the French city of Rouen, but at the age of 23 emigrated to Canada. Four years later, in 1670, he began an expedition south down the Ohio River, thinking it might take him to the Pacific. But the Ohio simply flows into the Mississippi, so La Salle decided to follow that river instead. After several years of great hardship he finally found his way, not to the Pacific, but to the Gulf of Mexico. He claimed the whole lower Mississippi for France, and called it "Louisiana" in honor of Louis XIV. In 1684 La Salle returned to the area to found a French settlement, but he was unable to find the mouth of the Mississippi from the sea. Having landed farther south, in Texas, he spent two years searching for the river before being murdered when his crew mutinied.

La Tour, Georges de (1593–1652)
La Tour was a French painter. He lived and worked all his life in the province of Lorraine, and painted a very small number of pictures. In fact, only about 40 works by La Tour are known to have survived. He painted several religious subjects, and experimented with dark, shadowy, candlelit scenes.

Laurel, Stan (Arthur Stanley Jefferson, 1890–1965)
Stan Laurel and **Oliver Hardy** (1892–1957) joined forces in 1926 to become one of the most successful comedy double acts in motion picture history. They made over 200 films in a simple, old-fashioned "slapstick" style.

Laver, Rod (1938–)
An Australian tennis player who on two occasions (in 1962 and 1969) won the "Grand Slam"—the French Open, the U.S. Open, the Australian Open, and the Wimbledon titles in a single year.

Lavoisier, Antoine Laurent (1743–94)
Antoine Lavoisier was a great French chemist. He was born in Paris. He found that nobody was willing to pay him to make chemical experiments, so in 1768 he accepted a job as a "farmer general," or tax collecter. That same year he became a member of the French Academy of Sciences. Over the next 25 years, Lavoisier made many important contributions to the birth of modern chemistry. He showed that air was a combination of oxygen and nitrogen (which he called "azote") and that oxygen was necessary to life. He experimented with combustion and discovered that when something is burned it combines with the oxygen in the air. In 1787 Lavoisier introduced a new system of names for chemical elements, and worked out a way of categorizing them. He worked for a time as director of the French gunpowder mills, and was able to improve the manufacture of explosives. He was a liberal who supported the aims of the French Revolution, which broke out in 1789, but disliked the violent methods of later revolutionaries such as Robespierre. One of the results of the revolution was the introduction of metric measurements, which Lavoisier helped plan. Despite Lavoisier's support of the revolution, his old job as a tax collector was held against him, and in 1794 he became a victim of the "Terror" and was executed.
○ PRIESTLEY, ROBESPIERRE

Lavoisier, the French chemist who worked out the first logical system of naming chemical compounds.

Lawrence, David Herbert (1885–1930)
D.H. Lawrence was an important and controversial English writer. He was born near the city of Nottingham, where his father was a miner. One of his earliest novels, *Sons and Lovers,* published in

1913, was inspired by Lawrence's intense relationship with his mother, who encouraged him to attend university and become a teacher. In 1914 he married a German woman, Frieda von Richthofen, but wartime suspicions that Lawrence might be a spy forced him to leave England. He spent the rest of his life traveling the world and writing. Lawrence wrote frankly about sex, and as a result two of his novels, *The Rainbow* (1915) and *Lady Chatterley's Lover* (1928), were prosecuted as "obscene."

Lawrence, Thomas Edward (1888–1935)
T.E. Lawrence was a British scholar and soldier who became known as Lawrence of Arabia after his exploits in the desert during World War I. At the beginning of the war he was working as an archaeologist in Syria, and his knowledge of the Arabs led to his being sent to help organize the "Arab Revolt" against Turkey. He became an aide and friend of the future King Faisal I of Iraq, and he described his experiences in a book called *The Seven Pillars of Wisdom*. Lawrence saw the settlement at the end of the war as a betrayal of the Arabs. He retired, changed his name, and joined the Royal Air Force. He was killed in a motorcycle accident.
○ FAISAL I

Lear, Edward (1812–88)
Edward Lear was an English writer and artist. Among his most famous works is the *Book of Nonsense*, which contains rhymes such as "The Owl and the Pussycat..." and which Lear wrote for his grandchildren.

There was a Young Lady whose bonnet
Came untied when the birds sat upon it;
But she said, "I don't care!
All the birds in the air
Are welcome to sit on my bonnet!"

Lebrun, Charles (1619–90)
Lebrun was a French artist who worked during the reign of King Louis XIV. He painted many of the decorations for the palace of Versailles, and was the principal founder of the Académie Royale. Because of his closeness to the king and his importance at the Académie, Lebrun was able to decide which other painters found work and in what style they should paint. He became almost the dictator of French art in the 17th century. ○ LOUIS XIV

Lee, Robert Edward (1807–70)
Robert E. Lee was a soldier who became supreme commander of the Confederate army during the American Civil War. He was born in the state of Virginia. His father, General **Harry Lee** (1756–1818), had played an important part in the War of Independence, and many other members of the Lee family had been politicians and diplomats. Young Robert attended the West Point military academy and took part in the Mexican War of 1846. He was quickly promoted and in 1852 was put in charge of West Point. When seven Southern states, including Virginia, decided to separate from the rest of the country and form the Confederacy in 1861, Lee remained loyal to his state and resigned from the U.S. Army. He organized the defense of Virginia and then invaded Maryland and Pennsylvania. In 1862 he took command of all the Confederate forces. Lee was always outnumbered and his soldiers were less well equipped than those in the

(Continued on page 156)

Civil War general Robert E. Lee.

Far left: An illustration from Lear's Book of Nonsense *and the accompanying limerick.*

The Russian Revolution

Lenin, Vladimir Ilyich (1870–1924)
When Karl Marx was writing his *Communist Manifesto* at the end of the 1840s, he believed that a Communist revolution would take place in one of the heavily populated, industrialized countries of western Europe, such as Great Britain or France. He thought that the factory workers, often poorly paid and living in terrible city slums, would be its leaders. But instead, the first Communist revolution took place in Russia, a vast, spread-out country, where there were few big cities and where most people worked on the land.

Lenin was the Russian Revolution's most important leader. He was born in the town of Simbirsk, where his father was a school inspector, and he studied at Kazan University. He began his career as a lawyer, but his life was changed by reading the works of Karl Marx, and in 1894 Lenin moved to the Russian capital, St. Petersburg, to organize the "Union for the Liberation of the Working Class." His activities were illegal, and he was arrested and spent three years imprisoned in Siberia. There he met and married Nadezhda Krupskaya, who had also been imprisoned for revolutionary activities. Unable to continue his work in Russia, Lenin left in 1900, but continued to organize and control the Russian revolutionary movement from abroad. He returned in 1905 for an attempted uprising against the government, but the revolution failed and in 1907 Lenin fled again to Switzerland where he continued to prepare for the revolution.

It was World War I (1914–18) that finally helped bring about change in Russia. For centuries the country had been ruled by autocratic tsars who governed almost alone, and millions of people had lived in poverty on land owned by a few rich noblemen. When the war began in 1914, Russians found themselves fighting in a distant country that they had no interest in. It put intolerable strains on the economy, and morale among the soldiers sank lower the longer it went on. When revolution broke out in February 1917, Tsar Nicholas II found himself powerless to stop it. Within a few days, he had been forced to abdicate and a new government had been formed, led by Alexander Kerensky. Lenin, hearing of the uprising, made plans to leave Switzerland. He was aided by Russia's enemy, the

In the evening of November 7, 1917, armed workers and Bolshevik-led soldiers and sailors attacked the Winter Palace in Petrograd (St. Petersburg and now Leningrad). The palace was the headquarters of the provisional government that had been established in March when Tsar Nicholas had given up the throne. The Bolsheviks seized the weakly defended palace and arrested members of the government. By November 15 the Bolsheviks controlled the city and formed a new Russian government headed by Lenin.

The Russian Revolution

1905 Attempted revolution in St. Petersburg fails. Tsar Nicholas II introduces some reforms.
1914 Russia enters World War I.
1917 February: Uprisings in Russian cities.
March 16: Tsar Nicholas II abdicates; Provisional government formed.
April: Lenin arrives in St. Petersburg. Urges workers to overthrow provisional government.
November 7: Revolution in St. Petersburg led by Lenin and the Bolsheviks. Lenin proclaimed head of state.
1918 Russia withdraws from World War I.
Nicholas II and family murdered by Bolsheviks.

Germans, who hoped to encourage trouble in Russia, and arranged for him to travel by train to St. Petersburg.

Throughout the summer of 1917 Kerensky's government and Lenin's Bolshevik Party struggled for power. In the "October Revolution" the government party finally collapsed, and the Bolsheviks took complete control. Lenin became sole leader of the new Soviet government.

The revolution had been successful in Russia's big cities, but it was some time before Lenin's government was able to claim control of the whole country. For several years the "Red Army," led by Trotsky, fought a civil war with the "White Army," made up of opponents of the revolution. Lenin agreed to peace with Germany and withdrew from World War I, but the economic and social problems of the country were vast, and lasted long after his death. He suffered from a gunshot wound and a stroke, and in January 1924 he died. Four days later St. Petersburg was renamed "Leningrad" in his honor.

○ KERENSKY, NICHOLAS II, TROTSKY

Union Army. But his great tactical skill enabled him to hold out, despite defeat at the Battle of Gettysburg in 1863 and a blockade of Southern ports which caused considerable hardship. He finally surrendered to General Grant in April 1865, and retired to become president of a university in Lexington. ○ GRANT, LINCOLN

Leeuwenhoek, Antony van (1632–1723)
Leeuwenhoek was a Dutch scientist. While working in a cloth warehouse in Amsterdam he began using a lens to examine the fibers in the cloth. This led him to develop the use of the microscope to study things such as blood, skin, hair, and eyes, as well as leaves and flowers. He was the first to describe blood corpuscles, and showed that blood circulates through tiny vessels called "capillaries."

Leif Eriksson (*c.*1000)
A Viking adventurer, son of Eric the Red. He is said to have been the first European to have visited North America. He sailed west from Greenland, and discovered a place which he called "Vinland" because he found vines growing there. This could have been Labrador, Newfoundland, or Massachusetts. ○ ERIC THE RED

Lenglen, Suzanne (1899–1938)
Suzanne Lenglen was a French tennis player who was virtually unbeatable between 1919 and 1926. She was fast, accurate, powerful, and a great crowd puller. She won six Wimbledon singles. She is regarded by some experts as all-time No. 1.

Suzanne Lenglen won six Wimbledon singles between 1919 and 1926.

Lenin, Vladimir Ilyich (1870–1924)
See pages 154 & 155

Lennon, John (1940–80)
John Lennon and **Paul McCartney** (1942–) wrote many of the songs that made the Beatles the most successful group in the history of pop music. The other members of the group were **George Harrison** (1943–) and **Ringo Starr** (1940–). They began performing in the Cavern Club in Liverpool in 1960 and signed their first recording contract in 1962. Songs such as "I Wanna Hold Your Hand" and "She Loves You" made them famous throughout the world, and they were greeted by crowds of screaming fans wherever they went. The band broke up in 1970 to continue separate musical careers. John Lennon was shot dead in New York City.

John Lennon (far right) with the other members of the Beatles—from the left: Paul McCartney, Ringo Starr and George Harrison.

Lenôtre, André (1613–1700)
Lenôtre was a French landscape gardener who laid out many parks and gardens in France. His most famous work is the garden of Louis XIV's palace at Versailles.

Leo X (1475–1521)
Leo X was the name taken by Giovanni de'Medici when he became Pope in 1513. He was the son of Lorenzo de'Medici and was made a cardinal at the age of only 13. He inherited a love of the arts from his father, and as Pope encouraged painters such as Raphael and Da Vinci to come to Rome and work for him. He began a vast and expensive project to rebuild St. Peter's Church in Rome, for which he was criticized by Luther, the leader of the Protestant Reformation. Leo took no steps to reform the Roman Church, despite the criticisms of people like Luther, but he was nonetheless honest and strict in his own conduct. ○ MEDICI, RAPHAEL

Left: Leonardo's self-portrait in old age.

Madonna of the Rocks*, one of Leonardo's masterpieces.*

Leonardo da Vinci (1452–1519)
Leonardo was one of the most extraordinary and talented figures of the Renaissance. As a painter, his style influenced a whole generation of younger artists, but he was also a sculptor, architect, and engineer. He investigated anatomy and almost discovered the circulation of the blood, planned schemes for irrigation and drainage, designed the first armored car, and foresaw the invention of the helicopter, the airplane, and the submarine. Very few of his ideas were ever carried out: either he lost interest in them, or his imagination had carried him beyond the technology of his time.

Leonardo was born at Vinci, near Florence, and in about 1470 became an assistant to the painter and sculptor Andrea del Verrochio. It is said that when Verrochio saw an angel Leonardo had painted for a picture of the baptism of Christ, he gave up painting forever. In 1482 Leonardo moved to Milan, where he became painter and a kind of "court genius" to the duke. When he painted his famous *Last Supper* on a wall in the convent of Santa Maria del Grazie in Milan he was experimenting with a new oil paint. Unfortunately, it did not stick to the wall very well, and the picture began to crumble almost as soon as it was finished. In about 1500 Leonardo returned to Florence and was employed to paint one wall of the government chamber there. His great rival Michelangelo was to paint the opposite wall, and the room would then contain the finest art of the time. But neither picture was ever finished, and Leonardo left Florence and traveled to Rome and then Paris. It was about this time that he painted his famous *Mona Lisa*. Leonardo left only a few finished pictures, and never wrote a "Treatise on Painting" which he had planned, but many drawings and notebooks have survived.

○ BOTTICELLI, MICHELANGELO

Lesseps, Vicomte Ferdinand Marie de (1805–94)
Lesseps was the French engineer who designed and constructed the Suez Canal. He worked for several years as a diplomat in the Middle East and became friends with Mohammed Said, who became governor of Suez in 1854. Said granted permission to build the canal and work began in 1860. Nine years later, the Suez Canal was opened to shipping, and Lesseps suddenly became an international celebrity for having found a way to save ships the long, expensive, and often dangerous journey around the Cape of Good Hope. A similar scheme to build a Panama canal ended in 1893 in failure and ruin for Lesseps.

Lessing, Doris May (1919–)
Doris Lessing is a novelist who lives and works in England. She was born in Iran and grew up in Rhodesia (now Zimbabwe) in southern Africa. She began writing and became involved in left-wing politics. Her first novel, *The Grass Is Singing*, was published after she moved to England in 1949. Among her other works are *The Golden Notebook* (1962) and *Briefing for a Descent into Hell* (1971).

Lewis, John Llewellyn (1880–1969)
Lewis was an American trade union leader. He worked as a miner from the age of 12, and in 1920

became the leader of the United Mine Workers' Union. He retained this position for the next 40 years and obtained better wages and conditions for miners throughout the country.

Lewis, Sinclair (1885–1951)
Sinclair Lewis was an American novelist, and the first American to win the Nobel Prize for Literature. He was born in Minnesota, where his father was a doctor, and after attending Yale University he became a journalist. His first novel, *Main Street,* appeared in 1920 and became a best-seller. Many of his works attack what he saw as the intolerance and narrow-mindedness of American small-town life. In 1925 he was awarded, but refused to accept, a Pulitzer Prize for his novel *Arrowsmith.* Other works include *Elmer Gantry* and *It Can't Happen Here.*

Abraham Lincoln at Sharpsburg in October 1862. The war that Lincoln hoped would be over in a few months dragged on for four years and cost the lives of half a million men.

Lincoln, Abraham (1809–65)
Abraham Lincoln is considered by many to have been the greatest of all the presidents of the United States.

He was born near the settlement of Hodgenville in Kentucky. After a move to Indiana in 1816, his mother died, but his father soon remarried, and Lincoln's stepmother encouraged him to read and gave him what education she could. In 1830 the family moved again, to Illinois where Lincoln first owned a small store, then became postmaster. He was captain of the local volunteer army, and in 1834 he was elected to serve in the state assembly.

Lincoln had never had any proper schooling, but by 1842 he had taught himself law and was allowed to practice as a lawyer. In 1847 he was elected to the House of Representatives, where he spoke out as an opponent of the war against Mexico and the extension of slavery into the north of the country. Until 1854, slavery was illegal in many Northern states, but in that year a new measure was proposed which would allow each state to choose for itself. Lincoln opposed this. At first he argued that Negro slavery would take jobs from white workers, but later he came to oppose slavery simply because he believed that it was wrong. In 1860 he was nominated as a presidential candidate. Because he was a well-known opponent of slavery, his victory in the election was seen as a threat by the Southern states, whose economies relied on slaves. South Carolina and six others decided to declare themselves independent of the United States, and in April 1861 the American Civil War broke out between the Southern Confederacy and the Northern Union. Lincoln believed that the country should remain united, and that it should offer freedom to all its people, both black and white. At Gettysburg in 1863 he said that democracy should be "government of the people, by the people, and for the people." In 1864, while the Civil War continued, he was re-elected on a policy of reconciliation with the South, saying: "Let us strive ... to bind up the nation's wounds ... to do all which may achieve a just and lasting peace." But five days after the end of the Civil War, in April 1865, he was assassinated in a Washington theater by an actor named John Wilkes Booth. A famous memorial in Washington commemorates his life and work. ○ GRANT, LEE

Lindbergh, Charles Augustus (1902–74)
Lindbergh was an American aviator who made the first solo flight across the Atlantic Ocean. He became devoted to flying at an early age, and gave up studying engineering in order to take flying lessons instead. He bought his first plane in 1923, paying $500 for it. Four years later he took off from Roosevelt Field in New York in a plane called the *Spirit of St. Louis.* Thirty-three hours and 3,600 miles later he landed in Paris to a hero's welcome. He described his journey in a book, also called *Spirit of St. Louis,* which won him a Pulitzer Prize.

Linnaeus, Carl (1707–78)
Linnaeus was a Swedish scientist who developed the system of classifying plants and animals according first to their genus, or family, and then by species, or individual, names. He was the son of a clergyman and studied at universities in the cities of Lund and Uppsala. He had at first wanted to become a doctor, but gave this up to study natural

history. He became professor of botany at Uppsala in 1742, and made a 4,000-mile journey through Lapland collecting new species and classifying them. After Linnaeus died, all his books and papers were given to the English Biological Association, which afterward became known as the "Linnaeus Society."

Lister, Lord Joseph (1827–1912)
Lister was an English surgeon who introduced the antiseptic system to modern medicine. After the invention of simple anesthetics in the 18th century, many more people were able to have operations—but more people were also dying as a result of infection. Lister discovered that infections were caused by microorganisms (or, simply, germs) and invented an antiseptic spray that killed them. As a result, many fewer people died in hospitals.

Liszt, Franz (1811–86)
Liszt was a Hungarian-born composer and pianist. He gave his first public performance at the age of nine. He studied in Vienna and toured Europe before settling in Paris in 1827. There he met composers such as Berlioz and Chopin, became friends with the novelist George Sand, and had a long love affair with the Comtesse d'Agoult. He taught, and gave recitals. Liszt was the first to give complete performances for the piano alone, and the first to play a whole recital from memory. His many compositions include two piano concertos (written in 1857 and 1863) and a famous piano sonata, as well as symphonies and other instrumental works. As well as over 400 original works, Liszt also transcribed some 900 others—which means that he took music written by another composer, and rewrote it for an instrument other than the one for which it was originally intended. In 1865, Liszt joined the Franciscan order of monks as a minor brother, and so became known as the "Abbé Liszt." His fame had made him wealthy, and in later life he helped other younger composers such as Schumann and Wagner, several of whose operas he produced. ○ CHOPIN, WAGNER

Livingstone, David (1813–73)
Livingstone was a Scottish missionary and explorer. He was born in Lanarkshire, where he worked in a cotton mill from the age of 10 until 24. He decided he wanted to become a missionary and went to London to train as a doctor. Originally, Livingstone had wanted to go to China, but war made that impossible and he was persuaded to travel to Africa instead. After some years in southern Africa he began a journey north into previously unexplored country, hoping to extend Christian teaching and discover new trade routes. He found Lake Ngami, traveled up the Zambezi River, and was the first European to see Victoria Falls. He returned to London amid great

Liszt playing the piano to a group of "romantic" musicians and composers.

excitement. Two more expeditions followed, although Livingstone had now resigned from the missionary society so as to be able to give all his efforts to exploration. In March 1866 he set out hoping to find the source of the river Nile. After nothing had been heard of him for several years a New York newspaper sent the explorer **Henry Morton Stanley** (1841–1904) to search for him. Stanley discovered Livingstone at Ujiji in 1871, where he greeted him with the famous words "Dr. Livingstone, I presume." Livingstone died in Africa two years later, still searching for the source of the Nile.

David Livingstone explored much of south and central Africa.

Lloyd George, David, 1st Earl (1863–1945)
Lloyd George was British Liberal prime minister from 1916 until 1922. He rose to prominence during Asquith's government (1908–16), when as Chancellor of the Exchequer he introduced radical new measures such as the Pensions and National Insurance Acts. Asquith's unpopularity during World War I led to his being replaced by Lloyd George as prime minister. He was a courageous and decisive war leader, but in the elections of 1918 he failed to get re-elected by a clear majority. As a result, he could only govern with the support of the Conservatives, and when they withdrew in 1922, Lloyd George was forced to resign.
○ ASQUITH

Locke, John (1632–1704)
Locke was an English philosopher who became particularly well known for his ideas about government. His most famous works are the *Essay Concerning Human Understanding* and *Treatises on Government* (both published in 1690). Locke said that government is a "contract" between a ruler and the people, and if the ruler breaks the contract by not serving the good of the people he should be deposed.

Lomonosov, Mikhail Vasilievich (1711–65)
Lomonosov was a Russian whose activities included writing poetry and history, collecting antiques, studying physics, chemistry, and geography, and keeping records of the weather. He ran away from home at an early age to seek an education, and eventually became professor of chemistry at St. Petersburg and the first person to lecture on the sciences in the Russian language.

London, Jack (1876–1916)
Jack London was an American novelist. He was born in San Francisco, did many odd jobs, became a sailor, a tramp, and a gold miner, and finally took up writing. His novels are based on his own experience in the wilds of America. They include *The Call of the Wild* (1903) and *The Iron Heel* (1907).

Longfellow, Henry Wadsworth (1807–82)
Longfellow was an American poet. He was born in the state of Maine, where he went to college and became professor of modern languages. He made several trips to Europe, during which he kept journals that were later published. From 1836 until 1854 he was professor of modern languages at Harvard University. He published his first collection of poetry in 1839. His best works are his long, narrative poems—poems that tell a story. They include *Hiawatha* and *Tales of a Wayside Inn.*

Lorca, Federico Garcia (1899–1936)
Lorca was a great Spanish poet and playwright. He was born near Granada in the south of the country. The countryside around Granada was the home of bands of gypsies who lived in caves on the hillsides. Many of Lorca's poems were inspired by gypsy storytelling, including the *Romancero Gitano* ("Gypsy Romance"), the poem that made him famous on its publication in 1928. Between 1929 and 1931 Lorca visited the United States. He became interested in Negro music and jazz, and tried to incorporate some of its sounds and rhythms into his poems. At about this time he also began writing plays. The best known is *Blood Wedding,* first performed in 1933. Lorca was not actively involved in politics, but at the outbreak of the Spanish Civil War in 1936 he was shot—probably as the result of a misunderstanding—by the Fascists.

Louis XIV (1638–1715)
Louis XIV became king of France in 1643. He became known as the "Great King" because his reign was one of prosperity and success for France,

and as the "Sun King" because he ruled in great splendor. Louis was only 5 years old when he inherited the throne, so for the next eighteen years his mother, Anne of Austria, and her skilled minister Mazarin governed the country. Louis took charge after Mazarin's death in 1661, and from then on every aspect of the government came under his strict personal supervision. He was energetic, intelligent, and persevering. He personally chose his ministers—men such as Colbert, who rebuilt the French economy, and Louvois, who reorganized and re-equipped the army.

Under Louis's rule, France quickly became a strong nation. In 1667 he began a series of wars against the Netherlands, which were at that time governed by Spain. By the 1680s, Louis had conquered territory in the Netherlands, as well as in Germany, and was recognized as the most powerful monarch in Europe. He reached the peak of his success when he took control of the city of Strasbourg in 1684. His decline began five years later, when the French army was defeated by William of Orange. In 1702 the War of Spanish Succession resulted in further defeats at the hands of Marlborough. Although Louis did not lose much territory, he lost a lot of prestige, and the French economy was ruined by the expense of the war.

Louis spent a fortune on the building and decoration of the palace of Versailles. He supported artists, and a great many French writers, including Corneille, Molière, and Racine, flourished during his reign. ○ COLBERT, LEBRUN, MARLBOROUGH, MAZARIN

The execution of Louis XVI in the Place de la Révolution, now the Place de la Concorde on January 21, 1793.

Louis XVI (1754–93)
Louis XVI was the king of France when the French Revolution broke out in 1789. Four years later, through a combination of foolishness, bad advice, and bad luck, he became the revolution's most famous victim when he was brought to trial and guillotined. Louis was the grandson of Louis XV, whom he succeeded as king in 1774. He inherited terrible economic and political problems: a series of wars had cost the French government large sums of money, and as a result the people suffered heavy taxes. Louis improved things a little by repealing the worst of the taxes, and for a while he was popular. But then France entered the American War of Independence and the government had to raise extra money to pay for the war. Louis's minister Necker proposed to tax the aristocracy, but the aristocrats, led by Louis's queen, Marie Antoinette, opposed this and forced Necker to resign. For several years the economy became steadily worse and the people of the country more discontented. Finally, in 1788, Necker was recalled to his old job.

Louis XIV of France (known as the Sun King) reigned for 72 years. He held a magnificent court at Versailles and ruled with absolute authority.

He demanded that the king summon the "States-General," an ancient French assembly made up of representatives from all over the country which could vote on taxes and other policies. The States-General met in May 1789. It was made up of aristocrats, bishops, and the "third estate"—middle-class businessmen and others. The third estate decided to form their own National Assembly and force the king to accept a new constitution for France. This was the first stage of the French Revolution. The king refused their demands, and tried to silence the calls for change by force. On July 14 revolutionaries in Paris stormed the Bastille fortress and took control of the city. Similar things happened throughout the country, and Louis quickly lost control. Eventually, in 1791, he and his family tried to flee, but they were caught and returned to Paris. He then began plotting with other countries to declare war on the revolutionary government, and it was this that led to his downfall. He was imprisoned, tried, and on January 20, 1793, executed. ○ DANTON, MARIE ANTOINETTE, NECKER, ROBESPIERRE

Lowell, Robert Traill Spence (1917–77)
Robert Lowell was one of the finest American poets of the 20th century. He was a member of a family which included several well-known poets, writers, and scientists. Lowell went to Harvard and lived much of his life in Massachusetts. Among his collections of poems are *Life Studies* and *Near the Ocean,* and he also translated work from other languages (*Imitations*). Robert Lowell was born in Boston. He was a conscientious objector during World War II.

Loyola, Saint Ignatius de (1491–1556)
Saint Ignatius was the founder of the order of Jesuits. The son of a nobleman from the Basque region of northern Spain, he became a soldier. After being wounded in battle he decided to give up soldiering and devote himself to the Church. Ignatius gathered a band of disciples which was officially recognized as the Society of Jesus by Pope Paul III in 1540.

Luke, Saint (d. *c.* A.D. 90)
Saint Luke was a companion of Saint Paul and the author of the third gospel and the Acts of the Apostles in the New Testament. He was a doctor—Saint Paul calls him "Our beloved Luke, the physician"—and he probably died in Greece, but little else is known about him. Luke is the patron saint of painters and doctors. ○ PAUL

Luther, Martin (1483–1546)
Martin Luther was a German religious reformer who became the most important of the founders of Protestantism. He was born in the kingdom of Saxony, and at first studied to become a lawyer. He gained his law degree in 1505, but Luther had already become interested in religion and joined a monastery. In 1507 he became a Catholic priest, and began preaching and lecturing at the University of Wittenberg.

Luther first became disillusioned with the Catholic Church when he visited Rome in 1511 and was shocked by the luxury and extravagance of the Pope's court. Then, in 1517, Pope Leo X began raising money by selling "indulgences"—that is, allowing people to buy forgiveness for their sins from the Church. Luther opposed this. He angrily nailed a paper with his "Ninety-five theses attacking the sale of indulgences" to the door of his church in Wittenberg. This was the beginning of a long series of disputes between Luther and the Church, and eventually the Pope excommunicated Luther. Luther, who denied the Pope's authority in many spiritual matters, burned the announcement of his excommunication in public. By now his opinions had support throughout Germany. The Emperor Charles V tried to bring about a reconciliation at the Diet of Worms in 1521, but Luther refused to change his views. He said: "Here I stand, I can do no other, so help me God." With the protection of various German princes, the Protestants finally separated from the Roman Catholic Church. Luther married Katharina von Bora in 1525. His most famous written work is his translation of the Bible, finished in 1532. ○ CALVIN, CRANACH, ERASMUS, KNOX, LEO X

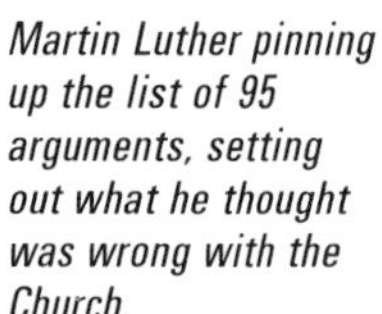

Martin Luther pinning up the list of 95 arguments, setting out what he thought was wrong with the Church.

M

McAdam, John Loudon (1756–1836)
The inventor of the "macadam" system of surfacing roads. He was born in Scotland, and made a huge fortune in business in the United States. In 1783 he returned to Britain and began experimenting with different methods of road building. Although he was successful and his advice was sought by many people, his experiments made him poor, until, in 1825, he was awarded a government pension.

MacArthur, Douglas (1880–1964)
General Douglas MacArthur was a soldier whose campaigns in World War II and the Korean War made him an American military hero. He was born at Little Rock in the state of Arkansas and went to the United States Military Academy at West Point. During World War I MacArthur served in France and gained a reputation as a brilliant leader. In 1919 MacArthur became the youngest ever superintendent of the West Point academy. This rapid rise continued: he was made an army head of the U.S. military forces in the Philippine Islands in 1935.

The Japanese air attack on Pearl Harbor in Hawaii in 1941 led to the American entry into World War II. MacArthur became commander of the U.S. forces in the Pacific and planned the defense of the Philippines against Japanese attack. His campaign to defend the islands was skillful, but unsuccessful, and in March 1942 he retreated and set up a new headquarters in Australia. The Japanese advance in the Pacific was halted in New Guinea, and MacArthur then carried out a clever island-hopping campaign which eventually enabled him to recapture the Philippines.

In 1950 war broke out between North and South Korea, and the South Koreans asked the United Nations to intervene on their behalf. President Truman sent MacArthur to take command of the UN forces. He was at first able to force the North Koreans to retreat, but in November 1950 the Chinese entered the war on the side of the North. MacArthur asked Truman for permission to bomb Chinese airbases and blockade Chinese ports. Truman refused, and in April 1951 removed MacArthur from his command. The general returned to the United States and a hero's welcome.
○ TRUMAN

Macbeth (d. 1057)
Macbeth became king of Scotland in 1040 when he killed King Duncan and seized the throne. His reign is said to have been a time of plenty, but in 1057 he was overthrown by Duncan's son Malcolm. Shakespeare's famous play *Macbeth* is based on accounts of his life found in historical chronicles, but most of the characters and events are imaginary. ○ SHAKESPEARE

Maccabaeus, Judas (d. 160 B.C.)
The Maccabees were a family of ancient Jewish leaders who opposed foreign persecution of their people. **Mattathias Maccabaeus** (d. 166 B.C.) was the founder of the family. He refused to give up the Jewish faith and led a revolt against King Antiochus of Syria. Judas Maccabaeus was his son. He took command of the Jewish army, recaptured Jerusalem from the Syrians, and re-established Jewish worship in the Temple. Having made the Jews strong again, he made an alliance with the Romans, but in 160 B.C. he was killed in battle. One of his brothers, **Simon Maccabaeus** (d. 135 B.C.), later became ruler.

Machiavelli, Niccolo (1469–1527)
Machiavelli was an Italian politician and writer at the beginning of the 16th century. He was born in the city of Florence, where he became a lawyer and then secretary of the "Council of Ten"—the council which governed Florence's affairs with other cities and states. He was sent on missions to France and Germany, and in 1502 he was the

Machiavelli was an Italian political philosopher of the Renaissance. In The Prince *he argued that rulers should use whatever methods they can to srengthen the state.*

Florentine representative at Cesare Borgia's court. This experience inspired his most famous book, *The Prince*, which was written in 1513 but not published until after Machiavelli's death. In *The Prince* he describes the qualities politicians must have in order to succeed and survive. He says they must be cunning and treacherous, and their evil deeds are justified because the people they rule are also evil. For a long time people thought that Machiavelli believed that this was right and that he intended his book as advice to ambitious princes. But in fact he simply described what he saw in Cesare Borgia and other princes like him. ○ BORGIA, MEDICI

Magellan, Ferdinand (*c.*1480–1521)
Magellan was the leader of the first expedition successfully to sail all the way around the world. He was born in Portugal and became a soldier. During a battle in Morocco he received an injury that left him lame for the rest of his life. He was then accused of stealing. He returned to Portugal to plead his innocence, but he was ignored, so he next decided to go to Spain. There, he proposed an expedition to sail westward to the East Indies. The king—the Emperor Charles V—approved and supplied Magellan with five ships. They left Seville in August 1519, and after sailing along the coast of South America discovered a narrow strait that led from the Atlantic to a vast new ocean. The strait is known as "Magellan's Strait," and Magellan named the new ocean the "Pacific," because he found it to be very peaceful. The expedition continued west, eventually reaching the Philippine Islands. Magellan was killed in a fight with natives of the islands, but his second-in-command sailed on, and in September 1522 arrived back in Spain, so completing the first "circumnavigation" (journey around) of the world.

Mahler, Gustav (1860–1911)
Mahler was an Austrian-born composer and conductor who lived and worked in Vienna and later in New York. He wrote long, dramatic symphonies and collections of songs. Among the most famous are his Eighth Symphony and *The Song of the Earth*. Mahler was conductor of several orchestras, including the Vienna Opera and the New York Metropolitan Opera.

Maimonides, Moses ben Maimon (1153–1204)
Maimonides was a Jewish philosopher. He was born in Spain, but after the Arab invasion of the country he and his family moved to Morocco and then to Cairo in Egypt. Maimonides was a doctor, and as well as being one of the leaders of the Jewish community in Egypt he became doctor to Saladin, the sultan. His most famous work is *The Guide for the Perplexed*, which describes his ideas about God and people's knowledge of God, but he also wrote about the law, science, and medicine. He remained one of the most influential of all Jewish thinkers for several centuries, and also influenced Christians such as St. Thomas Aquinas.

Malcolm X (Malcolm Little, 1925–65)
Malcolm X was the name used by a well-known leader of the black civil rights movement that grew in strength in the United States in the 1960s. Like his contemporary, Martin Luther King, Malcolm X wanted to improve the position of blacks in America, but he believed that they should seek self-government rather than equality with whites. He was a Muslim, and he became well known as a speaker and writer on racial issues and as a leader of the black Muslim community in America. In 1964 he formed the Organization for Afro-Americian Unity to promote links between blacks on the two continents. He was assassinated at a rally in New York City. ○ KING

Malcolm X, leader of the American Black Muslim sect in 1965.

Mallarmé, Stéphane (1842–98)
Mallarmé was a French poet. His works are known as "symbolist" because he gave certain words and phrases special meanings which were supposed to bring particular patterns or pictures to the reader's mind. He was influenced by Impressionist painters, and his most famous work, *L'Après-midi d'un faune*, was illustrated by Manet and inspired music by Debussy. ○ DEBUSSY, MANET

Malory, Sir Thomas (d. 1471)
An English knight who probably spent most of his life in prison and wrote the most famous English version of the story of King Arthur. It is called the *Morte d'Arthur* ("Death of Arthur") and describes the breakup of the famous Round Table and the quest for the Holy Grail. It was first printed by Caxton. ○ ARTHUR, CAXTON

Winnie Mandela, wife of jailed nationalist leader, Nelson, and herself an activist.

Mandela, Nelson Rolihlahla (1918–)
Nelson Mandela is one of Africa's most important political leaders. He was born in Transekei in South Africa and became a lawyer. After World War II, the white South African government introduced the policy of "Apartheid"—"separate development" for black and white people. Mandela and others formed the African National Congress in 1944 and began a campaign of non-violent opposition to the government, including strikes and demonstrations. In 1964 he was arrested and charged with several political offenses. He has been in prison ever since, but has remained a symbol of black opposition to white rule in South Africa. His wife, **Winnie Mandela**, has also been a powerful opponent of the South African system, despite restrictions imposed on her by the authorities.

Manet, Édouard (1832–83)
A French painter who rejected traditional "classical" French painting in the 19th century and developed a distinct style of his own. His work influenced the first Impressionist painters, including Monet and Renoir, and later artists such as Cézanne. His pictures include the *Bar at the Folies Bergères* and the *Déjeuner sur l'herbe* ("Lunch on the Grass").
○ CÉZANNE, MALLARMÉ, MONET

Mansfield, Katherine (1888–1923)
Katherine Mansfield was a New Zealand-born short-story writer. In 1908 she moved to Europe where she remained until she died, of tuberculosis. Her stories, which were influenced by those of Chekhov, are delicate and often ironic in style. Collections include *In a German Pension* (1911) and *The Garden Party* (1922). ○ CHEKHOV

Manzoni, Alessandro (1785–1873)
Manzoni was an Italian writer. He was born in the city of Milan and lived for a while in Paris, before returning to Italy to work. He wrote poems, criticism, and philosophical essays, but his greatest work is the novel *I Promessi Sposi* ("The Betrothed"), which is also thought of as one of the greatest novels ever written in Italian. It is a romance set in the 17th century, and it took Manzoni six years of careful work to complete. After its publication in 1827 Manzoni became increasingly involved in Italian politics and a keen supporter of the unification of the country under one government.

Mao Ze-dong (Mao Tse-tung, 1893–1976)
Mao Ze-dong was one of the twelve founders of the Chinese Communist Party. He led the Communists through a long period of struggle and civil war to become the leader of China in 1949.

Mao was born in the province of Hunan, the son of a farmer. During the Chinese Revolution, in which Sun Yat-sen overthrew the old Manchu dynasty of emperors, Mao served as a member of Sun's revolutionary army. Afterward, he worked in a laundry, as the secretary of a trade union, and eventually as a teacher. From 1918 he studied at the University of Peking, where he was able to read works by European philosophers such as Marx and Darwin. The Chinese Communist Party was founded by Mao and others in 1921. Mao came to believe that the Chinese Revolution must be different from the Russian Revolution. There were few big cities in China, so instead of being led by the working class, who lived in the cities and worked in factories, it would be led by peasants and small farmers from the countryside. At first, Mao cooperated with the government (now led by Chiang Kai-shek). But in 1927 the Communists withdrew their support for Chiang. Mao built up a peasant army in Hunan Province and declared the Communists leaders of a new "Chinese Soviet Republic." Chiang Kai-shek's army made several attacks on the Communists, until Mao and his supporters were forced to leave Hunan. With

Mao Ze-dong, first leader of Communist China.

80,000 others, he began the "Long March" to the safety of Yenan in northwest China. The journey took a year, from October 1934 until October 1935, and covered almost 6,000 miles. Three fourths of those who set out from Hunan died along the way.

When the Japanese invaded China in 1937, Mao's army cooperated with the government in resisting their attacks. But at the end of World War II in 1945, the Communists resumed the war with Chiang's government. By 1949, Chiang had been forced to retreat to the island of Taiwan, and Mao proclaimed the founding of the People's Republic of China. He remained the dominant figure in Chinese politics until his death, writing books and poetry as well as organizing the government. Mao's fourth wife, **Jiang Q'ing** (1910–), was also an important figure in the revolution, but since Mao's death she has fallen from favor.
○ CHIANG KAI-SHEK, SUN YAT-SEN

Marat, Jean Paul (1743–93)
Marat was a French revolutionary politician. He was a doctor and a scientist, and studied electricity and optics, publishing several scientific papers. When the French Revolution broke out in 1789 he began a newspaper called *L'Ami du peuple* ("The People's Friend") which became famous for its extreme opinions. He supported violence against the aristocracy and the old rulers. This made him popular with the "mob" in Paris, but also placed him in great danger from his opponents. He often had to flee, and once hid in the Paris sewers. Marat had a skin disease which forced him to spend much time in the bath. There, on July 13, 1793, Charlotte Corday stabbed him to death. ○ CORDAY, DANTON, ROBESPIERRE

Marconi, Guglielmo (1874–1937)
Marconi was an Italian inventor who became the first man successfully to transmit radio signals over a long distance. He studied at the University of Bologna, where discoveries made by other scientists such as Hertz led him to experiment with radio signals. His first major breakthrough came in 1895, when he was able to transmit signals between two points a mile apart. The British Post Office decided to support his research, and in 1898 he succeeded in sending signals between Britain and France. Then, in 1901, he sent the first radio signals across the Atlantic Ocean. He was awarded the 1909 Nobel Prize for Physics for his work.
○ HERTZ

Marconi, the Italian inventor. In 1901 he sent the first radio message across the Atlantic.

Maria Theresa (1717–80)
See Habsburg

Marie Antoinette (1755–93)
Marie Antoinette was queen of France at the time of the French Revolution. She was the fourth daughter of Maria Theresa, the empress of Austria, and the Emperor Francis I. In 1770 she married the future king of France, Louis XVI. After the couple's ascent to the throne in 1774, Marie Antoinette quickly became unpopular with the French people. She was extravagant and strong-willed. Many people thought she was trying to further the interests of Austria at the expense of France, and when men such as Necker and Turgot suggested reforms of the French economy, she bitterly opposed them. Louis XVI, who was as weak and indecisive as Marie Antoinette was strong, was often influenced by her. When the French

Revolution broke out in 1789, she opposed reform, and when the situation became desperate she tried first to bring the Austrian army to fight for the French crown, and then to flee the country. These things led to her and her husband's downfall. She was imprisoned by the revolutionaries, then brought to trial. After two days of questioning she was sentenced to death, and guillotined on October 16, 1793. ○ HABSBURG, LOUIS XVI, ROBESPIERRE

Marie de France (d. *c.*1200)
Marie de France was a French medieval poet. Her most famous works are her *Lais*, a collection of 14 romantic tales written in verse. She also wrote a collection of fables, in about the year 1170.

Mark Antony (*c.*82 B.C.–30 B.C.)
Mark Antony (also called Marcus Antonius) was a Roman soldier who after Julius Caesar's death became one of the three rulers of the Roman world. He is thought to have had a wild and irresponsible youth. He was often drunk, and was forced by people to whom he owed money to escape to Greece. However, he became a favorite of Julius Caesar, and when the civil war between Caesar and Pompey broke out, Mark Antony fought with great distinction on Caesar's side. After the war, Caesar left Antony in charge of Italy while he went on an expedition to Africa. In 44 B.C. Caesar was assassinated by a group of senators led by Brutus and Cassius. As a friend of Caesar, Antony was able to use the Roman people's anger at his murder to rise to power. The assassins were chased out of Rome, and together with Lepidus and Octavian (who later became the Emperor Augustus), Antony defeated Brutus and Cassius at the Battle of Philippi. Antony, Octavian, and Lepidus agreed to divide the world among themselves: Antony ruled Gaul in the north, Lepidus ruled Spain, and Octavian Africa and the Mediterranean. Antony now traveled to Egypt, where he met and was enchanted by Queen Cleopatra. The two became lovers, and Antony remained in Egypt, living with her in great luxury. Eventually, he was forced to return to Rome, where power was redivided between Antony and Octavian alone. But he was soon to return to Cleopatra. Octavian and the Roman people turned against Antony; in 31 B.C. Octavian's navy defeated the combined forces of Antony and Cleopatra at the Battle of Actium. When Antony, faced with capture, heard a false report of Cleopatra's death, he killed himself by falling on his sword.
○ AUGUSTUS, BRUTUS, CLEOPATRA, JULIUS CAESAR

Duke of Marlborough (right).

Marie Antoinette, wife of King Louis XVI of France at the time of the French Revolution, interfered in politics and was hated by the French people.

Marlborough, John Churchill, 1st Duke of (1650–1722)
John Churchill was a famous British soldier. He was the son of an English nobleman called Sir Winston Churchill, who had supported Charles I during the English Civil War. As a result, he was fined and became poor. The young Marlborough went to St. Paul's school in London, and then became a page to the Duke of York. There he met the beautiful Duchess of Cleveland, who gave him money and got him a post in the army. Meanwhile, his sister Arabella, who was the Duke of York's mistress, used her influence to have him promoted to the rank of colonel. He fought in Tangier and in the Dutch war which began in 1672. In 1677 he married **Sarah Jennings** (1660–1774), a lady-in-waiting to the queen, who used her influence over the queen to ensure her husband's advancement. Marlborough served King James II by crushing the Monmouth rebellion in 1685, but James was a weak and unpopular king and in 1688 William of Orange landed in England and claimed the throne. Marlborough switched his allegiance to William. In the War of Spanish Succession, which began in 1701, Marlborough led the British army to impressive victories at Blenheim, Malplaquet, and elsewhere over Louis XIV's French army. Meanwhile, Marlborough's enemies in England conspired to have him removed from his post. In 1711 he suddenly found himself dismissed, and his wife was no longer able to use her influence to protect him. Three years later he was reinstated by King George I, and he continued to act as a military adviser to the king until his death.
○ LOUIS XIV, WILLIAM OF ORANGE

Marley, Bob (1945–81)
Bob Marley was the Jamaican singer and songwriter who made "Reggae" music popular throughout the world. He was born in the city of Kingston, where he made his first record at the age of 19. The following year he formed the band "The Wailers," with whom he continued to make records until his death. Marley was a member of the Rastafarian religion. His songs are often political, and he became one of the most important spokesmen for West Indian culture.

The Jamaican singer Bob Marley. He made Reggae popular worldwide.

Marlowe, Christopher (1564–93)
Marlowe was, after Shakespeare, one of the greatest of the many playwrights who worked in England during the reign of Queen Elizabeth I. He was born in Canterbury, where his father was a shoemaker and where he went to school. From there, he went to study at Cambridge, and then moved to London where he immediately began writing plays. Little is known about Marlowe's life. He may have been involved in spying or some other dangerous and secret work, and he was killed in a fight in a tavern in east London at the age of only 29. His greatest plays are *The Tragical History of Doctor Faustus*, written in 1588, *The Jew of Malta* (1589), and *Edward II* (1592). Marlowe also wrote poetry, and he is thought to have written parts of two of Shakespeare's plays, *Titus Andronicus* and *Henry VI*. ○ SHAKESPEARE

Márquez, Gabriel Garcia (1928–)
Márquez is a Colombian novelist. His great book, *One Hundred Years of Solitude*, first published in 1967, helped increase interest in South American literature throughout the world. His other works include *The Autumn of the Patriarch* (1975), and he won the 1975 Nobel Prize for Literature.

Marshall, George Catlett (1880–1959)
George Marshall was an American soldier, diplomat, and administrator. After serving in World War I and with the American army in the Philippine Islands, he became chief of staff for all the American armed forces in World War II. During the war he supported a policy of completely defeating Hitler's Germany. But as the U.S. secretary of state he introduced the "Marshall Plan:" a program of American aid which would help the German and other European economies recover after the war.

Marvell, Andrew (1621–78)
Andrew Marvell was an English poet. Like his friend Milton, he was interested and involved in the politics of his time. He was a supporter of Cromwell, and in 1659 he was elected as the Member of Parliament for the town of Hull. Later, he became a diplomat and went on a mission to Russia. His poems include *To His Coy Mistress, The Garden*, and *The Bermudas*. ○ CROMWELL, MILTON

Marx, Karl (1818–83)
Karl Marx is among the most important and influential of all modern philosophers. He was the founder of the Communist movement, and his ideas about history and economics form the basis of socialist politics throughout the world. He was born in Trier in Germany and studied history and philosophy at universities in Berlin and Bonn. In 1842 he became the editor of a radical newspaper, but a year later the government forced it to close. Marx moved to Paris, but the French government refused to allow him to stay, so he settled for a time in Brussels. In 1848 Europe was convulsed by revolution. Marx took part in uprisings in Germany, and the same year he wrote the *Communist Manifesto* together with Engels. This book encouraged factory workers to overthrow rich and powerful people, and ended with the words: "The workers have nothing to lose but their chains. They have a world to win. Workers of the world, unite!" It made Marx unpopular with

George Marshall, the U.S. secretary of state who introduced the Marshall Plan to help Europe recover after World War II, and Karl Marx (right).

European governments, and he moved again, to London, where he remained until his death. There, he and his family lived in poverty, while Marx worked long hours in the British Museum. His great work *Das Kapital* says that history is a long series of conflicts between different classes. First the aristocrats and the feudal system were overthrown by the middle classes and the capitalist system. Next, said Marx, the workers must overthrow the middle classes. Eventually he believed that there would cease to be different classes at all, and that everybody would have an equal share of wealth and power. Marx's ideas have influenced not only politics and philosophy, but the study of history, literature, and art, as well as many other things. ○ ENGELS, HEGEL

Mary Queen of Scots (1542–87)
Mary was the daughter of King James V of Scotland. She was born as her father lay on his deathbed, so became queen when she was only a few days old. Scotland was at that time torn by religious disputes between members of the Roman Catholic faith and those who joined the new Protestant Church led by John Knox. Mary's family were devout Catholics. In order to protect her from the influence of Scottish Protestants, Mary's mother, Mary of Guise, took control of the government and sent the young queen to France. There she was educated, and eventually married the future King Francis II. He died in 1660, after only a year on the throne, and Mary returned to Scotland. At first she governed wisely. She continued to worship as a Catholic, but allowed the Protestants freedom to practice their own religion. But her marriage to Lord Darnley in 1565 was not a success. He claimed too much power for himself, and in 1566 he murdered Mary's chief adviser. In February 1567 Darnley caught smallpox. As he lay recovering in a house in Glasgow he was killed by a bomb explosion—only hours after being visited by the queen.

Many people thought that Mary knew of the plot, and three months later she married the man who carried it out, the Earl of Bothwell. This behavior outraged her subjects. Her army deserted her and Bothwell fled. In June 1567 she was forced to abdicate in favor of her son (by Lord Darnley), who became James VI of Scotland, and later James I of England. Mary took refuge in England, but the fact that she was a Catholic made people there suspicious of her. Queen Elizabeth kept Mary prisoner, while English Catholics plotted to depose Elizabeth and bring Mary to the English throne. When the "Babington Conspiracy" to kill Elizabeth was discovered to have had Mary's approval, she was brought to trial and executed.
○ ELIZABETH I, KNOX, JAMES I

The execution of Mary Queen of Scots.

Masaccio (1401–28)
One of the greatest painters of the first part of the Renaissance period. His most important surviving paintings are in the Church of Santa Maria della Carmine in the city of Florence. Masaccio's figures have interesting, individual expressions, like his predecessor Giotto's, but they also have strength and shape, which he learned from sculptors such as Donatello. ○ DONATELLO, GIOTTO, MILTON

Matilda (1102–67)
Matilda was the only child of King Henry I of England. When her father died in 1135 she was supposed to inherit the throne, but many English barons refused to accept her as queen. Instead, her cousin, **Stephen of Blois** (1097–1154), arrived in the country from France and claimed the throne for himself. Stephen and Matilda waged war on each other for several years. Stephen was at first successful, but he made many enemies because of the privileges he allowed to a few of his lords. In 1141 Matilda captured Stephen and held him prisoner. She now claimed the throne, but Stephen eventually escaped and chased her from the country. However, it was Matilda's son who became the country's next king, Henry II.

Matisse, Henri (1869–1954)
Henri Matisse was a French artist. While studying in Paris he was influenced first by the Impressionists, then by the works of Paul Cézanne.

But in about 1905 he became the leader of a new group of artists called the *Fauves* ("wild beasts"). They were interested in color above all else. Although Matisse was a fine drawer, his paintings often seem very badly drawn, and he did not make much use of perspective. Instead, he liked to use large areas of bold primary colors. Matisse spent much of his life living on the Mediterranean coast in the south of France, where the bright sunlight and the blue of the sea inspired many of his paintings. He painted sea-front scenes, still lifes, and figures. As he grew older his eyesight became bad, and he found it increasingly difficult to hold a paintbrush. For these reasons, he switched from painting to making pictures from pieces of brightly colored paper which he tore or cut to shape. These "paper cut-outs" are among the most colorful and enjoyable works in all of 20th-century art.

Matthew, Saint (C.A.D. 5–A.D. 85)
Matthew was one of Christ's twelve disciples and the author of the first of the four gospels of the New Testament. Very little is known about him, other than that he was working as a tax collector when Christ called him to become a disciple. He probably wrote the first version of his gospel in about A.D. 40. He is called "Levi" in the gospels of Saint Mark and Saint Luke. ○ LUKE

Maugham, W. Somerset (1874–1965)
Somerset Maugham was an English novelist and playwright whose work showed a fine understanding of people. He was born in Paris and orphaned at the age of ten. His best known novels are *Of Human Bondage,* a partly autobiographical account of the struggles of a young medical student, and *Cakes and Ale.*

Maupassant, Guy de (1850–93)
Maupassant was a French short-story writer and novelist. He was the son of an aristocrat, born in a château in the province of Normandy. After spending a short time as a soldier, he became a clerk in a government office. His mother introduced him to the writer Gustave Flaubert, and it was Flaubert who first encouraged Maupassant to write. In 1880 he published a story called *Boule de Suif* ("Bowl of Wax") in a magazine edited by Emile Zola. Its success made Maupassant decide to write for a living, and he went on to write over 300 more stories, as well as six novels. Like Zola and other French writers of the time he became interested in writing realistically and recording all the details of people's lives. His novels include *A Life* (1883) and *Bel Ami* (1885). Maupassant suffered from mental illnesses for much of his adult life, and eventually died of insanity. ○ FLAUBERT, ZOLA

Maximilian (1832–67)
Maximilian was archduke of Austria and the younger brother of the Emperor Francis Joseph. In 1864, on Napoleon III's invitation, he was made emperor of Mexico. His reign, opposed by the republican forces of Benito Juarez, ended in his execution soon after the French troops of Napoleon were forced to withdraw by the United States.

Maxwell, James Clerk
See Clerk Maxwell

Mazarin, Jules (1602–61)
Mazarin was a powerful French politician. He was born in Italy, where he was educated in a Jesuit monastery and eventually joined the Church as a priest. In 1634 he was sent to France as a diplomat on behalf of the Pope. He remained in the country and became a French citizen, and in 1641 he was given a job as assistant to the powerful Cardinal Richelieu. Richelieu made Mazarin a cardinal, and after Richelieu's death in 1642 Mazarin became chief minister of France. In 1643 King Louis XIII died, and because the new King Louis XIV was too young to govern, Mazarin ruled the country together with Louis's mother, Anne of Austria. Anne was in love with Mazarin. Mazarin carried on his government without the agreement of the

Giuseppe Mazzini, the Italian revolutionary who campaigned for the unification of Italy.

French parliament, and this led to a series of civil wars. But he negotiated a treaty ending the Thirty Years' War which favored France, and improved relations between France and Spain. ○ LOUIS XIV, RICHELIEU

Mazzini, Giuseppe (1805–72)
Mazzini was an Italian revolutionary politician. He spent his life campaigning for the unification of Italy under one republican government, as well as taking part in other uprisings and protests around Europe. He was born in the seaport of Genoa where he became a member of a secret revolutionary society. Next he moved to Marseilles and founded a society and a newspaper called *Young Italy* dedicated to Italian unity. He was banished from Italy, then from France, and eventually from several other European countries. During the revolution of 1849 he became one of the republican leaders of the city of Rome, and after the revolution's defeat he supported Garibaldi's guerrilla wars against the foreign troops occupying parts of Italy. Italian unity was eventually achieved through Garibaldi's and Cavour's efforts, but Mazzini was important in encouraging support for the change. ○ CAVOUR, GARIBALDI

McCullers, Carson (1917–67)
Carson McCullers was an American novelist, born in the Southern state of Georgia. In her early twenties she began having regular illnesses, and at the age of 31 she became paralyzed in her left side. Despite only being able to use one hand to type, she continued to write novels and stories. Among the most famous are *The Heart Is a Lonely Hunter* (1940) and *The Member of the Wedding* (1946).

McLuhan, Marshall (1911–80)
A Canadian critic who specialized in analyzing the role of the media—television, radio, film, newspapers, and so forth—in modern society. He taught at universities in the U.S.A. and Canada, and established a center for the study of culture and technology at Toronto University.

Mead, Margaret (1901–78)
Margaret Mead was an American anthropologist. She was one of the first people to study the customs and habits of primitive tribes by actually going to live with them. It was also thought very daring for a woman to go and live alone among people who were thought of as "savages." She spent many years in Samoa and New Guinea and published several books about her experiences.

Medici
See pages 172 & 173

Mehemet Ali (1769–1849)
Mehemet Ali was viceroy of Egypt from 1805 until 1848, when he became insane and was succeeded by his adopted son Ibrahim. He was an Albanian soldier who gained control of Egypt in 1805 after defeating the French army and the Arab tribe known as the Mamelukes. He introduced a modern economic system to the country, raising money through taxes to improve irrigation and other important agricultural projects, and raised an army with which he expanded his empire.

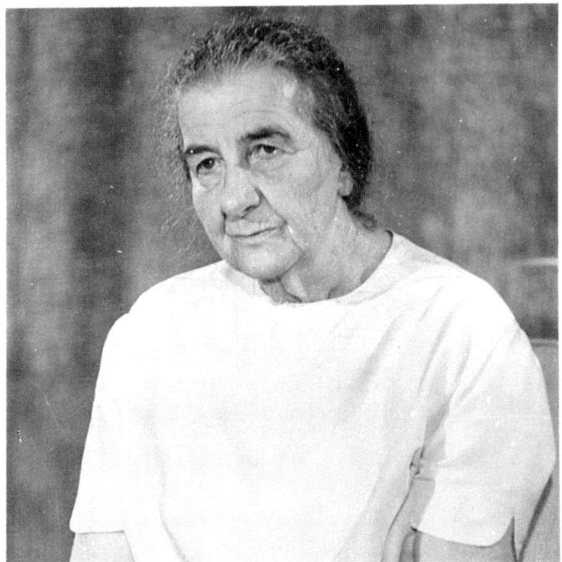

Golda Meir, the prime minister of Israel from 1969 to 1974.

Meir, Golda (1898–1978)
Golda Meir was the founder of the Israeli Labour Party and prime minister of the country from 1969 until 1974. She was born in Russia, from where her family moved to the United States. She moved to Palestine in 1921, where she worked on a farm and became involved in local politics. As prime minister, she tried to gain support for Israel from the United States and African countries.

Melville, Herman (1819–91)
Melville was an American novelist. Many of his books are based on his own adventurous life at sea. He was born in New York, where he was forced to leave school early when his father became bankrupt. Melville worked as a bank clerk, then as a teacher in an elementary school before he joined a ship bound for Liverpool in England. Next, in

Continued on page 174

The Cradle of the Renaissance

Medici

The Renaissance was a period lasting roughly from the beginning of the 14th to the end of the 16th century. The word means, literally, "rebirth," and describes the rebirth of art and learning after the long, barren centuries of the Middle Ages. It began in Italy, where the city of Florence is sometimes called the "cradle of the Renaissance," because many of the artists and writers whose geniuses are associated with the period lived and worked there: Dante, Giotto, Brunelleschi, Botticelli, and later Michelangelo and Leonardo Da Vinci all spent many years in the city, and left it some of their finest works. But these artists did not work for nothing; they needed people to buy their work. Florence was a city of bankers and businessmen. Their wealth prepared the way for the artists of the period.

Among the richest and most powerful of these businessmen were the Medici family. Their vast wealth was created by **Giovanni de'Medici** (1360–1429), the owner of a successful banking house. His son, **Cosimo de'Medici** (1389–1464), used the family fortune to try to gain political power in Florence. At first he was opposed by the city's rulers and forced into exile, but in 1534 he returned to a place in the government, and he quickly made himself absolute ruler of Florence. He was a strong leader who freed the city from constant disputes between different political groups, and maintained peace with neighboring states. He spent his own and the city's money on monuments and works of art. Among those he employed were Brunelleschi, Ghiberti, and Donatello.

Cosimo's son, **Lorenzo de'Medici** (1449–92), became ruler in 1469. The next 20 years were among the finest in the city's history, and Lorenzo became known as "Lorenzo the Magnificent." Like his father, he supported the finest artists and writers of the day. He encouraged printing, building, and learning, and was a just and generous ruler. There were, however, some who opposed Lorenzo, and in 1478 they attempted to overthrow him. The plot, known as the "Pazzi Conspiracy" after its leader, failed. Lorenzo escaped, and gained greater popularity for the courage he had shown—although his brother, **Giuliano de'Medici** (1453–78), was killed.

After Lorenzo's death in 1492, the Medici's power in

The Medici was the name of the family that ruled Florence at the height of the Renaissance. The picture shows the city's Piazza Signoria dominated by the magnificent Palazzo Vecchio with Michelangelo's statue of David.

Opposite: Botticelli's painting called Mystic Nativity.

Florence came to a temporary end. The city was ruled by a succession of different republican governments, including that of the religious leader Savonarola. They returned in 1512, when **Giuliano II de'Medici** (1478–1516) became ruler, supported by Pope Leo X—also a member of the family. The greatest of the later Medici rulers was **Cosimo I de'Medici** (1519–74), a distant relative of Lorenzo the Magnificent. He came to power in 1530 and ruled for the next 40 years, increasing the city's strength and security. He was made Grand Duke of Tuscany in 1569, and his descendants retained power until the middle of the 18th century. Other members of the family included two queens of France, **Catherine de'Medici** (1519–89) and **Marie de Medici** (1573–1642). ○ BOTTICELLI, BRUNELLESCHI, DONATELLO, GHIBERTI, LEO X, MICHELANGELO, SAVONAROLA

January 1841, he took a job aboard a whaling ship sailing for the Pacific Ocean. Melville found life aboard the whaler hard and his treatment by the ship's officers bad. When the ship reached the Marquesas Islands he deserted and hid out among the cannibals who lived there. This experience inspired his popular first novel *Typee*, written in 1846 after his return to the United States. He was rescued by an Australian whaling ship and made his way to Tahiti. There he was jailed for deserting, but escaped and again hid among the natives. Eventually, in order to return home, Melville joined the navy and sailed to Boston aboard the frigate the *United States*. He arrived in 1844 and immediately began to write books. In 1847 he married Elizabeth Shaw, and then bought a farm in the Massachusetts countryside. His great work is *Moby Dick* (first published in 1851). It tells the story of Captain Ahab and his ship the *Pequod*, and their search for a great white whale named "Moby Dick." It is thought of as one of the finest of all American novels. Later in life Melville turned to writing poetry, although he left an unfinished novel, *Billy Budd*, when he died.

The American novelist Herman Melville.

Mendel, Gregor Johann (1822–84)
Gregor Mendel was an Austrian scientist who did important research on the way characteristics (for example, the color of a person's eyes or hair) are passed on from one generation of living things to the next. He was a monk in the Augustinian monastery at the town of Brünn. The monastery paid for him to attend university in Vienna, where he studied science and became interested in the inheritance of characteristics. In 1868 he became abbot of the monastery, but he continued his research by studying families of pea plants which he grew in the garden there. Mendel published his conclusions in a small local magazine, so their importance did not become widely known until the beginning of the 20th century.

Mendelssohn-Bartholdy, Felix (1809–47)
Mendelssohn was a German composer born in Hamburg, the son of a wealthy banker. He was taught music from an early age and gave his first public performance at the age of ten. He began to compose soon afterward, and many of his finest works were written while he was in his late teens and early twenties. They include the overture to *A Midsummer Night's Dream* and the overture *The Hebrides*. This piece is also known as *Fingal's Cave* because it was inspired by a visit to the Scottish islands and the famous cave on the island of Staffa. Mendelssohn continued to perform, and he helped increase interest in the works of J.S. Bach by conducting some of the first performances of his choral works outside Germany. The death of Mendelssohn's sister in 1847 threw him into depression; he became ill and died a few months later at the age of only 38. ○ BACH

Menuhin, Yehudi (1916–)
An American violinist. He was born in New York, where he first performed while still a child. His sister, **Hephzibah Menuhin** (1922–81), was also a talented pianist.

Merckx, Eddy (1945–)
A Belgian racing cyclist who won the Tour de France five times and the world championship three times. He also holds the record for the fastest average speed over the period of an hour achieved on a conventional bicycle: 30.7 mph (49.4 km/h), set in Mexico in 1972.

Michelangelo Buonarotti (1475–1564)
Michelangelo was one of the greatest artists who ever lived. He is remembered above all for his sculptures and paintings, but he was also one of the Renaissance period's finest architects, and a talented poet.

Michelangelo was born near the city of Florence in Italy. At school he showed more interest in drawing than in his books, and at the age of 13 he was sent to become an apprentice in the workshop of the artist Domenico Ghirlandaio. Ghirlandaio recognized the boy's talent and introduced him to the powerful Lorenzo de' Medici, who allowed the young Michelangelo to study his splendid collection of ancient sculptures. His first works were sculptures: a *Madonna* and a scene showing the *Battle of the Centaurs.* After Lorenzo's death in 1492 Michelangelo moved to Rome, where he carved a magnificent *Pietà* (a statue of the Virgin Mary with the dead Christ in her arms) for St. Peter's. This work made Michelangelo famous. He returned to Florence in 1501 and began work on the gigantic figure of David which was to stand outside the Palazzo Vecchio (the city hall). Like other Renaissance artists and philosophers, Michelangelo believed that the beauty of the human body was a symbol of the most divine kind of beauty. His *David* stands 15 feet tall and shows the naked figure of the young king about to kill Goliath with a stone from his sling. In 1505 Michelangelo was summoned to Rome by Pope Julius II, who wanted the famous sculptor to design and build a tomb for him. This project was troubled by arguments and problems, and although Michelangelo worked on it for 40 years it was never finished. Meanwhile, he began work on his paintings on the ceiling of the Sistine Chapel in St. Peter's. Michelangelo was at first unwilling to do this work—he said that the young painter Raphael could do it better. But when the finished paintings were unveiled, Michelangelo was acclaimed as not only the greatest sculptor of his time, but the greatest painter as well. The work was incredibly difficult: he had to paint lying on his back, only a few inches from the ceiling, so he could never see the effect of his work. It is said that when Michelangelo went home he would read and write his letters lying on his back! The ceiling was finished in 1512. Later, in 1536, he painted another great work in the Sistine Chapel, the *Last Judgment*, on the wall above the altar. Many other projects occupied Michelangelo's time. He carved magnificent tombs for the Medici family in Florence, designed a library for the Church of San Lorenzo there, and became the chief architect of St. Peter's in Rome. He wrote over 100 sonnets for his friend, the poetess **Vittoria Colonna** (1492–1547). He became known as the "Divine Michelangelo" and was the first artist to have his biography published during his lifetime. When he died at the age of 89, Michelangelo was already thought of as the greatest genius in the history of art, and that remains his reputation to this day. ○ BOTTICELLI, JULIUS II, LEONARDO, MEDICI, RAPHAEL

A sculpture by Michelangelo called the Pietà*—the Virgin Mary with the dead Christ.*

Mill, John Stuart (1806–73)
John Stuart Mill was an English philosopher. His father, **James Mill** (1773–1836), was also a philosopher, and was so determined that his son should follow the same career that he began the boy's education almost at birth. At the age of three, John Stuart Mill was already learning Greek! Like Jeremy Bentham before him, Mill believed that happiness was the purpose of human activity, but unlike Bentham, he believed that happiness could be gained by spiritual as well as material means. His most famous works are *On Liberty* and the *Principles of Political Economy*. ○ BENTHAM

Miller, Arthur (1915–)
An American playwright. His best-known plays are *Death of a Salesman* (1949) and *The Crucible* (1953). He was married to the actress Marilyn Monroe. ○ MONROE

Milne, Alan Alexander (1882–1956)
A.A. Milne became famous for his children's books about the character "Winnie the Pooh," which he began writing for his son, Christopher Robin, in 1926. He also wrote children's poems, which were collected in the books *When We Were Very Young* and *Now We Are Six*.

Adam and Eve being driven from Paradise is the subject of this painting by the artist, Masaccio, and of Milton's Paradise Lost.

Milton, John (1608–74)
John Milton was an English poet. He was born in London, where his father worked writing up legal documents. He was an intelligent child, and he was sent first to St. Paul's school in London, then to Christ's College in Cambridge. Milton decided to become a poet at an early age, and after finishing his studies at university he spent several years at his father's country house, reading, and writing his first poems. These include *Lycidas,* which was written in memory of a friend of Milton's who drowned in the Irish Sea, and *Comus,* which was a "masque"—a kind of play set to music. In 1638 he traveled to Italy, where he met Galileo in prison. But when news reached Milton of the troubles in England which would eventually lead to the Civil War between Charles I and Cromwell, he returned home. He stopped writing poetry, and for the next 20 years devoted himself to politics. He wrote pamphlets in support of Parliament and the execution of King Charles. He also spoke out for the freedom of the press, and for allowing unhappy couples to divorce. When the monarchy was restored and King Charles II came to the throne, he went into hiding, but was eventually pardoned for his part in supporting Parliament. By 1651 Milton had become completely blind, but he continued working, and in 1662 began work on his great poem, *Paradise Lost,* which was published in 1667. It tells the story of Satan's rebellion against God and the fall of Adam and Eve in Paradise. He dictated the poem to members of his family, who painstakingly copied it down. ○ CHARLES I, CROMWELL, MARVELL

Mishima, Yukio (1925–70)
A Japanese author who wrote over 40 novels, as well as poetry, essays, and drama. His novels include *The Sea of Fertility* and *Confessions of a Mask*. Mishima was obsessed with traditional Japanese military values, which he saw as having disappeared from modern Japanese society. He formed a private army dedicated to these values, which attempted a takeover of the government in 1970. After its failure, Mishima committed suicide.

Mitchell, Margaret (1900–49)
An American novelist who was made famous by her novel *Gone With the Wind,* published in 1936. It sold over 8 million copies, won a Pulitzer Prize, and was made into a popular film.

Mitterrand, François Maurice (1916–)
François Mitterrand has been the president of France since 1981. During World War II he served as a member of the French resistance movement, and afterward entered politics. He is the first Socialist president of France to have been elected in many years.

Modigliani, Amedeo (1884–1920)
Modigliani was an Italian artist. He was born in the port of Leghorn, and his early pictures were influenced by early Italian Renaissance painters, such as Giotto. But in 1906 he went to Paris, where

he saw works by Cézanne and by the *Fauves* group led by Matisse. He developed a very individual style of painting figures. His nudes were thought indecent by many, and his first exhibition in Paris was closed down by the authorities.
○ MATISSE

Mohammed (570–632)
See Muhammad

Molière (Jean Baptiste Poquelin, 1622–73)
"Molière" was the name used by the French actor and playwright Jean Baptiste Poquelin. He was born in Paris and studied to become a lawyer. But Molière was always interested in the theater, and when his mother died and left him a large sum of money he decided to begin his own acting company. He rented an old tennis court in Paris and began giving performances. Unfortunately, the theater was not a great success, and after three years, in 1646, Molière and his friends left Paris for the country. For the next 12 years they gave performances in cities such as Rouen and Lyons, until they gained the support of the king's brother and were able to return to the capital. There, Molière gained the favor of the king, Louis XIV, and began organizing plays for the royal household. At the same time he began a public theater at the "Palais Royal," and began to give more time to writing his own plays. His plays are comedies, ranging from traditional farce and slapstick to savage and witty attacks on the people and manners of his time. They include *Tartuffe* (1665), *The Misanthrope* (1666), and *The Bourgeois Gentleman* (1671). Molière continued to act in his own and other people's plays, and he died after suffering a hemorrhage during a performance of his play *The Imaginary Invalid.* ○ CORNEILLE, LOUIS XIV, RACINE

A scene from Molière's Bourgeois Gentleman.

Monet, Claude (1840–1926)
Claude Monet was a French painter who became the leading member of the Impressionist group. Monet was born in Paris, but spent his youth in the seaport of Le Havre. There, he experimented with painting outside—something that was a new idea at the time. He became interested in the way light affects the way we see things, and began painting objects and scenes in different lights, using color and light alone to give them their shape. Eventually he returned to Paris, where he met Renoir and Pissarro. In 1874 he helped organize an exhibition at which he exhibited his picture *Impression: Sunrise.* It was this painting that gave the Impressionist movement its name. Monet continued to experiment with light, and painted objects such as haystacks at different times of day to get different effects. He took a room opposite Rouen cathedral so that he could study the effect of the sun on the stone. Among his most famous pictures are those of water lilies he made toward the end of his life at his country house at Giverny.
○ PISSARRO, RENOIR

The Water-Lily Pond *by Monet.*

Monroe, James (1758–1831)
James Monroe was the fifth president of the United States. He was a friend of Jefferson, and served as a diplomat in Europe during Jefferson's presidency. He was elected in 1816, and re-elected for a second term in 1820. Monroe is famous for the Monroe Doctrine, which banned European countries from trying to set up new colonies on the American continent. ○ JEFFERSON

Monroe, Marilyn (Norma Jean Baker, 1926–62)
Marilyn Monroe was an American actress, made famous as a "sex symbol" in films such as *Gentlemen Prefer Blondes* and *The Seven Year Itch.* She was exploited and unsatisfied by the Hollywood film industry, and committed suicide in 1962. She was for a time married to the playwright Arthur Miller. ○MILLER

Montessori, Maria (1870–1952)
Maria Montessori was the first woman medical student to graduate from Rome University, and she became famous for her theories about education.

She taught for a while in a school for mentally handicapped children and used what she had learned there to teach normal children. She thought children would learn best by being allowed to move freely from task to task in the classroom, with the minimum of discipline.

Maria Montessori.

Monteverdi, Claudio (1567–1643)
Monteverdi was an Italian composer. He was one of the pioneers of the opera—dramas set to music. Monteverdi was born in the town of Cremona. He first became known as a composer of fine madrigals, and for several years he was music master for the Duke of Mantua. Afterward, he became choirmaster of the Cathedral of St. Mark in Venice, where he began experimenting with opera, as well as with new types of religious music for the choir. His operas include *The Legend of Orpheus* and *The Coronation of Poppea.*

Montezuma II (1466–1520)
Montezuma was the last of the great Aztec emperors of Mexico. He came to the throne in 1502, and for a time ruled peacefully and gave his energy to reforming his people's laws. But in 1518 the Spanish *conquistador* Cortés landed in Mexico. Montezuma at first thought Cortés might be an Aztec god arrived in the world, and sent him gifts. Cortés used Montezuma's peaceful welcome as an opportunity to take him prisoner. Within two years, Montezuma's empire and civilization had been destroyed and Montezuma killed. The last of his descendants died in New Orleans in 1836.
○ CORTÉS

Montfort, Simon de (*c.*1208–65)
Simon de Montfort is remembered as the man who forced the king to grant powers to the first English "parliament." He was the leader of a party of barons who wanted to remove some authority from the king and give it to a council of nobles. In 1258 King Henry II accepted the "Provisions of Oxford" which did just this—but three years later he renounced them, and a civil war began between De Montfort and the nobles on one side, and the king and his army on the other. At the Battle of Lewes in 1264 both the king and Prince Edward were captured. The king was forced to accept the "De Montfort Parliament," made up of noblemen, knights, and representatives from certain towns. The king eventually escaped and defeated and killed De Montfort at the Battle of Evesham in 1265, but the history of the English Parliament began with these events.

Montgomery, Bernard Law, 1st Viscount of Alamein (1887–1976)
Montgomery was a British soldier. In 1942 he was sent to Egypt to take command of the British Eighth Army fighting against **Erwin Rommel** (1891–1944) and the German Afrika Korps. After a spectacular victory at El Alamein, he defeated the German forces and took control of North Africa. He commanded the British and American troops in the Normandy landings in 1944, and took an important part in the advance through France and Germany. ○ PATTON

Moore, Henry Spencer (1898–1986)
Henry Moore was an English sculptor. He worked with many different substances, and always paid careful attention to the qualities of the material itself (for example, the grain in a piece of wood) when he made his sculptures. His most famous works are his figures and groups of figures.

Moore, Marianne Craig (1887–1972)
Marianne Moore, who is often known as "Miss" Moore, was an important 20th-century American poet. She was born near the city of St. Louis, and studied biology at university. In 1918 she moved to the Greenwich Village district of New York, where many artists and writers lived. T.S. Eliot had published a few of her first poems in a London literary magazine, and in 1921 some friends published a collection of her work in England—without her knowledge. The same collection was later published in America, and she went on to win prizes and gain great admiration for her work. Miss Moore was a noted eccentric. She used to give readings of her poems dressed in bizarre costumes, or as famous characters such as Washington. Her works include *What Are Years?* and *The Arctic Fox.*

More, Saint Thomas (1478–1535)
Thomas More was an English politician and writer. After studying at the University of Oxford, More became a lawyer, and then, in 1504, a member of

Parliament. He was well known for his learning and his wit, especially after his book *Utopia* was published in 1516. It describes an ideal land where everything is shared and all the people are educated. More held several important government jobs, and in 1529 King Henry VIII made him Lord Chancellor—the country's most important judge. His fairness and honesty earned him great respect. But in 1532 he opposed Henry's wish to divorce his wife, Catherine of Aragon, and resigned from the chancellorship. More was a close friend of Henry's, but, in 1534, he refused to acknowledge Henry as the head of the Church of England, saying that the Pope remained the only head of the Church. For this he was imprisoned in the Tower of London, where he studied and wrote, and spent much time with his favorite daughter, Margaret Roper. Eventually he was tried for his refusal to obey the king, and sentenced to death. On the scaffold before being beheaded he said he was "the king's good servant—but God's first." ○ HENRY VIII, WOLSEY

Thomas More, the English writer and politician. He was sentenced to death for refusing to acknowledge Henry VIII as head of the Church.

Morris, William (1834–96)
William Morris was an English artist, poet, printer, and designer who worked during the second half of the 19th century. He despised the "mass-produced" objects being made by factories, and attempted to reintroduce an old-fashioned standard of craftsmanship. ○ ROSSETTI

Morse, Samuel Finley Breese (1791–1872)
Morse was the American inventor who developed the idea of the electric telegraph system for sending messages along a wire between places. He went to Yale University, and after graduating traveled to England to study painting. He became a successful portrait painter, and founded the National

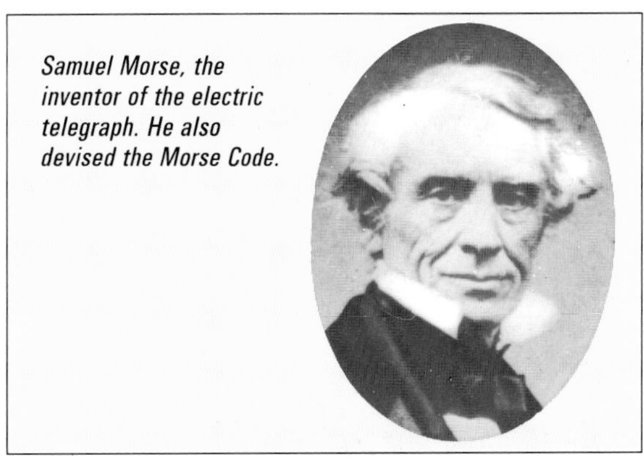

Samuel Morse, the inventor of the electric telegraph. He also devised the Morse Code.

Academy of Design in New York. From 1832 he experimented with the telegraph, although he had little money or support for his idea. Success came in 1843, when the American Congress agreed to spend $30,000 on a telegraph line between Washington and Baltimore. In 1844 he transmitted the first message between the two cities. Morse Code, the system of dots and dashes used to represent letters, is named after him.

Moses (15th–13th century B.C.)
Moses was leader of the Hebrew people. He was born and brought up in Egypt, where he had a vision that commanded him to lead the Jews from Egypt to the "Promised Land" in Palestine. On Mount Sinai in the desert he received the Ten Commandments from God. Finally, after many years in the wilderness, Moses and his people came within sight of the Promised Land.

Moses, Anna Mary (1860–1961)
"Grandma Moses" was an American artist. She was the wife of a farmer in a quiet town in New York State. At the age of 77 she began painting scenes from her childhood and life on the farm. These became popular after they were shown in an exhibition in New York in 1940.

Mountbatten, Louis Francis, Earl Mountbatten of Burma (1900–79)
Mountbatten was a British sailor and administrator. He had a distinguished career in the navy, and was made supreme commander of the Allied armies in Southeast Asia during World War II. He was viceroy and the governor-general of India during the period leading to Indian independence. Mountbatten was murdered by the IRA in 1979.

Mozart, Wolfgang Amadeus Chrysostom (1756–91)
See pages 180 & 181

Mozart – "the Most Divine Genius"

Mozart, Wolfgang Amadeus Chrysostom (1756–91) Mozart was one of the very greatest composers in the history of Western music. He died at the age of only 35, but in his short life he left a masterpiece of almost every kind: operas, such as *The Magic Flute* and *Così fan tutte*, symphonies, beautiful quartets, concertos for the piano, the violin, and other instruments, choral works, and a great deal of chamber music.

Mozart at the age of 21.

His career was as extraordinary as his talent. Mozart was born in Salzburg, a city on the edge of the Austrian Alps, where his father **Leopold Mozart** (1719–87) was a well-known musician and composer. At the age of 3, young Wolfgang suddenly began playing the harpsichord, without having had any formal tuition. Within two years he had mastered both the harpsichord and the violin, composed his first pieces of music, and given his first public performances. Leopold recognized his son's genius and organized tours of Europe for him from the age of 6. He played for the Habsburg Empress Maria Theresa, for the French court, and for the English king. At 9 Mozart composed his first symphony, and three years later his first opera was performed in Vienna. The same year he gave his first performance as a conductor, then left on a tour of Italy, where he was honored by the Pope and amazed all those who heard him play. On many of his early tours, Mozart was accompanied by his sister, **Maria Anna Mozart**, who was also a remarkable child musician. For a while, she shared her brother's fame, but her marriage put an end to her career.

Papageno, the comic bird-catcher from Mozart's opera The Magic Flute.

It was not until he was 25 that Mozart decided to settle down in one place. In 1781 he moved to Vienna, where he was employed by an archbishop. The following year he gave up this job, in which he was badly paid and badly treated, and married **Constanze Weber** (1763–1842). He gave concerts and lessons and wrote successful pieces, including the operas *The Marriage of Figaro* (1786) and *Don Giovanni* (1787). But despite his enormous fame Mozart was continually in debt. In 1787 the German Emperor Joseph II made him Imperial and Royal Chamber Composer, but his salary was miserable, and Mozart's difficulties only increased. The great opera *Così fan tutte* was written at the emperor's request, but Joseph died before it was finished and his successor, Leopold II, failed to pay him. He sold his last opera, *The Magic Flute* (1791), to a commercial theater, and it was the theater manager, and not the composer, who made a fortune from it. That same year Mozart died of typhoid while writing his great *Requiem* mass. With no money and only huge debts, he was buried in an unmarked pauper's grave. Mozart mastered every musical style and left over 600 pieces of music. His finest works include his string quartets, the "Paris" and "Jupiter" symphonies, his piano concertos, and his ever-popular operas.

○ BEETHOVEN, HAYDN

Manuscript of Mozart's setting of the psalm God Is Our Refuge.

Mozart plays the quartets that he dedicated to Haydn.

Muhammad (*c.*570–632)
Muhammad was the prophet-founder of Islam. He was born in the city of Mecca. His father was a poor merchant who died soon after the child's birth, and Muhammad's mother died when he was only 6 years old. He lived with his uncle and worked as a shepherd until he was 25, when he joined a merchant caravan setting out across the desert. The caravan was owned by a wealthy widow named Khadija, whom Muhammad eventually married, although she was 15 years older than he. Muhammad continued to work as a merchant, but spent more and more time alone. In the year 610 he had a vision of the angel Gabriel, who commanded him to preach a true religion to his people. The God worshiped by Muhammad was the same, single God that Jews and Christians worshiped, but he believed that they had departed from the true faith. He said that Muslims should live in complete submission to God's will. At first, Muhammad did not reveal his teaching, and it took many years to gather converts to his new religion. But eventually the powerful rulers of Mecca became suspicious, and forced Muhammad to leave. This took place in 622. It is known as the "Hegira" (flight), and is the first year in the Muslim calendar. At his new home in Medina Muhammad gained more followers, and soon became the city's governor. He began attacks on Mecca, and in 630 captured the city. It is now the sacred city of Islam, and can only be entered by the faithful. Muhammad's name means "praised." His sayings are written down in the *Qu'ran* (or "Koran"), the holy book of Islam.

Muhammad before the Battle of Uhad. Tradition prohibited the painter from showing the prophet's face.

Murasaki, Shikibu (978–*c.*1031)
Lady Murasaki was a Japanese noblewoman who wrote what is considered to be the world's first novel: *The Tale of Genji*. She was married at a young age, but after the death of her husband became a lady at the imperial court. She spent many years on her book, which gives a detailed picture of aristocratic life in ancient Japan.

Mussolini, Benito (1883–1945)
Mussolini was the Fascist dictator of Italy from 1922 until 1943. He served in World War I and afterward edited a nationalist newspaper. In 1919 he founded the Fascist political party, which dedicated itself to supporting the army and providing Italy with a strong government which would regain territories lost at the end of the war. In 1922 he organized the "March on Rome," in which his army of "blackshirts" took over the government and established Mussolini as prime minister. From then on he ruled as dictator. Mussolini dreamed of a new Roman Empire for Italy. In 1936 his troops overran Abyssinia (Ethiopia) in Africa, and in 1939 Italy annexed Albania. He made an alliance with Hitler's Germany, but avoided entering World War II until he felt sure that Germany would win. Unfortunately, Italian troops were defeated everywhere. In 1943 he was forced to resign as the Allied armies advanced on Rome, but was then rescued by German paratroopers and put in charge of a government in northern Italy. In April 1945 he was again forced to try to escape. He was captured by Italians and executed. ○ HITLER

Mussolini, the Fascist dictator of Italy during World War II.

Nagy, Imre (1895–1958)
Nagy was leader of Hungary from 1953 until 1955, and again in 1956. At the time of the 1917 Russian Revolution he was a prisoner in Siberia. He was freed and became a Russian citizen, and after World War II returned to Hungary as minister of agriculture in the Communist government. He became prime minister in 1953. In 1956, during Nagy's second spell as leader, the Hungarians rose against their Russian rulers. Nagy introduced free elections and other reforms. When the Soviets suppressed the revolution he appealed to the rest of the world for help, but none came. Nagy was arrested and later executed.

Nansen, Fridtjof (1861–1930)
Nansen was a Norwegian explorer and scientist. In 1893 he entered the thick pack ice in the north of the Arctic Ocean in a special ship called the *Fram*. He then allowed the ship to drift with the ice all the way across the Arctic. Meanwhile, Nansen and another member of the expedition spent the winter in Franz Josef Land, the farthest north anybody had yet been.

Napoleon I (1769–1821)
See pages 184 & 185

Napoleon III (1808–73)
Charles Louis Napoleon Bonaparte was the nephew of the Emperor Napoleon I. He was elected president of France after the revolution of 1848, and made himself emperor in 1852. Members of the first Napoleon's family had been exiled from France after his downfall, so the young Charles Louis was brought up in Germany and Switzerland. He hoped to overthrow the French king and re-establish the power of his own family, and in 1836 he attempted to organize a revolt in the city of Strasbourg. It failed, and he lived for a time in the United States before settling in London. In 1840 he attempted another rising, in the port of Boulogne, and this time the French government decided to keep him locked up instead of just expelling him from the country. He spent six years in prison, before escaping to England. In February 1848 revolution in Paris brought the reign of King Louis Philippe to an end, and Napoleon hurried back to Paris. He was supported by the working people of the city, and was elected first to the new French Assembly, then, in December, president of the republic. He gradually gave all the most important positions in the government and the army to his supporters, so that when, in 1851, he abandoned the constitution and took complete power into his own hands there was no resistance. A year later he declared himself Emperor Napoleon III. He ruled carefully, ensuring that bread prices were kept low so that poor people would support him, and beginning successful schemes to build roads, railways, and improve agriculture. He avoided becoming involved in expensive or unpopular wars until in 1870 he was provoked by Bismarck into declaring war on Prussia. The Franco-Prussian War was a disaster: Napoleon's armies were easily defeated, and he was captured. Two days later, a new republic was set up in France, and Napoleon was forced into exile in England. ○ NAPOLEON I, BISMARCK

Nasser, Gamal Abdel (1918–70)
President of Egypt from 1956 until 1958, and then of the United Arab Republic, a union between Egypt and Syria. Nasser organized the revolt that overthrew King Farouk in 1952. As president he brought the Suez Canal under Egyptian control and tried to bring about a union of Arab states. He led the Arab nations in the unsuccessful Six-Day War against Israel in 1967.

Navratilova, Martina (1956–)
Navratilova is the most successful modern woman tennis player. She was born in Czechoslovakia, but defected to the U.S.A. in 1975. Since then, she has dominated women's tennis, winning every major title (including six Wimbledons and two U.S. Opens) and has earned huge sums of money.

Nebuchadnezzar II (d. 562 B.C.)
Nebuchadnezzar became king of ancient Babylon in the year 605 B.C. He expanded his empire, captured Jerusalem, and took the people there into captivity. He made Babylon the most powerful state in the world. He rebuilt temples throughout his lands, and constructed the "Hanging Gardens" of Babylon—one of the seven wonders of the ancient world.

From Revolution to Empire

Napoleon I (1769–1821)
Napoleon was born on the island of Corsica in the Mediterranean. When the French Revolution broke out in 1789, he was a lieutenant in the French army. A supporter of the revolution, he returned to his home and took part in the uprising that overthrew the aristocratic government there. In 1793 he was made commander of the forces fighting outside Toulon, which had been occupied by the British. His skill led to the city's capture, and Napoleon was promoted to the rank of brigadier general. In 1796 he was put in charge of the French army preparing to invade Italy. His success was spectacular. The Austrian army in control of the country was defeated and driven backward toward Vienna.

Napoleon's next assignment was the defeat of the British. He realized that invasion was impossible, because the Royal Navy dominated the seas. Instead, he took his army to Egypt and tried to disrupt British trade with the East. This time his success was spoiled: although he quickly captured Egypt, he was cut off from France when Nelson destroyed his fleet at the Battle of the Nile. In November 1799 he returned to France alone, where he staged a *coup d'état* against the now unpopular Directory. He and his accomplices introduced a new constitution, and Napoleon was elected First Consul. He was now ruler of France.

Over the next five years, Napoleon introduced important reforms in almost every aspect of French government. In 1804, Napoleon had himself declared emperor and was crowned by the Pope in the cathedral of Notre Dame. Austria and Prussia were once again defeated by Napoleon's army, and he placed relatives or friends on thrones around Europe. But as Napoleon's power grew, so did his ambition. In 1808 he invaded Spain, beginning a long struggle with the British army in the Peninsular War. Then, in 1812, he invaded Russia. Not content with defeating the Russian army, Napoleon led his troops toward Moscow, which he captured and burned. But the fierce Russian winter quickly took revenge on the French. During the retreat, Napoleon lost most of his soldiers, and his army was so weakened that he found himself unable to resist the alliance of European nations that now formed against him. In April 1814, with his enemies advancing on

Important Dates

1769 (Aug. 15) Born at Ajaccio, Corsica.
1796 (Mar. 9) Married Josephine de Beauharnais.
1799 (Nov. 9) Seized power in France.
1804 (Dec. 2) Crowned himself emperor.
1805 (Dec. 2) Crushed the allied armies at Austerlitz.
1806 (Oct. 14) Defeated the Prussians at Jena.
1810 (Apr. 2) Married Marie Louise of Austria.
1812 (Sept. 14) Occupied Moscow.
1814 (Apr. 11) Abdicated his throne.
1814 (May 4) Exiled to Elba.
1815 (Mar. 20) Returned to power in France.
1815 (June 18) Defeated in the Battle of Waterloo.
1815 (Oct. 16) Exiled to St. Helena.
1821 (May 5) Died on St. Helena.

all sides, Napoleon abdicated. He retired to the island of Elba while the rest of Europe decided the fate of his empire.

But his career was not quite over. In March of the following year he escaped and returned to France, and the French army immediately joined him. His old enemies responded fast. At the Battle of Waterloo, on June 18, 1815, Napoleon's reign finally came to an end. He spent the rest of his life imprisoned on the island of St. Helena.

○ JOSEPHINE, NELSON, NEY, ROBESPIERRE, TALLEYRAND, WELLINGTON

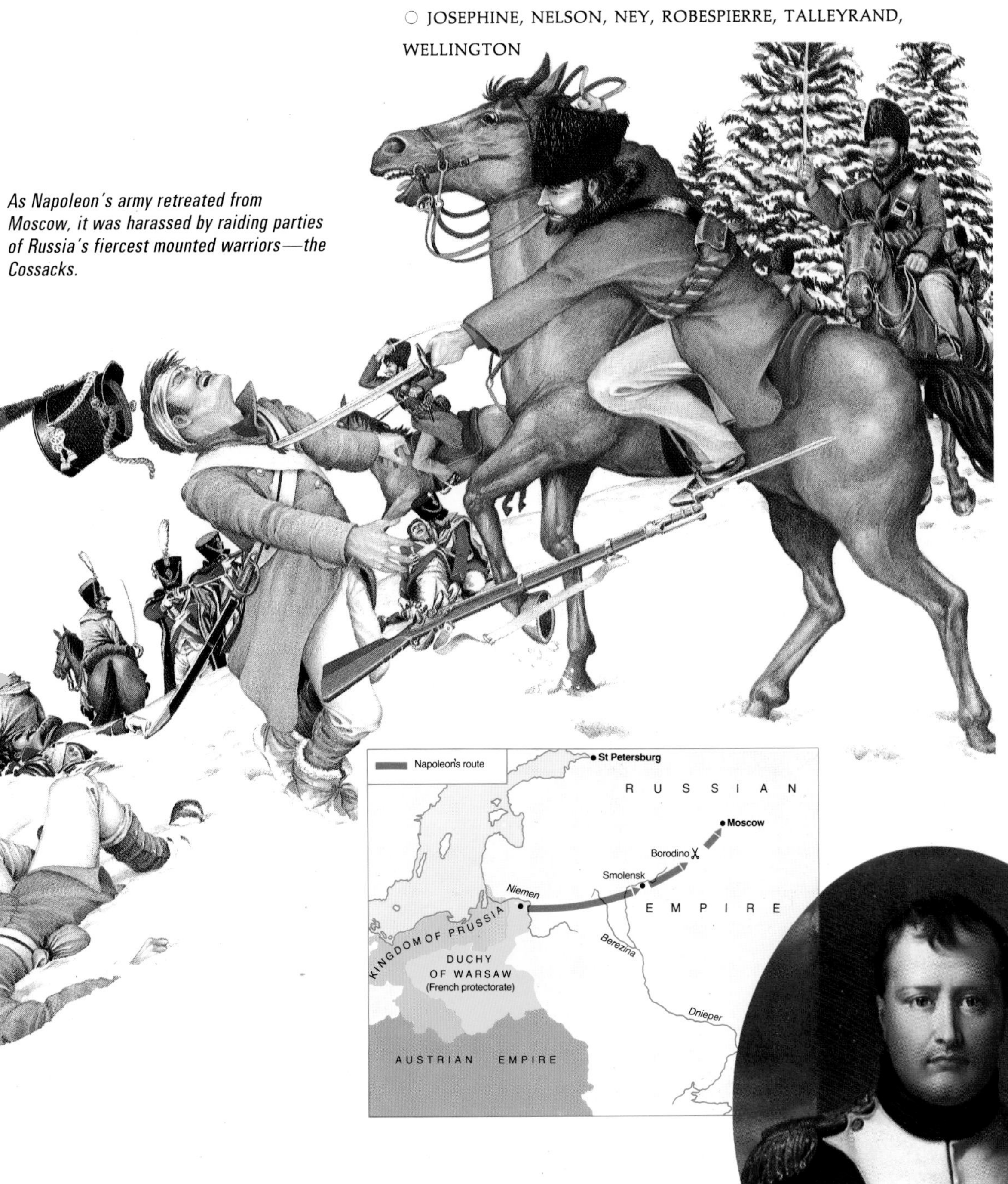

As Napoleon's army retreated from Moscow, it was harassed by raiding parties of Russia's fiercest mounted warriors—the Cossacks.

Necker, Jacques (1732–1804)
Necker was a French banker who served as minister of finance during the reign of King Louis XVI. He was given this job in 1771, at a time when the French economy faced ruin after a series of expensive wars. Necker successfully reorganized the system of tax and government spending, and for a while the economy improved. But he also suggested political reforms, including the setting up of elected assemblies in the French provinces which could vote on taxes. The aristocrats in the king's court opposed this, and Necker was dismissed. In desperation, Louis recalled him as France hung on the brink of revolution in 1788. Necker advised Louis to summon the States-General, but when the revolution broke out Necker again fell from favor. Eventually he became disillusioned and moved to Switzerland. His daughter was the famous Madame de Staël. ○ LOUIS XVI, MARIE ANTOINETTE, STAËL

Nehru, Jawaharlal (1889–1964)
Nehru was the first prime minister of India after the country became independent in 1947. He was a lawyer in the Indian high court in the city of Allahabad until he met Gandhi in 1918. From then on he devoted himself to the cause of Indian independence, and was imprisoned by the British several times for his activities. He disagreed with Gandhi about many things, but their aims were the same. He was a popular and respected leader, maintaining democracy in India and keeping a careful balance between powerful nations such as Russia, Britain, and the United States. His daughter, Indira Gandhi, became the Indian prime minister in 1966. ○ GANDHI

Nelson, Horatio, Viscount (1758–1805)
Nelson was an English admiral who won several famous naval victories and became a celebrated naval hero. He was the son of a country vicar in the county of Norfolk, and he joined the navy in 1770. Over the following years he sailed to many parts of the world, including the East and West Indies and the Arctic. His first command was a captured French ship, renamed HMS *Albermarle*, which he sailed to American waters during the American War of Independence. Injury and sickness forced Nelson to retire for a time, and he returned to his Norfolk home with his wife Francis, whom he had met and married during a trip to the West Indies. The French Revolution of 1789 began several years of war between Great Britain and France. Nelson sailed to the Mediterranean with Admiral Hood, where gunshot caused the loss of his right eye. In the Battle of Cape St. Vincent in 1797 Nelson captured two enemy ships, and as a result was promoted to the rank of rear admiral. Later that year he received a wound which led to the amputation of his right arm, but he continued in his command. In August 1798 he found Napoleon's fleet at anchor off the coast of Egypt. Although outnumbered, Nelson won a dramatic victory and destroyed nearly all the French ships. He was welcomed as a hero in Naples, where he met **Emma Hamilton** (1765–1815), the beautiful wife of the English ambassador. The two immediately became lovers, and Nelson temporarily resigned his post in order to remain with her in Italy.

Horatio Nelson led the British navy to an overwhelming victory over the French fleet at the Battle of Trafalgar in 1805. In the moment of victory he was wounded by gunshot and later died.

In 1801 Nelson was sent as second-in-command to attack the Danish fleet in Copenhagen. Leading the attack, Nelson was suddenly ordered by a signal from another ship to retreat. This he would not do, and he raised his telescope to his blind right eye, saying, "I see no signal"—before going on to win the battle. His most famous victory took place at the Battle of Trafalgar in 1805, which prevented Napoleon's invasion army from being able to cross the English Channel. He chased the French admiral, Villeneuve, in and out of the Channel, until the fleets confronted each other off Cape Trafalgar. During the fighting Nelson was wounded by gunshot while talking to his first mate, Hardy. He died some hours later with the words "Kiss me, Hardy!" ○ NAPOLEON

Nero (A.D. 37–A.D. 68)
Nero was proclaimed Roman emperor by his mother Agrippina in the year A.D. 54. Things began peacefully, but Nero's reign turned into one of

A statue of the Roman Emperor Nero. He was famous for his cruelty, vanity, and corrupt nature.

great cruelty. He had his mother, his first wife, and the previous emperor Claudius' son killed; he murdered his second wife, persecuted Christians, and acted without mercy against anybody he even suspected of opposing him. In A.D. 64 a great fire destroyed much of Rome—which Nero is thought to have started. Eventually he was overthrown by his own soldiers. ○ AGRIPPINA, CLAUDIUS

Neruda, Pablo (1904–73)
Neruda was a Chilean poet who is thought of as one of the most important modern poets to have written in Spanish. His first work was published in 1923. After World War II he entered politics as a member of the Communist Party. He received the Nobel Prize for Literature in 1971.

Newman, John Henry (1801–90)
An English cardinal. He began as a priest in the Church of England, preaching at St. Mary's Church in Oxford. In the 1830s Newman became more and more attracted to the Roman Catholic Church, and he led the "Oxford Movement" which tried to make the English Church more like the Catholic. Eventually, in 1845, he became a Catholic. He won great admiration for his work with the poor and the sick, and for his support for tolerance between different faiths. Newman was made a cardinal of the Church in 1879.

Newton, Sir Isaac (1642–1727)
Isaac Newton was an English scientist. His great achievement was to develop a few simple laws which described the complicated and varied aspects of the physical world. Newton was born in a village in the county of Lincolnshire. He was fascinated by science from an early age, and at school he spent his time inventing sundials and water-powered clocks. In 1661 he was sent to the University of Cambridge, but his college was later closed due to plague, and Newton returned to Lincolnshire. There, in the autumn of 1665 or 1666, he was sitting in an orchard when an apple dropped from a tree. This event first set Newton thinking about gravity, and—at the age of only 23—he was able to develop laws describing gravity and the movements of the planets and the tides. Unfortunately, a mistake in his estimate of the size of the earth led him to abandon this work for several years, although his ideas were correct. Instead, he experimented with light, and discovered that "white" light was in fact made up of several different colors which could be separated and then recombined by the use of a piece of special glass

Isaac Newton, the English scientist who made some of the world's most important discoveries in physics, mathematics, and astronomy.

called a "prism." This enabled him to build the first "reflecting" telescope in 1668, which focused light by using a curved mirror instead of a lens. In 1667 he returned to Cambridge, where he was made professor of mathematics. He published the results of his work in 1687 in the *Principia*, which described gravity, motion, and Newton's many discoveries in the field of mathematics. He was elected president of the Royal Society in London in 1703, and was re-elected every year until his death. He remains one of the greatest scientists of all time.

Ney, Michel (1769–1815)
Marshal Ney was a French general who served in Napoleon's armies during the Napoleonic Wars. At the time of the French Revolution he was a junior officer in the French army. He was quickly promoted, until Napoleon made him a marshal. He became the Duke of Elchingen in recognition of bravery in storming the defenses of the town in 1805; he was distinguished again at the Battles of Jena and Friedland, and during Napoleon's advance into Russia he played a crucial part in the Battles of Borodino and Smolensk. For this he was made Prince of Moscow by Napoleon. During the less glorious retreat from Russia Ney fought bravely, defending the rear of the column. After Napoleon's abdication in 1814, Ney remained in charge of the army under the new King Louis XVIII, but when Napoleon returned in 1815, Ney immediately joined him. After the defeat at Waterloo, Ney attempted to escape to Switzerland, but he was captured and executed as a traitor. Napoleon called him the "bravest of the brave." ○ NAPOLEON I, WELLINGTON

Nicholas II (1868–1918)
Nicholas II was the last tsar of Russia. He was a well-meaning but weak man who fell under the influence of powerful advisers. He was persuaded to suppress liberal movements in the country, and became unpopular after Russia's humiliating defeat in the war of 1905 with Japan. Discontent with Nicholas' government turned into revolution in 1917, and Nicholas abdicated. He and his family were shot by the Bolsheviks in Siberia in 1918, although a woman named **Anna Anderson** (d. 1983) later claimed to be his surviving daughter Anastasia. ○ LENIN

Tsar Nicholas II of Russia with his family before World War I.

Nicholas, Saint (4th century)
Saint Nicholas was a bishop in Asia Minor sometime during the fourth century. As the patron saint of children, he gave rise to the legend of "Santa Claus" as the bringer of gifts. "Santa Claus" comes from a Dutch form of his name, *Sinte Klaas.*

Nicklaus, Jack (1940–   )
Jack Nicklaus emerged as the world's leading golfer in the 1960s and 1970s, and went on to win numerous important tournaments.

Niepce, Joseph Nicéphore (1765–1833)
Niepce was the French inventor who took the world's first photograph in 1826. He was an army officer and administrator who devoted all his spare time to experiments with photography. The first successful picture showed a farmyard and took over eight hours to expose. He later worked with Louis Daguerre to improve the process.
○ DAGUERRE

Nietzsche, Friedrich Wilhelm (1844–1900)
Nietzsche was a German philosopher. He was a brilliant student—so much so that the University of Basel offered to make him professor of philosophy there before he had even earned his first degree. His first book, *The Birth of Tragedy,* was published in 1871. Nietzsche believed that the thirst for power was the most important source of human actions, and that great individuals were more important than groups of people. His most important book is *Thus Spake Zarathustra* (1885). Nietzsche's ideas have been misunderstood by some extreme political groups, such as the German Nazis, who used them to justify their policies.

Nightingale, Florence (1820–1910)
Florence Nightingale was an Englishwoman who reformed military hospitals and founded the modern nursing profession. She was named after the city of her birth—Florence, in Italy—and in 1851 she began training to be a nurse, despite the opposition of her parents. In 1854, at the beginning of the Crimean War, she traveled with 38 other nurses to Scutari to run a military hospital. She found the place crowded, filthy, and badly managed. Against the opposition of the military commanders, she introduced new rules of cleanliness and hygiene, organized food supplies, and ensured that the wounded were properly cared for. Almost immediately the numbers of soldiers who died in hospital fell, and Florence Nightingale became known to them as "the Lady of the Lamp."

Florence Nightingale at work in the wards at Scutari hospital during the Crimean War. She brought down the death rate in the hospital from 42 percent to 2.2 percent.

News of her success reached England, and on her return she raised money to found a proper nurses' school at St. Thomas's Hospital.

Nijinsky, Vaslav (1890–1950)
One of the greatest of all male ballet dancers. Nijinsky danced with Diaghilev's *Ballets Russes,* where his grace and strength made him famous throughout the world. He later became a choreographer, but mental illness brought his career to an early end. ○ DIAGHILEV

Nixon, Richard Milhous (1913–)
Nixon was the 37th president of the United States, and the only one ever to resign. He was defeated by J.F. Kennedy in 1960, but elected by a narrow margin in 1968. During the 1972 campaign, some of his supporters broke the law—most famously when they burgled the Democratic Party headquarters in the Watergate Hotel. Nixon was shown to have known of this, and in 1974 a committee voted that he be "impeached" (removed from office). To avoid this, Nixon resigned. ○ KISSINGER

Nobel, Alfred (1833–96)
Alfred Nobel was a Swedish inventor. He developed a way of making explosives which could be used safely in quarries and other industries. He called his invention "dynamite" and it brought him great success. He also invented other explosives in the form of a jelly. When he died he left over $9 million for the founding of five Nobel Prizes. These are awarded every year for literature, medicine, physics, chemistry, and the encouragement of peace.

Nostradamus (1503–66)
Nostradamus was a French astrologer—somebody who claimed to see meaning in the movements of the stars and planets and other omens. He was a trained doctor and became well known for his devotion to his patients during a period of plague. In about 1547 he suddenly claimed to be a prophet, and began recording his prophecies in books called the *Centuries.* He won great fame for his predictions about the future, eventually becoming court doctor to King Charles IX. Even today people claim to see his predictions fulfilled in events around the world.

Nureyev, Rudolf Hametovich (1939–)
Nureyev is a Russian-born ballet dancer. His remarkable ability has often been compared to that of the famous Nijinsky, and he became celebrated for a partnership with Margot Fonteyn. ○ FONTEYN, NIJINSKY

Nyerere, Julius Kambarage (1921–)
Nyerere was president of the African country of Tanzania. He was a teacher, and after spending some time studying at Edinburgh University he returned to his country (which was then called Tanganyika) to organize a nationalist political party. His aim was complete independence for the

Julius Nyerere, ex-president of Tanzania.

country, and this was achieved in 1960. Nyerere was made prime minister, and became president the next year. In 1964 a revolution took place in the neighboring country of Zanzibar. Nyerere arranged the union of Tanganyika and Zanzibar, which became known as "Tanzania," and he became president of the new country.

Oates, Titus (1649–1705)
Titus Oates was an English conspirator who claimed to have information about a "Popish Plot" to kill the king in 1678. He was a clergyman who had been dismissed from his post as a naval chaplain for misbehavior. Obsessed by his dislike of Roman Catholics, he pretended to be a convert to their religion and joined a Jesuit monastery. A few months later he appeared in London saying that the Catholics were plotting to kill the king and massacre Protestants. At first he was ignored, but when the magistrate to whom he had told his story was found murdered, people began to believe him. Soon many Catholics had been imprisoned, and 35 executed for treason. But there was no plot; Oates had made the whole thing up, and probably murdered the magistrate himself. In 1685 he was tried for perjury (lying before the law) and sentenced to life imprisonment.

O'Brien, Flann (Brian O'Nolan, 1911–66)
"Flann O'Brien" is the pseudonym (false name) used by the Irish novelist Brian O'Nolan. He wrote columns for the *Irish Times*, and in 1939 attempted to publish a novel, *At Swim-Two-Birds*. The book was praised by writers such as James Joyce, but was not recognized as a great work until much later, in the 1960s. His other works include *The Hard Life* and *The Third Policeman*.

O'Casey, Sean (1884–1964)
Sean O'Casey was an Irish playwright. He was born in a poor part of Dublin, and this, together with an eye disease, meant that he had no proper schooling. He later taught himself to read, but he could only find work as a builder's laborer. O'Casey began writing plays based on the lives of the poor people in Dublin in about 1919. The poet W.B. Yeats read his work and encouraged him to write more, and in 1923 his first play, *The Shadow of a Gunman*, was staged at the city's Abbey Theatre. His most famous play, *Juno and the Paycock*, was put on there the next year, but in 1926 O'Casey moved to England to escape hostile criticism. He remained there, and some but not all of his plays were successful in London. ○ GREGORY, YEATS

O'Connell, Daniel (1775–1847)
Daniel O'Connell was an Irish politician who spent his life fighting for the end of the Act of Union between Great Britain and Ireland—the law that meant Ireland was governed from London. He was a Catholic. Catholics were not allowed to serve in the House of Commons, so when he was elected as MP for County Clare in 1828 he was unable to take his seat. He campaigned for Catholic Emancipation, which would give Irish Catholics the same rights as everybody else, and in 1829 this was achieved and O'Connell took his seat. He became the leader of a group of Irish members of Parliament who wanted to end the union with Britain. Eventually, younger, more revolutionary campaigners became impatient with O'Connell and his influence became less.

O'Connor, Flannery (1925–64)
An American short-story writer and novelist. She was born in the town of Savannah, Georgia, and spent much of her life confined to bed by illness. Her novels include *Wise Blood* and her stories "A Good Man Is Hard to Find" and "Revelation."

Oersted, Hans Christian (1777–1851)
Oersted was professor of physics at the University of Copenhagen in Denmark. He was the man who discovered the connection between electricity and

The Danish physicist Oersted at work.

magnetism when he found that electric current passing through a wire sets up a magnetic field. The "oersted," a unit used for measuring the strength of a magnetic field, is named after him.

Offa (d. 796)
Offa became king of the ancient English kingdom named Mercia in 757. He conquered the kingdom of Wessex to the south and made alliances with other powerful lords. Offa soon controlled all of the country south of the river Humber, and he built a defensive ditch (called "Offa's Dyke") all the way along the border with Wales, to protect his kingdom from invasion. It is said that he founded abbeys at Bath and St. Albans, and introduced new laws.

O'Higgins, Bernardo (1776–1842)
O'Higgins was the first president of the new republic of Chile after the country had been freed from Spanish rule. He was the son of the Irish-born viceroy of Chile, and in 1791 he was sent to England to school. There he met a group of revolutionaries planning to overthrow the Spanish governments of South America. After his return to Chile he took part in the revolution of 1811, and then became a commander in San Martín's army of liberation. When Chile became independent he was made president, but he turned out to be an unpopular leader and had to resign. ○ SAN MARTÍN

Ohm, Georg Simon (1787–1854)
Ohm was a German physicist. He made important discoveries about the behavior of electricity, and the "ohm," a unit used to measure electrical resistance, is named after him. He was professor of physics at Nuremberg and Munich universities.

Olivier, Laurence Kerr, Lord (1907–)
An English actor and theater director. His performances in Shakespeare's plays made him famous all over the world in the 1950s. He was the director of the English National Theatre and the Old Vic Company. Some of his performances, including those as Henry V and Hamlet, have been recorded in popular films.

O'Neill, Eugene Gladstone (1888–1953)
O'Neill was an American playwright. He began writing while recovering from tuberculosis in a hospital. His first full-length play, *Beyond the Horizon*, performed in 1920, won him a Pulitzer Prize, and he went on to write many more fine plays. Among the most famous are *The Iceman Cometh* (1946) and *Long Day's Journey into Night* (1957). They are both long plays lasting several hours; the second is based on O'Neill's own life. He is thought of as America's greatest dramatist, and was awarded the Nobel Prize for Literature in 1936.

Oppenheimer, James Robert (1904–67)
Oppenheimer was an American scientist who became an expert in nuclear physics. From 1943 until 1945 he was director of the Los Alamos laboratory in New Mexico, where the first atomic bombs were constructed. He argued for the sharing of all nuclear technology between nations, and particularly between the United States and the Soviet Union. In 1953 he was suddenly accused of disloyalty by the American government and forbidden to see secret documents, but he was later cleared.

Orwell, George (Eric Arthur Blair, 1903–50)
Orwell was an English writer. He was born in India, but after serving for five years in the Burma police he returned to Europe and decided to abandon his past and become a writer. He changed his name and spent some time living with tramps and poor people. He recorded his experiences in his first book, *Down and Out in Paris and London* (written in 1933). A later book, *The Road to Wigan Pier* (1937), describes the problems facing the unemployed in the north of England. Orwell is most famous for two political novels. *Animal Farm* (1945) describes what happens to a farm when the animals take over its government, but it is also a satire about the Soviet system under Stalin's rule. *Nineteen Eighty-Four* (1949) is a vision of a future in which everything people do is controlled by the government. Orwell died from tuberculosis.

American playwright Eugene O'Neill (left); and British actor Laurence Olivier playing Hamlet.

Oswald, Lee Harvey (1939–63)
Lee Harvey Oswald was the man who assassinated President Kennedy of the United States in 1963. On November 22, as the President's car passed through the center of Dallas, Oswald fired two fatal shots from a high building. He was never brought to trial because he was himself shot by Jack Ruby in a Dallas police station. Since his death, several theories have been put forward suggesting that Oswald was either part of a Soviet conspiracy, or being used by American opponents of Kennedy. ○ KENNEDY

Ovid (43 B.C.–A.D. 17)
Ovid was a Roman poet at the time of the Emperor Augustus. His masterpiece is the *Metamorphoses,* which tells stories of people, animals, and things that change their shape. After its publication he was banished by the emperor, although it is not known why. At his new home on the Black Sea he wrote poems lamenting his ill luck. ○ AUGUSTUS

Owen Glendower (*c.*1350–*c.*1416)
Owen (Owain) Glendower was the last independent prince of Wales. He ruled lands in north Wales. He was educated at Oxford and studied law in London. For many years he fought against English rule. The fighting began after a dispute over some land. Owen attacked English soldiers, and in 1402 he captured two English lords, who then decided to join him. He made an alliance with Harry Hotspur, but they were defeated at the Battle of Shrewsbury in 1403 by King Henry IV. After this, Owen's power declined, although he kept up the battle until his death. ○ HENRY IV

Owen, Robert (1771–1858)
Owen was a Welsh factory manager and social reformer. In 1799 he married the daughter of a Scottish mill owner, and eventually became manager and part owner of the mill. There, he improved safety and cleanliness in the mill, and shortened the length of the working day. He had new housing built for the workers in the factory and began schools for their children. The success of these measures led him to propose cooperative villages where people lived and worked for their own good, instead of for the profit of a factory owner. Several of these were begun, including one in the United States, although they were not a success.

Owen, Wilfred (1893–1918)
Wilfred Owen was the most famous of the many poets who wrote about their experiences in the trenches during World War I. His poems include *Anthem for Doomed Youth* and *Dulce Et Decorum Est,* and some of them were later set to music by the composer Benjamin Britten. He was killed only a week before the end of the war. ○ BRITTEN

Owens, Jesse (1913–80)
Jesse Owens was a great black American athlete. In 1935 he broke three world records at one meeting, including a new long jump record which was not broken again until 1960. Owens went to the 1936 Berlin Olympics, where Hitler—who believed in the superiority of white people—was forced to look on as Owens won four gold medals. After the games he became a professional.

Jesse Owens, the American athlete, running in the 1936 Olympics in Berlin. A black man, he embarrassed the Nazis by winning four gold medals.

P

Paderewski, Ignace Jan (1860–1941)
Paderewski was a Polish musician, composer, and politician. His career began at the age of 3, when his mother began teaching him the piano. He went to study in Warsaw and Strasbourg, and made successful tours of Europe and the U.S. In 1909 he was made director of the Warsaw musical conservatory, where he continued to perform and compose. He entered politics during World War I, and afterward became prime minister of the new Polish Republic. He retired soon afterward to live in Switzerland, but entered politics again briefly as a member of the provisional Polish government set up in France during World War II.

Paganini, Nicolo (1782–1840)
An Italian violinist and composer. His virtuoso playing astonished audiences wherever he went—so much so that some said he must be in league with the devil. Paganini introduced many new techniques to violin playing, as well as composing extremely difficult pieces for the instrument.

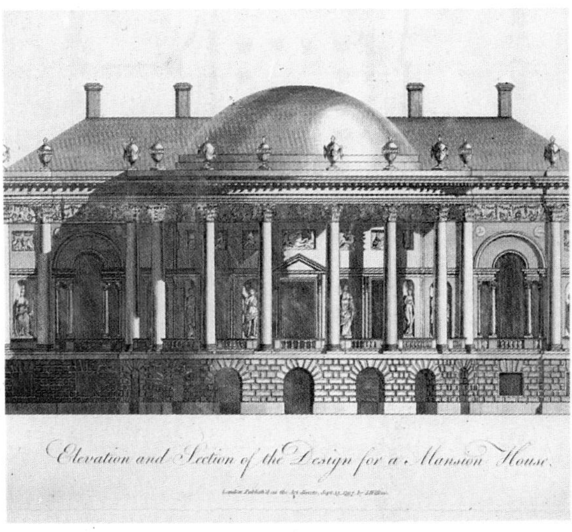

A drawing by the Italian architect, Palladio, of a section of the design for a mansion house.

Paine, Thomas (1737–1809)
Thomas Paine was an English radical. He wrote pamphlets and books, and became involved in both the American and French Revolutions. His father was a stay maker (stays were an old-fashioned type of lady's corset), and young Thomas too tried stay making for while. He was also a schoolmaster, a tobacconist, a sailor, and a customs officer before he left England for the United States in 1774. There he met the revolutionaries seeking independence from Britain. He wrote two books and several pamphlets supporting American independence, and joined Washington's army fighting against the British. He left America in 1787 and returned to England, where he published his famous *Rights of Man* in 1792. The book got him into trouble with the authorities, so he left for France. He was elected to the French National Assembly, but after opposing Robespierre's decision to execute King Louis XVI he was imprisoned. After nearly a year, during which he began writing his book *The Age of Reason*, he was released. Paine returned to his seat in the National Assembly, but he became totally disillusioned with French politics. He returned to the United States in 1802, where he died.
○ ROBESPIERRE, WASHINGTON

Palestrina, Giovanni Pierluigi da (1525–94)
Palestrina was an Italian composer of church music. He wrote almost 100 settings for the Mass, as well as many motets, hymns, and other pieces. There is a legend that the beauty of his music persuaded the heads of the Roman Catholic Church not to forbid the singing of choral music, but this is probably not true.

Palladio, Andrea (1508–80)
Palladio was a great Italian architect of the Renaissance period. He was born in the city of Padua, but he moved to nearby Vicenza where he got a job in a stonemason's yard. The mason noticed his skill at designing things, and encouraged him to go to Rome to study. There he saw the remains of many ancient Roman buildings, and these became the most important influence on his own work. He designed villas, churches, and other public buildings. Among the most famous are the Teatro Olympico, a theater in Verona, and the Church of Il Redentore ("The Savior") in Venice. He is thought of as the pioneer of modern Italian architecture. ○ JONES

British suffragettes in 1908 celebrating the release of two of their members from prison. In 1918 women over 30 were given the vote.

Pankhurst, Emmeline (1858–1928)
Emmeline Pankhurst was an English feminist who led the campaign to gain the vote for women at the beginning of the 20th century. Together with her daughters, **Christabel Pankhurst** (1880–1958) and **Sylvia Pankhurst** (1882–1960), and many other women, she adopted dramatic (and sometimes violent) methods to gain attention and sympathy for her cause. Emmeline was born in the city of Manchester, one of a large family of ten children. She went to school first in Manchester, then in Paris, and in 1874 she married a radical politician, **Richard Marsden Pankhurst** (1839–98). Together they campaigned for votes for women and for new laws allowing women to keep control of their property after they were married. In 1885 they moved to London, where they founded the Women's Franchise League to continue the campaign.

After Richard Pankhurst's death in 1898, Emmeline moved back to Manchester. In 1903 she and her daughter Christabel began the Women's Social and Political Union (known as the WSPU), the organization that became the center of the women's movement. In 1905 Christabel was arrested when she stood up at a Liberal Party meeting in Manchester and shouted, "Votes for Women!" Most politicians—who were, of course, all men—simply ignored the WSPU, so as time went on the women's campaign became more and more dramatic. Members chained themselves to lampposts and railings (throwing away the keys), slashed paintings, attacked policemen, and threw stones through windows. Newspapers began calling them "suffragettes"—women who campaigned for "suffrage" (the vote). Emmeline's second daughter, Sylvia, became one of the most active suffragettes. When she was arrested she began "hunger strikes," threatening to starve herself to death unless she was released. The authorities introduced a new law which meant that the women could be released, then rearrested as soon as they were well again. This happened to Sylvia 13 times after she was imprisoned for bombing Lloyd George's house.

When World War I began in 1914 the suffragettes halted their campaign and organized war work instead. During the war many very young men fought and died for their country, and the government could no longer deny them the vote. In 1918 a new law allowed all men over the age of 18 to vote. The government could no longer ignore women either, but the law allowed only women over 30 the vote. The suffragettes continued campaigning, and eventually, in 1928, they gained a vote equal to men's.

Parker, Dorothy (1893–1967)
Dorothy Parker was an American writer. She worked as a journalist in New York, where she became well known for her wit. This wit is reflected in her many stories, essays, and poems.

She was actively involved in politics, and worked as a newspaper reporter in Spain during the Civil War there.

Parnell, Charles Stewart (1846–91)
Parnell was an Irish politician who led a campaign for "home rule" (a government for Ireland that was separate from the British government). He was elected to the House of Commons in 1875 and became leader of the Irish party in 1880. The Irish party were in a position to be able to cast their votes to make either one of the British parties the more powerful, and they used their influence to ensure that Irish home rule became the most important political issue of the time. Parnell was forced to resign after a scandal in 1889.

Pascal, Blaise (1623–62)
Pascal was a French scientist, mathematician, and philosopher. He was a brilliant child, helping his father with experiments and calculations as well as developing theories of his own about geometry, physics, and other things. Descartes admired one of his treatises so much that he would not believe it had been written by a 16-year-old! He did important work on the effects of air pressure, which led to the invention of the barometer. In 1654 he suddenly joined his sister in a monastery, where he gave his energy to defending certain Christian philosophies against the attacks of Jesuit thinkers. His famous *Pensées* are a collection of notes he made for a book on Christian theology.
○ DESCARTES

Pasteur, Louis (1822–95)
Pasteur was a French scientist who proved that the existence of bacteria in the air caused wine to ferment or milk to go sour. He taught chemistry at the University of Dijon and later became professor of science in Paris. In 1857 he began studying the fermentation of wine and showed that it did not "just happen," but was caused by invisible organisms carried in the air—bacteria, or "germs." He was then able to invent a process for killing bacteria in milk, called "pasteurization" in his memory. His research led to great advances in the treatment of disease. Lister based his methods of antiseptic treatment on Pasteur's discoveries. The Pasteur Institute in Paris was founded in his honor in 1885. ○ LISTER

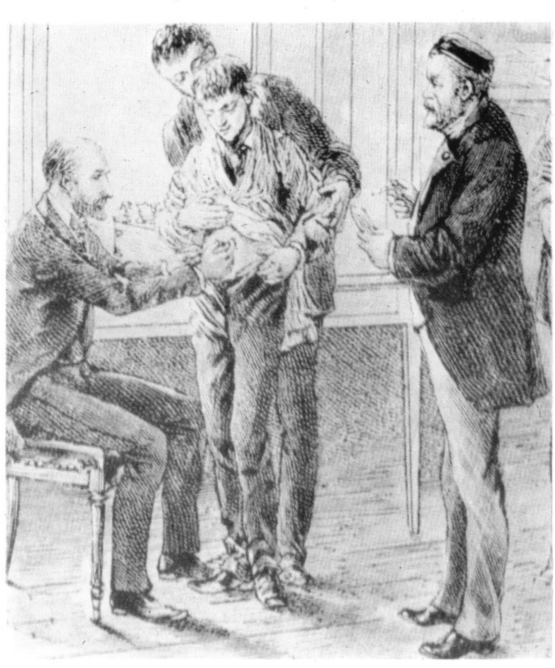

Louis Pasteur at his clinic. He proved that bacteria and other germs cause disease. He invented pasteurization*—a way of heating milk and cooling it quickly to make it safe to drink.*

Patrick, Saint (*c*.385–*c*.461)
Saint Patrick is the patron saint of Ireland. He was born somewhere in the west of England or Wales, and at the age of 16 was kidnapped by pirates and forced to work as a slave in County Antrim in Ireland. After many years he escaped to France, where he became a monk. He returned to Ireland to spread Christian teaching, fearlessly confronting powerful chieftains and druids. He founded the Irish Church, and in about 444 became bishop of Armagh.

Patton, George Smith (1885–1945)
Patton was an American general who became one of the most successful commmanders of World War II. He led the United States Third Army in North Africa, Italy, and then in France after the Normandy landings of 1944. It was Patton who made the breakthrough that allowed the Allied armies to escape from Normandy and advance quickly through France, and he led the division that liberated Paris. He was killed in a car accident in Germany after the end of the war. ○ MONTGOMERY

Paul, Saint (d. *c*.A.D. 67)
Saint Paul is known as the "Apostle of the Gentiles" because he made missionary journeys to convert Gentiles (people who are not Jews) to Christianity. In doing so, he established Christianity as an independent religion, separate

from the Jewish faith. He was a Jew and a Roman citizen, born at Tarsus. As a young man he took an active part in the widespread persecution of Christians by Jews. But suddenly, as he was traveling to Damascus, he had a vision in which Christ appeared and told him to preach Christianity to non-Jews. He was baptized, and after spending some time in meditation he went to Jerusalem, where Peter was preaching. He began his missionary journeys in A.D. 45, visiting Asia Minor, Syria, and Greece. He preached to both Jews and non-Jews, founding churches wherever he went. These journeys involved danger and hardship. This is how Paul described them: "In journeyings often, in perils of waters, in perils of robbers... In weariness and painfulness, in watchings often, in hunger and thirst, in fastings often, in cold and nakedness." His arrival in a town caused great excitement, and his teaching made him many enemies. Eventually, in Jerusalem, he was arrested by the Roman governor. As a Roman citizen, he demanded to be tried in Rome. He was shipwrecked on his way there, and after his arrival he remained under "house arrest" for two years, writing letters to the churches he had founded. He was eventually tried and, according to tradition, beheaded at the place now called *Tre Fontane.*
○ LUKE, PETER

Pauli, Wolfgang (1900–58)
Pauli was an Austrian physicist, born in Vienna, where his father was professor of chemistry at the university. He became professor of physics at Zurich in 1928. His most important work concerns the structure of atoms—the tiny particles that make up all substances. He developed something called the "exclusion principle," and in 1931 he suggested the existence of the "neutrino," later proved by Enrico Fermi. ○ FERMI

Pauling, Linus Carl (1901–)
Pauling is an American chemist. He taught at the California Institute of Technology, where he worked out a technique to discover the structure of complicated molecules. This became useful in the treatment of certain diseases, and he was awarded the Nobel Prize in 1954. After World War II he led a group of scientists who opposed the construction of nuclear weapons by the United States. He won a second Nobel Prize, for Peace, in 1962.

Pavlov, Ivan Petrovich (1849–1936)
Pavlov was a Russian scientist who worked at the Institute of Experimental Medicine at St. Petersburg. In his most famous experiment he rang a bell before feeding some dogs he kept in his laboratory. When the dogs saw the food, glands in their mouth would produce saliva. After a while, Pavlov rang the bell, but did not feed the dogs. He found that they continued to produce saliva, because they had learned to expect food when they heard the bell. This demonstrated what Pavlov called the "conditioned reflex"—a discovery of great importance in the study of animal and human behavior. He won the Nobel Prize for Medicine in 1904.

Pavlova, Anna (1885–1931)
Anna Pavlova was a great Russian ballerina. She was born in St. Petersburg, where she trained at the Imperial Ballet School. In 1909 she joined Diaghilev's *Ballets Russes* in Paris. Her performances immediately made her famous. She went on to form her own ballet company. Among her most famous roles were *The Dying Swan* and *Giselle*.

Paxton, Sir Joseph (1801–65)
Paxton was an English landscape gardener and architect. While working for the Duke of Devonshire at Chatsworth House he built many greenhouses, and these inspired his most famous creation, the Crystal Palace. This was a huge steel-framed glass pavilion built for the Great Exhibition in London in 1851. The building stood until 1936, when it was destroyed by a fire.

Peary, Robert Edwin (1856–1920)
Peary was the American explorer who was the first man to reach the North Pole. He was a sailor in the U.S. Navy, and first became interested in the Arctic on a navy expedition to Greenland. He made several more journeys to the area, and in 1892

American explorer Peary—the first man to reach the North Pole.

crossed the ice pack from west to east on a sledge. In April 1909 he reached the North Pole by sledge. He wrote several books about his adventures, including *The North Pole* (published in 1910).
○ AMUNDSEN

Pedro the Cruel (1334–69)
Pedro the Cruel was a notorious king of Castile in the south of Spain. He murdered anybody suspected of opposing him, including three of his half brothers. The fourth, Henry, attempted to overthrow Pedro, but Pedro defeated him with the help of Edward the Black Prince of England. But Edward then became disgusted at Pedro's cruelty and abandoned him; Henry returned and defeated his half brother in hand-to-hand combat.

Peel, Sir Robert (1788–1850)
Peel was the British prime minister from 1841 until 1846. He was a member of the Tory Party, first elected to the House of Commons in 1809. While serving as Home Secretary he introduced the Metropolitan Police, who became known as "peelers," or "bobbies" (from Peel's first name, Robert). When he became prime minister his main aim was to encourage free trade between Great Britain and other countries, so he took steps toward eliminating the tax that had to be paid on corn imported from abroad. In 1846, as a result of the potato famine that was causing starvation throughout Ireland, he abandoned these taxes altogether in order to make food cheaper. His own party opposed him, and although the measure was passed, Peel was forced to resign. ○ DISRAELI, VICTORIA

Peisistratus (*c.*600 B.C.–528 B.C.)
Peisistratus was a ruler of ancient Athens. He was the owner of several gold and silver mines, and he used his great wealth to hire soldiers willing to fight for him. In about 560 B.C. he took control of the Acropolis, and although other Athenians continued to oppose him, he was able to maintain himself as ruler. He used his power and wealth wisely. He fortified the city, built new public monuments and buildings, supported farmers, and helped the poor in times of need. He is said to have been the first person to collect Homer's poems in one volume.

Pelé (Edison Arantes do Nascimento, 1940–)
Pelé is regarded as the greatest soccer player of all time. He was born into a poor family, but became a star at the age of only 16 when he scored his first goal for his club Santos. He appeared in his first World Cup in 1958 still only 17—which Brazil won. Pelé played in three more World Cups, scoring 97 goals for Brazil in only 110 games.

Penda (*c.*577–655)
Penda was a warlike Anglo-Saxon king of Mercia (an ancient English kingdom) who ruled from the year 633. He built up an army and, by making an alliance with the king of Wales, he was able to defeat King Edwin of Northumbria. For a while he was the most powerful chieftain in the land, but eventually he was defeated and killed by Oswy of Northumbria.

Penn, William (1644–1718)
William Penn was an English Quaker who founded the state of Pennsylvania. Puritan religious groups such as the Quakers were not tolerated in England during the 17th century, and when the young Penn was discovered attending Quaker meetings in Oxford he was expelled from the university. His father sent him on a tour of Europe, and then made him manager of his estates in Ireland. But Penn was

(Continued on page 200)

William Penn selling cloth to North American Indians.

Plato's Republic

Plato (*c*.427 B.C. – 347 B.C.)
Plato was an ancient Athenian philosopher. He was a pupil of Socrates, and because the master left no books or manuscripts it is only through Plato's writings that we know about his ideas. Aristotle, the third great Athenian philosopher, was in turn a pupil of Plato. Plato's ideas have, more than any others, dominated Western thought. All the books he is known to have written have survived, and in the 15th century they were translated into Latin and inspired many of the thinkers, writers, and artists of the Renaissance period. Since then, they have been a constant source of ideas and principles for philosophers of many different kinds.

A bust of Plato, one of the most important of the Greek philosophers. He was the pupil of Socrates and the master of Aristotle, two other great philosophers.

Very little is known about Plato's life. He was probably born into a family of Athenian nobles, and he served in the army during the Peloponnesian War against Sparta. Afterward he returned to Athens and met Socrates. Socrates was a very informal teacher: he liked to go to the city's public places and get into discussion with whoever he found willing to give up the time. When Socrates was brought to trial and executed in 399 B.C., Plato made a point of writing down his ideas. Socrates appears as a character in most of Plato's works, and at first Plato faithfully recorded the master's words. But in later works the ideas become those of Plato himself, and Socrates' role became that of a "voice" alone. These works are "dialogues": Plato invents discussions in which various characters ask questions (such as "What is knowledge?" or "What is beauty?"), and discuss the answers.

Plato and students engaging in a "dialogue" in the garden of the Academy Plato established in Athens in about 388 B.C. It was called the Academy because it was near the grove of Academus.

After Socrates' death, Plato traveled around the Mediterranean, visiting Italy, Egypt, and other places. He returned to Athens in 388 B.C. and founded a school where young noblemen could study mathematics and politics, as well as philosophy. It became known as the "Academy" because it was near a grove dedicated to the mythical character Academus.

Among Plato's most important ideas are those he had about government. He believed that behind the confusing world seen and understood by humans there lay certain unchanging and absolute truths, which he called simply the "good." In the book called the *Republic* Plato says that government should be entrusted to philosopher-kings who

A Happy Soul

Plato proposed the theory that all people desire happiness. People sometimes act in ways that do not produce happiness. They do this because they do not know what actions will produce happiness. Plato claimed that happiness resulted from a happy state of the soul. Because moral virtue produces health in the soul, everyone should strive to be virtuous. The reason why many people do not seek to be virtuous is because they do not realize that virtue produces happiness. So the basic problem for all people is the problem of knowledge.

have the ability and education to see the "good." They would rule with the best interests of ordinary men and women in mind. In 368 B.C. Plato got the chance to try out his ideas, when he was invited to educate Dionysus II to become such a philosopher-king in Sicily. Unfortunately, Dionysus was not interested in his studies, and soon fell out with Plato and with his guardian. Plato was forced to leave, and later he wrote a more practical version of these ideas in the *Laws*. Plato's republic would have a strict hierarchy, compulsory military and athletic training, censorship of art and literature (which Plato thought could mislead the uneducated), and property would be owned not by private individuals, but in common.

Plato is traditionally said to have died during a wedding. His ideas on politics, art, and society, as well as the more abstract area of philosophy, have made him one of the most influential thinkers in history. ○ ARISTOTLE, SOCRATES

again arrested for going to Quaker meetings in the city of Cork, then later imprisoned in the Tower of London for publishing a book supporting his beliefs. After his father's death, the Duke of York persuaded Penn to go to America and found a colony for Quakers. He was granted a large area of land to the west of the Delaware River, which he named "Pennsylvania" in honor of his father. He arrived there in December 1682. He drew up a democratic constitution, which insisted on toleration for all religions that were compatible with Christianity. The capital of the new state was founded at Philadelphia—which means "City of Brotherly Love." Penn remained governor until 1684, when he returned to England to campaign for greater religious tolerance there. As a result of his efforts, many imprisoned Quakers were set free.

Pepin III, "the Short" (*c.*715–768)
Pepin the Short was the son of Charles Martel. He became king of the Franks in 751 after the old king, Childeric, had been deposed. In 754 he led an expedition to Italy to support the Pope against the invading Longobard tribe, and his victory made him one of the most powerful rulers in Europe. His son, Charlemagne, extended the empire to make it the greatest since the time of the Romans.
○ CHARLEMAGNE, CHARLES MARTEL

Pepys, Samuel (1633–1703)
Samuel Pepys was an English government official at the end of the 17th century. He left an extraordinary record of his life and times in his famous *Diary*, which he kept every day from January 1, 1660, until May 31, 1669—when his eyesight became too bad. Pepys was secretary to the Admiralty. He was one of those imprisoned as a result of Titus Oates's "Popish Plot" in 1679, although when the plot was discovered to be an invention he was released and given his old job back. His diary describes all the famous events of the 1660s: the Great Plague of 1665, the Fire of London in 1666, and the sea battle with the Dutch in the Thames Estuary in 1667. It reveals the gossip and scandal of King Charles II's court—as well as revealing much of Pepys's own home life. Pepys wrote the diary in code, and it remained undeciphered in a Cambridge college until the 19th century, when it was first published. ○ OATES

Pericles (*c.*490 B.C.–429 B.C.)
Pericles was the greatest of the leaders of the ancient Greek state of Athens. He is sometimes known as the "father of democracy" because he was able to restrict the power of the city's magistrates and increase the influence of the assembly of citizens. Under his leadership Athens reached the height of its power in the ancient world. He spent large sums of money on beautifying the city with new buildings and works of art, and supported the drama competitions at which Sophocles' and Euripides' plays were performed. Eventually, Athens was defeated by its powerful and jealous neighbor, Sparta. Pericles died during a plague. ○ AESCHYLUS, PHIDIAS, SOCRATES, SOPHOCLES

Pericles, the Athenian known as the "father of democracy." He was responsible for the building of the Parthenon and other famous buildings in Athens.

Perón, Juan Domingo (1895–1974)
Juan Perón was a president of Argentina. He was elected in 1946, after taking part in an army coup d'état which overthrew the old regime of President Castillo. Although he was the head of a right-wing military party, he became popular with Argentina's working people. He introduced social welfare schemes and encouraged the development of industry. In this he was supported by his wife, **Eva Perón** (1919–52), who devoted herself to relieving poverty and to social reform. She organized a union of women workers, and used her influence to gain the vote for women. Eva became popular with the Argentines, and was known as "Evita." She died of cancer in 1952. Juan Perón was overthrown in 1955, although he returned to power in 1973. After his death he was briefly succeeded as president by his third wife, **Isabella Martinez Perón** (1931–).

The diarist Samuel Pepys (left). Philip II of Spain (above). Eva Perón praying in the Vatican.

Peter, Saint (d. *c.* A.D. 64)
Saint Peter was the leader of Christ's disciples. He was a fisherman on the Sea of Galilee when Jesus called him to be a "fisher of men," together with his brother, Andrew. The New Testament tells how, after the Resurrection, Jesus appeared to Peter and told him to spread Christian teaching. He went on missionary journeys to Samaria and Antioch and continued to preach in Palestine, against the opposition of Roman and Jewish authorities. Eventually he went to Rome, where he was executed during the reign of the Emperor Nero. Peter's name was originally Simon; the name "Peter" was given to him by Jesus and means "Rock," because Jesus said that Peter would be the rock upon which the Christian Church was built.
○ JESUS OF NAZARETH, NERO, PAUL

Peter I, "the Great" (1672–1725)
Peter the Great was one of the most powerful and enterprising of all the tsars of Russia. He came to power in 1682, sharing the throne with his half brother, Ivan. After Ivan's death in 1696, Peter took full control of the country. A series of military campaigns, against Turkey to the south and Sweden to the west, eventually brought him large areas of extra territory, as well as important ports on the Baltic and Black Seas. Meanwhile, he reformed the tax system and the government, introduced schools, opened the first Russian museum, and edited the first newspaper, and brought the Church under the control of his government. On a visit to England and the Netherlands he worked as a common shipbuilder in order to learn the trade, then persuaded skilled workers to travel to Russia to build the country's first navy. Finally, he decided to build a new capital city, which he planned himself, on the swampy land near the Baltic. He called the beautiful new city "St. Petersburg" (now Leningrad). After his death he was succeeded by his mistress, who became **Catherine I** (*c.*1684–1727). ○ CHARLES XII

Petrarch (Francesco Petrarca, 1304–74)
Petrarch was thought of by the people of his own time as a great scholar, although today he is remembered more for his beautiful love poetry. He was born in Arezzo, and lived for some years at Avignon in France. There, at Easter, 1327, he saw the beautiful "Laura" in a church. He celebrates his love for her in over 300 sonnets—although he never did any more than write about it. Petrarch traveled widely, collecting ancient Roman manuscripts, and became an important figure in the sudden explosion of interest in the ancient world that would lead to the Italian Renaissance. He died at a villa near Padua, where he was found with his head resting on a book. ○ BOCCACCIO

Phidias (*c.*490 B.C.–*c.*430 B.C.)
The most famous of ancient Greek sculptors. He worked for Pericles, designing statues and friezes for the city of Athens. Although none of his work has survived, his contemporaries said that the figures of Athena (in Athens) and Zeus (at Olympia) were among the most beautiful objects in the world. ○ PERICLES

Philip II (1527–98)
Philip II became the king of Spain when his father, the Emperor Charles V, abdicated in 1556. He was a stubborn, tyrannical ruler whose policies had little success. His main aim was to ensure Europe continued to be ruled by Catholics, and he opposed the growth of the new Protestant Church. He carried on a long and bloody war with the Netherlands, which finally ended in a Spanish defeat in 1579. He was more successful against the powerful Turks, who were defeated and held at bay by his brother Don John at the Battle of Lepanto in 1571. In 1554 he married **Mary Tudor** (1516–1558), the queen of England, hoping that way to bring England under his influence. But the couple had no children, and after Mary's death the new queen, Elizabeth I, made herself Philip's new

enemy. In 1588 he sent the Spanish Armada to conquer England—with disastrous results. Meanwhile, English pirates had reduced the strength of the Spanish navy, and the Spanish economy was in ruins. Philip died leaving the country weaker than when he had come to power.
○ CHARLES V, ELIZABETH I, JOHN OF AUSTRIA

Philip IV, "the Fair" (1268–1314)
A strong king of France, who came to power in 1285. He began a dispute with Pope Boniface VIII over the amount of authority the Pope should have over his country. After Boniface's death Philip was able to get a French Pope (Clement V) elected, and the papacy then moved from Rome to Avignon in the south of France.

Piaf, Edith (Edith Giovanna Gassion, 1915–63)
Edith Piaf was a French singer and songwriter. Her name, which means "sparrow," was given to her by a host in one of the nightclubs where she began her career in the 1930s. She became successful in clubs, on the radio, and in films.

Picasso, Pablo Ruiz y (1881–1973)
Pablo Picasso was a Spanish artist. As the founder of the "Cubist" movement, he became the most important and influential artist of the 20th century. Picasso was born in Málaga and studied in Barcelona, where his extraordinary talent for drawing and painting was apparent even while he was still a boy. At the age of 20 he moved to Paris, which was at that time the artistic capital of Europe. Under the influence of Post-Impressionist painters such as Toulouse-Lautrec, Van Gogh, and Gauguin he began painting people he saw in the city—beggars, harlequins, circus performers, actors, and others. These pictures are often dominated by deep blues or pinks. Picasso then began to study the works of Paul Cézanne, and to collect African sculpture. They gave him revolutionary new ideas, and in 1907, he suddenly broke with the artistic styles of the past: his picture *Les Demoiselles d'Avignon* showed a group of distorted figures, their bodies broken up into simple, angular shapes. Together with another artist, **Georges Braque** (1882–1963), Picasso developed this style of distorting objects and exaggerating the different shapes he found in them. It came to be called "Cubism." One of his most famous pictures is *Guernica*, which commemorates the bombing of the town of Guernica during the Spanish Civil War. The horror of the bombing is conveyed in the tangled, distorted shapes of the people in the

A Cubist painting by Picasso called The Seated Nude.

picture. For many years it hung in the Museum of Modern Art in New York City, but with the return of democracy to Spain in the 1980s it was moved to the town of Guernica itself. Picasso produced not only thousands of paintings, but prints, sculptures, and book illustrations as well.
○ CÉZANNE, TOULOUSE-LAUTREC

Piero della Francesca (*c.*1420–92)
Piero was one of the finest painters of the early part of the Renaissance period in Italy. Most of his pictures are of religious subjects, among the most famous being *The Baptism* and the *Flagellation of Christ*. Piero studied mathematics and wrote about perspective and geometry, and his compositions are beautifully arranged and delicately colored.

Pilate, Pontius (d. *c.* A.D. 36)
Pilate was the Roman governor of Judea who sentenced Jesus of Nazareth to be crucified. Pilate attempted to avoid responsibility for trying Jesus by referring the case to the Jewish King Herod, but Herod refused to become involved. During Pilate's government, which began in A.D. 26, there were several outbreaks of violence in Judea, and eventually he was summoned to Rome charged with cruelty. He then either committed suicide or was banished. ○ HEROD, JESUS OF NAZARETH

Pirandello, Luigi (1867–1936)
Pirandello was an Italian writer. He was born on the island of Sicily, and wrote many stories based on the traditional folk tales told by the people who lived there. He is most famous for his plays, which include *Six Characters in Search of an Author* (written in 1921). It is set at a play rehearsal and involves characters looking for somebody to give them a script.

Pisano, Niccola (*c.*1225–*c.*1284)
Pisano was an Italian sculptor, architect, and engineer who is celebrated for the beautiful pulpits he carved for the Baptistery in the city of Pisa and the cathedral in Siena. He was assisted by his son, **Giovanni Pisano** (*c.*1250–*c.*1320), who also went on to become a well-known sculptor.

Pissarro, Camille (1830–1903)
Pissarro was a French painter. He became an important member of the Impressionist group, and was the only one to exhibit in all of the Impressionist exhibitions held in Paris. He lived for a while in London, but spent most of his time in the countryside near Paris. ○ CÉZANNE, MANET

Pitt, William, "the Elder" Earl of Chatham (1708–78)
William Pitt the Elder was an English politician. Although he only served as a prime minister for a year (1766–67), his ideas and influence had dominated the British government for several years before. He was famous for the many fine speeches he gave during his career, and for his organizational skill. In 1746 he became paymaster to the armed forces, a job he carried out with great efficiency and honesty, refusing to take advantage of his position for his own profit. His policies during the Seven Years' War brought Britain success in Europe, as well as new colonies in India and Canada. Pitt was troubled by illness and depression, and was eventually forced to retire from politics. His son, **William Pitt "the Younger"** (1759–1806), was also a successful politician. He became prime minister in 1783, at the age of only 25, and governed for the next 17 years. He introduced an act sharing control of India between the government and the East India Company, abolished public hangings, and in 1800 abolished the Irish Parliament, bringing the country's government under the control of the English Parliament in London.

The Baptism of Christ by the Italian artist Piero della Francesca.

Pizarro, Francisco (*c.*1478–1541)
Francisco Pizarro was the Spanish *conquistador* who conquered Peru. He first sailed to the Americas with Balboa in 1509, before attempting to invade Peru in 1526. This first expedition failed, and Pizarro returned to Spain. He received weapons and support from the Emperor Charles V, and was made governor of Peru in advance of his arrival. In May 1532 he began a campaign against the Incas who lived there. He captured their ruler, Atahualpa, first demanding a huge ransom for his release, then treacherously murdering him. Pizarro founded the city of Lima in 1535, and by 1540 the Spaniards had conquered the whole country. He was killed during a dispute with some of his own people.
○ CHARLES V, CORTÉS

Planck, Max Ernst Ludwig (1858–1947)
Max Planck was a German scientist. He became professor of physics at Berlin University in 1889. In 1900 he published his Quantum Theory, which concerns the nature of energy, and in 1918 he received the Nobel Prize for his work. ○ BOHR

The German scientist Max Planck. He revolutionized physics with his Quantum Theory.

Plath, Sylvia (1932–63)
Sylvia Plath was an American writer. Her works include a novel, *The Bell Jar* (1963), but she is best known for her poems, collected in two books, *The Colossus* (1960) and *Ariel*, which was published in 1965, two years after she committed suicide. She was married to the English poet, Ted Hughes.
○ HUGHES

Plato (*c.*427 B.C.–347 B.C.)
See pages 198 & 199

Plutarch (*c.* A.D. 46–*c.*120)
Plutarch was the first person to write a book like this one—a collection of the lives of the most famous people in history. He was born in Boeotia, a region of ancient Greece, and went to school in Athens. Later he became a diplomat, and made several visits to Rome, where he gave lectures on philosophy. His *Parallel Lives* contains 46 biographies of soldiers and politicians. They are arranged in pairs, one from ancient Greece, and one from ancient Rome, and Plutarch compares them with each other. He also wrote some single *Lives*, as well as essays on philosophy, history, politics, and other subjects.

A portrait of the North American native princess, Pocahontas, in Elizabethan dress.

Pocahontas (1595–1617)
Pocahontas was a famous North American native princess. She was the daughter of Powhatan, the chief of a tribe living near the European settlement at Jamestown, Virginia. In 1606, at the age of 11, she saved the life of an English colonist, Captain John Smith. The next year she was in turn captured by the settlers and taken to Jamestown. There, another Englishman, John Rolfe, fell in love with her. Pocahontas was baptized, took a new name, "Rebecca," and in 1616 they were married. She traveled to England with him, where she became famous but was unhappy at being separated from her home. She decided to return to America in 1617, but died before her ship had even left the river Thames.

Poe, Edgar Allan (1809–49)
Edgar Allan Poe was an American writer. He is best known as the author of grotesque mysteries and horror stories. *The Pit and the Pendulum* and *The Tell-Tale Heart* are among his most famous short stories. Poe also wrote some of the first detective stories. But he was also admired as a poet, particularly in France, where Baudelaire and others were influenced by his work. Poe was born in Boston and, after his mother's death, adopted by a wealthy merchant named John Allan. He began a career in the army, but found he could not afford the training, so he turned to writing instead. His poems received little notice, but a story called "MS. Found in a Bottle" won a prize in 1833, and he became editor of a newspaper. He continued to write, and in 1840 he moved to New York and a job as editor of a magazine. The magazine became successful, partly because of the popularity of Poe's own stories, which he published there. A collection of his poems, *The Raven and Other Poems*, published in 1845, was also a success, but after the death of his wife in 1847 Poe became depressed, and wrote less. He died in Baltimore, shortly before he was supposed to marry a second time.

Pollock, Jackson (1912–56)
Pollock was an American artist. He was the inventor of "Action Painting"—a method of dripping or splashing paint onto canvases to get instant, abstract patterns. He even tried spreading paint by riding a bicycle through it. He has been ridiculed by many people, but his works have taken an important place in 20th-century art.

Polo, Marco (1254–1324)
See pages 206 & 207

Pompey (106 B.C.–48 B.C.)
Pompey was a Roman general. He won many impressive military campaigns, including the conquest of much of Syria and Palestine. After capturing Jerusalem in 63 B.C. he returned to Rome, and became one of the three "triumvirs" who governed the empire. While Caesar was campaigning in Gaul, Pompey ruled Rome alone. The two men had been close friends and Pompey had married Caesar's sister, Julia, but eventually the desire for power made them rivals. In 49 B.C. they quarreled and began a civil war. Pompey was defeated at the Battle of Pharsalus and forced to flee to Egypt, where he was murdered. ○ JULIUS CAESAR

A bust of Pompey, the Roman general.

Pompidou, Georges Jean Raymond (1911–74)
Pompidou was a French politician. He entered politics in 1944 as an adviser to General De Gaulle. He became prime minister in 1962, but was forced to resign after the riots of 1968. He was president from 1969 until his death. ○ DE GAULLE

Pope, Alexander (1688–1744)
Alexander Pope was an English poet. He grew up in the countryside around Windsor, just outside London. Because his family were Catholics, and because Pope suffered from a crippling disease, he had no proper schooling. Instead, he educated himself at home with the help of his father. When he was 15 he went to London to learn French and Italian. He met several famous men of letters, and they helped him publish his first works. His poem *The Rape of the Lock*, published in 1712, brought him fame, and his translations of Homer's *Iliad* and *Odyssey* made him wealthy enough to buy a house in West London. His famous *Dunciad* (1728) made fun of many of the writers and politicians of the day. He made many enemies through his writing. ○ SWIFT

A painting by the American artist, Jackson Pollock.

Porter, Cole (1891–1964)
An American songwriter. He specialized in witty, sophisticated lyrics, and wrote songs for several popular musicals, including *Kiss Me Kate* and *Anything Goes.*

Potter, Beatrix (1866–1943)
Beatrix Potter was the author of a famous series of children's stories, featuring animal characters such as "Peter Rabbit," "Jemima Puddleduck," and "Mrs. Tiggy-Winkle." She was born in London, but lived for much of her life in the beautiful Lake District in the north of England. She both wrote the stories and painted illustrations for them.

Pound, Ezra Loomis (1885–1972)
Ezra Pound was an American poet. He was born in Idaho and worked for a short time as a teacher. In 1906 he made a tour of Europe, then settled in England. He worked for literary magazines and became friends with many other writers, including T.S. Eliot, James Joyce, and Ernest Hemingway. Pound was particularly interested in Far Eastern writing, and made use of Chinese and Japanese poems in developing his own "Imagist" style. From 1924 he lived in Italy, where he became a supporter of the Fascist government. After World War II he was arrested and taken to the United States to stand trial for treason, but he avoided prosecution by being certified as insane.

Travels in the East

Polo, Marco (1254–1324)
When Marco Polo returned to his home in Venice after 20 years in the Far East, he had probably traveled farther than anybody before him. Not even Arab explorers, who had reached China by sea, had ventured far from the coast. Marco Polo traveled overland, from Acre on the coast of Palestine, through Persia and Turkestan, across the vast Gobi Desert and into China itself. There, at the city of Khan-balik, he became a favorite of the great Mongol Emperor Kubla Khan, who sent him on further journeys—to the south, to Burma and Indochina, to Tibet in the west, and to the city of Karakorum and northern China.

People in Europe had known of vast lands to the east for centuries, since Alexander the Great had conquered parts of India in the 4th century B.C. But there were many reasons why nobody had tried to explore them. In the first place, great distances and many natural dangers were involved. Marco Polo described some of these: wild animals, hostile warriors belonging to the nomadic tribes living in central Asia, bandits—and the landscape itself, sometimes arid, sometimes mountainous, and always unknown. Besides, for centuries nobody had had any good reason to go venturing into unfamiliar and dangerous territory. By Marco Polo's day, however, this had changed. Europe had become a community of merchants and traders, and Venice was one of its wealthiest and fastest-growing states. The East was a rich source of gems, spices, silks, and other precious goods, and merchants began looking for new and more profitable trade routes.

There were other problems: politics and religion. The Middle East was controlled by Muslims, and centuries of conflict between them and the Christians meant that any journey to the East by a European could be dangerous. Beyond the Muslim communities lived the Mongols, an alliance of Asian tribes deeply feared for their ferocity and military skill. By the 13th century, the Mongol Empire stretched from the edge of Europe to China.

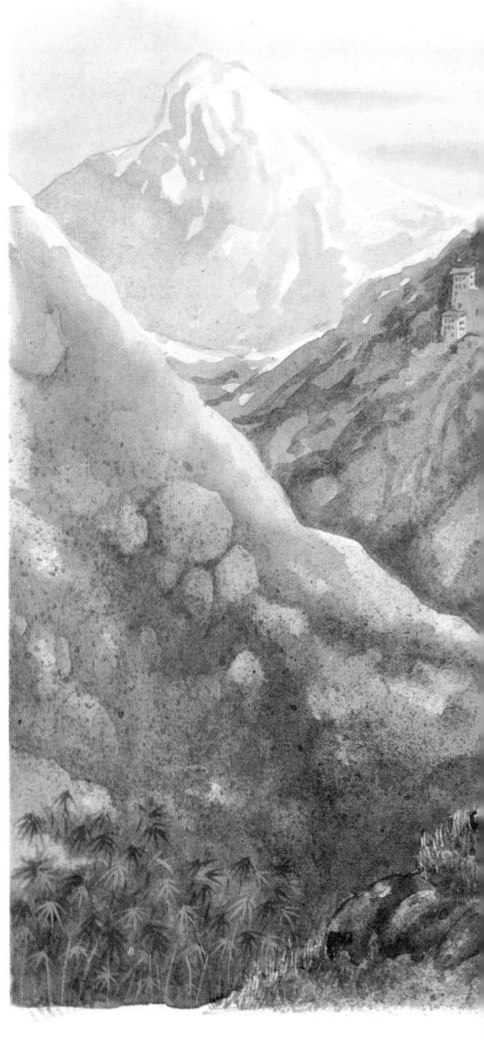

Marco Polo and his party in the Tibetan mountains. In order to scare off wild animals they lit bamboo cane fires. They blindfolded their horses to keep them calm.

Despite the dangers, in 1260 two of Marco Polo's uncles set out for China, and eventually visited the Emperor Kubla Khan. He instructed them to return, and this they did, leaving Venice in 1271, and this time taking the 17-year-old Marco Polo along with them. After

The province of Tibet is terribly devastated, for it was ravaged by the campaign of Mogul Khan.

This country produces canes of immense size and girth. . . . Merchants who are passing through this country at night use these canes as fuel, because when they are alight, they make such a popping and banging that lions and bears and other beasts of prey are scared away in terror. When they have horses that have never heard this noise, they bandage their eyes and shackle their feet so that they cannot bolt.

Travels of Marco Polo

crossing Asia, the party reached the Khan's palace at Khanbalik in 1275. For the next 20 years Marco acted as a diplomat for the Khan, traveling on missions throughout the empire, and recording what he saw. In 1293, Marco and his uncles left, escorting an imperial princess to her wedding in Persia. Two years later they reached Venice.

Marco did not write anything of his adventures until he was captured during a war between Venice and the city of Genoa and imprisoned. There he met a writer named Rustichello, and together they composed Marco Polo's *Description of the World* (now known simply as the *Travels*). It became one of the best-known books of the age before the invention of printing. Marco Polo's name has survived to this day as belonging to one of history's greatest travelers. ○ KUBLA KHAN

Merchants appear on a map of Marco Polo's travels in the East.

Presley, Elvis Aron (1935–77)
Elvis Presley was one of the first rock 'n' roll stars. He was born in the state of Missouri, where he first sang in a local church choir. He was still working as a truck driver when he signed his first recording contract in 1954. Within two years he had become the idol of teenagers all over the United States and had made several hit records. He was accused of causing hysteria and of obscenity, and some radio stations even banned his records. During the late 1960s he performed less and less frequently, spending more time alone at his mansion in Memphis. He died after an accidental drug overdose.

American singer Elvis Presley established the popularity of rock 'n' roll in the 1950s.

Joseph Priestley, one of the founders of modern chemistry.

Priestley, Joseph (1733–1804)
Joseph Priestley was an English clergyman who took up chemistry in his spare time and made important discoveries about gases. He was minister at a church in Leeds. He was the first person to make pure ammonia gas, and he invented soda water by using carbon dioxide to make the bubbles. Priestley is most famous for being the first to make pure oxygen, which he called "dephlogisticated air," in 1774. Meanwhile, he had become involved in religious controversies, and eventually emigrated to the United States.

Prokofiev, Serge Sergeievich (1891–1953)
Prokofiev was a Russian composer. He began playing the piano and composing while still a young child, before traveling to St. Petersburg to study at the conservatory there. He became celebrated as a pianist, moved to London and then to the United States, before returning to Russia in 1934. His works include *Peter and the Wolf*, a musical "story" in which different instruments represent different characters.

Proudhon, Pierre Joseph (1809–65)
Proudhon was a French writer and revolutionary. During the uprising in Paris in 1848 he was elected to the new French Assembly, where he proposed extreme socialist policies. He was eventually sentenced to prison for his views, but escaped to Geneva before he could be locked up. He returned in 1849 to serve his sentence, and he was imprisoned several more times in later years. His most famous work is *What Is Property?* which he wrote in 1846.

Proust, Marcel (1871–1922)
Marcel Proust was a French novelist who devoted much of his life to the writing of a single great work, the *Remembrance of Things Past*. He was born in Auteuil, a suburb of Paris. Periods of illness interrupted his education, and he finally gave up his studies altogether. Instead, he became a member of fashionable Paris society, spending his time at parties and in the "salons" of the wealthy and famous. Proust described himself as a "social butterfly," but this existence came to an end after the death of his mother in 1905. He had been deeply attached to her, and without her he suffered more and more from the asthma and other illnesses that had troubled him as a boy. Eventually, he confined himself to a soundproofed room in Paris. He slept by day and worked by night on his novel. The *Remembrance of Things Past* is a vast work, nearly 4,000 pages in length. It is made up of 13 separate volumes, the first of which, called *Swann's Way*, was published in 1913. It is based on Proust's own life, and paints a fascinating picture of Paris at the end of the 19th century. He continued working for the rest of his life, and the last part was not published until after his death.

Marcel Proust, the French novelist, author of the semi-autobiographical, 16-volume novel Remembrance of Things Past.

Prynne, William (1600–69)
William Prynne was an English writer and politician. He was a Puritan who opposed all forms of extravagance and luxury, and while he was still at the University of Oxford he began publishing pamphlets attacking some of the many things he disapproved of. In 1632 he got into deep trouble for his pamphlet *Histrio-Mastix*, which attacked acting and the theater. Queen Henrietta Maria, who liked play acting, took it to be an attack on her. Prynne was tried, and sentenced to pay a £5,000 fine, have his book burned in public, have both his ears cut off, and be imprisoned for the rest of his life. This did not stop him. In 1635 he published an attack on Archbishop Laud, and as a further punishment he had "S.L." (which stood for "Seditious Libeler") branded on both his cheeks. After the Civil War and the fall of Charles I, Prynne was released and became a member of Parliament. But he was expelled in 1648 for writing attacks on the army, and eventually became a supporter of restoring the monarchy. When King Charles II came to power in 1660, Prynne was made the keeper of the government records at the Tower of London. ○ CHARLES I, CROMWELL

Ptolemy (*c.*A.D. 90–168)
Ptolemy was an ancient Greek astronomer. He realized that the earth was a sphere, but he wrongly believed that it was the center of the universe and that all the other planets and the stars moved around it. Ptolemy was also a great mapmaker. He published a *Treatise on Geography* which was in effect the world's first atlas, which introduced the idea of identifying places by latitude and longitude.

Puccini, Giacomo (1858–1924)
Puccini was an Italian composer, famous for his romantic operas. He was born in Lucca, where he became choirmaster and composed his first pieces of music. His first operas failed badly, but *Manon Lescaut* was a great success on its first performance in 1893. His other works include *La Bohème* (1896), *Tosca* (1900), and *Madame Butterfly* (1904). Puccini was not only a skillful composer, but he had a great sense of drama, and this contributed to the popularity of his operas.

Pulitzer, Joseph (1847–1911)
Pulitzer was an American journalist. After working as a reporter for several years he began to buy failing newspapers and make them successful again. When he died he left money to establish the annual Pulitzer Prizes for journalism, literature, and music.

Pullman, George Mortimer (1831–1897)
An American businessman who invented the idea of the "sleeping car" to enable people to travel long distances by train. They were introduced in 1863, and Pullman went on to develop luxury coaches and begin the "Pullman Palace Car Company." He built a town named Pullman near Chicago, for the people who worked in his factory.

Pyrrhus (319 B.C.–272 B.C.)
Pyrrhus was ruler of the ancient kingdom of Epirus. From about the year 280 B.C. he was involved in a campaign against Rome. After a battle at the river Siris at which he lost a great many troops, he said: "Another such victory, and I must return home alone." Ever since, the phrase "Pyrrhic victory" has meant one that is achieved at such expense that it seems almost a defeat. His campaign in Italy was unsuccessful, and Pyrrhus returned to Epirus.

Pythagoras (*c.*550 B.C.)
Pythagoras was an ancient Greek mathematician and philosopher. He was born on the island of Samos, and as a young man he traveled around Greece and the Mediterranean, absorbing the learning of the different peoples he met. In about 530 B.C. he set up a school at Croton in southern Italy. He and his followers came to believe in the "transmigration of souls"—that is, that when a human or an animal dies, its soul passes into the body of another human or animal. They lived a life of religious discipline, and eventually became the leaders of the Croton government. Pythagoras himself is remembered for his mathematical theories. He believed that the whole universe was arranged on a mathematical basis and is said to have discovered that the earth rotates. After about 20 years at Croton, Pythagoras and his followers were forced to leave by an uprising.

A cigarette card showing the Italian operatic composer Puccini.

Quant, Mary, OBE (1934–)
Mary Quant is a British fashion designer and hairstylist. She is perhaps best known for the "Chelsea Look" of the "Swinging Sixties."

Quasimodo, Salvatore (1901–68)
Quasimodo was an Italian poet, born in the city of Syracuse on the island of Sicily. He was trained to be an engineer, and spent several years traveling the country as a government inspector before turning to poetry. His works include *And Suddenly It Is Evening* (published in 1942) and *Life Is Not a Dream* (1949). He was awarded the Nobel Prize for Literature in 1959.

Quintilian (*c.* A.D. 30–*c.* A.D. 96)
Quintilian was a Roman writer. He was born in Spain, but lived in Rome for most of his life. His book *The Training of an Orator* is a guide to public speaking. It gives detailed instructions on how to write and give speeches, including advice on the correct clothes and gestures. Quintilian established a school to teach speaking and rhetoric (the science of presenting an argument), and several Roman politicians became his pupils. He was given a pension and made a consul of Rome by the emperor.

Quisling, Vidkun (1887–1945)
Quisling was the leader of Norway during the German occupation of the country between 1940 and 1945. He was an army officer who held several positions in the Norwegian government in the 1920s and 1930s. In 1933 he founded a Norwegian Nazi Party, and in 1939 visited Hitler in Berlin. When Germany invaded in 1940 he was made head of state and tried to introduce Nazi policies. After the liberation of the country in 1945 he was tried as a traitor and executed. The word "quisling" later came to stand for "traitor."

Rabelais, François (1494–1553)
Rabelais was a French author. He wrote a series of books telling of the lives, travels, and adventures of two giants, called Pantagruel and Gargantua, and their friend Panurge. The first two, *Pantagruel* (1632) and *Gargantua* (1534), were published under the name "Alcofri bas Nasier," which is an anagram of "François Rabelais." Rabelais was a monk, and he realized that the books would be condemned by the Church, for as well as containing much good sense and learning, they are also full of bawdy humor and make fun of priests and churchmen. But Rabelais did publish the third and fourth volumes under his own name. They were extremely popular, both in France and later in England, where translations began appearing in the 1650s.

Racine, Jean (1639–99)
Jean Racine was a French tragic playwright who lived and worked at the time of King Louis XIV. He was born in the region of Picardy, where his father was a solicitor in a small country town, but he was sent to a strict religious school in Paris. His talent for writing verses was frowned upon by his teachers, but after completing his studies Racine decided to seek his fortune through writing. He made friends with other, more famous writers, and published poems dedicated to the king. In 1664 his first play, *La Thébaïde,* was performed by Molière's acting company at the Palais Royal theater. Molière and Racine became friends, but the following year they quarreled over Racine's second play, *Alexander the Great.* Racine thought that the company were not performing it well enough, so after only a week he removed it from the Palais Royal and gave it to Molière's rivals to produce at another theater. The two were never reconciled—perhaps because (so it is said) Racine seduced Molière's mistress at the same time.

Most of Racines greatest plays were written

during the next ten years. They include *Andromache* (1667), *Berenice* (1670), and *Phaedra* (1677). His plots (which were often borrowed from ancient Greek plays) were simple, having few characters or events and covering only a short time. But they present extreme emotions, such as love, hate, and jealousy, in poetry which is among the most beautiful ever written in French. After 1677 he wrote less, although one of his greatest plays, *Athaliah*, was not written until 1691.

○ CORNEILLE, LOUIS XIV, MOLIERE

English navigator, Sir Walter Raleigh.

French tragic playwright, Jean Racine.

Raleigh, Sir Walter (1552–1618)
Walter Raleigh was an English navigator and adventurer. His manners, good looks, and charm won him the favor of Queen Elizabeth I, who gave him gifts of land and licenses to trade in wine, wool, and other goods. In 1584 he organized the first of three expeditions to explore and colonize the southeastern coasts of North America, in the area of what is now Florida. This led to the founding of Virginia (named in honor of Elizabeth, the "Virgin Queen") and the introduction of potatoes and tobacco to England, but none of the colonists managed to remain in the area. Raleigh fell briefly into disgrace when he was discovered to be having an affair with one of the queen's ladies-in-waiting, Elizabeth Throckmorton, whom he later married. In 1595 he sailed to the West Indies looking for gold, but found none, and in 1596 he led a successful attack on a Spanish fleet in Cadiz harbor. After Elizabeth's death, Raleigh was treated with suspicion by the new king, James I, and imprisoned on a false charge of treason. While locked up in the Tower of London he wrote the most famous of his many books, the *History of the World*. He was released in 1616 to lead another expedition to the West Indies, but on his return he was executed on the same charge of treason.

○ ELIZABETH I, ESSEX, JAMES I

Ranjit Singh (1780–1839)
Ranjit Singh became leader of the Sikh people living in the Punjab region of India at the age of only 12. Within 10 years he had driven foreign invaders out of the area and made his state the most powerful in India. He made an alliance with the British East India Company which helped maintain peace and stability in the area.

Raphael (Raffaello Sanzio, 1483–1520)
Together with Michelangelo and Leonardo Da Vinci, Raphael was one of the three great Italian artists of the 16th century. He was born at the town of Urbino and studied in Perugia with the painter known as **Il Perugino** (*c*.1445–1523). For a while he carefully imitated his master's style, but in about 1505 he went to Florence to begin his own workshop. He painted a large number of Madonnas and other religious pictures, as well as some portraits, and soon became well known. In about 1509 he was summoned to Rome by Pope Julius II to decorate the walls of the papal apartments in the Vatican. He remained in Rome for the rest of his life, working on these and other projects for the Pope, as well as more portraits and church paintings. He died of fever at the age of only 37.

○ LEONARDO, JULIUS II, MICHELANGELO

Rasputin, Grigori Yefimovich (1871–1916)
Rasputin was a Russian monk who greatly influenced the Tsarina Alexandra and the court. After a debauched life he was murdered by nobles.

Reagan, Ronald Wilson (1911–)
Ronald Reagan is the fortieth president of the United States. He began his career as a sports commentator on the radio. From there, he went on

(Continued on page 214)

Madonna and Child, by the great Italian painter Raphael. He painted numerous Madonnas in soft coloring and outline.

Painter of Light and Shade

Rembrandt Harmensz van Rijn (1606–69)
Rembrandt was among the very greatest of all European artists. Unlike Titian, Michelangelo, Velazquez, and the other great painters of the south, whose subjects were popes, princes, and royal households, Rembrandt was a northerner. His subjects were the merchants and townsmen of his native Holland.

Rembrandt was born in the city of Leyden, where his father was a well-to-do miller. He studied for about a year at Leyden University, but at the age of 15 he gave up his books and took up painting instead. For three years he was an apprentice in the workshop of a minor artist in his home town. Then, in 1624, he went to Amsterdam, where there were better teachers and more paintings by other artists to be seen. Although he only stayed six months, Rembrandt absorbed all that he saw and heard, and when he returned to Leyden he set up his own workshop and quickly became the town's most successful painter.

In 1631 Rembrandt returned to Amsterdam and went into business as a portrait painter. Not only was there great demand for portraits in the city, but painting people's faces deeply interested him. Rembrandt's style was not flattering to his subjects. Instead, he painted revealing pictures that seem to express the entire personality of the sitter in a single expression. He liked to paint precious fabrics and jewelry, and often dressed his subjects up in elaborate costumes so that he could capture the way light fell on these fine materials. However, Rembrandt did not confine his talents to portraiture alone. He also painted fine biblical scenes, and became well known as a printmaker. Among his biblical paintings is *The Return of the Prodigal Son,* which he first did as an etching print in 1636 when he was successful and rich. When he painted the large picture (a detail of which is shown here) he was old and bankrupt.

A popular type of portrait in 17th-century Holland was the "group portrait." The members of various organizations would club together to pay the artist's fee, and they would all appear in the picture. Rembrandt announced his arrival in Amsterdam with a painting of this type: *The Anatomy Lesson of Dr. Tulp,* painted in 1632. It was a great success, and a steady stream of new patrons came to have their pictures made—alone, in pairs, or in

One of Rembrandt's many self-portraits.

Return of the Prodigal Son, *based on the parable in the New Testament.*

larger groups. Rembrandt's great contemporary, Frans Hals, had also made a specialty of group portraits, and had taken care in his works to give each member of the group (who had paid an equal amount) equal importance in the composition. Rembrandt did no such thing. He planned the painting in what he thought was the most interesting way, and those who appeared in the background or shadow simply paid a smaller share. The most famous of these paintings is *The Company of Captain Frans Banning Cocq* (better known as *The Night Watch*), which shows a company of the volunteer militia set up to defend Amsterdam.

In 1634 Rembrandt married Saskia van Uylenborch, and for several years the couple lived very well. But when Saskia died in 1642, Rembrandt began to get into debt and lose his customers, and by 1656 he was completely bankrupt. His most remarkable portraits are those he painted of himself, beginning as a young man, but continuing throughout his years of success, then through poverty and old age. Of almost 700 paintings by Rembrandt, about 60 are self-portraits, a complete painted autobiography that reveals all the painter's moods and styles. ○ HALS

Pictures by Rembrandt around the World

Scholar in a Lofty Room
(National Gallery, London)

The Anatomy Lesson of Dr. Tulp
(Mauritshuis, The Hague)

Portrait of Himself with Saskia
(Dresden)

The Reconciliation of David and Absalom
(The Hermitage, Leningrad)

The Company of Captain Frans Banning Cocq
("The Night Watch," Rijksmuseum, Amsterdam)

The Jewish Merchant
(National Gallery, London)

Man with a Magnifying Glass
(Metropolitan Museum, New York)

Woman with a Plume
(National Gallery, Washington, D.C.)

The Night Watch *or* The Company of Captain Frans Banning Cocq, *one of Rembrandt's most famous paintings. It is a dramatic picture in which the artist uses deep shadows and groups the figures irregularly.*

to become a film actor, and between 1937 and 1964 he appeared in over 50 films. In 1967 he became governor of the state of California. He failed to be nominated as the Republican presidential candidate in 1976, but in 1980 he ran and defeated President Jimmy Carter. He was re-elected in 1984. ○ CARTER

Reed, John (1887–1920)
John Reed was an American writer. He became a committed Communist, and in 1918 he traveled to the Soviet Union to witness the revolution taking place there. He wrote a book about what he saw called *Ten Days That Shook the World* (published in 1919) and he is one of the very few Americans to be buried in the Kremlin.

Remarque, Erich Maria (1897–1970)
Remarque was a writer who served in the trenches with the German army in World War I. He wrote a realistic novel based on his experiences, called *All Quiet on the Western Front* (published in 1929), which was later made into a dramatic film.

Rembrandt (1606–69)
See pages 212 & 213

Renoir, Pierre Auguste (1841–1919)
Renoir was a French Impressionist painter. He was born in the city of Limoges, where, at the age of only 13, he got a job painting figures and patterns on porcelain objects made in a local factory. In 1861 he moved to Paris to teach in an artist's studio, and there he met Monet. The two men became friends and spent time painting together—often outdoors, on the banks of the river Seine. Like Monet, Renoir was particularly interested in effects of light and color, but he also took time to visit the Paris museums and study the works of old painters. He exhibited his pictures at the Impressionist exhibitions of the 1870s. His early works include the famous *Moulin de la Galette*, showing a busy outdoor scene lit by sunlight filtering through trees. Later, Renoir painted a great many female nudes, pictures characterized by vivid pink and orange tones. Renoir's son, **Jean Renoir** (1894–1979), was a well-known film director.
○ MONET

Reuter, Paul Julius (1816–99)
Reuter was the German founder of the famous Reuter's Press Agency. When he was a young man, news traveled very slowly, as it was carried either by horse, or sometimes by pigeons. While working in a bank Reuter saw the need for information to move faster, so he set up a small company in the city of Aachen which would collect news and send it by electric telegraph. In 1851 he moved to London. His organization gradually grew, until it had offices all over the world.

Revere, Paul (1735–1818)
Paul Revere was one of the heroes of the American War of Independence. He was born in Boston, where he grew up to become first a soldier, then a goldsmith. In 1773 he was one of a party of Boston citizens who dumped large amounts of tea into the city's harbor as a protest against the British tax on imported tea. This event became known as the "Boston Tea Party" and was one of many incidents that led to the beginning of the War of Independence. Revere was among the leaders of a secret society formed to spy on the British troops. In April 1775 he made two famous rides from Charlestown to Lexington. The first was to warn the revolutionaries to hide their arms; then, two days later, Revere rode back again to tell them that the British troops were on the move. The next day, at the Battle of Lexington, the American revolutionaries defeated the British, and the American Revolution had begun.

Paul Revere continued in his trade as a goldsmith and made many beautiful objects.

Reynolds, Joshua (1723–92)
Reynolds was an English artist who is famous for his portraits of well-to-do members of 18th-century society. He was born in the county of Devon. He studied for a while in London, then made a visit to Italy, where he was able to see the work of the greatest painters of the past. He returned to London in 1753. Reynolds painted over 2,000 portraits of fashionable men and women, and his skills were in constant demand. In 1768 he became the first president of the Royal Academy, and delivered a series of lectures on art to students there known as the *Discourses*. Toward the end of his life Reynolds began to go blind, and in 1789 he had to give up painting altogether.

Richard I, "the Lionheart" (1157–99)
Richard I was king of England from 1189 until his death. He spent much of his life on a crusade against the Muslims, and was given the nickname "Lionheart" (or, in French, "Coeur de Lion") for his bravery. In 1187 the city of Jerusalem was captured by the Muslim Emperor Saladin. Richard and King Philip of France vowed to return the city to

Christian rulers and set out on the Third Crusade in 1190, only a few months after Richard had become king. In 1191 Richard captured the island of Cyprus and won a great victory at the town of Acre. But he had quarreled with Philip and was forced to make a truce without ever reaching Jerusalem. On his way home Richard was shipwrecked. He put on a disguise and tried to make his way to England through lands ruled by his enemy, the Duke of Austria. Unfortunately, he was captured and held for a huge ransom. After being released, Richard went to war with Philip of France, and was killed at a siege by a stray arrow. He spent only a few months in England, and could probably not even speak English. ○ ELEANOR OF AQUITAINE, SALADIN

Richard II (1367–1400)
Richard II was king of England from 1377 until 1399. Because he was only ten years old when he inherited the throne, the country was governed by a council of powerful lords. These lords had become more and more unpopular with the people, and when they tried to impose a new tax in 1380, a crowd of as many as 100,000 peasants and farmers marched on London to protest. Some were persuaded to return home, but a party from the county of Kent broke into the Tower of London and killed the Archbishop of Canterbury. Richard and his ministers met them at Smithfield on June 15, 1381, where the Lord Mayor of London killed the peasants' leader, Wat Tyler. Richard, seeing the trouble this might cause, rode into the crowd and told them that he would settle their complaints.

Richard II's meeting with the rebels at Smithfield during the Peasants' Revolt. This picture from Froissart's Chronicles *shows Wat Tyler about to be killed by the mayor of London.*

Richard took control of the government of the country in 1389. He managed to limit the power of his lords, and for a time ruled wisely. But after 1397 he became more tyrannical. He forced his cousin, Henry Bolingbroke, into exile and later confiscated his family estates. In July 1399 Henry landed with an army in Yorkshire while Richard was abroad. Richard hurried back, but it was too late. He saw he could not defeat his cousin, so he surrendered. Henry became King **Henry IV** (1367–1413), and Richard was imprisoned in Pontefract Castle, where he died, probably murdered.

Richard III (1452–85)
Richard III became king of England in 1483. He was the brother of King **Edward IV** (1441–83), who died leaving only his young son **Edward V** (1470–83) to succeed him. As the boy's uncle, Richard became "Protector" of the country until Edward grew up. But he found the old queen and the country's lords opposed to him. He arrested some of Edward's closest relatives, and accused one of the most powerful of the noblemen, Lord Hastings, of treason and had him beheaded. Meanwhile, the young king was locked up in the Tower of London, together with his brother, the Duke of York. They had been put there "for safety"—but it was Richard himself who was plotting the boy king's downfall. He persuaded Parliament that King Edward IV's marriage had been illegal, that Edward V was therefore an illegitimate child and could not inherit the throne. Parliament agreed, and on July 16, 1483, Richard was crowned king. The two "Princes in the Tower" were murdered, perhaps on Richard's command, although this has never been proved. He was a strong and very efficient ruler, but when the murder of the princes was discovered some months later he suddenly became unpopular. Rival noblemen gathered around Henry Tudor. In August 1585 Henry landed in England with an army, and defeated and killed Richard at the Battle of Bosworth. He became King **Henry VII** (1457–1509).

Richelieu, Armand Jean du Plessis (1585–1642)
Richelieu was chief minister and the most powerful man in France during the reign of King **Louis XIII** (1601–43). He began his career as a soldier, but he was forced to give up the army and entered the Church instead. At the age of 21 Richelieu was already a bishop. He rose to become a cardinal, and in 1624 he was made Louis's minister. By supporting the Protestant countries in the Thirty Years' War and declaring war on Spain (in 1635), he was able to ensure the decline of the power of the Habsburg family, and make France Europe's most powerful nation. Meanwhile, in France, he set out to defeat the king's opponents (known as Huguenots). Eventually, they were besieged by Richelieu's army at the port of La Rochelle. Richelieu organized the building of a dike across the harbor mouth so that the Huguenots could not be supplied by British ships, and in 1628 the city fell. Gradually, Richelieu reduced the power held by France's noblemen, placing it instead in his own or the king's hands. This made him many enemies, and there were many plots against him. But Richelieu had organized an efficient network of spies and informers, and he defeated every attempt to overthrow him. He died at the height of his power. ○ CORNEILLE, LOUIS XIV, MAZARIN

Rilke, Rainer Maria (1875–1926)
Rilke was an Austrian poet. He was born in Prague, but traveled widely in Europe. On a trip to Russia he met Tolstoy, and in 1901 he settled in Paris, where he became secretary to the sculptor Auguste Rodin. Collections of his poems were published in 1906 and 1926, and he also wrote a novel based on his own life. His most famous work is *Sonnets to Orpheus*, written in 1923. ○ RODIN

Robert I (the Bruce), king of Scotland, won the independence of his country and ensured an undisputed succession.

Robbia
See Della Robbia

Robert Bruce (1274–1329)
Robert was a king of Scotland who led the country to independence from the English. He had originally sworn allegiance to the English king, but in 1306 he made himself the leader of the Scottish lords and was crowned king of Scotland at the castle of Scone. At first Robert was forced into the hills by the English army, but in 1307 the English king died, and Robert was able to return and take control of much of the country. At the Battle of Bannockburn on June 24, 1314, his army, although outnumbered by three to one, defeated the English King Edward II. Fighting continued for another 14 years, but in 1628 the Scots' independence was finally recognized by the English. ○ EDWARD II

Robeson, Paul (1898–1976)
Robeson was a black American singer and actor. He was born in Princeton, New Jersey. At university he became an excellent sportsman, then went on to study law in New York. He gave up the law to become an actor. After several successes on the stage during the 1920s he began making films, and became well known as a singer. One of his most famous performances was singing "Ol' Man River" in the film *Showboat*, made in 1936. During the 1940s and 1950s he spoke out on many political issues. The American government suspected him of being a Communist and took away his passport.

Robespierre, Maximilien Marie Isidore de (1758–94)
Robespierre was one of the most important of the leaders of the French Revolution. He was born in Arras in the north of the country, where he eventually became a lawyer, a judge, and one of the town's leading citizens. When King Louis XVI and his minister Necker summoned the ancient assembly called the "States-General" to Paris in 1789, Robespierre was elected to represent the province of Artois. During the early part of the revolution he spoke regularly in the assembly. His uncompromising opinions made him unpopular with extremists and with the revolutionary mob in Paris. In 1791 he was elected to the "commune" that governed the city, and became a member of the "Jacobin Club," a meeting place for extreme revolutionaries. The Jacobins' opponents were known as the "Girondists," and over the next two years the two groups struggled for control of the government of France. The Girondists succeeded in declaring war on Austria in 1793, against the opposition of Robespierre and the Jacobins. When the war turned out badly for France, the Girondists were weakened. The following year the Jacobins insisted on the execution of King Louis XVI, despite the doubts of the Girondists. The battle between the two groups was finally won by the Jacobins. Robespierre introduced a new constitution and was elected to the "Committee of Public Safety." In this position he became more or less absolute ruler of France. He introduced strict economic measures and programs to feed and care for the poor. In 1794 he proposed a new state religion, based on the worship of the "Supreme Being." Meanwhile, the Committee of Public Safety mercilessly arrested and executed his opponents—

Robespierre, one of the leaders of the French Revolution. He voted for the execution of King Louis XVI, supported the Reign of Terror, but himself fell victim to it.

In 1789 the people of Paris attacked the Bastille, a prison, in an attempt to capture weapons and free political prisoners. The fall of the Bastille marks the beginning of the French Revolution.

men who were either too moderate (like Danton), or too extreme. This period became known as "The Terror," for Robespierre believed the revolution could not succeed without the use of force. But as the number of executions increased and the state of the economy grew worse, he became increasingly unpopular. In July 1794 the assembly refused to approve his decrees. Members attacked Robespierre, and his supporters were shouted down. He was arrested, and the next day he became a victim of the guillotine he had used so often against his opponents. ○ CORDAY, DANTON, LOUIS XVI, MARAT, NECKER

Robin Hood
Robin is a legendary English outlaw. Folk tales and ballads tell how he lived in the depths of Sherwood Forest, in the English Midlands, with his "Merry Men." He was a skilled archer, and he and his men robbed wealthy noblemen (such as the wicked sheriff of Nottingham) and then handed out their takings to the poor and needy. There is no evidence that such a man ever existed, but the stories about him were very popular, especially during the 15th century. They were first written down as part of Langland's poem *Piers the Plowman.* ○ LANGLAND

Rockefeller, John Davison (1839–1937)
John Davison Rockefeller was the founder of the Standard Oil Company in 1870. His business was so successful that by 1878 Rockefeller controlled almost all of the American oil industry. He was forced to give up some of his power in 1898, but the profits he made were huge. He gave over $500 million to support medical research, education, and churches and was the founder of Chicago University.

Rodin, Auguste (1840–1917)
Rodin was a French sculptor. Like the painters of the Impressionist movement, he was interested in the effects of light. He experimented with different surfaces that caught the light in different ways, and with dramatic shadows in his sculptures. Among his most famous works are *The Kiss* (1898) and *The Thinker* (1904). Both of these were originally intended for a vast frieze of almost 200 figures illustrating Dante's *Divine Comedy*. Rodin's sculptures include a controversial statue of the writer Balzac, made in 1898. When it was unveiled the literary society that had paid for it refused to recognize it, saying that it dishonored the writer's memory. ○ AUGUSTUS, JOHN, RILKE

Roger I (1031–1101)
Roger was a Norman king of Sicily. Together with his brother, **Robert Guiscard** (*c.*1015–85), he conquered much of southern Italy by defeating the Muslim rulers of the area. He became king of Sicily in 1085. His son, **Roger II** (1095–1154), also became king of the island, but he went on to unite the territories of southern Italy under his leadership. During his reign the city of Palermo became a center of both Arab and European learning.

Rollo (*c.*860–*c.*932)
Rollo was a Viking chieftain. In about the year 912 Charles, the ruler of France, granted him territories in the west of the country. In return, Rollo was baptized a Christian and swore allegiance to Charles. This territory eventually became the Duchy of Normandy, the home of William the Conqueror and the Norman kings of England.

Romulus
According to legend, Romulus was the founder of Rome. He and his twin brother **Remus** were the sons of a princess named Rhea Silvia. Her husband imprisoned her and threw the infants into the river Tiber, where they were found by a she-wolf. The wolf fed and cared for them until a shepherd took

A bust by Rodin of the French novelist Balzac.

The twins Romulus and Remus being suckled by a she-wolf.

them home and brought them up. When Romulus and Remus were young men they returned to avenge the wrongs done to them and their mother, and founded the city of Rome on the banks of the Tiber. Later, Romulus killed Remus in a quarrel and became king. This story is told by many people, including Plutarch, who wrote a *Life* of Romulus, and there are many statues of the twins being fed by the wolf. ○ PLUTARCH

Ronsard, Pierre de (1524–85)
Ronsard was a French poet. He began life as a page in the service of the French court, but he was forced to give up this life when he became deaf. As a poet, he tried to establish the French language as an equal to Greek, Latin, and Italian. His works include the *Odes* and the *Amours.*

Röntgen, Wilhelm Konrad (1845–1923)
Röntgen was the German scientist who discovered X rays and the possible uses they could have for the medical profession. He was professor of physics at the University of Würzburg, where he made his discovery in 1895. He was awarded the Nobel Prize for Physics in 1901.

Roosevelt, Franklin Delano (1882–1945)
Franklin D. Roosevelt was the thirty-second president of the United States. He overcame a crippling disease to become one of the country's most popular leaders, serving for a record four terms. Roosevelt was born in New York State, a member of a well-known and wealthy American family. He became a lawyer, and was elected as senator for New York in 1910. During Woodrow Wilson's presidency he served as assistant secretary of the navy, and in 1920 he was the Democratic candidate for the job of vice-president. Unfortunately, the Democrats lost the election, and Roosevelt's career suffered a further blow the following year when he was struck down by polio. It took him a year of great effort to recover, but he returned to his law work and to politics with renewed determination. From 1928 until 1932 he was governor of New York; then, in the 1932 presidential election, he inflicted a huge defeat on President Hoover. America, like the rest of the world, was suffering from a terrible economic depression: businesses were failing, and vast numbers of people were unable to find work. Roosevelt's policy became known as the "New Deal." The government spent large amounts of money on dams, roads, and other projects which provided jobs. Social welfare programs were introduced, and businesses were forced to negotiate with labor unions over pay and conditions. Roosevelt's popularity grew. He was re-elected in 1936, 1940, and again in 1944.

President Franklin D. Roosevelt with his wife Eleanor, a distinguished and popular woman.

A U.S. postage stamp commemorating the centenary of Roosevelt's birth.

At the beginning of World War II, Roosevelt tried to remain neutral. But he soon began providing support to Great Britain under a program called "Lend-Lease." After the Japanese air raid on Pearl Harbor in 1941, the United States was forced to enter the war on the Allied side. Roosevelt played an important role in the diplomacy of the time, attending conferences in Casablanca, Cairo, Teheran, and Yalta. He died only a few weeks before the war's end. Throughout his life he had been supported by his popular wife, **Eleanor Roosevelt** (1884–1962). She continued to take an active role in politics after 1945, and was a U.S. delegate at the first United Nations Assembly.
○ CHURCHILL, HOOVER, STALIN, WILSON

Roosevelt, Theodore (1858–1919)
Theodore Roosevelt was the twenty-sixth president of the United States. He came to power in 1901 after the assassination of President **William McKinley** (1843–1901), and was re-elected in 1904. Franklin D. Roosevelt was his distant relative.

Rosenberg, Julius (1917–53)
Julius Rosenberg and his wife, **Ethel Rosenberg** (1916–53), were convicted of spying for the Soviet Union against the United States and executed in 1953. Julius was an electrical engineer in the United States Army. After the trial of a British scientist, **Klaus Fuchs** (1912–), in 1950, Julius and Ethel were found to be part of an international spy network. They were convicted on evidence supplied by Ethel's brother, who had also been involved, but gave evidence in order to save himself. In April 1951 they were sentenced to death. Several other countries appealed for a lighter sentence, but two years later they were both sent to the electric chair.

Rose of Lima, Saint (1586–1617)
Saint Rose was the first person from the American continents to be made a saint. She was born in the city of Lima in Peru. Her parents were very poor, and Rose had to work hard to look after them. She did odd jobs: needlework and embroidery, growing and selling flowers, and similar things. In 1606 she became a Dominican nun. She spent most of her time alone in prayer, often inflicting cruel penances on herself. But she also devoted great energy to caring for the sick and poor in Lima, especially for Indians and slaves, and she is regarded as an unofficial patron saint of social services in Peru.

Rossetti, Dante Gabriel (1828–82)
Rossetti was a 19th-century English painter and poet. In 1848, together with other artists such as **John Everett Millais** (1829–96) and **William Holman Hunt** (1827–1910), he formed the "Pre-Raphaelite Brotherhood." They dedicated themselves to a medieval style of painting, producing pictures on very moral or religious subjects, painted with great attention to detail. They were at first ridiculed, and Rossetti gave up painting to devote himself to poetry. In 1860 he married Elizabeth Siddal, but her death two years later threw him into such despair that he buried all his poems with her. They had to be retrieved a few years later, and were published in 1870. Meanwhile, he began painting again. The model for many of his later pictures was June Burden, the beautiful wife of the artist and philosopher William Morris, who was also involved with the Pre-Raphaelite movement. Rossetti's sister, **Christina Georgina Rossetti** (1830–94), was a talented poet. She published her first work in 1847, and her most famous poems include *Goblin Market* and *The Prince's Progress.* ○ MORRIS

Roublev, Andrei (*c.*1360–*c.*1430)
Andrei Roublev was a Russian medieval icon painter. "Icons" were paintings which were thought of as sacred because they showed sacred figures. Among his most famous works is the icon of the *Trinity*, which can still be seen in Moscow.

Rousseau, Henri (1844–1910)
Henri Rousseau was a French painter. His pictures are unusual in style. They show brightly colored scenes ranging from ordinary streets to jungles crowded with animals, all painted exactly as Rousseau imagined them. He was not in the least bit influenced by the great artistic movements of his time, such as Impressionism or the beginnings of Cubism, although he was a friend of Pissarro, Picasso, and others. He is sometimes nicknamed "Le Douanier"—"the customs officer"—because he worked for many years in a customs house, and did not take up painting until he reached age 41.

A painting by the French artist Henri Rousseau.

Rousseau, Jean Jacques (1712–78)
Jean Jacques Rousseau was a French writer and philosopher. He was born in Geneva, the son of a watchmaker, but his father abandoned him while he was still young, and he soon ran away from the relatives to whom he had been left. He traveled to France and to Italy, and eventually became the

The French philosopher Jean Jacques Rousseau in old age, contemplating nature.

servant and lover of Madame de Warens, a wealthy woman living in the French town of Annecy. Rousseau gained what education he could, from reading and singing in a church choir, which taught him music and some Italian. In 1741 he went to Paris, where he worked copying music. He also tried writing, and in 1747 published a successful opera. He wrote articles for Diderot's *Encyclopedia,* and in 1749 won a prize for an essay in which he said that art and science are not good for people, but in fact corrupts them. Rousseau came to believe that people are born "good," and that it is society, with its systems and institutions, that makes them "bad." In 1762 he published his famous book, *The Social Contract,* which began with the words: "Man is born free, but everywhere he is in chains." In the same year he also wrote a novel, *Émile,* in which he expressed his ideas about education. Children, he said, should not be forced to learn, but should learn by using their natural curiosity. The purpose of education, according to Rousseau, was to encourage curiosity. Meanwhile, he had been living with a kitchenmaid named Thérèse Levasseur, who bore him five children, all of whom he abandoned to an orphanage. *Émile* was censored by the French authorities, and Rousseau was forced to leave France for a time. After his death his *Confessions* were published, in which he tries to give an honest account of his life. ○ DIDEROT

Rubens, Sir Peter Paul (1577–1640)
Rubens was a Flemish painter. As well as learning to paint, he studied the literature of ancient Greece and Rome, and learned six different languages. His skill as an artist made him welcome in the royal households of Europe, and he was employed as a diplomat on missions to France, Spain, and England. Among his most famous works are a series of huge paintings illustrating the life of Marie de'Medici, the queen of France, finished in 1621, and the ceiling of the Whitehall banqueting hall in London which he painted for King Charles I. ○ JONES

Ruskin, John (1819–1900)
Ruskin was an English author who wrote about painting and the history of art. His works include *Modern Painters* (begun in 1843) and *The Stones of Venice,* a study of the architecture of the city of Venice that was published in 1851. Ruskin admired Turner's paintings, and he defended Rossetti and the Pre-Raphaelite painters against the attacks of other critics. Like the Pre-Raphaelites, he admired medieval art: he thought that it was a truer expression of the artist's spirit than the art of the Renaissance and later periods. Ruskin also supported social reforms such as free education, and old age pensions. ○ MORRIS, ROSSETTI, TURNER

Ruth, George Herman, "Babe" (1895–1948)
Babe Ruth was one of the most famous of all American baseball players. He was both a great pitcher and a great hitter. His career total of 714 home runs was not beaten until 1974, and in his best season (1927) he hit 60 home runs. He played for Baltimore, Boston, and the New York Yankees.

Rutherford, Lord Ernest (1871–1937)
Ernest Rutherford was a New Zealand-born scientist whose work on radioactivity and the structure of atoms began the "nuclear age." He discovered that radioactivity is given off by atoms (the tiny particles that make up all substances) as they disintegrate. Then he showed that this disintegration can cause one element to turn into another. With this knowledge he was able (in 1920) to transform atoms of nitrogen into atoms of oxygen and hydrogen by bombarding them with radioactive particles. Perhaps his most famous work was his suggestion (made in 1911) that an atom was mostly empty space, and that its mass was concentrated in an even tinier "nucleus." This discovery was of great importance to the development of nuclear power and nuclear weapons, for Rutherford realized that great amounts of energy would be released if this nucleus was broken open or "split." ○ BOHR, EINSTEIN, FERMI

S

Sacajawea guided the explorers Lewis and Clark on their expedition across western lands to the Pacific Ocean.

Saarinen, Eero (1910–61)
Eero Saarinen was a Finnish-born American architect who designed the Trans World Airlines terminal in New York and the John Foster Dulles Airport in Virginia.

Sacajawea (1787–1812)
Sacajawea was a Shoshone Indian guide and interpreter. She was sold to a French Canadian trapper, Toussaint Charbonneau, who in 1804 married her. When the explorers Lewis and Clark came to winter in North Dakota they engaged Charbonneau and his wife as interpreters and guides to travel with them for the rest of their historic journey to the Pacific coast.

Sackville-West, Vita (1892–1962)
Victoria (Vita) Sackville-West was an English writer. She was the author of poems, including *The Land* (1927), and novels, and in her book *Knole and the Sackvilles* (1922) she described her family and the beautiful country house where she grew up. She was married to the British diplomat and writer **Harold Nicolson** (1886–1968), and was the friend of the novelist Virginia Woolf. ○ WOOLF

Sadat, Mohamed Anwar el (1918–81)
Anwar el Sadat was president of Egypt from 1970 until his death in 1981. He was one of the army officers who took part in Nasser's coup against King Farouk, and he afterward served in Nasser's government. His main achievement as president was the signing of a peace treaty with Egypt's old enemy, Israel. He met Prime Minister **Menachem Begin** (1913–) of Israel in Jerusalem in 1977 and at Camp David in the United States in 1978. Sadat and Begin were jointly awarded the Nobel Peace Prize for their achievement in 1978. Many Arabs were very critical of the Egyptian agreement with Israel, the first made by an Arab country. Sadat was assassinated by an extreme Muslim group.
○ CARTER, NASSER

Saladin (Salah-al Din Yusuf ibn Ayyub, 1137–93)
Saladin became sultan of Egypt and Syria in 1174. He expanded his empire and eventually captured Jerusalem. This brought about the Third Crusade, led by Richard the Lionheart, which forced Saladin to allow Christian pilgrims to visit Jerusalem.
○ RICHARD I

Salazar, Antonio de Oliveira (1889–1970)
Salazar was dictator of Portugal from 1932 until 1968. He ruled efficiently and improved the country's economy, but he would not allow any political opposition. He was forced to retire from politics after an illness in 1968.

Jonas Salk, the American scientist who developed a successful vaccine against the disease poliomyelitis (polio).

Salk, Jonas Edward (1914–   )
Jonas Salk is an American scientist who successfully developed and introduced the first effective vaccine against the disease poliomyelitis (known as "polio" for short). He was born in New York. His parents were not wealthy, so Salk paid for his college education by earning scholarships and working in his spare time. He graduated from the New York School of Medicine in 1939, but instead of becoming a doctor he decided to devote himself to research into disease. Polio is caused by a "virus," a tiny disease-causing organism. Salk developed a technique of weakening the virus enough to prevent the disease, but not enough to stop it provoking a person's body into developing its own natural protection (known as "antibodies") against it. These weakened viruses formed the basis of the vaccine, which was injected into people so they could develop antibodies. Tests began in 1953, when Salk injected himself and members of his family. The following year nearly two million schoolchildren were injected as part of a mass testing program. The tests were successful, and in 1955 a huge advertising campaign was launched to persuade people to have themselves and their children vaccinated. Salk has continued to research into the effects of viruses, and he has made important contributions to understanding of the disease influenza ("flu"), which still kills many old or weak people.

Sand, George (Amandine Aurore Lucie Dupin, 1804–76)
George Sand was a French writer. Her father died while she was an infant and she was brought up by her grandmother. At the age of 18 she married a nobleman, but the marriage was not a success. She eventually left her husband and moved to Paris to devote herself to writing. Her first novels, which include *Indiana* (1832), express her dislike of marriage. Her pen name, "George Sand," was partly taken from the surname of the man she lived with at the time, Jules Sandeau. She was involved with several artists and writers, including the composer Chopin and the poet Alfred de Musset. Her novels, meanwhile, were very successful. They include *Mauprat* (1837) and *François le Champi* (1846). In 1848 she left Paris for her country home, where she continued to write until her death.
○ CHOPIN

San Martín, José de (1778–1850)
San Martín was a South American revolutionary leader. After the Argentinian government declared itself independent of Spanish rule in 1816, San Martín led an army across the Andes Mountains to liberate Chile. Then the Chileans and Argentinians combined forces and entered Peru. When the army reached Lima in 1821, San Martín was declared "Protector" of Peru, but after a dispute with another revolutionary, Simón Bolívar, he resigned. He left South America three years later, and died in unhappy exile in France. ○ BOLÍVAR, O'HIGGINS

Sappho (*c.*600 B.C.)
Sappho was the greatest poetess of ancient times. Little is known about her life, and most of her poems only survive in fragments. They consist of love poems, poems addressed to the gods, and marriage poems, and they were written with great passion and in exquisite language. There are many traditions about her life. In one, she is said to have thrown herself off a cliff in despair at unreturned love; in another she was the leader of a group of women devoted to each other and to the goddess of love, Aphrodite.

Sargent, John Singer (1856–1925)
John Singer Sargent was an American artist. He was born in the Italian city of Florence, and lived for most of his life in London, although he made frequent visits to the United States. He is most famous as a portrait painter: many fashionable and well-known people of the Victorian and Edwardian ages had their pictures painted by Sargent. He had a high reputation, although sometimes he upset his subjects by being unflattering in what he painted.
○ JAMES, TERRY

The French novelist, George Sand. She was a pioneer of "women's lib."

Sartre, Jean Paul (1905–80)
Jean Paul Sartre was a French writer and philosopher. He was born in Paris, where he was a teacher of philosophy before the outbreak of World War II. During the war, he became one of the

leaders of Paris's intellectual life. Sartre and other men and women like him gathered in cafés in the Left Bank district of the city to discuss politics and ideas. There he met the writer Simone de Beauvoir, who remained his lover for many years. Sartre's philosophy is called "Existentialism": he did not believe in God, and said that people arrived in the world as "nothing." They only develop personality and became "something" through the things they choose to do. He wrote about these ideas in his book *Being and Nothingness,* published in 1943. He also wrote several novels and plays, including *Nausea* (1938) and *The Flies* (1942).
○ DE BEAUVOIR, HEGEL

Savonarola, Girolamo (1452–98)
Savonarola was a monk who became the governor of the Italian city of Florence after the downfall of the Medici family in 1494. He was a Dominican monk in the monastery of San Marco in the city. He spoke out against vices such as gambling, and was a fierce opponent of all forms of luxury, including fine clothing and jewelry. Gradually, Savonarola built up a large following among the citizens of Florence, and he prophesied that the city would soon be purged of wickedness and vice. He saw his prediction fulfilled in 1494, when the French army invaded and the Medici fled. Savonarola became the city's leader, saying that Florence would become a Christian republic, ruled by the laws of God. Huge bonfires were built in the squares, and people flocked to burn their fine clothes, which Savonarola called "vanities." But his strictness quickly made him unpopular, and in Rome the Pope objected to his growing power and his claim that he could make prophecies about the future. In 1498 he was brought to trial for religious "error" and together with two of his followers he was hanged and burned. ○ MEDICI

Scarlatti, Alessandro (1659–1725)
Scarlatti was an Italian composer. He was born in Sicily, and at various times worked for the king of Naples and Queen Christina of Sweden. He wrote about 120 operas and many pieces of music for religious services, as well as madrigals and other choral works.

Scheele, Carl Wilhelm (1742–86)
Scheele was a Swedish scientist. In 1772 he discovered the gas oxygen and showed that air is made up mainly of two gases. This was two years before the English chemist Joseph Priestley made the same discovery (without any knowledge of Scheele's work), but Scheele did not publish his findings until 1777. He also discovered many types of acids. ○ PRIESTLEY

Schiller, Johann Christoph Friedrich von (1759–1805)
Schiller was a German writer of plays, poems, essays, and works of history. As a young man, he was persuaded by his father to join the army, although he always intended to devote himself to literature. In 1783 he was arrested for taking leave without permission to watch one of his own plays, and after that he fled, to become a playwright in the city of Mannheim. He later lived in Leipzig, Dresden, and Weimar, where he became a close friend of the writer Goethe. His plays include *Mary Stuart* (1800), about Mary, Queen of Scots, and *The Maid of Orleans* (1801) about Joan of Arc. ○ GOETHE

Schliemann, Heinrich (1822–90)
Schliemann was a German archaeologist. As a boy he had been fascinated by the stories of the Siege of Troy told by Homer in his *Iliad,* and he decided to try and prove that the events described by the poet had actually happened. He made a fortune in business, then retired and set out for Turkey to investigate the "mound of Hissarlik," said to have been the site of ancient Troy. He began work in 1872, and showed that there had been at least nine different cities built there over the ages. He also discovered much ancient treasure, and excavated other ancient sites, including Mycenae. ○ HOMER

The gold mask of Agamemnon discovered by the German archaeologist Heinrich Schliemann at what is thought to be the site of ancient Troy.

Schoenberg, Arnold (1874–1951)
A 20th-century composer. Schoenberg invented what is known as the "12-note" system of writing music, based on principles completely different from those of traditional music.

Schrödinger, Erwin (1887–1961)
An Austrian scientist who made important contributions to the study of the structure of the atom, which had been begun by Rutherford. He was awarded the Nobel Prize for Physics in 1933 for his "wave equation." ○ RUTHERFORD

Schubert, Franz Peter (1797–1828)
Schubert was an Austrian composer, born in Vienna, where he became a choirboy in the imperial school. He composed his first symphony at the age of 16, and the next year he wrote his first opera. For most of his life, Schubert lived on whatever money he could make by giving occasional music lessons or performances, and (when times were hard) on the good will of his many friends. He wrote several symphonies, including his famous Eighth "Unfinished" Symphony, as well as cycles of songs. Often these songs were settings of poems written by romantic authors such as Goethe or Schiller. Schubert was a devoted admirer of Beethoven: he often visited the same cafés as the great composer, but was too nervous to introduce himself. Eventually, Schubert dedicated some piano pieces and songs to Beethoven, and Beethoven's praise helped make him more famous. He never became wealthy, and ended his life poor and in bad health. ○ BEETHOVEN

Schumann, Robert Alexander (1810–56)
Robert Schumann was a German composer, famous particularly for his piano pieces and songs. He began studying the law but, inspired by the performances of Paganini and others, he decided to take up music instead. He studied the piano, wrote music, and contributed articles about young composers such as Chopin and Mendelssohn to a newspaper. After breaking a finger in 1832, he was forced to give up his hopes of becoming a concert pianist, but he continued to compose pieces of his own. Meanwhile he had fallen in love with his piano teacher's daughter, **Clara Josephine Wieck** (1819–96). She was a well-known concert pianist. Her father attempted to keep the couple apart by taking Clara on long European tours, but, unknown to him, they had already become engaged. In 1840, without his consent, they were married. Clara Schumann played and championed her husband's music wherever she went. His best works, including the "Spring" Symphony and many songs and piano pieces, were written during these years. But Schumann had often been troubled by mental illness. He tried to kill himself by jumping into the river Rhine and he died in an asylum. ○ BRAHMS

Schweitzer, Albert (1875–1965)
Schweitzer was a French scholar, missionary, and theologian. He decided that he would study until the age of 30, then dedicate the rest of his life to the service of other people. He became a musician, a teacher, and published books on religion and on the works of J. S. Bach. In 1905 he began studying medicine, and went to Africa to open a mission hospital, where he remained until his death. He won the Nobel Prize for Peace in 1953.

Scipio, Publius Cornelius (237 B.C.–183 B.C.)
Scipio was a Roman general. During the long Punic War against the North African city of Carthage he fought against Hannibal in Italy, and was then made Roman commander in Spain. To force Hannibal to leave Italy, he invaded Carthage itself, and defeated Hannibal at the Battle of Zama in 202 B.C. For the next 15 years he remained the most powerful man in Rome, although he was eventually forced to retire from public life. ○ HANNIBAL

Scott, Robert Falcon (1868–1912)
Scott was an English explorer who died during a famous expedition to the South Pole in 1912. He first visited the Antarctic between 1901 and 1904 in HMS *Discovery*, when he explored the Ross Sea and discovered King Edward VII Land. Six years later, in 1910, Scott was made commander of the ship the *Terra Nova* and planned an expedition to reach the South Pole by sledge. In January 1911 he and his crew arrived in the Ross Sea and began setting up supply bases for the journey. In November, at the beginning of the brief Antarctic summer, Scott set out. At first, he and his companions carried equipment on motor sledges and ponies. But as conditions became worse the sledges broke down, and eventually they were forced by hunger to shoot and eat the animals. Some of the crew returned to the ship, while Scott

The German romantic composer Robert Schumann.

and four others continued toward the pole. They arrived on January 17, 1912, only to find that Amundsen had arrived a month earlier. They now had to face the almost impossible return journey across frozen wastelands and glaciers and through worsening blizzards. One member of the party died on February 17, another on March 17. Scott and his two remaining companions perished while sheltering from a blizzard ten days later. At the beginning of the following summer their bodies, and Scott's diary, were found by a search party. Scott's son, **Peter Markham Scott** (1909–), is a well-known ornithologist and campaigner for the preservation of wildlife. ○ AMUNDSEN

Scott, Sir Walter (1771–1832)
Walter Scott was a Scottish writer. He grew up on his grandfather's farm near the border between England and Scotland, and the landscape around him inspired many of his novels and poems. Scott's first works were ballads and poems, which made him both wealthy and famous. But he is best known for the romantic novels that he wrote later in his life, including *Rob Roy* and *The Heart of Midlothian* (both published in 1818). They are often known as the "Waverley" novels because Scott always called himself the "author of *Waverley*" (the title of his first novel).

The Scottish novelist, Sir Walter Scott. He began writing historical romances with Waverley *in 1814.*

Segovia, Andrés (1893–1987)
A Spanish guitarist. He taught himself to play the instrument, and developed a playing technique that used the nails and very tips of the fingers to achieve a wide range of tones. Segovia gave his first performance at the age of 14. His popularity helped to re-establish the guitar as a serious concert instrument.

Service, Robert William (1874–1958)
Robert Service was a Canadian poet and novelist. He was born in Preston, in England, and emigrated to Canada to become a reporter for a Toronto newspaper. His poems, songs, and ballads are written in the rough language of the American frontier. The most famous is *The Shooting of Dangerous Dan McGrew.*

Scott was beaten in his attempt to be the first to reach the South Pole by the Norwegian Amundsen. The North Pole was first reached by the American Robert Peary in 1909. The picture shows an earlier expedition in the Arctic Ocean by the Norwegian scientist Nansen in the Fram.

Sévigné, Madame de (1626–96)
Madame de Sévigné was a French noblewoman who has remained famous for the hundreds of letters she wrote to her daughter. She began them when her daughter married in 1669, and continued them for the next 25 years, describing life in French society and at the royal household.

Shakespeare, William (1564–1616)
See pages 228 & 229

Shaw, George Bernard (1856–1950)
George Bernard Shaw was an Irish playwright, journalist, and critic. He was born in Dublin, where he eventually became an office clerk, and left Dublin to live in London, where his mother was a singing teacher. He spent his time studying in the British Museum, and writing a series of five novels, none of which was successful. In 1888 he was made music critic for a London newspaper, and then later he began reviewing plays. He admired the works of the Norwegian playwright Henrik Ibsen, which were at that time thought scandalous, and at the same time attacked Shakespeare—something that made him unpopular with many people. His first plays did not do well, and it was several years before Shaw became well known. His most successful plays include *Arms and the Man* (1894), *Man and Superman* (1903), and *Saint Joan* (1923). Shaw became a socialist as a young man, and for many years he was involved in local politics in London and wrote pamphlets for the socialist "Fabian Society." At the end of his life he began campaigning to simplify spelling and left much of his money for this purpose.

Shelley, Percy Bysshe (1792–1822)
Shelley was an English poet. He went to school at Eton and to university at Oxford, but in 1811 he was expelled for publishing a book attacking religion. He moved to London, where he met and married the 16-year-old daughter of a coffeehouse keeper, Harriet Westbrook. Their marriage was not a particularly happy one, and in 1814 Shelley fell in love with the beautiful **Mary Wollstonecraft Godwin** (1797–1851), the daughter of Mary Wollstonecraft, the writer and feminist. Shelley, who believed in "free love," abandoned Harriet, and two years later she drowned herself in the Serpentine lake in London's Hyde Park. Mary and Percy Shelley were married, and left England to travel in Europe. They eventually settled in Italy, where Shelley wrote many of his fine lyric poems. Meanwhile, Mary Shelley had written her novel

The poet Percy B. Shelley. He was expelled from Oxford for writing a book attacking religion.

Frankenstein. She began the story while she and her husband and some friends were staying in Switzerland, and all agreed to write a ghost story. Mary was the only one to finish hers, and it remains famous to this day. Shelley was killed in the summer of 1822, when a small boat he was sailing capsized in a sudden storm and he was drowned. ○ KEATS, WOLLSTONECRAFT

Sherman, William Tecumseh (1820–91)
Sherman was an American Civil War general. As commander of a division he played an important part in the Battles of Shiloh (in April 1862) and Vicksburg (1863) under General Grant. In 1864 he was put in charge of the Union Army's campaign in the southwestern United States. He led his 65,000 troops through Georgia, capturing the cities of Atlanta and Savannah, but the destruction he left behind caused lasting resentment in the area. When General Grant became President, Sherman was made head of the U.S. Army. ○ GRANT

Shih Huang Ti (259 B.C.–210 B.C.)
Shih Huang Ti became emperor of China in 221 B.C. and founded the Ch'in dynasty. He brought all of China under his personal rule, introduced standard systems of writing and measurement, and built the Great Wall of China to protect his empire. His name means "First Sovereign Emperor."

Sibelius, Jean (1865–1957)
Sibelius was a Finnish composer. He began playing the piano while he was a child, but went on to university to study law. He gave this up in 1885 to devote all his time to music. Sibelius was deeply interested in the folklore and traditions of his country, and many of his works are based on Finnish myths and legends. He wrote many orchestral "poems," seven symphonies, and a violin concerto.

Shakespeare's Theater

A portrait of the playwright, William Shakespeare.

Many playwrights, including Shakespeare, lived and worked at the end of the 16th century. Here are just some of them, together with the plays they wrote.

1588
Doctor Faustus, by Marlowe
1590
The Jew of Malta, by Marlowe
1592
The Spanish Tragedy, by Kyd
*Richard III**
1594
*Romeo and Juliet**
1595
*A Midsummer Night's Dream**
1596
*The Merchant of Venice**
1599
Julius Caesar and *Twelfth Night**
1600
*Hamlet**
1605
King Lear and *Macbeth**
1606
Volpone, by Jonson
*Antony and Cleopatra**
1607
Bussy d'Ambois, by Chapman
The Revenger's Tragedy, by Tourneur
1610
The Alchemist, by Jonson
*A Winter's Tale**
1611
The Roaring Girl, by Middleton
1614
The Duchess of Malfi, by Webster

*By Shakespeare

Shakespeare, William (1564–1616)
The plays of William Shakespeare are among the best known of all works of art. They have been translated into almost every language, and performed around the world. Shakespeare lived at a time when the theater was popular entertainment: new theaters were being built, the public clamored for new plays, and playwrights competed with each other to satisfy them. For about 50 years, from the 1580s until the 1620s, the English stage flourished as never before. Christopher Marlowe, Thomas Kyd, George Chapman, Cyril Tourneur, Ben Jonson, John Webster, Thomas Middleton, and others—as well as Shakespeare—were famous writers of the age.

Most of the details of Shakespeare's life are a mystery, although there are many stories and traditions about it. He was born in the town of Stratford-on-Avon, where his father was a wealthy glove-maker and town councilor, and his mother a farmer's daughter. He went to the local grammar school and probably became a teacher himself. In 1582 he married **Anne Hathaway** (1556–1623), and about three years later the couple moved to London. There he worked as both an actor and a playwright. His first plays, probably the comedies *Love's Labour's Lost* and the *Comedy of Errors*, were produced about 1590. There is no certainty about the dates of any of his plays, but for the next 20 years they appeared in a steady stream—37 in all. In several of these he was probably helped by others.

Most of his first plays were comedies or histories. Shakespeare's version of history has become so familiar that it is often taken as, simply, "true." But in his plays about English history, for example, he was very careful not to offend his own queen, Elizabeth I, by abusing her ancestors. In the middle of his career, Shakespeare wrote the tragedies for which he is perhaps most famous, among them *Hamlet*, *Macbeth*, and *King Lear*. He also wrote a number of poems, including a collection of over 100 sonnets, several of which are addressed to a mysterious "dark lady." But he returned to comedy in his last plays, although it is not "comedy" in the sense of "funny," so much as "romantic." His last production was *The Tempest*, staged in 1611. He ended his life back in Stratford, where he died on his birthday in 1616. ○ ELIZABETH I, JONSON, MARLOWE

A reconstruction of the Globe Theatre. It was a circular wooden building with an apron stage overlooked by covered galleries.

Siddons, Sarah (1755–1831)
"Mrs. Siddons" was the greatest actress of her time. She was born in Wales and was the daughter of a theater manager—so she appeared on the stage from an early age. Although she became successful in the theaters in English country towns, her talent was at first unnoticed in London. But after 1782, when she gave a brilliant performance at the city's Drury Lane Theatre, she was London's most celebrated actress. She retired in 1812, after 30 years of continuous success.

Signoret, Simone (1921–86)
Simone Signoret was a French film actress. Among her most famous films are *Thérèse Raquin* (based on a novel by Émile Zola) and *Les Diaboliques.*

Sihanouk, Norodom (1922–)
Prince Sihanouk succeeded his grandfather as king of Cambodia in 1941. In 1955 he abdicated (leaving the throne to his parents) so that he could take part in his country's politics, and he founded a socialist party. He was prime minister between 1955 and 1960 and head of state until 1970, but he was then deposed and forced into exile in China.

Sikorsky, Igor Ivan (1889–1972)
Sikorsky was the engineer who developed the first helicopter to be flown in the West. He was born in Russia, where he built and flew the first four-engined airplane in 1913. In 1918 he left Russia for the U.S.A. and founded his own aero engineering company. The company built flying boats, and in 1939 successfully flew a single-rotor helicopter.

Sitting Bull (1834–90)
Sitting Bull was a Dakota Sioux Indian warrior, and one of the leaders of the American Indian army that defeated General Custer's U.S. Cavalry division at the Battle of the Little Big Horn in 1876. Sitting Bull was a highly respected "medicine man"—that is, a man possessing the power of magic. Some days before the battle he said that he had a vision of the cavalry soldiers "falling upside down" into his camp, and by this knew that the Indians would be successful. Sitting Bull and his tribe were among about 7,000 Indians camped by the Little Big Horn River. When Custer and only a few hundred soldiers attacked the camp on June 25, Custer isolated himself from the rest of his division, and he and his men were completely wiped out. Sitting Bull and the other Indians realized that their victory would bring more soldiers after them, so two days later they dismantled their camp and left. Sitting Bull traveled to Canada to escape the U.S. Army, but surrendered in 1881. He was killed during an Indian rebellion in 1890. ○ CRAZY HORSE, CUSTER

Sitting Bull, one of the leaders of the American Indian army that defeated General Custer at the Battle of The Little Big Horn.

Smith, Adam (1723–90)
Adam Smith was a Scottish economist and philosopher whose book *The Wealth of Nations* (published 1776) began the modern science of economics. He believed that old-fashioned government controls over trade, such as the granting of "monopolies" (a privilege allowing only one company to trade in particular goods or regions) should be abandoned. Instead, he thought that the nation's economy would flourish, and people would be better off, if free, unrestricted trade was allowed. His work had great influence over the governments of the 19th century.

Smith, Ian Douglas (1919–)
Ian Smith was a white Rhodesian politician. He opposed the idea of giving political power to the country's black population. When it became clear that black rule was favored by the British government, Smith declared Rhodesia independent of Britain. He ruled for 13 years, between 1965 and 1978, until forced to grant power to the country's black opposition.

Smuts, Jan Christian (1870–1950)
Smuts was a South African soldier and politician. He fought in the Boer War against the British, and after the establishment of South Africa he held several important government posts. He was prime minister from 1919 until 1924, and throughout the period leading to the World War II he took an important role in international politics.

Socrates (*c.*469 B.C.–399 B.C.)
Socrates was an ancient Greek philosopher. The sacred oracle in the city of Delphi declared that he was the "wisest man in the world," but Socrates never wrote a book. His life and ideas were recorded by his pupil, the great philosopher Plato, and by the historian Xenophon. He was a soldier in

the Peloponnesian War, and afterward returned to Athens. Socrates liked to spend his time in the streets and marketplaces of the city, talking with whoever would listen to him. He claimed to receive a kind of divine guidance in his wisdom, and eventually this got him into trouble with the Athenian government, who thought his claim was blasphemous. In 399 B.C. he was brought to trial, charged with blaspheming, as well as corrupting young men. He defended himself skillfully, and was only found guilty by a tiny majority of those who tried his case. He was sentenced to death, and although he had the opportunity to escape, killed himself by drinking poison. ○ PERICLES, PLATO

Solomon (*c.*1015 B.C.–*c.*977 B.C.)
Solomon was a king of ancient Israel. He was the son of King David and his wife Bathsheba. Solomon was said to have been very wise, and his reign was one of great splendor. He built magnificent new palaces, and is said to have ordered the construction of the great Temple in Jerusalem, which became known as the "Temple of Solomon." But he was not popular with all his people: many were offended by the luxury in which he lived, as well as by the number of wives he chose to keep. Solomon was a strong ruler, but after his death rebellion and war broke out. He is traditionally said to have written parts of the Bible, including the Song of Solomon. ○ DAVID

Solon (*c.*640 B.C.–*c.*559 B.C.)
Solon was an ancient Greek governor and poet. In about the year 594 B.C. he was made "archon" of Athens—that is, chief of the nine magistrates who governed the city. Athens was at that time suffering under an economic depression, and Solon was given complete power to introduce reforms. He freed everybody who had been made a slave as punishment for getting into debt, introduced a new system of money, and encouraged farmers to grow food to feed the citizens. He also reformed the system of government, allowing more people to join the city's assemblies. Solon's popularity with the people is said to have been due to the great skill with which he expressed his political ideas in the form of poetry.

Solzhenitsyn, Aleksandr Isayevich (1918–)
Aleksandr Solzhenitsyn is a Soviet-born writer who now lives in the United States. He was critical of Stalin's government and as a result he was sent to a labor camp in Siberia. In his book *One Day in the Life of Ivan Denisovich* (published in 1962) he described the effort it took to get through just one day in the terrible conditions of the camp. Later, Solzhenitsyn found himself suffering from cancer. After his recovery he wrote a novel called *Cancer Ward* (1965) in which he compares the Soviet Union to a body infected by the disease. His criticism of the Soviet system brought him the disapproval of the government. He was first expelled from the Soviet Writers' Union, then, when he was awarded the Nobel Prize in 1970, he was not allowed to travel to Sweden to receive it. In 1974 he was finally forced into exile.

The Soviet-born writer Solzhenitsyn. He was forced into exile for his dissident views.

Sophocles (*c.*496 B.C.–*c.*405 B.C.)
Sophocles was an ancient Greek playwright. It is said that he took to writing after trying unsuccessfully to begin a career as an actor. Only seven of his plays have survived, but he is known to have won the magnificent drama competition held in honor of the god Dionysus at least eighteen times. Like the other great playwrights of his time, Aeschylus and Euripides, Sophocles wrote about events surrounding the siege of Troy and the heroes who fought there. But his finest works describe the fate of Oedipus, the king of Thebes. In these plays, Thebes is suffering under a terrible plague. In order to end it, Oedipus decrees that the man who murdered his father Laius must be brought to trial. But the plays reveal that Oedipus himself had unknowingly killed his own father—and then married his mother, the Queen Jocasta. Oedipus blinds himself and leaves Thebes. The two plays describing the story are *Oedipus the King* and *Oedipus at Colonus*. They are considered among the most powerful tragic plays ever written.
○ AESCHYLUS, EURIPIDES, PERICLES

Spartacus (d. 71 B.C.)
Spartacus was a gladiator who led a rebellion against the government of ancient Rome. He was a shepherd, who became a bandit and was then

captured and sold to the circus in the city of Capua. But in 73 B.C. he escaped with a group of other gladiators and began a revolt. Many slaves joined Spartacus, until his army numbered about 100,000 men. After several successful battles he was finally defeated near the river Silarius. Spartacus was killed during the fighting, and afterward his followers were gradually captured and executed.

Spenser, Edmund (*c.*1552–99)
Spenser was an English poet who worked at the time of Queen Elizabeth I. He was the secretary of the governor of Ireland, and spent much of his life there. His greatest work is a long poem called *The Faerie Queene,* to which he devoted many years. It tells of the adventures of knights, magical kings and queens, and other fantastical characters. Many others are meant to represent real people: for example, the queen of the poem's magic land, Gloriana, is supposed to be Queen Elizabeth herself. The poem was left unfinished when Spenser died.

Spinoza, Benedict de (1632–77)
Spinoza was a Dutch philosopher. He lived in Amsterdam, where he worked as a lens grinder in order to support himself, while giving his spare time to philosophy. In 1670 he published a treatise arguing for greater freedom, which made him unpopular with the government and religious authorities. His greatest work, the *Ethics,* was not published until after his death, which was caused by the glass dust from his lens-grinding work getting into his lungs.

Spitz, Mark Andrew (1950–   )
Mark Spitz is an American swimmer who became famous at the 1972 Olympic Games in Munich. He won a record seven gold medals—four for individual events, and three for team relay events. In each case, he set a new world record.

Staël-Holstein, Anne Louise Germaine (1766–1817)
Madame de Staël was a French woman writer who lived during the age of Napoleon. She was the daughter of the banker Necker, who had been Louis XVI's minister, and she married the Swedish ambassador to France, the Baron of Staël-Holstein. She was famous for her literary "salons"—gatherings of the most famous, artistic, and wealthy people of the time, at which she was the hostess. These were held in her Paris home until the outbreak of the French Revolution, when she moved to Switzerland and then to England, together with many other French aristocrats who were afraid for their lives. After the rise of Napoleon, Madame de Staël returned to France and attempted to make friends with the emperor, but he was suspicious of her, and eventually exiled her from Paris. Her works include two novels, as well as books on history and literature. She knew almost all the great European writers of her time, including Goethe, Schiller, and Benjamin Constant, with whom she had a long and close friendship.
○ CONSTANT, LOUIS XVI, NAPOLEON, NECKER

Joseph Stalin, leader of the Soviet Union, was a ruthless and cunning tyrant.

Stalin, Joseph Vissarionovich (1879–1953)
Joseph Stalin was leader of the Soviet Union from 1924 until 1953. He was a ruthless and cunning politician who refused to tolerate opposition, and who used the secret police to send many thousands of Soviet citizens to their deaths in labor camps. But he was also an efficient administrator and a great war leader: his policies ensured that the Soviet Union became an important world power after the revolution, and his determination to resist and defeat Hitler's Germany ensured the Allies' victory in the World War II, 1939 to 1945.

Stalin was born in the province of Georgia. He became a revolutionary at an early age and as a result was expelled from his college and imprisoned several times. During the Russian Revolution of 1917 he worked closely with Lenin and the other Bolshevik leaders, and gradually became one of the most important men in the new government. He was made general secretary of the Communist Party in 1922, and after Lenin's death in 1924 he made himself absolute ruler of the country. During the 1930s he conducted vicious purges of the Communist Party, eliminating all those he

suspected of opposing him. Important politicians such as Trotsky were forced into exile or murdered, while the secret police imprisoned or killed thousands of ordinary Russians. Meanwhile, Stalin had introduced a policy of building up the Soviet Union's industrial and military power. In 1939 he made a pact with Hitler in order to avoid war, but two years later Germany attacked Russia. World War II was a time of intense hardship for Russia. Millions of people died, either of starvation or in the fighting, but their determination eventually ensured Hitler's defeat. The result of the war was that the Soviet Union came to control Eastern Europe. Stalin inflicted great cruelty on his people, but he was also responsible for making the Soviet Union the powerful nation that it is today.
○ CHURCHILL, KHRUSHCHEV, LENIN, ROOSEVELT, TROTSKY

Standish, Miles (*c.*1584–1656)
Miles Standish was hired by the Pilgrims who sailed to America on the ship the *Mayflower* in 1620 to navigate, manage, and protect their expedition. He led the settlers in Massachusetts against the natives, and his exploits are the subject of a poem by Longfellow. ○ LONGFELLOW

Stanley, Sir Henry Morton (1841–1904)
Stanley was a British journalist and explorer who is remembered for his famous words: "Dr. Livingstone, I presume." He emigrated to the United States at the age of 15, where he fought in the Civil War and then became a journalist. He went on several expeditions to Africa before being sent by the New York *Herald* to find Livingstone. His success made him famous throughout the world, and he spent much of the rest of his life exploring Africa. ○ LIVINGSTONE

Stein, Gertrude (1874–1946)
Gertrude Stein was an American writer. She was born in Pennsylvania and studied medicine and psychology at university. In 1905 she moved to Paris, where she remained for much of the rest of her life, and became friends with artists such as Picasso. Her poems and other pieces of writing experimented with strange and sometimes confusing ways of using words and punctuation. She developed a technique of repeating words several times to fix them in the mind of her reader. Her works include *Tender Buttons*, a book of poems, and *The Autobiography of Alice B. Toklas*.

Steinbeck, John Ernst (1902–68)
Steinbeck was an American novelist. He was born and lived in California, and some of his novels portray the poor people and hoboes who lived in the towns where he grew up. His first successful book was *Tortilla Flat*, published in 1935. His best known is *The Grapes of Wrath*, which tells the story of poor farmers forced to leave their homes and move west to find work. His descriptions of the hardships they faced drew attention to the plight of poor farmers in some parts of the United States, and led to new laws and reforms to protect them. The book won a Pulitzer Prize when it was published in 1940. Steinbeck's other novels include *Of Mice and Men* (1937) and *East of Eden* (1952). He was awarded the Nobel Prize for Literature in 1962.

Steinway, Heinrich Engelhard (1797–1871)
The founder of a famous firm of piano makers. Steinway was born with the name "Steinweg" in Germany, where he started his first piano factory. But in 1851 he moved to the United States and began a new company, changing his name and calling it "Steinway."

Stendhal (Marie Henri Beyle, 1783–1842)
"Stendhal" was the name used by the French writer Marie Henri Beyle. He was a member of Napoleon's army and took part in the unsuccessful Russian campaign of 1812. He then spent several years traveling, and in 1830 he was made French consul in the Italian city of Trieste. He wrote many works, including biographies of composers and books on painting, but he is best known for his

A portrait of Gertrude Stein by Picasso.

novels. They include *The Red and the Black* (published in 1830) and *The Charterhouse of Parma* (1839). They are both vivid descriptions of the politics and intrigues of his time, and *The Charterhouse of Parma* contains a famous description of the Battle of Waterloo.

Stephenson, George (1781–1848)
George Stephenson was the English engineer who developed and built the first successful railway locomotive. He was born near the city of Newcastle and began working in a coal mine at the age of only 7. As a young man he used his wages to pay for the education he had never received as a child, and meanwhile invented several improvements to equipment used in the mines. In 1815 he won a £1,000 prize for his invention of the miner's safety lamp. The scientist Sir Humphry Davy invented a similar lamp at the same time, and the two men were involved in a bitter argument over who should get the credit. Stephenson built his first railway engine in 1814. It was called *My Lord* and it was capable of a steady six miles per hour. In 1825 he built the world's first public railway, between Stockton and Darlington in Yorkshire, although for some years horses were used to pull the carriages. In 1829 a competition was held to find the best design for a steam engine. Stephenson's "Rocket" won a prize of £500 for achieving a speed of 30 mph. A year later he completed a 28-mile railway line between Manchester and Liverpool. Stephenson's son, **Robert Stephenson** (1803–59), also became an engineer, and is especially well known for the bridges he built.

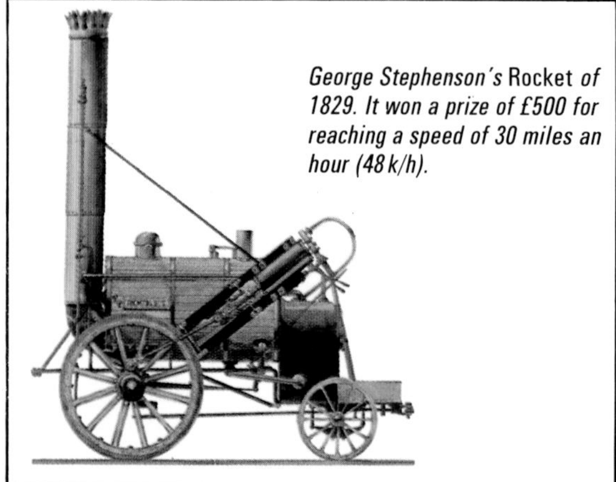

George Stephenson's Rocket *of 1829. It won a prize of £500 for reaching a speed of 30 miles an hour (48 k/h).*

Sterne, Laurence (1713–68)
Sterne was an English novelist. His masterpiece is *The Life and Opinions of Tristram Shandy* (known as *Tristram Shandy* for short), which he begun in 1759 and continued until his death. It is an eccentric and often very funny book. Sterne pretends that he is going to tell the life story of his hero, Tristram Shandy, but he gets so overwhelmed by details and digressions that he only covers the first few years of his life.

Stevens, Wallace (1879–1955)
Wallace Stevens was an American poet. He went to Harvard and then became vice-president of a big insurance company. Unknown to the company's other employees, Stevens began writing. He was over the age of 40 when his first book of poems, called *Harmonium*, was published in 1923. His other works include *Ideas of Order*. His *Collected Poems* were published in 1954. Stevens had a unique writing style. Much of his work is diffcult to understand.

Stevenson, Robert Louis Balfour (1850–94)
Robert Louis Stevenson was a Scottish writer whose most famous books, including *Treasure Island* and *The Strange Case of Dr. Jekyll and Mr. Hyde*, remain popular to this day. He was born in Edinburgh, where he studied first to become an engineer like his father, then to become a lawyer. In 1875 he began journeying around Europe. His first books describe his travels, including a canoe trip he took through France and Belgium. *Treasure Island* was his first novel, published in 1883. It was very successful, and was followed by several more, including *Kidnapped* (1886), *The Master of Ballantrae*, and *Dr. Jekyll and Mr. Hyde* (1886). In 1889 Stevenson left Scotland for the South Seas, hoping to recover from tuberculosis in the better climate there. He settled on the island of Samoa with his wife and family, where he died.

Stewart
Stewart is the name of the Scottish royal family. It is derived from the post of steward of Scotland. The name was modified to the French form Stuart. James VI of Scotland became James I of the United Kingdom in 1603. Thus the Tudors were replaced by the Stuarts.

Stowe, Harriet Beecher *see Beecher Stowe*

Stradivari, Antonio (1644–1737)
Antonio Stradivari was the most famous of the family of violin makers who gave their name to the "Stradivarius" violin. They worked in the Italian town of Cremona and perfected the craft of violin

making. Today, their beautiful instruments are worth hundreds of thousands of dollars.

Strauss, Johann (1825–99)
Johann Strauss was the most famous of a family of Austrian musicians and composers. They lived and worked at a time when Vienna was one of the busiest and most romantic cities in Europe, famous for its glittering society and the magnificent balls and parties that were held there. The waltzes, dances, and operas written and performed by the Strauss family captured the spirit of Vienna in the mid-19th century.

Johann's father was also called **Johann Strauss** (1804–49), so he is usually known as "Johann the Elder," and his son as "Johann the Younger." Johann the Elder was born in Vienna, where his father owned a beerhall. He studied music and eventually became well known in the city as a violinist, and then as a conductor. He began composing in 1825, and the following year he organized his own orchestra. They played in all the great cities of Europe, including London, where they performed at Queen Victoria's coronation in 1838. Among Johann the Elder's most famous compositions is the *Radetzky March*, which was written in honor of an Austrian general. Although he had been very successful, Johann the Elder did not wish his son to become a musician. Instead, he inisisted that Johann the Younger go to college and study law. But in the 1840s the young man gave up his studies, and his fame as a composer soon overshadowed that of his father. He formed an orchestra of his own in 1844, and like his father he toured all over Europe. He even visited the United States, where he appeared as a conductor in Boston and New York City in 1872. His waltzes are among the finest ever written. They include, "The Blue Danube" (1867), "Tales from the Vienna Woods" (1868), and "The Emperor Waltz" (1888). He also wrote successful operas, including *Die Fledermaus* ("The Bat," first performed in 1874) and *A Night in Venice* (1883). Johann the Younger became known as the "Waltz King." He died in Vienna.

Two more of Johann the Elder's sons became successful musicians: **Joseph Strauss** (1827–70) was supposed to be studying architecture, but eventually became a conductor and wrote several hundred pieces of music, and **Eduard Strauss** (1835–1916) became director of the balls held at the Viennese court.

Strauss's wonderful music started a craze for waltzing that spread everywhere.

Strauss's Waltzes

The Blue Danube
1867
Artist's Life
1867
Tales from the Vienna Woods
1868
Voices of Spring
1882
The Emperor
1888

Johann Strauss the Younger became known as the "Waltz King."

Strauss, Richard (1864–1949)
Richard Strauss was a German composer. He was born in the city of Munich, and was no relation of the famous Viennese Strauss family. He began to compose at the age of 6, published his first works at the age of 11, and later studied music at university in Munich and Berlin. In 1883 he became assistant conductor at an opera house, and he was quickly recognized as both a fine conductor and a great composer. His works include songs, symphonic "poems," and many operas. The most famous of his operas include *Salome*, first performed in 1905, and *Der Rosenkavalier* (1911). In 1933 he was made president of the German Music Chamber by Hitler's government, but he later resigned in disagreement with their policies.

Stravinsky, Igor Fedorovich (1882–1971)
Stravinsky was the greatest composer of the 20th century. He was born near St. Petersburg in Russia. He studied the law until he was 20 years old, then gave it up to devote himself to music. Throughout his life, Stravinsky experimented with many different ideas and techniques of composition. His first works were influenced by Russian folk music. They include three ballets he wrote for Diaghilev's *Ballets Russes* company: *The Firebird, Petrushka*, and *The Rite of Spring*. When the last of these was first performed in Paris in 1913, the audience were so outraged by it that the police had to be called to restore order in the theater. Stravinsky wrote music for many more ballets, and worked closely with choreographers, such as George Balanchine. He left Russia in 1910, and lived in France, Switzerland, and the United States. He experimented with music based on Schoenberg's revolutionary "12-note" system of composition, as well as with pieces inspired by classical composers such as Bach. Together with the poet W. H. Auden he wrote the opera *The Rake's Progress* (1951). Among Stravinsky's other works are a violin concerto, symphonies, and a choral work called *Symphony of Psalms*. ○ AUDEN, BALANCHINE, DIAGHILEV, SCHOENBERG

Strindberg, Johan August (1849–1912)
August Strindberg was a Swedish writer. He is most famous for his plays, including *The Father* (1887) and *Miss Julie* (1888). Strindberg had had an unhappy childhood, and his plays contain scenes of families in conflict. As well as plays, he wrote novels, stories, poems, and essays. He spent many years outside Sweden, but returned there at the end of his life to found a theater company to perform his plays.

Stubbs, George (1724–1806)
Stubbs was an English artist who is most famous for his paintings of horses and other animals. He studied anatomy at the hospital in the city of York, while making a living as a portrait painter. After a visit to Italy he settled in a remote farmhouse in the English countryside. He studied and dissected animals, and as a result his paintings are incredibly accurate. Among his most famous works are *The Grosvenor Hunt*, and a book called *Anatomy of the Horse*, published in 1776.

Sturluson, Snorri (1179–1241)
Snorri Sturluson was an Icelandic poet whose works describe the history of his own and the Norwegian people. They include the *Edda*, and the *Heimskringla*, which tells of the lives of the kings of Norway. In 1215 he was made chief judge of Iceland, but he provoked the Norwegian King Haakon by interfering in Norwegian affairs. As a result, Haakon had Snorri murdered.

The Russian-born composer, Stravinsky. His music, full of dissonances and strange rhythms, alarmed people at first.

Stuyvesant, Peter (1593–1672)
Peter Stuyvesant was governor of the Dutch colony of "New Netherland," which later became New York. He was born in Holland and was governor of other Dutch colonies before being sent to New Amsterdam (now New York City) in 1646. He was a harsh administrator who refused to allow political freedom and insisted that settlers follow strict religious rules. But he encouraged trade, and under his government New Amsterdam became a prosperous port. In 1664 the British, who were at war with the Dutch, annexed the colony of New Netherland and forced Stuyvesant to surrender. "New Amsterdam" was then renamed "New York."

A painting by the English artist, Stubbs, who is famous for his pictures of horses.

Sulaiman the Magnificent (1494–1566)
Sulaiman the Magnificent was the greatest of the sultans of Turkey. He inherited his throne from his father, Selim I, in 1520. Over the next 20 years the Turkish Empire reached its height. Sulaiman's armies captured Belgrade, Budapest, Baghdad, and territories in North Africa. The island of Rhodes came under his control as his navy expanded the empire westward through the Mediterranean. Turkey's great enemy in Europe was the Italian city-state of Venice, because the two nations competed for control of ports and trading routes in the Middle East. Under Sulaiman, Venetian power was reduced (although this was later reversed at the Battle of Lepanto in 1571). Meanwhile Sulaiman introduced legal reforms in Turkey, and spent large amounts of money on new palaces and mosques in his capital, Constantinople. He died during a war with Austria.

Sulla, Lucius Cornelius (138 B.C.–78 B.C.)
Sulla made himself dictator of ancient Rome in the year 82 B.C. He was a powerful general in the army serving under the command of **Gaius Marius** (157 B.C.–86 B.C.). The two men gradually became involved in a long rivalry for power in Rome. In 88 B.C. Sulla was made a consul, but when Marius was given command of the army he took control of the city by force. Later, while Sulla was fighting in Greece, Marius' supporters gained power once again. Sulla returned, and after defeating Marius' supporters he was made dictator. He took harsh revenge on his enemies, but afterward proved himself an effective ruler.

Sun Yat-sen (1866–1925)
Sun Yat-sen was a Chinese revolutionary who inspired the overthrow of the Chinese emperor in 1911, and later became the country's president. His activities forced him to live in exile, but he tried several times to organize a revolution in China from abroad. The Chinese government attempted unsuccessfully to kidnap and kill him. In 1911 revolution broke out in China, the emperor abdicated, and Sun returned to become the country's provisional president. But he stepped down in favor of an army general, and did not become president until 1916. His aim was to unify China under a single government, but this was not achieved until after his death, when Chiang Kai-shek formed a government inspired by Sun's ideas.
○ CHIANG KAI-SHEK, MAO ZE-DONG

Sutherland, Joan (1926–)
Joan Sutherland is an Australian opera singer. She made her debut in 1952, but became world famous in 1959 for her performance in the opera *Lucia di Lammermoor* by Donizetti. Since then she has toured throughout the world.

Swift, Jonathan (1667–1745)
Jonathan Swift was a writer who is most famous as the author of *Gulliver's Travels*, the story of Gulliver's adventures in Lilliput (a country of little people) and other strange lands. Although Swift had English parents, he was born and lived much of his life in the Irish city of Dublin. He was not very successful at college, but with the help of his family he was given a job as secretary to an English diplomat. At the same time, he began to write political pamphlets and "satires"—works that made fun of people or political parties. Apart from *Gulliver's Travels*, Swift published all his works without being paid and without his name being mentioned. *Gulliver* was published in 1826. As well as being part adventure, part fairy tale, it also attacks human weaknesses and institutions. Swift also wrote poems and essays, and from 1713 he was the dean of St. Patrick's Church in Dublin.

Swithin, Saint (d. 862)
Saint Swithin was a loyal counselor to two old kings of Wessex (a kingdom in the south of England), Egbert and Ethelwulf. He was made bishop of Winchester. According to tradition, heavy rain delayed the transfer of his remains from Winchester churchyard to the cathedral itself. Thus, it is said, if it rains on Saint Swithin's Day, it will rain for 40 days more.

Tacitus, Publius Cornelius (*c.* A.D. 55–120)
Tacitus was an ancient Roman historian. In his *Annals* and *Histories* he describes the history of the Roman Empire from the death of Augustus in A.D. 14 until the death of Domitian in A.D. 96. He also wrote a book about Germany and the people living there, and his *Agricola* contains an interesting description of Britain. (Agricola was the Roman general who conquered Britain, and Tacitus was married to his daughter.) Tacitus himself was a well-known orator, and he became a diplomat during the reign of the Emperor Trajan.

Taglioni, Marie (1804–84)
Marie Taglioni was an Italian ballerina. She is said to have introduced the technique of dancing *sur les pointes*—on the points of the toes. In 1832 her father, who was a dance master, choreographed the ballet *La Sylphide* especially for her. She moved with such lightness that he once said: "If I heard my daughter dance, I would kill her." After a successful career as a dancer, Marie Taglioni became a teacher to the children of the English royal family, but she died in poverty.

Talleyrand-Périgord, Charles Maurice de (1754–1838)
Talleyrand was an important French politician of the Napoleonic age. During the French Revolution of 1789 he was elected head of the new French Assembly, but when Robespierre came to power he was forced to leave the country for a time. After Robespierre's fall, Talleyrand returned to become foreign minister. He supported Napoleon's takeover of the government in 1799 and remained as foreign minister under the new leadership. He negotiated several important treaties on Napoleon's behalf, but he eventually became disillusioned with the emperor's policies. He made secret agreements with the governments of France's enemies, and after Napoleon's fall he became a member of the new King Louis XVIII's administration. ○ NAPOLEON

Talleyrand, a French politician during the revolution and under Napoleon.

Tamerlane (1336–1405)
Tamerlane was a great Tatar chieftain. He became ruler of the kingdom known as Samarkand in 1369 and began a long series of wars with neighboring tribes and kingdoms. He conquered Persia, Georgia (now part of the Soviet Union), and large parts of central Asia, and then returned home with vast amounts of captured treasure. After taking control of parts of Turkey and the Middle East, he died while marching toward China. He was given the name "Timur the Lame" because he had been born crippled.

Tasman, Abel Janszoon (1603–59)
Tasman was a Dutch navigator. In 1642 he discovered Tasmania, the island off the southern coast of Australia, which he named "Van Dieman's Land" in honor of the Dutch governor of the East Indies. The following year he discovered New Zealand, and the islands of Tonga and Fiji.

Tasso, Torquato (1544–95)
Tasso was an Italian poet. His greatest work is *La Gerusalemme liberata* (published in 1575), which describes the First Crusade. Like his play *Aminta,* the poem was very successful, but Tasso showed signs of madness, and in 1579 he was imprisoned for seven years in the city of Ferrara. After his release he wandered the country, visiting Rome, Mantua, and Naples and working on a new edition of his great poem. He died while on his way to Rome to be crowned "poet laureate" by the Pope.

Tchaikovsky, Piotr Ilyich (1840–93)
Tchaikovsky was a Russian composer. He showed a talent for music while he was still a child, but he did not begin studying the subject until he was 21, when his family moved to St. Petersburg and he was able to join the music school there. His first symphonies and operas made him well known, and in 1877 a rich widow called Nadezhda von Meck

Marie Taglioni moved with amazing lightness and grace. Her father, who trained her, once said: "If I heard my daughter dance, I would kill her."

provided Tchaikovsky with an income so that he could compose without having to worry about money. The two wrote letters to each other, but when they finally met they were too embarrassed to speak. Tchaikovsky married in 1877, but the marriage lasted less than a month before he left his wife. Meanwhile, his compositions were very popular. They include several symphonies and concertos, and Tchaikovsky is best known for his ballets, which include *Swan Lake* (1876), *The Sleeping Beauty* (1889), and *The Nutcracker* (1892). He was always the victim of illness and fits of depression, and in 1893 he died during an outbreak of cholera in St. Petersburg.

Teilhard de Chardin, Pierre (1881–1955)
Teilhard was a French scientist and philosopher. He made expeditions to China and other parts of Asia to study geological evidence of life in prehistoric times. He was also a Jesuit priest, but he was forbidden by the Jesuits either to teach or publish his theories, because they were thought incompatible with Christian teaching. His philosophical works were therefore published after his death.

Telford, Thomas (1757–1834)
Thomas Telford was a Scottish engineer. He designed and built over 1,200 bridges and 1,550 miles of road, as well as churches, houses, and docks, and he organized the draining of large areas of waterlogged land in East Anglia. Among his most famous achievements are the road between London and the Welsh port of Holyhead, St. Katherine's Docks in London, and the Menai suspension bridge in Wales.

Tennyson, Alfred, Lord (1809–92)
Tennyson was one of the most popular poets in the history of English literature. He was born in the county of Lincolnshire and went to university at Cambridge. There, he met Arthur Hallam. The two men became close friends, and Hallam's unexpected death in 1833 led Tennyson to write his great poem *In Memoriam*—although it was not published until 1850. Meanwhile, Tennyson had gradually become successful. He was made "poet laureate" in 1850 by Queen Victoria; his books sold in huge numbers, and it seemed that everybody in England read his work. He wrote many poems commemorating important events, such as the famous *Charge of the Light Brigade*. Another popular subject was the legend of King Arthur. Tennyson wrote his own version of the *Morte d'Arthur* early in his career, and he later began a long series of poems based on Arthurian legends, called *Idylls of the King*.

Tenzing Norgay (1914–86)
Tenzing was a Nepalese mountaineer who, together with Edmund Hillary, became the first man to reach the summit of Mount Everest in 1953. He began climbing in 1935 with the first expeditions to the Himalayas, and later became the president of the Sherpa Association and head of a Nepalese mountaineering institute. ○ HILLARY

Terence (Publius Terentius Afer, *c.*190 B.C.–159 B.C.)
Terence was an ancient Roman playwright. He was born in the North African city of Carthage, where he was sold as a slave to a Roman senator named Terentius. Terentius took him to Rome and educated and then freed him. Terence's plays are comedies, often based on earlier Greek works. They include *Andria* (first performed in the year 166 B.C.), *Hecyra*, and *Adelphi*.

Teresa of Calcutta, "Mother"
(Agnes Gonxha Bojaxhiu, 1910–)
Mother Teresa is a Roman Catholic missionary whose name has become well known throughout the world as a result of her work with the poor and homeless in India. Her parents were Albanians, and Mother Teresa was born in Yugoslavia. She became a nun at the age of 18 and traveled to the Indian city of Calcutta, where she eventually

became head of a school. After seeing the terrible conditions in which many of the city's poorest people lived, she decided to leave the school and give all her time to caring for them. She went to Paris to learn medicine, then returned to the slums and founded a school for destitute children. Many other nuns joined her, and in 1950 she began the Missionaries of Charity, a foundation dedicated to looking after the poor. As well as the homeless and the starving, Mother Teresa has also cared for the ill, especially those with leprosy, and she has set up many schools and hospitals throughout India. In 1979 she was awarded the Nobel Peace Prize.

Mother Teresa of Calcutta holding one of the many orphans her Missionaries of Charity care for.

Tereshkova, Valentina Vladimirova (1937–)
The first woman in space. Tereshkova was a Russian textile worker who trained to be an astronaut and began her historic flight on June 6, 1963, in a Vostok spacecraft. She returned to earth three days later after completing 48 orbits.

Terry, Dame Ellen Alice (1847–1928)
Ellen Terry was an actress who dominated London's theater world at the end of the 19th century. She gave her first performance at the age of only 9 in Shakespeare's *The Winter's Tale.* After some years performing in London and other English cities she gave up the stage and married an

Ellen Terry (on the right) in a painting depicting a scene from The Merry Wives of Windsor *by Shakespeare.*

artist, George Watts. The marriage was a disaster, and after less than a year Ellen Terry returned to acting. She became most famous for her performances in plays by Shakespeare, and particularly for those she gave together with another famous actor, **Henry Brodribb Irving** (1838–1905). Their partnership began in 1878 and lasted over 20 years.

Thackeray, William Makepeace (1811–63)
Thackeray was an English writer. He was born in the Indian city of Calcutta, where his father was a wealthy official in the East India Company. Thackeray expected to inherit his father's wealth, but the company did badly and he was forced to try to make a living by writing instead. He began contributing articles to the most popular magazines of his time, and soon became well known. In 1848 he began publishing his first and most famous novel, *Vanity Fair.* It is set at the time of the Napoleonic Wars and tells the story of Becky Sharp, a poor but very clever girl who manipulates those around her to gain wealth and power. Like many other 19th-century novels, it was published in weekly parts in a magazine. Thackeray's other works include *Pendennis* and *The Virginians,* and a story for children called *The Rose and the Ring.*

Thant, U (1909–74)
U Thant was a Burmese diplomat who was adviser to the country's prime minister and later a member

of the United Nations Assembly. From 1962 until 1971 he was general secretary of the United Nations.

Thatcher, Margaret Hilda (1925–)
Margaret Thatcher is a British politician. In 1979 she became the first woman to be elected prime minister of her country. She was born in the town of Grantham in Lincolnshire, where her father owned a small shop. After studying chemistry at Oxford University she became a lawyer and entered politics. During the 1960s and 1970s she held important posts in Conservative governments, then, in 1975, she became leader of the Conservative Party. The Conservatives' victory in the 1979 General Election made her prime minister, and she was re-elected in 1983 and 1987. Among her most controversial acts as prime minister was her declaration of war with Argentina in 1982 over the future of the Falkland Islands in the Atlantic Ocean, which are governed by Britain but which Argentina claims as its own.

Themistocles (*c.*523 B.C.–*c.*458 B.C.)
Themistocles was an Athenian general. He set out to build a vast new navy for Athens and in ten years more than doubled the number of ships in the Athenian fleet. At the sea battle at Salamis in 480 B.C. Themistocles led the Greeks to a great victory over the Persians. The Persians were forced to give up their campaign against Greece, Themistocles later became unpopular with his own people and was forced into exile.

Theodora (*c.*500–548)
Theodora was a Byzantine empress. She was first an actress, then a courtesan, and she eventually became the mistress and then the wife of the Emperor Justinian. She played an important part in the government of the empire, and during riots in the year 532 her courage was said to have saved Justinian's government. ○ JUSTINIAN

Theresa of Ávila, Saint (1515–82)
Theresa was a Spanish saint who devoted herself to founding or reforming monasteries throughout her country. She was born in the town of Ávila in the kingdom of Castile and became a nun at the age of 20. At first she was homesick for her family and sometimes ill, but she gradually became more committed to the life of a nun. As she grew older she began having ecstasies and other spiritual experiences. Eventually she decided to leave her convent and found another, based on older, stricter religious principles. In 1562, after many hardships, she opened a new convent, dedicated to Saint Joseph, in the town of Ávila. She and her followers were known as the "barefooted" Carmelites because of their strictness. Theresa traveled around Spain encouraging other convents to adopt her system, and founded 17 new ones. They were poor, and completely devoted to prayer. Theresa also wrote several books describing her life and her ideas about religion and the Church. In 1970, she and Saint Catherine of Siena became the first women to be declared doctors of the Roman Catholic Church. ○ CATHERINE OF SIENA

Thomas, Dylan Marlais (1914–53)
Dylan Thomas was a Welsh writer. He is best known for his poems, and for his famous radio play *Under Milk Wood*. It was first broadcast in 1954, and describes a day in the life of an imaginary Welsh seaside town. It was very popular, on the radio, and later in the theater and as a film. He died, partly as a result of drinking too much, while on a tour of the United States.

Thoreau, Henry David (1817–62)
Henry Thoreau was an American writer. He was born at Concord, in Massachusetts, where he lived for much of his life. In about 1839 he began taking long walks in the countryside and carefully studying nature. In 1845 he built a small hut near Walden Pond, in a remote part of Massachusetts, where he lived for two years, writing and watching what he saw around him. His description of this experience, *Walden*, was published in 1854. Later in his life he visited Maine and Canada, but he always returned to Concord, where he died. His other works include *Civil Disobedience* (1849), which inspired Mahatma Gandhi, and the *Week on the Concord and Merrimack Rivers* (1849).

Thorpe, James (1888–1953)
"Jim" Thorpe was an American athlete, probably the most outstanding all-around sportsman of all time. He won the pentathlon and decathlon in the 1912 Olympics.

Thurber, James Grover (1894–1961)
James Thurber was an American writer. He is best known for his humorous stories and drawings, which were published in magazines. His books include *My Life and Hard Times* and *Men, Women, and Dogs*. As he grew older, he found it more and more difficult to draw as his eyesight got worse.

Tiglath Pileser III (d. *c.*727 B.C.)
Tiglath Pileser III was a great king of Assyria. He came to the throne in 745 B.C. and conquered parts of Syria and Phoenicia. His greatest achievement was the capture of Babylon in 729 B.C. He is sometimes known by the name "Pulu."

Tintoretto (Jacopo Robusti, 1518–94)
Tintoretto was an Italian painter. He lived and worked in the city of Venice; he was a pupil of the great Titian. It is said that Titian grew jealous of Tintoretto's skill and dismissed him. By about 1540 he had set up his own workshop, where he produced large numbers of paintings for the churches and public buildings of the city. He enjoyed his work, and he would often reduce the price he charged for a painting simply in order to be given the job; sometimes he even imitated other painters' styles in order to get more work. Among Tintoretto's most important clients was the government of Venice. In the 1570s two disastrous fires destroyed parts of the Doge's Palace (the government headquarters). Tintoretto was one of the painters employed in redecorating the building. He painted portraits of the doges and counselors, scenes from Venetian history, and a vast vision of Paradise in the government's main council chamber. Another important project was the great series of pictures Tintoretto painted in the "Scuola di San Rocco"—the headquarters of a charitable society of which he was a member. He spent 12 years working on the walls and ceiling, which he covered with scenes from the New Testament. In all these things Tintoretto was helped by assistants from his workshop. They included two of his sons, Domenico and Marco, and his daughter Marietta, who was one of the very few women painters of the Renaissance period. ○ TITIAN

Titian (Tiziano Vecelli, *c.*1488–1576)
Titian was one of the greatest painters of the Renaissance period. Unlike artists such as Michelangelo and Raphael, who spent their lives in Florence or Rome, Titian lived and worked in the city of Venice, and he and the other Venetian painters developed their own, distinct style.

Titian had two great teachers: Giorgione and Giovanni Bellini. Bellini died in 1516, and Titian took over his job as the Venetian government's "official" painter. He also completed many of the paintings that Bellini had left unfinished. In 1518 he began work on a magnificent new altarpiece for the Church of the Frari in Venice. It showed the Assumption of the Virgin Mary into heaven, and was painted in a dramatic style, in bold, bright colors. Together with another altarpiece in the same church, it established Titian's fame, and over the next few years he received orders for paintings from many important people. He produced pictures on religious and mythological subjects, and many very fine portraits. In 1632 he met the Emperor Charles V, who made him his official court painter. Among the many paintings Titian made for Charles is a portrait showing the emperor with his dog (○ CHARLES V). The two men became good friends, and when Charles died Titian continued to work for his son, Philip II. It was very unusual for a painter to be considered an "equal" by a king. At the beginning of the Renaissance, artists were thought of as simple craftsmen, but by the time of Titian and Michelangelo they were considered gifted, even "divine," and the wealthy and famous competed for their favor. There is a story that when Titian dropped his brush during a sitting, the emperor himself bent down to pick it up! Titian gained great fame and lived to be a great age. He left a painting called the *Pietà,* which he intended for his own tomb, unfinished when he died.
○ BELLINI, GIORGIONE, TINTORETTO

Tito (Josip Broz, 1892–1980)
Tito was a Communist leader of Yugoslavia. He was born with the name "Josip Broz" in the area known as Croatia, and during World War I (1914–18) he served in the Austrian army. He was taken prisoner by the Russians, but at the end of the war he remained in Russia where he became a member of the Red Army and took the name "Tito." During World War II (1939–45) he led a group of Yugoslav partisans in attacks against the German invaders. He was supported by the Allies, and after the war set up a Communist government for Yugoslavia. He was prime minister from 1945 until 1953 and then president from 1953 until his death. He skillfully followed a neutral policy, maintaining relations with both Russia and the West, but favoring neither.

Tolstoy, Count Leo Nikolayevich (1828–1910)
Tolstoy was a Russian novelist and philosopher. His first books were inspired by his experiences as an army officer during the Crimean War, which began in 1853. At the end of the war he traveled around much of Europe before marrying and returning to his family estates in the Tula province of Russia. He was a liberal landlord who introduced modern farming methods and built schools and proper homes for the people who lived and worked

Portrait of a Man with a Blue Sleeve *by the Venetian artist Titian.*

on his land. In 1865 he began his great novel *War and Peace,* which is considered by some people to be the finest novel ever written. It tells the story of two Russian families at the time of the Napoleonic Wars. Tolstoy followed *War and Peace* with another great novel, *Anna Karenina* (finished in 1876). After this, he gave his time to philosophy. His ideas eventually led him to give up his family estates and wealth, and caused a quarrel with his wife that was never healed. He died in October 1910 of fever at a railroad station.

Tone, Theobald Wolfe (1763–98)
Wolfe Tone was an Irish leader who wanted to free his country from British rule. He organized the "United Irishmen" and tried to gain support from the United States and France. After the failure of a rebellion in 1798 he killed himself while in prison.

Torquemada, Tomás de (1420–98)
Torquemada was a Dominican monk who persuaded King Ferdinand and Queen Isabella to introduce the Inquisition in Spain to persecute those who were not Catholics. In 1493 he became Inquisitor-General and organized a campaign of imprisonment and torture against Jews, Arabs, and other non-Catholics. ○ FERDINAND II

Torricelli, Evangelista (1608–47)
Torricelli was an Italian scientist and mathematician. He was born in the town of Faenza, from where he went to Florence and became Galileo's pupil. After the master's death, Torricelli became professor of mathematics at the Florentine Academy. He experimented with the effects of atmospheric pressure on water and mercury, with vacuums, and with the behavior of different liquids. He also experimented with microscopes. ○ GALILEO

Toulouse-Lautrec, Henri de (1864–1901)
Toulouse-Lautrec was a French artist. His favorite subjects were actresses, circus performers and clowns, prostitutes, and the people he saw around him in the bars and cafés of Paris. He worked quickly and was a fine drawer: he could catch a figure or a movement with just a few strokes of his brush. As well as paintings, he made prints and poster designs. His main interests were in color and movement, not (like the Impressionists) the effects of light.

A poster by the French artist Toulouse-Lautrec. Toulouse-Lautrec was injured as a child so severely that he remained dwarflike.

Toussaint L'Ouverture, Pierre Dominique (1743–1803)
Toussaint was a slave who made himself leader of the Caribbean island of Haiti. Despite the hardships of his youth he was able to learn French and he read a great many books. In 1791 the Negroes in Haiti rebelled against their French rulers, and Toussaint became their leader. Slavery was abolished in 1794 and the French made Toussaint the island's governor. His military skill enabled him to keep first the British, then the Spanish from conquering Haiti, and he governed the island with fairness and good sense. In 1801 he introduced a new constitution and attempted to make Haiti completely independent of France. Napoleon resisted this, sent an army to invade the island, and proposed the reintroduction of slavery. Toussaint was forced to surrender in 1802. He was taken to France, where he died in prison. ○ NAPOLEON

Trajan's column in Rome records the emperor's campaigns.

Trajan (Marcus Ulpius Trajanus, *c.* A.D. 53–117)
Trajan succeeded Nerva as Roman emperor in A.D. 98. He is best remembered for his military campaigns; in fact, he spent most of his reign abroad, attempting to expand the empire. His first action was against Dacia, an area of central Europe. The campaign was long and hard, but by 106 the Romans had defeated the Dacians. Trajan next left for the east, where he captured parts of Armenia and Mesopotamia. "Trajan's Column" in Rome records the emperor's campaigns in a series of carvings. His government was efficient, and new roads, canals, harbors, and bridges were built during his reign.

Trevithick, Richard (1771–1833)
Trevithick was an English engineer. He was born in Cornwall, where there were many tin mines, and he made several inventions and improvements in mining equipment. In 1802 he developed a steam engine which he used to power railway and road vehicles. Unfortunately, he and his inventions were forgotten when he went to South America, and he died in poverty.

Trotsky, Leon (Lev Davidovich Bronstein, 1879–1940)
Trotsky was one of the most important figures in the Russian Revolution. He became a Communist as a young man, and as a result was expelled from university and spent three years in a prison in Siberia. He escaped and traveled to London, where he joined Lenin and other exiled Russian revolutionaries. During the unsuccessful attempt to overthrow the government of Russia in 1905, Trotsky was leader of the St. Petersburg revolutionaries. He was once again imprisoned, but he escaped a second time and fled. In 1917 he

Trotsky, a minister in the first Russian Soviet government.

returned to Russia to join the Bolsheviks, and together with Lenin he planned the overthrow of Kerensky's provisional government. He became the minister responsible for war and foreign affairs, and he built up and led the "Red Army" to victory in the civil war that followed the 1917 Revolution. After Lenin's death in 1924, Trotsky opposed the new leader, Stalin. As a result he was expelled from the Communist Party, and in 1929 exiled from the country. He eventually settled in Mexico City, but in Russia a Soviet court had sentenced him to death. In 1940 he was murdered by Ramon Mercador, an agent of Stalin's secret police.

○ KERENSKY, LENIN, STALIN

Trudeau, Pierre Elliott (1919–)
Pierre Trudeau is a Canadian politician. He was prime minister of Canada from 1968 until 1979 and again from 1980 until 1984. One of the most important issues in Canadian politics during this time was whether or not the French-speaking province of Quebec should separate from the rest of Canada. Trudeau opposed this, and tried to bring about a compromise that would satisfy both French- and English-speakers, but keep the country together.

Truffaut, François (1932–84)
François Truffaut was a French motion-picture director. He was one of those who introduced the "new wave" in French cinema—films that upset traditional film-making styles. Among his films are *Jules et Jim* (1961) and *Day for Night* (1973).

Truman, Harry S. (1884–1972)
Harry Truman was the thirty-third president of the United States. He was born in the state of Missouri, where his family were farmers. After World War I, Truman became a partner in a clothing shop, but the business collapsed and he had to spend the next 15 years working to pay back those who had supported it. He entered politics in the mid-1920s, and in 1935 he was elected senator for the state of Missouri. In 1944 he became vice president to Franklin D. Roosevelt, and when Roosevelt died the following year he became president. One of his first decisions was to drop the atomic bombs that destroyed the Japanese cities of Hiroshima and Nagasaki. After the war he adopted a policy of "containing" Communist countries such as the U.S.S.R. and China—by force, if necessary. This led to his decision to send U.S. troops to fight in the Korean War in 1950. In 1951 he took the difficult step of removing the powerful General MacArthur from command of the army in Korea after MacArthur publicly disagreed with Truman over the correct policy for fighting the war. He was re-elected president in 1948, but refused to stand in the 1952 election. The "S." in his name does not stand for any single name, but for the names of both his grandfathers.

○ MACARTHUR, ROOSEVELT

A U.S. postage stamp showing Harry S. Truman, the thirty-third president of the United States.

Truth, Sojourner (Isabella, 1797–1883)
Sojourner Truth was a black American woman who campaigned for the abolition of slavery in her country. She was born into slavery in New York State, but in 1828 a law was passed which made keeping slaves illegal. She was set free and moved to New York City. Some years later, she had what she believed was a call from God to preach, and it was then that she took the name "Sojourner Truth." She began holding meetings in New York, but as her fame spread she toured all over the north-eastern part of the United States. Her message was simple: that Christians should show love for others, and this meant they must oppose the appalling evil and degradation of slavery. In 1864 she went to

(Continued on page 248)

Sojourner Truth, former slave and celebrated abolitionist.

America's Greatest Humorist

Twain, Mark (Samuel Langhorne Clemens, 1835–1910) "Mark Twain" was the pseudonym (false name) used by the American writer Samuel Langhorne Clemens. He is best known for writing *The Adventures of Tom Sawyer* and *The Adventures of Huckleberry Finn*, books that have remained best-sellers since they were first published, popular with both adults and children.

Tom Sawyer and *Huckleberry Finn* are set in the waterside country along the Mississippi River, where Clemens grew up, and he included much from his own life in the adventures of his two heroes. Clemens was born in the town of Hannibal, Missouri. His father was a lawyer, but died poor when the boy was only 12 years old. He had to leave school and take a job in order to survive. He worked as a printer and traveled through the South, eventually making his way north to New York City. For a while he planned to go to South America, but in 1857 he returned to New Orleans and became an apprentice steamboat pilot on the Mississippi. At the same time, he began writing occasional articles for newspapers and magazines under the name "Mark Twain." He took the name from steamboatmen's language: when in shallow water a man would stand at the front of the boat and lower a weighted line to the bottom. When the depth reached two fathoms he would cry "Mark twain!" meaning "Two fathoms deep."

A caricature of Mark Twain, the great American humorist. A white linen suit became his trademark in public appearances.

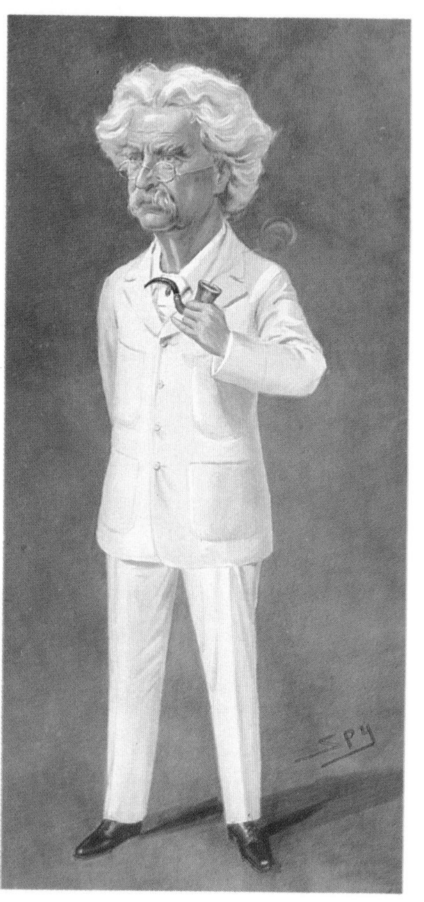

When the Civil War broke out, Twain traveled west with his brother to look for gold, but found nothing. Meanwhile his articles were very successful, and he devoted more time to writing. He traveled abroad, visiting the Mediterranean, and publishing a witty and very successful account of his travels called *Innocents Abroad* in 1869. In 1870 he married Olivia Langdon, and became editor of a newspaper in New York State. *Tom Sawyer* was published in 1876. It tells the story of Tom and his friends Joe Harper and Huckleberry Finn. They get tired of school and leave town to live on an island, are thought to have died, but return home in time for their funerals; they witness a murder, get lost in caves, discover a hoard of treasure—and have numerous other adventures besides. *Tom Sawyer* was unlike other children's books of the time because there was nothing very "good" about its heroes: Tom is lazy, mischievous, and almost entirely selfish—yet he and his friends have great adventures, and everything turns out well despite their "badness."

The same thing was true of *Huckleberry Finn*, which was published in 1884. Huck smokes a pipe, several of the characters drink whiskey, and the story has the same mischievous quality as *Tom Sawyer*. Many people criticized it as unsuitable for children when it was published, and there are still libraries in some parts of the United States that do not keep it on their children's shelves.

> *Now the master began to draw a map of America on the blackboard. . . . But he made a sad business of it and a smothered titter rippled over the house. . . . The tittering continued; it even manifestly increased. And well it might. There was a garret above, pierced with a scuttle over his head; down through this scuttle came a cat suspended around the haunches by a string; she had a rag tied about her head and jaws to keep her from mewing; she slowly descended. The tittering rose higher and higher, the cat was within six inches of the absorbed teacher's head; down down a little lower, and she grabbed his wig with her desperate claws, clung to it, and was snatched up into the garret in an instant.*
>
> The Adventures of Tom Sawyer

Washington, where she met President Lincoln. Many white women publicly opposed slavery, but Sojourner Truth was the first black woman to speak out. ○ LINCOLN, TUBMAN

Tubman, Harriet (1820–1913)
Harriet Tubman was one of the black Americans who risked their lives organizing the "underground railroad" which helped slaves escape from captivity during the 1850s. She and others like her traveled to the Southern states in which slavery was legal to help slaves escape and reach the safety of Canada or the "free" states in the north of the country. After 1850, when the United States Congress passed the Fugitive Slave Act, it was illegal to help an escaped slave, and large rewards were offered for those operating the underground railroad.

Harriet Tubman, a runaway slave who became a leading "conductor" of the underground railroad and guided many slaves to freedom. She served as nurse, scout, and intelligence agent for the Union Army in the South during the American Civil War.

Tubman was born into slavery in the state of Maryland. At the age of 13 she was badly injured when she tried to stop a foreman from beating another slave. She escaped in 1849 and traveled to Philadelphia. She made 19 trips back to the South to escort parties of escaping slaves to freedom. Neither she nor any of the 300 people she helped were caught, and in 1857 she was able to bring her parents to safety. After the outbreak of the American Civil War in 1861, Harriet Tubman continued her work by joining the Union Army. She served as a spy, and helped free several hundred more slaves. After the war and the end of slavery she helped set up schools, homes, and other services for black people. ○ LINCOLN, TRUTH

Tull, Jethro (1674–1741)
Jethro Tull was an English inventor and agricultural reformer. He is most famous for his seed drill, a device for planting seeds in straight rows. But he also explained *why* seeds should be planted this way, and his ideas led to great improvements in crops. He recognized the importance of turning the soil to "aerate" it. Tull published his work in a book called *Horse-hoeing Husbandry* in 1733.

Turgenev, Ivan Sergeyevich (1818–83)
Turgenev was a Russian writer. For much of his life he was in love with a famous singer, Pauline Garcia, but she was already married, and Turgenev's devotion to her proved to be hopeless. Partly to be near her, and partly because he was unpopular in Russia, he traveled around Europe, spending several years in Paris, where he eventually died. He wrote short stories and novels. Among them are *Fathers and Sons*, published in 1862, and *Virgin Soil*.

Turner, Joseph Mallord William (1775–1851)
Turner was an English artist. He is most famous for his dramatic oil paintings of sea and landscape scenes, and for his watercolors. Like the Impressionists who came after him, Turner was interested in the effects of light, and he liked to paint landscapes and skies flooded with color. He was unpopular with many people in his own time. The painter Constable said that his pictures looked like "tinted steam." But others, such as the critic John Ruskin, defended him, and he gradually became successful. When he died he left thousands of paintings and drawings to the nation.

Twain, Mark (1835–1910)
See pages 246 & 247

Tyler, Wat (d. 1381)
Wat Tyler was one of the leaders of the "Peasants' Revolt" in England in 1381. He marched with thousands of poor farmers from the county of Kent to demand reforms from the king, Richard II. During his conference with the king, Tyler was killed by the Lord Mayor of London. Richard saw that this would anger the crowd, and he stepped in and promised to answer their complaints. His bravery probably saved him, but afterward he did little to fulfill his promise. ○ RICHARD II

U V

Uccello, Paolo (1397–1475)
Paolo Uccello was an Italian painter who worked during the early part of the Renaissance period. He was one of the first to experiment with perspective as a way of arranging the figures in his compositions, and he liked to use real plants and animals as his subjects. Among his most famous works are three scenes showing the Battle of San Romano, painted in about 1455, and a charming picture of Saint George and the Dragon. Although he was well known for a time, Uccello never became really popular, as his style was overtaken by the newer techniques of artists such as Masaccio. ○ MASACCIO

Updike, John Hoyer (1932–)
John Updike is an American writer. He has published poems, stories, essays, and novels, many of which have been best-sellers. They include *Rabbit, Run,* his first book, published in 1960, *Couples* (1968), and *Rabbit Is Rich,* which won a Pulitzer Prize in 1981.

Urban II (1042–99)
Urban II became Pope in 1088. He drove foreign princes such as Henry IV of Germany and Philip I of France out of Italy, and in 1095 he inspired the First Crusade, which captured Jerusalem from its Arab rulers.

Ursula, Saint
Ursula is a legendary saint who is said to have been slaughtered, along with a number of other women, by barbarians in the city of Cologne. According to tradition, she was a British princess who fled when her parents tried to force her into marriage. She and her companions were killed for being Christians. Different versions of the story give different numbers for those who died with Ursula, some as few as 10, others as many as 1,000. She is the patron saint of many schools and colleges.

Valois, Dame Ninette de (1898–)
Ninette de Valois was a British dancer and choreographer. While still a young girl she joined Diaghilev's *Ballets Russes* company which toured Europe, and she eventually became a soloist. In 1931 she founded the Vic-Wells Ballet company in London. She choreographed several successful ballets, including *The Rake's Progress* and *Don Quixote.* The choreographer Frederick Ashton joined her, and in 1956 the company became the Royal Ballet. ○ ASHTON, DIAGHILEV

Van Allen, James Alfred (1914–)
Van Allen is an American scientist who has made many important contributions to rocket design and space exploration. During World War II (1939–45), he developed a system for guiding explosive rockets to their targets, and afterward he was involved in the building of the first U.S. space satellites. His most important discovery was the existence of the Van Allen Belts, two "zones" in the earth's atmosphere that trap radioactive particles before they can reach the ground. He proved their existence by placing special scientific instruments that measured radioactivity on the first American spacecraft, the *Explorer* satellites.

Vanderbilt, Cornelius (1794–1877)
Vanderbilt was an American ship and railroad owner. He bought his first boat at the age of 16 and began ferrying goods and passengers between New York City and Staten Island. His business expanded, and within 20 years he was the owner of steamship lines throughout America and the rest of the world. At the age of 70 he entered the railroad business, which gradually became as successful as his shipping lines. He left a million dollars to found Vanderbilt University in Tennessee. His son, William Henry Vanderbilt (1821–85), expanded and improved the railroad system.

Van Dyck, Sir Anthony (1599–1641)
Van Dyck was a great Flemish portrait painter. He was born in the city of Antwerp, where he became the most brilliant pupil of the great painter Rubens. By the age of 16, Van Dyck was already Rubens' chief assistant, and at the age of 21 he left the Netherlands to visit England and then Italy. His skill at painting portraits quickly made him famous, and when he returned to Antwerp in 1627 he and Rubens competed for commissions from the wealthy and famous. In 1632 Van Dyck moved to England, where he became court painter to King Charles I. He remained in England until his death, and painted many pictures of the king and his lords during the period leading up to the Civil War.
○ CHARLES I, RUBENS

Van Eyck, Jan (*c.*1389–1441)
Van Eyck was a Flemish painter, who from time to time also worked as a diplomat for the princes of Europe. His greatest work is the *Adoration of the Lamb,* which was painted in about 1432 as an altarpiece for Ghent cathedral. The painting has an extraordinary history: it was first almost destroyed by Protestant reformers, stolen by Napoleon, and then by the German army during both World War I and World War II. The Nazis hid the picture in a salt mine, from where it was rescued and returned to its home in 1945. Another famous painting by Van Eyck is the *Arnolfini Wedding.*

Van Gogh, Vincent Willem (1853–90)
Van Gogh was a Dutch painter. As a young man he had several different jobs, none of which satisfied him. He worked for an art dealer, as a teacher in England, and then in a bookshop. Eventually he joined a missionary society and began preaching to coal miners in Belgium, but he was dismissed and spent the next few years living in great poverty. He began painting in the mid-1880s, and in 1886 his devoted brother Theo invited him to Paris. There he was inspired by the works of painters such as Gauguin and Toulouse-Lautrec, and in 1888 he left Paris to work in the bright sunshine of the south of France. Many of his most brilliant paintings show the landscapes and vegetation of the countryside around the town of Arles, where Van Gogh lived. But he was troubled by attacks of depression and insanity and spent a lot of time in an asylum at Arles. In 1889, after a quarrel with Gauguin, he cut off his ear. The following year he shot himself in the cornfield that had been the subject of his last painting, *Cornfields with Flight of Birds.* ○ GAUGUIN

Vasari, Giorgio (1511–74)
Vasari was an architect and painter who worked in the Italian city of Florence during the 16th century. He is most famous as the author of a book: *The Lives of the Most Excellent Painters, Sculptors, and Architects,* which was first published in 1550. It was the first book to be written about art history, and it tells us much of what we know about many Renaissance artists.

Veblen, Thorstein (1857–1929)
Veblen was an American economist and a pioneer of the study of society, known as "sociology." He taught at universities in Chicago, California, and New York, and his best-known book is *The Theory of the Leisure Class,* published in 1899.

Velázquez, Diego Rodriguez de Silva (1599–1660)
Velázquez was a Spanish painter. He was born in the southern city of Seville, where he began studying art at the age of about 14. In 1622 he traveled to the capital, Madrid, and painted a portrait of King Philip IV. The king liked the

Van Gogh's Self-Portrait with Bandaged Ear. *Like most self-portraits, this is really a mirror image. It was in fact part of the left ear that Vincent cut off after a quarrel with Gauguin.*

picture, and the following year Velázquez was appointed the court's official painter. Apart from two trips to Italy, he spent the rest of his life in Madrid. He painted a few landscapes and scenes from Spanish history, and a famous nude woman known as the *Rokeby Venus*. His finest works were portraits—of the king and queen, their courtiers, and especially of their children. In 1656 he painted the magnificent *Las Meninas* ("The Maids of Honor"). It shows Velázquez himself, working on a portrait of the king and queen (who can be seen in a mirror behind him); around him are the Infanta (Princess) Margarita and her maids. Many people consider it one of the greatest works in the history of Western art. Velázquez did not become well known outside Spain during his lifetime, and it was not until much later, in the 19th century, that he became recognized as a great artist throughout the world.

Verdi, Giuseppe (1813–1901)
Verdi was an Italian opera composer. He was born in a small country village, where his father owned a grocer's shop, and he learned music in the nearby cathedral of Busetto. Some wealthy local people admired Verdi's talent, and they helped him to study at La Scala opera house in the city of Milan. His first success was *Nabucco* ("Nebuchadnezzar"), which was performed at La Scala in 1842. Ten years later three great operas, *Rigoletto* (1851). *La Traviata* (1853), and *Il Trovatore* (1853), had made him famous throughout Europe. They remain among the most popular of all operas to this day. Verdi continued to compose, although he often returned to his country home to relax. In 1871 his opera *Aïda* was performed in Cairo to celebrate the opening of the Suez Canal, and he finished his career with two works based on Shakespeare: *Othello* and *Falstaff*. He also wrote some religious music, including a *Requiem*.

Vermeer, Jan (1632–75)
Vermeer was a Dutch artist. He left very few paintings; in fact, only about 4 works by him are known to exist. He spent all his life in the city of Delft, and one of his pictures is a famous landscape, the *View of Delft*. The others all show indoor scenes, often with young women, reading, playing musical instruments, or doing other, ordinary domestic things. They are beautifully arranged and carefully painted so that the marks of the artist's brush do not show. Vermeer was popular in his own time, but he did not paint enough to make any money and he died in debt.

Verne, Jules (1828–1905)
Jules Verne was a French novelist who invented "science fiction" stories. He was born in the city of Nantes, and worked for a time writing the words for operas. In 1863 he published *Five Weeks in a Balloon*. It was very successful, and he continued to write books in which science and fantastic inventions lead people to adventure. They include *Twenty Thousand Leagues Under the Sea* and *Around the World in Eighty Days*.

The French novelist Jules Verne.

Veronese, Paolo (1525–88)
Veronese was an Italian painter. He decorated many palaces, villas, and churches in and around the city of Venice, and, together with Tintoretto, he painted scenes for the Venetian government headquarters. In 1573 he was tried by the Inquisition because many of his religious paintings contained unnecessary figures (such as dwarfs and clowns), which Veronese had added just for decoration. Among the most famous of these is the *Feast of the House of Levi*, painted in 1573. Veronese had intended the picture to be of the Last Supper, but the objections of the Church forced him to change its title to a less important biblical story.
○ TINTORETTO

Vesalius, Andreas (1514–64)
Vesalius was a Belgian scientist. He was professor of medicine at the University of Padua in Italy, and he carried out many investigations into the structure of the human body. He was one of the first to dissect dead bodies to find out how they were made. In 1643 he published a book describing what he had learned. As a result, he was condemned by the Church, which disapproved of dissection. His punishment was to make a pilgrimage to Jerusalem. He died while on his way home.

Vespucci, Amerigo (1451–1512)
Amerigo Vespucci was an Italian sailor. The continents of "America" are named after him. He was a businessman and an agent of the wealthy Medici family, and at the time of Columbus' voyage to America he was living in the Spanish city of Seville. He claimed that he had made four voyages to the New World in the years after Columbus, and to have traveled up and down the coast of South America. In fact, he probably only sailed on one or two expeditions, and his claim to have discovered the mainland is probably also false. ○ COLUMBUS

Victor Emmanuel II (1820–78)
Victor Emmanuel II became king of Sardinia in 1849, when his father abdicated. Together with his chief minister Cavour, he led the struggle to free Italy from foreign rule and unite the country under one government. After defeating the Austrians (with French help) in 1859, Sardinia was joined by several other Italian states, and in 1860 Garibaldi conquered Sicily and Naples and handed them over to Victor Emmanuel. In February 1861 he was crowned Victor Emmanuel I, the first king of a united Italy. The remaining states of Venice and Rome joined the union in 1866 and 1870 respectively. ○ CAVOUR, GARIBALDI

Victoria (1819–1901)
Victoria was queen of Britain for over 60 years, from 1837 until her death in 1901. Although only 18 when she came to the throne, she soon showed that she had a strong will and a clear understanding of the political system. Throughout her reign she made her political opinions known, but she never acted against the advice of Parliament and her ministers. She worked closely with her husband, **Prince Albert of Saxe-Coburg and Gotha** (1819–61). After his death she was so stricken with grief that she retired completely from public life for some years. This was one of the few times in her reign when she was unpopular with her people. It was Disraeli, the prime minister, who persuaded her to take up public life again, and in 1877 he succeeded in having her proclaimed "Empress of India." Her popularity was now at its height, and her Jubilee (to commemorate 50 years on the throne) and Diamond Jubilee (60 years) involved huge public celebrations. She was succeeded by her son, Edward VII. ○ DISRAELI, EDWARD VII, GLADSTONE

Villa, "Pancho" (1877–1923)
Pancho Villa was a Mexican bandit, revolutionary, and hero. He and his gang took part in the successful overthrow of the Mexican government in 1911, but then fled to the north of the country. He fought for improvements in the treatment of the poor, and made himself unpopular with both his own and the United States governments. In 1916 the U.S. Army tried to catch him, but failed, and their invasion of Mexican territory upset many Mexicans.

Vincent de Paul, Saint (*c.*1580–1660)
Saint Vincent de Paul founded societies of missionary priests and nuns dedicated to helping the poor and destitute. He was a generous and single-minded man who gave all his energy to looking after those in need. His example inspired

The British royal family in 1846. Prince Albert's and Victoria's marriage was outstandingly successful. When Albert died at the age of 42, Victoria was devastated.

many others, both members of the priesthood, and ordinary men and women. The "Vincentian" order of monks was founded in 1625, and the Daughters of Charity, an order of nuns, in 1633.

Virgil (Publius Vergilius Maro, 70 B.C.–19 B.C.)
Virgil was an ancient Roman poet. He was born in the north of Italy, but in about 41 B.C. his family estates were confiscated and he had to move to Rome. There he became a court poet and a friend of Maecenas, an important political and literary figure. With Maecenas' help he was given a villa in the countryside, where he wrote many of his poems. They include the *Georgics* (written in about 30 B.C.), which describe the skills needed to grow vines, keep animals, and cultivate olive trees. His greatest work was the *Aeneid*, an epic poem written at the request of the emperor. It tells of the fate of one of the warriors at the siege of Troy, Aeneas, who escaped after the capture of the city, and after many adventures settled in Italy, where his descendants eventually founded Rome.

Vivaldi, Antonio (1678–1741)
Vivaldi was an Italian composer, born in the city of Venice. He was a priest, but he gave up officiating in church to work at a school for orphans. As well as composing, he taught the pupils music. He is best known for his concertos, four of which are arranged together in the well-known piece called *The Four Seasons*.

The music of Vivaldi is highly ornamental, elaborate, but clear.

Volta, Count Alessandro (1745–1827)
Volta was an Italian scientist who made important discoveries about electricity. He came up with the theory of electric currents and invented the first battery. For a while he was professor at the University of Pavia, but he did most of his work at his home in the beautiful lakeside town of Como. His fame spread, and he was even summoned to demonstrate his discoveries to Napoleon.
○ GALVANI

The philosopher Voltaire greeting King Frederick of Prussia.

Voltaire (François Marie Arouet, 1694–1778)
Voltaire was a French writer who is remembered as one of the great geniuses of the 18th century. He was born in Paris, where his father was a lawyer, and he went to a strict religious college. His father intended him to become a lawyer, but Voltaire studied history instead, and began to write. His first work, *Oedipe*, was very successful, but meanwhile Voltaire had been in trouble for making fun of a French nobleman. In all his writings, Voltaire was a merciless critic of people or things he thought narrow-minded or stupid. He attacked all forms of oppression and injustice, and he was scornful of organized religion and people who unthinkingly believed in God. He admired English politics, and this often got him into trouble with the French government. Voltaire's works include plays, poems, and essays. One of the most famous is a short story, *Candide*, published in 1760. He died, at the height of his fame, at the age of 84.
○ DIDEROT, FREDERICK II

Von Braun, Wernher Magnus Maximilian (1912–77)
Von Braun was a German-born engineer. During World War II (1939–45) he developed the V-1 and V-2 rockets, which were launched against London. After the war he went to the United States where he worked first on missiles, then on the giant Saturn V rockets that sent man to the moon.

Wagner, Wilhelm Richard (1813–83)
Richard Wagner was a German composer. He is most famous for his operas, some of which were so long and required such complicated scenery that a special theater had to be built for them. He was an orphan, born in the city of Leipzig. For many years, Wagner struggled to become a composer. He had badly paid jobs conducting small orchestras and his compositions were not successful. But in 1842 his opera *Rienzi* was performed to great acclaim in Dresden. Other successes followed, including *The Flying Dutchman* and *Tannhäuser*, although Wagner was still in debt and forced to live on the generosity of his friends. In 1853 he began work on *The Ring*, his greatest achievement. It took over 20 years to complete, and it was this opera that required the special theater that was eventually built at Bayreuth in southern Germany. It is written in four parts and lasts more than 15 hours. Meanwhile, Wagner had completed several other works, including *Tristran and Isolde* and *The Mastersingers*. He also wrote some orchestral music, including the beautiful *Siegfried Idyll* which celebrated the birth of his son, Siegfried. ○ LISZT

Walesa, Lech (1943–)
Lech Walesa is a Polish trade union leader. In 1980 he led the shipyard workers in the northern city of Gdansk in protests against the Polish government and helped found the "Solidarity" union. The unions were eventually defeated and Walesa imprisoned, but he has remained an important figure in Polish politics. He was awarded the Nobel Peace Prize in 1983.

Wallace, Alfred Russel (1823–1913)
Wallace was an English naturalist. After exploring parts of Brazil and Malaysia he developed a theory of "natural selection" similar to Darwin's. He and Darwin discussed their ideas and published them at the same time. ○ DARWIN

Walton, Sir William Turner (1902–83)
William Walton was an English composer. Among his finest works are concertos for the viola and the violin, and a choral work called *Belshazzar's Feast* (written in 1931). He also wrote dramatic film music, particularly for the films of Shakespeare's plays *Henry V, Hamlet*, and *Richard III.* ○ HEIFETZ

Washington, Booker Taliaferro (1856–1915)
Booker T. Washington was a black American educationalist and reformer. He was born into slavery in the state of Virginia, but in 1872 he began attending college, paying for his courses by working as a caretaker in his spare time. After he graduated he became a teacher, and in 1881 he was made head of a school for blacks in Alabama. Meanwhile he wrote articles and gave lectures on education, and on the problems faced by his people. His school became well known as a center for black education, and Washington's influence spread. He wrote about his life and work in an autobiography called *Up from Slavery*.

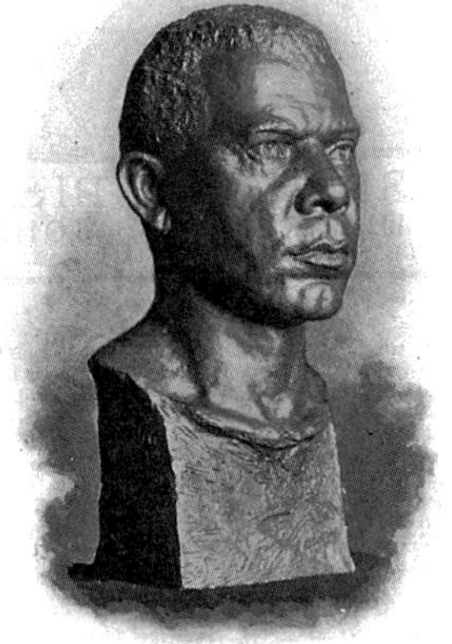

Booker T. Washington, the black American educationalist and reformer.

The German composer of operas, Richard Wagner (above left).

Washington, George (1732–1799)
See pages 256 & 257

Watson-Watt, Sir Robert Alexander (1892–1973)
Watson-Watt was a Scottish scientist. He is most famous for his work on radar systems, which played a crucial role in World War II. During the 1930s he persuaded the government that enemy aircraft could be detected while still far away by sending radio waves toward them. The radio waves would be reflected off the aircraft, and their position revealed.

Watt, James (1736–1819)
James Watt was a Scottish engineer who made several important improvements to the steam engine. It is said that he first realized the possibility of using steam as a source of power when he noticed how it lifted the lid of a boiling kettle. In 1764 he was working in a laboratory and was asked to repair a model of a primitive steam engine. This he did, and he saw several improvements he could make. Over the next 20 years he built and improved steam engines of his own design which were many times more efficient than the old kind, and which could for the first time be used by all kinds of factories. He also invented a copying machine, and the unit used to measure electrical power, the "watt," is named after him.

Watteau, Jean Antoine (1684–1721)
Watteau was a French artist. He was born in the north of the country, but he studied and eventually settled in Paris. His pictures are colorful scenes, often based on ancient myths, but showing the people and costumes of his own time. Among the most famous are the *Embarkation for Cytherea*, finished in 1717, and the *Fêtes Galantes*. He died of tuberculosis.

Wayne, Anthony (1745–96)
Anthony Wayne was a soldier who fought in Washington's army during the American War of Independence. He recruited his own regiment after the Declaration of Independence, and they fought in several important battles. During Washington's winter at Valley Forge, Wayne led expeditions to capture food for the army. His daring led him to be nicknamed "Mad Anthony." ○ WASHINGTON

Webb, Sidney James (1859–1947)
Sidney Webb was an English writer and social reformer. He and his wife, **Beatrice Webb** (1858–1943), campaigned for many years for the introduction of socialist policies in Britain. Sidney was born in London. In 1885 he met the playwright George Bernard Shaw, who introduced him to the socialist Fabian Society. He became one of the society's most active members, and he published many pamphlets and books. Beatrice was born in the west of England. During the 1880s she collected information for a study of Britain's poor and working people. She and Sidney were married in 1892. They wrote many books about history and economics, began the socialist newspaper the *New Statesman*, and helped found the London School of Economics.

Webster, Noah (1758–1843)
Noah Webster was an American lexicographer. He compiled *An American Dictionary of the English Language*. This was published in two volumes in 1828. It contained 20% more entries than any previous English dictionary. It also rationalized between American and English usage and introduced many Americanisms. Between 1783 and 1785 Webster had published the "Blue-Backed Speller" in which he declared that "America must be as independent in literature as she is in politics" from England.

Wedgwood, Josiah (1730–95)
Wedgwood was the founder of the famous English pottery that is named after him. He opened his first factory in 1759, and began by producing plain, everyday pots. Later he introduced fine-quality porcelain, improved glazing techniques, and employed some of the best artists of his time to invent designs. Among the most famous are the plain blue objects with raised white figures on them in white, which remain popular to this day.

Josiah Wedgwood, the English pottery manufacturer. He developed new processes in the making of fine porcelain.

Weil, Simone (1909–43)
Simone Weil was a French writer and philosopher. She was interested in the lives of working people, and spent several years working in factories or on farms to find out about them. At other times she taught philosophy in a number of French colleges, and during the Spanish Civil War she was a member of the Republican forces. Later, although she disliked the institution of the Church, she became interested in religion, and had a number of mystical experiences.

Weissmuller, Johnny (1904–84)
Weissmuller was an American swimmer who won five Olympic gold medals, three in 1924 and two in 1928. He later became famous as the star of many "Tarzan" films.

American Independence

Washington, George (1732–99)
Modern America was born in the 1770s, when the colonists rebelled against their British governors, formed their own constitution, and elected their first president: George Washington.

Washington was born at Bridges Creek in the British colony of Virginia. His father died when he was 11, and he spent his youth living with his elder brother Lawrence, who had inherited the family estates. He educated himself, became a surveyor and then a member of the Virginia militia. The first fighting he did was against the French, when he was sent to Ohio to warn French settlers away from British territory. His mission ended in defeat, but he showed great skill in organizing his men's retreat, and when he returned he was made commander of all the Virginian troops.

George Washington, the first president of the United States of America.

In 1758 Washington became a member of the Virginia Assembly. The following year he married a wealthy widow, **Martha Dandridge Custis** (1732–1802).

Trouble between the American colonists and their British rulers began in the mid-1760s, when the British imposed taxes on Americans. The Virginia Assembly was the first to challenge this, saying that the British did not have the right to gather taxes from the colony. In Boston, large public protests took place against the taxes imposed on goods imported into America, such as tea, paper, and dye. The British responded to the opposition by suspending the colonial assemblies, first in New York, then in Massachusetts and Virginia. The Virginia Assembly continued to meet in secret, and in 1774 they called the first Continental Congress in Philadelphia to discuss opposition to the British. Washington was one of the delegates sent from Virginia. Meanwhile, the situation became increasingly tense, and in 1775 fighting broke out between the citizens of Massachusetts and the British army. The British were defeated at the Battle of Lexington and forced to retreat. At a second Continental Congress in 1775 Washington was made commander of the colonial army. The following year the Congress drew up the Declaration of Independence.

From the saddle General Washington directs his men across the Delaware River to capture Trenton, New Jersey. Ice-choked waters and blinding snow hindered the nighttime crossing.

Washington was a great organizer, and soon turned the inexperienced farmers and townsmen of America into an

The Pennsylvania State House (now Independence Hall), Philadelphia. Here in May 1775 the second Continental Congress met and appointed George Washington commander-in-chief of its forces.

army. He could not, however, expect to defeat the British at once. After forcing them out of Boston in 1776, Washington made a fighting retreat south through New York and New Jersey, winning important battles at Princeton and Trenton in 1777. He and his men spent the winter of 1777–78 at Valley Forge in Pennsylvania. Poorly clothed and equipped, they nonetheless survived the bitter cold and were able to continue the fight the following spring. With the help of the French, who entered the war against the British in 1777, the tide turned in the Americans' favor. At Yorktown in October 1781 the British army surrendered, bringing the fighting to an end. Two years later, by the Treaty of Versailles, the British recognized American independence.

The United States Constitution was drawn up at a convention in Philadelphia in 1787. It provided for a federal government over all the member states, led by a president. Washington was chosen to be the country's first president and was inaugurated in 1789. He was re-elected to serve a second term in 1792, but refused to serve a third and spent the last two years of his life at his home in Virginia. He helped to plan the capital of the United States, which was named in his honor. ○ ARNOLD, JEFFERSON, LA FAYETTE, REVERE

Welles, George Orson (1915–85)
Orson Welles was an American film maker, actor, and writer. He first appeared as an actor at the age of 16, and he acted in many films and theater productions throughout his life. But he is best known as a director. His films include *Citizen Kane*—one of the greatest of all American films, which he made at the age of only 25—and *Touch of Evil*. Welles also made a famous radio play based on H. G. Wells's book, *War of the Worlds*. It tells of a Martian invasion of earth, and the play was so realistic that many people hearing the play in America thought that it had actually happened.
○ WELLS

Arthur Wellesley, Duke of Wellington. His ability to inspire his troops to hold a position against seemingly overwhelming odds earned him the nickname the "Iron Duke."

Wellington, Arthur Wellesley, Duke of (1769–1852)
Arthur Wellesley, the Duke of Wellington, was a British soldier and politician. He fought against France during the Napoleonic Wars and won a great victory at the Battle of Waterloo, and he later became prime minister of Great Britain.

Wellington was born in Ireland and he joined the army immediately after leaving school. In 1793 war broke out between France and several other European countries as a result of the French Revolution. The fighting continued for over 20 years, first because foreign powers opposed the revolution, then as Napoleon tried to expand his empire across the continent. Wellington fought briefly in the Netherlands, but in 1797 he and his regiment were sent to India. He won several campaigns, and returned to Britain as a well-known military commander. In 1808 he was sent to Portugal to defend the Spanish peninsula against Napoleon's troops, in what became known as the "Peninsular War." His strategy was to exhaust the French troops before defeating them. Gradually, this worked, and Wellington was able to advance through Spain and finally defeat the French at the Battle of Toulouse in 1814. Napoleon had by now abdicated and been imprisoned on the island of Elba, but in 1815 he escaped and returned to lead the French army. Wellington gathered his troops at Waterloo in Belgium, where, on June 8, 1815, Napoleon was finally defeated. Wellington was the hero of the hour, and after his return to Britain he took an important part in political life. He was a minister in several Tory governments, and from 1828 until 1830 he was prime minister.
○ NAPOLEON

Wells, Herbert George (1866–1946)
H. G. Wells was an English writer. He is remembered for several science fiction novels, including *The Time Machine* and *The War of the Worlds*. But his finest works were based on his observations of society in the early part of the 20th century. They include *Anne Veronica* (1909) and *Marriage* (1912). ○ WELLES

Wenceslas, Saint (*c.*907–929)
Wenceslas was a duke of Bohemia. Because of his support for Christianity he was murdered by his brother, Boleslav. Although he is remembered as "Good King Wenceslas" he was not actually a king, but one of the lords who governed the country. He is the patron saint of Czechoslovakia.

Wesley, John (1703–91)
John Wesley was the founder of the Methodist Church. The name "Methodist" was first used by Wesley and a group of his friends at the University of Oxford, who vowed to live their lives after the "method" described by Christ. But the new church did not come into existence for many years. Wesley was a priest in the Church of England, and in 1735 he traveled to America to be a missionary. After his return he experienced a "call" to carry Christ's message to others. But he found that his enthusiasm made him unpopular with the Church, and he was refused permission to preach in many places. As a result, in 1739 he began preaching outside. His passion attracted huge crowds wherever he went, and he was especially popular with poor and working-class people. Wesley traveled over a quarter of a million miles in his lifetime and preached about 40,000 sermons. He

also wrote many books, and used the money he made to help the poor. He never intended to break away from the official Church of England, but when he began to appoint Methodist priests to serve in America and elsewhere, a split was unavoidable. His brother, **Charles Wesley** (1707–88), wrote over 8,000 hymns.

West, Rebecca (Cicely Isabel Fairfield Andrews, 1892–1983)
Rebecca West was a British writer. She began her life as an actress, but later became a journalist. Her books include studies of other writers, such as Henry James, travel books, and a series of famous reports on the trials of Nazi war criminals at Nuremberg after World War II. Her novels include *The Judge* (1922) and *The Birds Fall Down* (1966).

Whistler, James Abbott McNeill (1834–1903)
Whistler was an American artist. He attended West Point, intending to become a soldier, but failed his exams. After working as a surveyor in the navy, he left the United States to live in Paris, and never returned home. He was a skilled etcher, and his prints of Paris, London, and Venice sold well. But he was never a popular painter. In 1877 the critic John Ruskin criticized one of his pictures, and Whistler was so offended that he sued Ruskin. Although he won his case, he was awarded only a farthing (a quarter of a cent) in damages, and the costs left him in debt. He is best known for the painting of his mother called "Arrangements in Gray and Black."

White, Patrick Victor Martindale (1912–)
Patrick White is an Australian novelist. His works include *Voss* (1957), *The Eye of the Storm* (1973), and *The Twyborn Affair* (1979). He won the Nobel Prize for Literature in 1973.

Whitman, Walt (1819–92)
Together with Edgar Allan Poe, Walt Whitman is thought of as the first great American male poet. But unlike Poe, who followed traditional methods of writing, Whitman invented a style that expressed his ecstatic vision of American life. He was born near the city of New York, where he had several different jobs in offices, schools, and printing shops. In 1846 he became editor of a newspaper. His greatest work is called *Leaves of Grass*, which he began in 1855 and continued to work on and expand for many years. He intended his poetry to be "American," not European in style, and he wrote in free, natural language. Whitman continued to move from job to job, and at the end of his life he was very poor and only survived thanks to the generosity of friends and admirers.

Walt Whitman, the first great American male poet.

Whitney, Eli (1765–1825)
Eli Whitney was an American who invented the cotton gin in 1792. This was a machine that could separate the valuable fibers of the cotton plant from the seeds and other waste. One cotton gin could do the same amount of work as more than a hundred men, and so the machine revolutionized the cotton-growing industry. Unfortunately, Whitney made very little money from his idea, but he did become rich from other inventions.

A cotton gin. Eli Whitney's invention helped cotton growing to become big business.

Whittier, John Greenleaf (1807–92)
John Greenleaf Whittier was an American writer, born in the state of Massachusetts. He is best known for his poetry, but he also wrote stories and spent much of his life working as a journalist and newspaper editor. Whittier was a Quaker, and he devoted himself to campaigning for the abolition of slavery. Many of his poems and stories, as well as his articles and pamphlets, were written on this theme. His books include *Legends of New England,* published in 1831, and *In War Time* (1864). Although he was well known in his own time, Whittier's poetry is not so popular today.

Wilberforce, William (1759–1833)
William Wilberforce was an English politician who campaigned for the abolition of the slave trade. He was the son of a rich merchant, and after studying at the University of Cambridge he became a priest in the Church of England. In 1780 he was elected member of Parliament for his home town of Hull. At that time, large numbers of African people were being transported from their homes to colonies in the Americas, where they were sold as slaves. Conditions on the ships were terrible, and many died. In 1784, Wilberforce began campaigning to end this trade. He worked tirelessly for over 20 years, and gained a great deal of support—especially from religious groups such as the Quakers. In 1807 a law was finally passed making it illegal for slaves to be bought or sold anywhere in the British Empire. Wilberforce then began campaigning to free those already enslaved in the British colonies. Eventually he became ill, and was forced to retire from politics. He died just a few weeks before another law completely abolishing slavery was passed.

William Wilberforce, who campaigned for the abolition of the slave trade.

Wilde, Oscar Fingall O'Flahertie Wills (1854–1900)
Oscar Wilde was an Irish writer. His mother, Lady Wilde, was a poet who was well known for the "salons" (gatherings of artists, writers, and others)

The Irish dramatist and poet, Oscar Wilde, in 1878. While in prison he wrote The Ballad of Reading Gaol.

that she held in her Dublin home. Oscar Wilde won prizes for his poems while he was still a student at Oxford University. He also became famous for his wit, and many of his sayings have remained well known. He published his first collection of poems in 1881. This was followed by a novel, *The Picture of Dorian Gray,* and several successful plays. They include *Lady Windermere's Fan* (1893) and *The Importance of Being Earnest* (1899). In 1895 Wilde was accused of homosexual practices by the Marquis of Queensberry. Homosexuality was against the law then, and Wilde was tried and sentenced to two years in prison. After he was released he moved to France and took the name "Sebastian Melmoth."

Wilder, Thornton Niven (1897–1976)
Thornton Wilder was an American writer. He was born in the state of Wisconsin, and he was a soldier in both World Wars I and II. He began writing novels in the 1920s. They include *The Bridge of San Luis Rey,* which was a best-seller in 1927. Later he turned to drama. His plays include *Our Town* (1938) and *The Skin of Our Teeth* (1942).

Wilkes, John (1727–97)
John Wilkes was an English politician who successfully challenged the government's right to control what was published in newspapers and elsewhere. He was a member of Parliament, and in 1763 he attacked the government in an article published in a newspaper called the *North Briton.* The government tried to imprison him, but he was eventually released. He was then outlawed from Parliament. Wilkes fought back. After some years abroad he became Lord Mayor of London, and was re-elected to Parliament several times. At first he was not allowed to take his seat, but in 1774 he finally returned.

William I, "the Conqueror" (1027–87)
William the Conqueror was a duke of the French kingdom of Normandy who invaded England in 1066. He was the son of Duke Robert III of Normandy, and he became ruler when his father died in 1035. At first, the other Norman lords opposed William, but he gradually strengthened his rule. William was the cousin of Edward the Confessor, the king of England, and in 1051 Edward promised William the English crown when he died. Later, Harold, an English lord, swore an oath of loyalty to William, but when Edward the Confessor died in 1066 it was Harold, not William, who was crowned king. William prepared an invasion of the country, and in October he and his men landed near the town of Hastings. At the Battle of Hastings on October 14, Harold was defeated and killed. William was crowned in Westminster Abbey on Christmas Day. He spent the next four years bringing the country under his complete control. He was an efficient king who made sure that neither the Church nor the country's lords gained too much power. In 1086 he ordered the writing of the "Domesday Book," a list of all the property in the land, together with its value and the name of its owner. He was killed when he fell off his horse during fighting in France.
○ EDWARD THE CONFESSOR, HAROLD II

William of Orange landing in Britain in 1688 after his father-in-law, the Roman Catholic James II, was driven into exile. He, as King William III, reigned jointly with his wife Mary, daughter of James II. James's attempt to raise an army in Ireland was frustrated when William defeated him at the Battle of the Boyne. The battle is each year celebrated by Ulster Protestants. Mary died in 1694, William in 1702.

William I (1797–1888)
William (Wilhelm) was king of Prussia from 1861 and the first emperor of Germany from 1871. His reign was dominated by Bismarck, whom he appointed chancellor in 1862. His reign saw the defeat of Denmark (1864), of Austria (1867), and France (1871).

William II (1859–1941)
William II was king of Prussia and emperor of Germany from 1888 until 1918. One of his first decisions after inheriting his throne was to dismiss the powerful Chancellor of Germany, Bismarck. From then on he governed alone, choosing only ministers who would not oppose his policies. He wanted Germany to remain a great military power, and in the early 1900s he began the construction of a huge new navy. Eventually his policies alienated the other European countries and led to the outbreak of World War I in 1914, in which Germany was defeated by the combined forces of Great Britain, France, Russia, Italy, and the United States. Germany then became a republic, and William lived in the Netherlands. ○ BISMARCK

William the Silent (1533–84)
William the Silent was the leader of the Dutch Protestants in their rebellion against Spain in the late 16th century. He is called the "Prince of Orange" because he inherited the kingdom of Orange (in south France) from his cousin. He was brought up a Catholic, but when he was made governor of the Spanish territories in the Netherlands he was horrified by the persecution of Protestants there. In 1568 he began a revolt against the Spanish and became a Protestant. He and his followers had to remain abroad until they captured the port of Brielle in 1572. For several years they fought the Spanish, until the "free" Netherlands was established in 1584. He was assassinated in Delft.

William Tell
William Tell was a legendary Swiss leader. The best-known story about him tells how he was commanded to show homage to a duke's hat placed on top of a pole. William refused, and as a punishment he was forced to try to shoot an apple off his son's head. He was successful, and later killed the duke and made himself leader of the Swiss. The most famous version of his story was written in the 18th century by Johannes von Müller, but there is no evidence that William Tell ever really existed.

Williams, Tennessee (Thomas Lanier Williams, 1911–83)
Tennessee Williams was an American writer. He is best known for his plays, which are set in America's Southern states. They include *A Streetcar Named Desire* (first performed in 1947) and *Cat on a Hot Tin Roof* (1955), both of which won Pulitzer Prizes and were later made into successful films. He also wrote novels and short stories.

Wilson, Thomas Woodrow (1856–1924)
Woodrow Wilson was the twenty-eighth president of the United States. After teaching and lecturing in universities for many years, he became governor of the state of New Jersey in 1911. The following year the Democratic Party chose him as their candidate in the presidential elections. He won the election, and began his term of office by introducing many reforms, especially in the laws governing working conditions and child welfare. When World War I began in 1914, Wilson decided that the United States would remain neutral and not support either side. This policy was popular with the American people, but in 1915 a United States ship, the *Lusitania*, was sunk by a German submarine. Other attacks on American ships followed, and eventually (in 1917) the United States entered the war on the Allied side. After the war Woodrow Wilson played an important part in arranging the Treaty of Versailles between the Germans and the Allies. One of his ideas was a new international organization, called the League of Nations (very similar to the modern United Nations). The League first met in 1920, but this and other parts of the treaty were unpopular with the American people, and the United States did not join the League. Wilson was defeated in the 1920 elections. ○ ROOSEVELT

Woodrow Wilson, the twenty-eighth president of the U.S.A. He reluctantly brought the United States into the World War I and played a leading part in the Treaty of Versailles between the Allies and the Germans.

Wolfe, James (1727–59)
James Wolfe was a British general. He entered the army in 1741 and fought in the Scottish campaigns of the 1745 rebellion. His great opportunity came when he was chosen to attack the French settlements along the St. Lawrence in North America during the Seven Years' War. He won the decisive Battle of Quebec (1759). The citadel was strongly defended by Louis de Montcalm. In a night attack Wolfe was able to scale the Heights of Abraham above the city. In the battle that followed both Wolfe and Montcalm were killed. Thereafter Canada became a British territory.

Wollstonecraft, Mary (1759–97)
Mary Wollstonecraft was a writer and feminist. She was born in London, and worked as a schoolmistress and governess before starting to write. In the *Vindication of the Rights of Woman*, published in 1792, she argued for complete equality between men and women. Her other books include a history of the French Revolution, which she wrote after visiting Paris at its height. Her daughter, Mary Shelley, became famous as the lover and later wife of the poet Percy Shelley and as the author of *Frankenstein*. ○ SHELLEY

Wolsey, Thomas (*c.*1475–1530)
Wolsey was an English politician during the reign of King Henry VIII. He was Henry's private chaplain, and the king thought so highly of him that he quickly advanced to become the Archbishop of York. In 1515 Henry made Wolsey his Lord Chancellor—the country's most powerful minister. It was Wolsey who was sent on diplomatic missions to the Holy Roman Emperor, Charles V, to King Francis of France, and to the Pope. Meanwhile, in England, he ensured that the king's power was not challenged by any of the country's noblemen or by Parliament. This made him many enemies. When Henry decided he wanted to divorce Catherine of Aragon and marry

Anne Boleyn, he first asked Wolsey to try to gain the Pope's agreement. But when it became clear that the Pope would not agree, Wolsey found himself in disgrace. With so many enemies among the nobles, there was nobody to save him. He was charged with treason, but he died while on his way to London to stand trial. ○ BOLEYN, CRANMER, HENRY VIII

Wonder, Stevie (Stevland Morris, 1950–)
Stevie Wonder is a black American singer and songwriter. His compositions include rock songs, love songs, and songs about politics and religion. He has been blind since birth, but has performed all around the world.

Woolf, Virginia (1882–1941)
Virginia Woolf was an English writer. She was the daughter of a famous Victorian writer and mountaineer, **Leslie Stephen** (1832–1904), and her sister Vanessa became a well-known artist. She lived in London, where she and other writers and artists became members of a group known as the "Bloomsbury Set." In 1912 she married **Leonard Sidney Woolf** (1880–1969), a journalist and political writer, and together they founded their own publishing company, called the Hogarth Press. As well as her own books, the press published works by other important writers of the time. Virginia Woolf's first novel appeared in 1915. She developed a style of writing novels as though they were poetry—using rhythms that imitated the flow of the mind and the experience of time passing. It was considered very difficult in her day, but has since been very influential. Among her novels are *Mrs. Dalloway* (1925), *To the Lighthouse* (1927), and *Orlando* (1928). ○ SACKVILLE-WEST

Woolworth, Frank Winfield (1852–1919)
F. W. Woolworth's name can be seen on stores all over the world. He was an American farm worker who opened his first store in 1879. By selling cheap, general household goods he expanded his chain of shops until there were over a thousand in the United States, and several in Britain, at the time of his death.

Wordsworth, William (1770–1850)
William Wordsworth was a great English romantic poet. He and the poets who followed him were called "romantic" because they were inspired by nature and wrote in a plain, simple style. Wordsworth was born in the north of England, studied at Cambridge University, and visited France during the French Revolution. He returned to England in 1792, and in 1799 he and his devoted sister, **Dorothy Wordsworth** (1771–1855), moved to a house in the beautiful Lake District of England. Together with his friend Coleridge, Wordsworth published *Lyrical Ballads* (1798), the first collection of English romantic poetry. Inspired by the scenery around him, he continued to write, and as his fame spread other writers made the journey north to visit him. He married an old friend, Mary Hutchinson, in 1802. Wordsworth's later works include *The Prelude*, a long poem describing his development as a poet, and *The Recluse*, another long poem which he worked on for many years, but never finished. He became the poet laureate in 1843 ○ COLERIDGE

This model of St. Paul's Cathedral shows Wren's original design. Londoners were fortunate to be able to make use of Wren's genius when rebuilding their city after the Great Fire of 1666.

Wren, Sir Christopher (1632–1723)
Christopher Wren was an English architect, most famous for designing St. Paul's Cathedral in London. As well as being an architect, he was also a mathematician and astronomer, and for several years he was professor of these sciences at Oxford University. His first building was a theater in Oxford. After the fire that destroyed much of the City of London in 1666, Wren was asked to re-design St. Paul's and the city's churches. St. Paul's, with its huge dome, was completed in 1710, and together with the many elegant church spires he designed it dominated the London skyline for 250 years, until the age of modern high buildings. With such buildings as the modifications he made to Hampton Court or the building of the Royal Hospital at Chelsea Wren was able to graft a sense of baroque grandeur onto the existing English tradition of brickwork and steep gables. ○ PALLADIO

Wright, Frank Lloyd (1869–1959)
Frank Lloyd Wright was one of the 20th century's most important architects. He was born in the state of Wisconsin and studied engineering at the university there. When a new building on the university campus collapsed, Wright decided to become an architect and use his knowledge of engineering to design better buildings. He studied with one of the first people to use iron and steel and build high "skyscrapers," **Louis Henri Sullivan** (1856–1924). Wright's first designs were not, however, for tall buildings. Instead he built a series of very low-lying "prairie houses" near the city of Chicago. He believed that a building should fit in with its surroundings, and these large flat houses were supposed to blend with the land. Inside the houses he experimented with "open planning"—that is, having large, multi-purpose rooms, and few walls. At the same time as he was designing these prairie houses, Wright also built his first large offices, and began to use modern materials such as concrete reinforced with pieces of steel to make them strong. In 1916 work began on the Imperial Hotel in the Japanese capital, Tokyo. It was so well designed that it was one of the only large buildings to survive an earthquake that struck the city in 1923. One of the last buildings to be completed before Frank Lloyd Wright died was the Guggenheim Museum of modern art in New York City. It is designed as a continuous spiral that rises gently from the pavement. The paintings are hung on the inside walls, and so the building forms one long gallery with curved walls. It was finished in 1956. Wright described his life and work in *An Autobiography*, published in 1932, and wrote several other books about architecture.

Wright, Orville (1871–1948), and **Wilbur** (1867–1912)
Orville and Wilbur Wright were American engineers who designed, built, and flew the first powered aircraft in 1903. They were born in Ohio, where they went to school, but had no special training in engineering. What they learned about the subject they got from books, or from their experiences as bicycle manufacturers. When they became interested in flying, the only aircraft to have been flown were gliders. The only engines available were too heavy to power an airplane. So the Wrights first designed and built a lightweight, 12-horsepower gasoline engine. But they also found that controlling an airplane in flight was a problem. They experimented with different wing designs, and eventually came up with the idea of

The Guggenheim Museum of modern art in New York City, one of Wright's most famous buildings. It is a continuous spiral that rises gently from the ground. His first important commercial structure, the Larkin Building in Buffalo, New York, was the first air-conditioned building and the first in which plate glass and metal furniture were used.

Frank Lloyd Wright, outside the Capitol in Washington. One of the more spectacular buildings designed by this brilliant American architect is the Johnson's Wax Factory at Racine, Wisconsin, a structure of giant mushroom columns and glass tubing. Its design expressed the streamlined style common in automobiles of the 1930s.

Orville and Wilbur Wright.

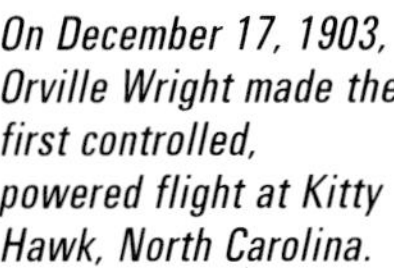

On December 17, 1903, Orville Wright made the first controlled, powered flight at Kitty Hawk, North Carolina.

putting "ailerons" (movable flaps) on the wings and tailplane, and a rudder on the tail. This basic design has hardly changed since. On December 17, 1903, they made their first flights at Kitty Hawk in the state of North Carolina. The first, made by Orville, lasted only 12 seconds and covered only 120 feet, but by the end of the day Wilbur succeeded in flying for almost a minute at a speed of 30 mph. Within three years they had so improved the design of the plane that they could fly for over an hour, but it took some time to interest people in buying their invention.

Wycliffe, John (*c.*1329–1384)
John Wycliffe was an English church reformer. He and his followers became known as "Lollards," which means "mumblers." He served the English king as a diplomat, and during the period when there were two popes—one at Rome and one at Avignon in France—he began to oppose the authority of the Church. First he attacked corruption among priests and in the papacy, then he denied that the Church had authority to interfere in matters of government. He organized and helped write a new English translation of the Bible, but as his views became more extreme he was condemned by those who had at first supported him. He was forced to retire in 1382, and died in disgrace at his country parish.

Xavier, Saint Francis (1506–32)
Xavier was a Jesuit and missionary who became known as the "Apostle of the Indies" for his devotion to spreading Christianity in the Far East. He was a close friend of the Jesuits' founder, Loyola, and made his first journey to India in 1541. Over the next ten years he traveled through much of the Indian subcontinent, and in 1549 he visited Japan. He died of fever on his way to China.
○ LOYOLA

Xenophon (*c.*435 B.C.–354 B.C.)
Xenophon was a Greek soldier and writer. He was an Athenian who fought in several wars, and was eventually banished from Athens for joining the Spartans. During his exile he wrote a great deal. His works include a number of books about the great Socrates, who was Xenophon's teacher in Athens. ○ PLATO, SOCRATES

Xerxes I (*c.*519 B.C.–*c.*465 B.C.)
Xerxes was a warlike king of ancient Persia who began an invasion of Greece in the year 480 B.C. His army is said to have numbered over two million men—and to have been brought to a standstill by only 300 Spartan warriors at the Battle of Thermopylae. After finally defeating the Spartans, Xerxes attacked Athens, but was defeated both at sea (in the Battle of Salamis) and on land.
○ THEMISTOCLES

Ximenes (Francisco Jiménez de Cisneros, 1436–1517)
Ximenes was a Spanish cardinal who became the most powerful man in Spain during the reign of King Ferdinand II. As the country's chief minister, he reorganized the economy and strengthened the power of the king. He also founded a new university, and patronized artists and writers.
○ FERDINAND II

Y Z

Yeats, William Butler (1865–1939)
W. B. Yeats was an Irish poet and playwright. Together with other writers such as Sean O'Casey and Lady Gregory, he helped encourage the revival of interest in Irish literature and culture that took place at the beginning of the 20th century. He was born in Dublin, but moved to London to study. At first Yeats intended to become a painter, but in 1898 he published his first book of poetry, and he gradually came to devote all his energy to writing. Many of his early works were plays, written for the Abbey Theatre, which Yeats helped found with Lady Gregory. They include *The Countess Cathleen* (first performed in 1899), *The Land of the Heart's Desire* (1894), and *Cathleen ni Houlihan* (1903). Meanwhile, Yeats also wrote poetry. He was interested in Irish myths and legends, as well as in the country's actual history, and he successfully used both in his work. In the years after 1910, political tension in Ireland grew as the country struggled for independence from Britain. Yeats eventually became a senator in the Irish government. His collections of poetry include *The Wanderings of Oisin* (1898) and *The Winding Stair* (1933), and he also wrote a mystical philosophical essay called *A Vision*. His brother, **Jack Butler Yeats** (1873–1958), was a successful painter and writer who was also deeply influenced by Irish history and culture in his work.
○ GREGORY, O'CASEY

Young, Brigham (1801–77)
Brigham Young was the leader of the "Mormons" (members of the Church of Latter-Day Saints) who settled in Salt Lake City in Utah in the late 1840s. He was governor of the city for a time, but the U.S. Government removed him because he preached—and practiced—polygamy (having more than one wife). The phenomenal growth in prosperity of the community was entirely due to his organizing genius. His pioneering efforts rank him as one of the most important colonizers of the American West.

Zapata, Emiliano (1879–1919)
Zapata was a Mexican revolutionary who campaigned for changes in the system of landownership in his country. He took part in the successful uprising against the government in 1911, but when the reforms he wanted were not introduced he began a guerrilla war against the new government. He failed to gain control of the country, but after his death many of the reforms he had suggested were actually introduced. ○ VILLA

Zeppelin, Graf Ferdinand von (1838–1917)
Zeppelin was a German general who developed and built the huge, hydrogen-filled airships that used to carry passengers across the Atlantic. He constructed his first craft in 1900, but it was not until 1912 that he was able to find enough support to build them commercially. During World War I, Zeppelins were used by the German army in attempts to bomb London, but the giant shapes were easy targets and very inflammable. After the war they were used to ferry passengers between Europe and the Americas, but they were dangerous (there were several terrible accidents), and soon overtaken by airplanes. Recently, however, airships filled with less dangerous gases have been used to carry freight.

Zhou Enlai (1898–1976)
Zhou Enlai (who is also sometimes known as "Chou En-lai") was a Chinese Communist politician. He was a member of the party leadership, called the "Politburo," for almost 50 years, from 1927 until his death. For a time he served in Chiang Kai-shek's army, but in 1927 he left Chiang to join the Communists, who had already broken with Chiang's government. He was one of the leaders of the "Long March" in 1934 and afterward worked with Chairman Mao to set up a Commnist government. When the Communists finally gained control after World War II, Zhou was made prime minister, a position he held until his

Irish poet, William Butler Yeats.

Brigham Young, the Mormon leader.

death. He was also foreign minister from 1949 until 1958, and so he became well known outside China. ○ CHIANG KAI-SHEK, MAO ZE-DONG

Zhukov, Georgi Konstantinovich (1896–1974)
Zhukov was the Russian general who led the Red Army to victory over the Germans in World War II. When the Germans invaded in 1941 he successfully defended Moscow, and then took charge of the forces fighting the long and bitter battle for the city of Stalingrad. As the Germans began to retreat he led the central divisions of the Russian army that finally captured Berlin. It was Zhukov who accepted the German surrender. After the war he was governor of the German territories occupied by the Soviet Union, and later minister for defense. ○ STALIN

Zola, Émile (1840–1902)
Zola was a French writer. His father died while he was still young, and he was brought up in poverty in the south of France. He wrote many short stories, and became well known when his novel *Thérèse Raquin* was published in 1868. It tells the story of a woman who encourages her lover to murder her husband, but who is then plagued by remorse. Like all Zola's novels, it is very realistic. Zola always took care to research the settings and characters for his novels so that he could create a completely convincing picture of their lives. After the success of *Thérèse,* he began a long series of books which dealt with different aspects of 19th-century France, as the country gradually became industrialized. They include *La Terre* (about a peasant) and *Nana* (about prostitution). He also wrote essays and articles for newspapers, and in 1898 he wrote a famous letter to the president demanding that the falsely imprisoned army officer Dreyfus be given a new trial. His attack on the army got him into trouble, and he had to escape to England for a time. He died in Paris when he accidentally suffocated himself. ○ DREYFUS, MAUPASSANT

Zoroaster (6th century B.C.)
Zoroaster was an ancient Iranian religious leader who founded the Parsee religion. The sacred writings of this religion are known as the *Ayesta,* parts of which were written by Zoroaster himself. He believed that there was a constant struggle between good and evil forces in the world.

Zwingli, Ulrich (1484–1531)
Zwingli was a Swiss Protestant leader. In 1518 he was made minister of the cathedral in Zurich, and he was able to influence the city's government. He aimed to simplify church rituals, and challenged many established traditions and beliefs. Some of the changes he made, such as removing images from the cathedral, were made only after being debated in public. Zwingli was killed during fighting when Catholic forces from other parts of Switzerland invaded Zurich.

Zworykin, Vladimir Kosma (1889–1982)
Zworykin was a Russian-born scientist who emigrated to America and developed the "Iconoscope" which replaced John Logie Baird's system of producing television pictures. He also helped develop the electron microscope, which could magnify tiny objects to sizes far greater than an ordinary microscope. ○ BAIRD

Emile Zola, French novelist and journalist. In a celebrated article, J'Accuse, *he defended Alfred Dreyfus, a French army officer of Jewish blood who in 1894 was unjustly convicted of giving evidence to Germany and was imprisoned on Devil's Island, off the coast of French Guiana.*

Glossary

Definitions of some of the names, technical terms, and abbreviations used in this book.

A.D. "The year of our Lord" (Latin: *Anno Domini*), used to date events after Christ's birth.
Allegory A story in which the obvious meaning also symbolizes a hidden meaning.
Anthropology The study of humankind, its habits, customs, and social organization.
Avant garde A French term, often used to describe the most advanced or experimental artistic movements of a particular period. It means literally the "forefront" or "vanguard."
b. Stands for "born" when used before a date.
Barbarians A word meaning, in general, "uncivilized" or "wild." The Romans used it to describe the the non-Roman tribes of the north and east, and Christians. Europeans once used it to describe non-Christians.
Baroque A style of art and architecture common in Europe between about 1600 and 1750, heavily decorated and with a violent emotional appeal.
B.C. "Before Christ," used to date events before the birth of Christ.
Broadway The term used for the American professional theater, from the New York street where many theaters were once situated.
Byzantine The Byzantine Empire was the eastern division of the Roman Empire, which survived after the fall of Rome to become a powerful force in Eastern Europe. Byzantine art was the style of art and architecture produced or inspired by the empire, which had its capital at Constantinople. ○ JUSTINIAN
c. Stands for *circa*, a Latin word meaning "about," used when the accuracy of a date is in doubt.
Canonize Formally to declare somebody a saint. Used by the Roman Catholic Church.
Choreography The art of dance position and composition.
Civil war War between different people living in the same country.
Classical In art or architecture, "Classical" means the style of ancient Greece or Rome. In the 1700s and 1800s the **Neo-classical** movement aimed for a style of art as simple and elegant as that of the ancient world.
Coup d'état A term used to describe the overthrow of a government, usually by other members of the same government or the armed forces. *Coup* is French for "cut"; *état* French for "state" or "nation."
Cubism A style of art developed in the early 20th century which painted objects using very strong, angular shapes. ○ PICASSO
d. Stands for "died" when used before a date.
Democracy A system of government in which the citizens choose their own leaders, usually by voting.
Dictator An absolute ruler or governor, one whose word is law.
Feminism Support or advocacy of the rights, claims, or qualities of women. A feminist is somebody who supports these things; something that is feminist is written, said, or produced with these things in mind. The term *women's movement* is sometimes used to describe modern popular feminism.
Franks German tribes who conquered Gaul in about the 6th century, and who gave it the name "France."
Gothic A medieval style of art and architecture, developed in France. Gothic buildings often have pointed arches, narrow columns, flying buttresses, vaulted roofs, and large windows.
Goths German tribes who successfully fought both the eastern and western parts of the Roman Empire between the 3rd and 5th centuries. They ruled parts of Italy, France, and Spain.
Holy Roman Empire A confederation of European states and princes that lasted from 800 until 1803. ○ CHARLEMAGNE

Illegitimate Often used to describe somebody conceived and born outside marriage, who therefore could not inherit the parents' titles or property.
Impressionism A late 19th-century artistic movement interested mainly in the effects of light. The Impressionists set out to capture their immediate "impressions" of nature. ○ MONET
Left wing Political group or party holding radical views. The term comes from where the radicals sat in the French Revolutionary Assembly.
Medieval Of the Middle Ages.
Middle Ages The period from about 1000 to about 1400, before the beginning of the RENAISSANCE.
Monarchy A system of government that has a king or queen as its head, who rules by right of birth.
Monastery or abbey A community of monks under an abbot. They live in buildings especially designed for a life of Christian work and prayer.
Mongols The people of central Asia. In the late Middle Ages they commanded a vast empire; now they live mainly in Mongolia.
Nationalism Devotion to one's own country. Nationalist political movements often seek independence from foreign invasion or government.
Philanthropy A word meaning love of people, usually used for charitable or generous acts aimed at improving the lives of others. A **philanthropist** is somebody who performs such acts.
Philosophy The study of knowledge; the search for "truth" or "reality."
Physics The study of the physical world, its laws and mechanisms.
Pope Title of the head of the Roman Catholic Church; recognized by Catholics as the lawful successor of St. Peter, the first Pope.
Post-Impressionism was a movement that developed from Impressionism a little later.
Psychology The study of the nature and functions of the human mind.
Quaker The Quakers are a religious group devoted to plainness and simplicity in their religion. Also known as the "Society of Friends."
Reformation The 16th-century movement headed by Martin Luther to reform the Church. It resulted in the Church splitting into Roman Catholics and Protestants.
Renaissance The period from about 1400 to about 1600 during which people suddenly rediscovered the CLASSICAL art and learning of ancient Greece and Rome. This encouraged an explosion of new art and literature based on ancient ideas. ○ MEDICI
Republic A republic is a democratic country, one in which power is held by the citizens themselves and which does not have a MONARCH. A **republican** is somebody who supports such a system.
Revolution An uprising of the people that completely changes the system of government. Revolutions are often violent.
Right wing Conservative, traditionalist political group. From where the conservatives sat in the French Revolutionary Assembly.
Romantic The romantic movement in art and literature began at the end of the 18th century. It emphasized imagination and inspiration by nature.
Saxons Saxons were a German tribe. In about the 5th century some of them conquered Britain and became known as the **Anglo-Saxons.**
Socialism A political theory that favors ownership of all resources—land, industry, property, services, etc.—by all the people, rather than by private individuals. ○ MARX
Species Every *genus* of animal consists of one or more species. For example, the genus *Equus* includes the horse, three species of zebra, and two kinds of wild ass. These six species are alike in their basic structure, but they differ in certain details.
Surrealism A 20th-century artistic movement, mainly interested in the subconscious mind as a source of inspiration.
Theology The study of God and religion.

Index

How to use this Index

The names of the people in this book are listed here according to subject. You can look up events in history, the names of countries, sayings, nicknames, the names of books, paintings, inventions, and many other things. If, for example, you wish to know about the personalities involved in the French Revolution, you can find a list of their names under **French Revolution**. You will find **Corday, Danton, Guillotin, La Fayette,** etc. You can also look up specific events, for instance, **Bastille, Storming of** (you will find **Louis XVI**). And if you simply want to know about the history of France, look under **France** for a list of kings, ministers, and other important people.

You will also find the names of certain people who are mentioned in the book, but do not have separate entries of their own. If you cannot find persons you are interested in, try looking up their names in the index. If they are mentioned somewhere else, the index will tell you where to look.

Acknowledgments

The publisher and author wish to thank the following for kindly supplying photographs for this book:

Page 20 & 22 Mary Evans Picture Library; 23 Ronald Sheridan; 26 Royal Geographic Society; 27 middle Robert Harding, bottom Bettmann Archive/BBC Hulton; 29 Mary Evans; 30 Sonia Halliday; 31 middle Hulton, bottom Mansell Collection; 32 left National Portrait Gallery, right Jane Austen Memorial Trust; 33 Mansell; 34 bottom & 35 Mary Evans; 36 left Canterbury Cathedral, bottom Picture Point; 37 Mansell; 39 top National Gallery London, bottom Sonia Halliday; 40 Mansell; 41 top Tate Gallery, bottom Mansell; 42 & 43 Mansell; 44 Popperfoto; 45 left Lord William Taylor; 46 left German Embassy, right Bettmann Archive/BBC Hulton; 47 middle Bridgeman Art Library, bottom NPG; 48 top Brontë Society; 50 Hulton; 53 Mansell; 54 top British Museum; 55 Mary Evans; 56 Popperfoto; 57 Tate Gallery c. ADAGP, Paris 1987; 58 Mansell; 59 left National Gallery London, right Kobal; 60 By Gracious Permission of Her Majesty the Queen Mother; 61 Scala Milan; 62 Mansell; 63 Popperfoto; 64 Cavendish Laboratory Cambs; 65 top Mansell, bottom Popperfoto; 66 National Palace Museum, Taiwan; 67 top Sonia Halliday; 70 Musée Royaux des Beaux Arts de Belgique Brussels/Bridgeman; 71 Mansell; 72 National Gallery London; 74 Bettmann Archive/BBC Hulton; 75 left Hulton, right Bettman Archive/BBC Hulton; 77 bottom Scala; 78 Hulton; 79 Photosource; 82 Popperfoto; 83 Hulton; 85 left Mary Evans, right Scala; 86 NPG; 87 Phaidon Press; 88 Mansell; 89 Hulton; 92 left Bettmann Archive/BBC Hulton, middle Stanley Gibbons Stamps, right Hulton; 93 top National Gallery London, bottom Mansell; 94 left Mansell, right Popperfoto; 96 top Mansell, middle & bottom Atomic Energy Commission; 97 top Tate Gallery, bottom Mansell; 99 top Mansell, bottom Hulton; 100 Bettmann Archive/BBC Hulton; 101 left NPG, right top & bottom Ford Motor Company; 102 Scala; 103 Mansell; 104 Popperfoto; 105 left National Gallery London, right Science Museum London; 108 Popperfoto; 109 top Hulton, bottom Photosource; 110 left Black Star, right Biblioteque National Paris; 111 & 112 Scala; 114 National Gallery London; 115 & 116 Mansell; 117 left Mary Evans, right Musées de la Ville Strasbourg; 120 Mansell; 121 top Michael Holford, bottom & 122 Hulton; 123 NPG; 125 top Popperfoto, bottom National Maritime Museum; 126 left Hulton, right Cleveland Museum of Art; 127 Fitzwilliam Museum Cambridge; 128 top Michael Holford, bottom & 129 Mary Evans; 130 Stanley Gibbons Stamps; 132 right National Gallery London; 134 Fotomas; 135 left Mansell, right Sonia Halliday; 137 top Stanley Gibbons Stamps, bottom Popperfoto; 138 Mansell; 139 Ronald Sheridan; 142 Mansell; 145 right Radio Times Collection; 146 Keystone; 147 left Bettmann Archive/BBC Hulton, right 148 & 149 Popperfoto; 153 & 156 left Hulton, right Popperfoto; 157 left Scala, right National Gallery London; 158 Hulton; 159 & 160 Mansell; 161 left Giraudon; 163 Scala; 164 & 165 Bettmann Archives/BBC Hulton; 166 right & 167 left Mansell, 167 right Hudson Bay Co.; 168 Popperfoto, bottom left Bettmann Archive, bottom right Hulton; 170 Mansell; 171 Hulton; 173 bottom National Gallery London; 174 Hulton; 175 & 176 Scala; 177 top National Gallery London, bottom Mary Evans; 178 Popperfoto; 179 left NPG, right Mansell; 181 top British Museum; 185 bottom & 186 NPG; 187 left Sonia Halliday; 188 Mansell; 189 bottom Keystone; 191 left Bettmann Archive/BBC Hulton, right Kobal; 192 All-Sport; 193 Mansell; 194 Mary Evans; 197 Mansell; 198 Ronald Sheridan; 200 Michael Holford; 201 top left Michael Holford, right NPG, bottom Popperfoto; 202 Tate Gallery; 203 left National Gallery London, right BBC Hulton; 205 top Mansell; 207 bottom British Museum; 208 left Kobal, right BBC Hulton; 209 Mary Evans; 211 left NPG, right Mansell, bottom Pitti Gallery; 212 right Mozarteum Salzburg; 213 top Novosti, bottom Rijkmuseum Amsterdam; 215 Bodleian; 218 Tate Gallery; 219 left & top right Mansell, bottom right Stanley Gibbons Stamps; 220 National Gallery London; 221 BBC Hulton; 222 top Peter Newark's Western Americana, bottom Bettmann Archive/BBC Hulton; 223 French Institute; 225, 226 & 227 Mansell; 228 NPG; 231 & 232 Popperfoto; 233 Metropolitan Museum of Art; 235 and 236 BBC Hulton; 237 National Gallery London; 238 BBC Hulton; 239 Victoria and Albert Museum; 240 ET Archive; 241 Popperfoto; 243 top National Gallery London, bottom Picture Point; 244 left ZEFA, right BBC Hulton; 245 top Stanley Gibbons Stamps, bottom Peter Newark's Western Americana; 246 Mary Evans; 248 Peter Newark's Western Americana; 250 Burhte Collection; 251 BBC Hulton; 252 By Gracious Permission of Her Majesty the Queen; 253 left Ullstein Bilderdienst; 254 Mansell; 255 NPG; 256 Robert Hunt Library; 257 Pennsylvania Bureau of Travel Development; 258 NPG; 259 Mansell; 260 top Popperfoto, bottom NPG; 261·Mansell; 262 BBC Hulton; 263 Ronald Sheridan; 264 left Guggenheim, right Bettmann Archive/BBC Hulton; 265 top Science Museum, bottom British Aircraft Corporation; 267 top left NPG, bottom Mansell.